# L.A. BIZARRO

# L.A. BIZARRO

## THE ALL-NEW INSIDER'S GUIDE TO THE OBSCURE, THE ABSURD, AND THE PERVERSE IN LOS ANGELES

ANTHONY LOVETT · MATT MARANIAN

CHRONICLE BOOKS

SAN FRANCISCO

Library of Congress Cataloging-in-Publication Data:

Lovett, Anthony R.
  L.A. bizarro : the all-new insider's guide to the obscure, the absurd, and the perverse in Los Angeles / by Anthony Lovett and Matt Maranian.—2nd rev. ed.
    p. cm.
  ISBN 978-0-8118-6511-1 (pbk.)
  1. Los Angeles (Calif.)—Guidebooks. 2. Curiosities and wonders—California—Los Angeles—Guidebooks. I. Maranian, Matt. II. Title.
  F869.L83L7 2009
  917.94′940454—dc22

Manufactured in Hong Kong
Designed by Katie Hanburger

Photo Credits:

Courtesy of Aetherius Society: 232; Jennifer Bastian/The Museum of Jurassic Technology: 247 middle, 248; Mark Berry: 171; M.A. Flores: 243 top; Courtesy of Ireland Entertainment: 136 top; Isis: 336; Ed Lange/Elysium Institute: 349; Randi Liberman: 89 top, 368 bottom; Anthony Lovett and Matt Maranian: 16–17, 18, 19, 21, 23, 25, 26, 27, 28, 29, 30, 31, 32, 33, 34, 35, 36, 37, 39, 40, 41 top, 43, 44, 45, 46, 47, 48, 49, 51, 53, 54, 55, 57, 59, 64–65, 66, 68, 69, 70, 71, 72, 73, 74, 75, 76, 77, 78, 80, 81, 82, 84 top, 85 top, 89 middle and bottom, 90, 91, 92 top and bottom, 93 top, middle (bottom), and bottom, 94, 95, 96 top, middle (top), middle (bottom), 97 top, 98, 99, 100–101, 102, 103, 105, 106, 107, 108, 109, 110, 111, 112, 113, 114, 115, 117, 118, 119, 121, 122, 123, 124, 125, 126, 128, 129, 130, 131, 132, 133, 134–135, 136 bottom, 137, 138, 142, 143, 144, 145, 149, 151, 152, 153, 154, 155, 156, 158, 159, 160, 161, 162, 163, 164, 165, 167, 168, 169, 170, 172 bottom, 175, 176, 177, 178–179, 180, 182, 185, 186, 187, 188, 189, 192, 193, 194, 195, 197, 199, 202, 203, 204, 205, 206, 207, 208, 209, 211, 213, 214, 215, 217, 219, 220, 221, 225, 226, 227, 228, 230, 231, 233, 234, 235, 236, 237, 238, 239, 240, 241, 242, 243 middle and bottom, 246, 247 top and bottom, 249, 250–251, 252, 253, 254, 255, 256, 257, 260, 261, 262, 263, 264, 265 middle and bottom, 266, 267, 268, 269, 271, 272, 275, 277, 278, 280, 281, 282, 283, 284, 285, 286, 287, 288–289, 291, 292, 293, 294, 295, 296, 297, 298, 300, 302, 303, 304, 305, 306, 307, 308, 311, 312, 313, 314, 315, 316, 318, 319, 324, 325, 326, 327, 328, 329, 330, 331, 332–333, 334, 335, 337, 338, 339, 340, 341, 342, 343, 344, 345, 348, 350, 352, 354, 355, 356, 357, 358, 359, 362, 363, 365, 366, 367, 368 top; Phyllis Madonna: 140, 141; Courtesy of Malibu Horizon: 84 bottom, 85 bottom; Courtesy of National Archives: 353; Loretta Palazzo: 15; Anthony Rich: 92 middle, 96 bottom, 97 bottom; Carol Rosenthal: 41 bottom, 63, 191, 223; Shutterstock Images LLC/Copyright Brasiliao: 148 top; Shutterstock Images LLC/Copyyright ChipPix: 320 bottom; Shutterstock Images LLC/Copyright Ivan Cholakov: 148 bottom; Shutterstock Images LLC/Copyright Kiselev Andrey Valerevich: 320 top; Shutterstock Images LLC/Copyright Benko Zsolt: 147 bottom; Yair Smolinisky: 265 top; Saskia Vogel: 93 middle (top), 166, 259.

Page 172 top: *White Power* by Ed Mironiuk

10 9 8 7 6 5 4 3 2 1

Chronicle Books LLC
680 Second Street
San Francisco, CA 94107

www.chroniclebooks.com

# ACKNOWLEDGMENTS

**Matt:** I'd like to thank my very lovely and charming wife Loretta, who barely raised an eyebrow as I hopped from nudist resort to colon hydrotherapy session to professional dungeon, all in the good name of *L.A. Bizarro* of course. Thanks also go to my parents, who probably never imagined their retirement years would include *L.A. Bizarro* recon missions into the hinterlands of Torrance, but hey, I didn't ask to be born. Thanks, too, to one of my favorite Jews, Carol Rosenthal, who wasted hours with me on red hot leads that turned ice cold and never once complained, and most especially to Don Favareau—wearer of both the *L.A. Bizarro* Badge of Honor and our Purple Heart—for whom no L.A.B. field trip was either too sleazy, dangerous, or stupid. And I would also like to dedicate 100% of my 50% of this book to my late, great, talented pal Tracy Thielen, without whom Los Angeles is even more crappy than usual.

**Tony:** First, I owe a debt of gratitude to my *other* partner, Randi, who displayed heroic patience while she endured as many cemeteries, curio shoppes, bad restaurants, seedy bars, and seemingly endless day trips as I could throw at her. I would also like to thank my dear mother, Mary, who has always supported my dubious career decisions no matter how much shame they brought to the family. Sorry about that. Finally, to my daughter, Ivy, I know this book will raise many questions, and I look forward to answering them sometime after your 21st birthday. Kudos also go out to Jennifer Traig, who made our writing much better than it actually is; Jessica Gelt, without whose *L.A. Times* article this new edition may never have come to pass; Jesse Dena, for creative triage; and Steve "The Tree Killer" Mockus at Chronicle Books, since his largesse allowed this book to become two times longer than planned.

**Matt:** And I'd like to take another moment to thank you, Tony Lovett, because I made a solemn promise to myself that I would never work with you again, which either goes to show that my word means nothing or that you're amazing. Or both. It was even more fun the second time around.

**Tony:** We've worked together before?

**Matt:** Never mind. Finally, we should thank all the wonderful people who bought our books and will undoubtedly love our Web site, www.labizarro.com.

**Tony:** Shameless plug. Cha-*ching!*

# TABLE OF CONTENTS

## IOI CHAPTER № 3 CONSPICUOUS CONSUMPTION

## 251 CHAPTER № 6 AFTERLIFE, THEN WHAT?

# 289 CHAPTER № 7 GO AWAY

# INTRODUCTION

## Hello, and welcome to the long-awaited, much-anticipated, totally renovated *L.A. Bizarro*.

Much has changed for us in the dozen or so years since the first edition of *L.A. Bizarro* was published. Rashes and rehabs came and went. Wrinkles appeared, waistlines expanded, and hairlines receded—as did our tolerance for living in the city that inspired the book. Don't get us wrong, it's not that we lost our affection for L.A.'s seedy side, but like anyone who's had too much of a good thing, we decided it would be better to enjoy our subject matter in moderation. And from afar. It's tough to accurately describe the beast when you're living in its belly—plus we really hate the traffic.

L.A. is a tough city to love—*truly love*—because it's an even tougher city to know. Its sheer immensity is daunting—an endless patchwork of disparate neighborhoods, communities, and cities all crammed together without any apparent rhyme or reason. Aside from earthquakes and conflagrations, life is fairly consistent if you remain within the confines of your own safe enclave; plenty of Angelenos are content to live and die inside the boundaries of their dull yet familiar worlds. Then there are those who thrive on curiosity and exploration, citizens intrigued by the potential for adventure that only a city this diverse can offer. From highbrow to lowbrow, civil to sinful, inspirational to evil, getting to know the real L.A. is a lot like having a manic-depressive lover who is great in the sack one day, then defecates in your shoes the next. You learn to live with it—and to watch where you step.

Anyone who makes it a point to explore places that others would not give a second thought will quickly become aware of the city's multiple personalities. L.A.'s unpredictability is not just about the shifting fault lines, but the shape-shifting phantom of the culture itself. In the world capital of make-believe, beware the moment you finally feel comfortable with your surroundings. Undoubtedly, that is the moment when everything will change. Go to bed one night in a neighborhood rich with history; wake up the next morning to a Kafkaesque tableau in which entire city blocks have been razed and replaced with hideously colorful condos, rat-race fitness centers, stucco mini-malls, and self-storage facilities with all the architectural zest of an East German abattoir. As a friend who cherished her prime, rent-controlled West Hollywood digs once confessed, "I'm reluctant to leave my apartment for too long for fear it'll get turned into a Mrs. Fields Cookies." Only now it might be more likely to become a Pinkberry. And who knows what tomorrow holds? We're putting our money on a successful franchise of anal-bleaching parlors.

Laugh now, but you know we're right.

In the wake of the longest political season in U.S. history, Hope and Change have taken on new meanings on a national level, but change in L.A. hasn't given us much in the way of hope. Sadly, for every L.A. oddity that bites the dust, there is nothing to take its place that is even of remote interest. The vast chem lab superstore (Tri-Ess Sciences), the nudist gang-bang retreat (Naked City), and the enduring pagan amusement park (Santa's Village) are but a few of the original *L.A. Bizarro* casualties we mourn; future generations of camp connoisseurs will only be able to read about these wonders . . . and wonder.

As far as we're concerned, a business need not declare bankruptcy to go belly-up. After years of slumming it, a treasured curiosity might suddenly find itself in the center of L.A.'s neighborhood *du jour*, or experience a fortuitous and unforeseen comeback by virtue of a local "Best Of" listing, or worse, an A-list celebrity spotting. Presto! Seemingly overnight, the incontinent winos who once dampened the barstools of a crusty dive are replaced with pretty youngsters in full control of their involuntary muscles, and whose low-slung jeans reveal conspicuously pee-free undies.

Sadly, many of our longtime favorites underwent misguided upgrades; they finally found their spotlight, but lost their charm in the process. New owners, fresh décor, hot clientele, chronic overexposure . . . whatever the reason, we lost interest, and with a casual swipe of our red pen, they were gone. Love and God are fickle like that. And so are we.

Not long ago, one had to possess at least a modicum of style and DIY resourcefulness to stay abreast of what's what. You had to know the right people, read the right rags, and get off your ass once in awhile. When you made a great find, you kept it within your little circle of friends lest it be overrun by frat boys and valley girls and what used to be called "yuppies." Those glory days are gone. Now, thanks to the Web, everyone's a critic, and anyone with a cell phone camera and an Internet connection can ruin a little-known gem for the regulars with the click of a mouse. Jesus Creeping Christ, we can remember when you had to publish a book to do that.

Which is one of the reasons we're doing it again.

The long march of progress has burdened us with an overload of information from a seemingly endless array of social networks, user-generated content sites, and annoyingly cutesy hyper-gadgets like Twitter. Just because the technology exists to let the world know what you're thinking at any given moment doesn't suddenly a) give your thoughts merit, or b) mean the world gives a shit about you. There was a time when the folks who ranted on street corners or muttered to themselves all day long were known as cranks or crazies. Now everyone does it and we call them "bloggers." (You can read our blog at *www.labizarro.com*!)

We're the first to admit that there is a certain guilty pleasure to be had in going online to read a completely retarded and spurious "user review," especially for something as ubiquitous as, say, a 7-Eleven store. Behold this genuine, unexpurgated gem:

*"Went here to get my paper today. Sometimes parking can be a problem here. I guess it happens everywhere. I will be back. I normally get my lottery at this one or Overland one."*

Although these kinds of reviews provide reassurance that there is actually someone lower on the food chain than yourself, we regret that space constraints for *L.A. Bizarro* prohibited us from indulging in writing about anything more banal than Famima!! and Bubba Gump Shrimp Company. We apologize in advance, and encourage fans of the obvious to check out our Web site *www.labizarro.com* for reviews on manhole covers, homeless people, and the wind.

Now, given the way we wax lyrical over those perfectly preserved joints that have yet to be co-opted by the self-consciously cool, one might assume that we lose sleep about Los Angeles culture, its landmark historic architecture, and the iconic establishments that have managed to hang tough through the decades. While it's certainly a downer to see the world's only Dudley Do-Right Emporium turn into a taco stand, we're hardly preservationists. Fact is, we take perverse pleasure in watching the thrill-a-minute horror show called "progress" unfold before our very eyes; nothing makes our hearts race like seeing another cherished L.A. landmark French-kissed by the wrecking ball. It's like witnessing the messy reality of a boob job, only on a vast, metropolitan scale: Flabby, decrepit, unwanted history is hauled to the county's landfills in order to make way for bigger and better retail, and housing developments so conspicuously perfect that they defy the imagination. This obsessive race to replace the almost old with the brand spanking new is as much a part of Los Angeles as any sacred relic whose demise would elicit copious boo-hooing. Without this callow tradition, L.A. would be allowed to grow old gracefully, and then we'd have nothing to write about.

Which brings us back to this new edition.

We wasted untold gallons of gas, polluted the environment, drank ourselves stupid, stuffed ourselves silly, scorched naked in the Jacumba sun, subjected ourselves to indescribable sexual humiliations, endured grueling detox sessions, talked to Scientologists, and even had our colons cleansed *just for you*. This is a vicarious thrill ride as much as it is a guidebook; how you choose to use it is entirely up to you. Should you insist in following in the folly of our footsteps, you hereby acknowledge and agree that we accept no responsibility nor shall we be held liable for your actions.

Enjoy.

Anthony Lovett and Matt Maranian

Matt Tony

ENJOY LIFE,
EAT OUT
MORE OFTEN

CHAPTER
№ 1

# VISIT YOSEMITE WITHOUT LEAVING DOWNTOWN LOS ANGELES AT

# CLIFTON'S CAFETERIA

**Clifton's Cafeteria**
**648 Broadway**
**Los Angeles**
**213.627.1673**
**www.cliftonscafeteria.com**

Let's say you're a Make-a-Wish kid and your time is running out. And let's say your wish—your one wish to provide the final days of your tragically abbreviated young life with an unyielding crescendo—is to experience our City of Angels, *L.A. Bizarro*-style (let's say you're a Make-a-Wish kid who aims low). Since you wouldn't have the luxury of frittering away lots of extra hours in freeway traffic or waiting in line at Pinkberry, we'd suggest you tell your driver to make but one stop: Clifton's Cafeteria.

If *L.A. Bizarro* had a centerfold, Clifton's would surely find a staple in its navel and the corners of its pages dog-eared and sticky. It could be said that Clifton's is *all* of Los Angeles, right in one spot. Here you will find carefully manufactured illusion, well preserved with frequent face-lifts and occasional upgrades (in fact, the concrete deer that once stood precariously perched in a lofty corner grotto was replaced with an actual taxidermied moose head sometime in the past decade). Clifton's isn't short on Tinseltown glamour, either, since it's been on TV, and it's got history too, having outlived once-thriving institutions like The Brown Derby, Chasen's, and Perino's by decades. And although Clifton's can't compete with the geographic desirability of the Self-Realization Fellowship in Pacific Palisades or the real estate holdings of the Church of Scientology, you'll find that faith-based initiative is not lost here either, with a private two-dimensional nature sanctuary-cum-chapel (recorded sermon at the push of a button), Clifton's A-plus exercise in low-end surrealism. Think Los Angeles is overpopulated with boring white people? Watch Clifton's thumb its cosmopolitan nose with a steam table that includes traditional fare like coleslaw and Jell-O right alongside homemade enchiladas and Polish sausage with sauerkraut—and a clientele representing more nations than the "Small World" ride at Disneyland.

Don't be fooled by Clifton's modest façade; you're in Los Angeles, after all, where appearances are routinely deceiving. The main floor of Clifton's spectacular dining room features a wall stretching two stories high, painted floor to ceiling to look like a forest clearing in Yosemite complete with a cedar tree trunk relief and an illuminated full moon. When was the last time you nibbled potato salad alongside a babbling brook trimmed with Astroturf that finished off-gassing while you were still in diapers? Featuring themed seating on no less than five levels, this delightfully wooded wonderland scores extra points with a waterfall and an absence of real windows. Don't be alarmed if you begin to feel a bit punchy. You'll soon lose all sense of day or night because Clifton's has thoughtfully painted forest scenes over all the original windows (and added some nice fake ones too), which help to shelter patrons from the nasty reality of downtown Los Angeles.

## *"Is it day or night?"*
—THE RUNAWAYS

Marginally informative historic note: E. J. *Clinton* was a Salvation Army captain who established Clinton's "Cafeteria and Puritan Dining Rooms" in San Francisco at the turn of the century. He came to Los Angeles (changing one consonant in his last name for no reason that we've ever been able to discern and don't care enough about to research) and founded Clifton's Cafeterias in 1931.

A visit to Clifton's is the duty of every Angeleno worth their weight in rice pudding; it would be like living in Rome and having never visited St. Peter's.

Don't be a loser. Visit Clifton's now and often.

## WHEN SOME GOON HITS YOUR EYE LIKE A MAFIA GUY, THAT'S THE

# SINATRA ROOM

The Sinatra Room /
Casa De Pizza
16161 San Fernando Mission
Boulevard
Granada Hills
818.366.6311

*Rediscovering
the Chairman
of the Bored*

Yes, smartass, "That's Amore" was actually made famous by Dean Martin, but grant us a little poetic license, would you? We've been searching for The Sinatra Room for over a decade and we're freakin' exhausted here.

Our obsession began sometime in the early nineties, when we literally stumbled into an Italian restaurant that featured something called "The Sinatra Room." Upon sobering up, our collective memory of the place was hazy at best: we recalled it was *somewhere* in Los Angeles, had a sign on the wall which read, "If you have anything bad to say about Francis Albert Sinatra, don't say it here," and we thought it was the cat's meow. Yet our best efforts to retrace our steps were in vain. We began to think we had hallucinated the whole thing, which, considering our state of mind at the time, was a distinct possibility. Like a wild, drunken, one-night stand, we never forgot The Sinatra Room . . . but we couldn't remember it, either. Like so many disconsolate souls, we turned to she-male porn and bags of Bugles for succor. If repeated screenings of *Tranny and the Professor* and handfuls of salty corn snacks couldn't fill the void, nothing would.

Fortunately, we were lifted from our perverted malaise by "the Google," as our former president likes to call it, and suddenly The Sinatra Room went from being a tawdry memory to a tawdry reality. We could hardly contain our joy, and decided to make it our first stop for this new edition of the book.

The rest, as they say, is denouement.

Going back to the trope about a one-night stand, we were initially underwhelmed when finally reunited with Casa de Pizza, a small, nondescript, hole-in-the-wall Italian restaurant wedged into an unassuming strip mall in Granada Hills. Not that there's anything wrong with the joint—other than the spelling, of course, which in Italian would be "Casa *di* Pizza"—but it just didn't seem as magical as we kind of remembered it. Then again, when one is talking about a Technicolor memory fueled by powerful chemicals, reality is always going to be a disappointment. That's the first thing they teach you at the Owsley Academy for Boys. So, despite the fact that the sign we so adored was gone (sequestered in the owner's house, it turns out), The Sinatra Room was still there, which is more than we could say for most of our favorite haunts. We decided to soldier on and attempt to relive the unmistakable thrill we weren't even sure we'd had in the first place. Boy, are we glad we did. We think.

If you can imagine someone turning their rumpus room into a living shrine to Frank Sinatra, where they would serve pizza and stuffed mushroom caps to the faithful, that would be something like The Sinatra Room, the walls of which are packed with portraits, posters, placards, records, and any other kind of Sinatrian memorabilia that can be nailed to a flat surface. In other words, *tutto magnifico!*

The same goes for the food, which was a pleasant surprise (again, in the one-night stand paradigm, one is expected to expect the worst). High points: the thin-crust pizza was distinctly homemade, the mushroom caps were big, bold, and very New Jersey, and the lasagna was . . . filling. *Very* filling. Unbutton-your-pants-and-let-out-an-audible-groan filling.

We worked up the nerve to talk to our waitress, who just happened to be the daughter of the owner, and she looked at us like we were a little crazy when we griped about the "Don't talk

# OUT '*n*' ABOUT
# ODE TO HENRY'S TACOS

Over forty years of life have you, a sleepy Moorpark icon,
Though better fare the city offers us to set our sights on.

But love in us you have instilled with crisp shell and greasy meat,
And we maintain for nuance dear, that Henry's can't be beat.

Your picnic table in the sun, or to our car, we go,
For you were never of the kind to indulge us in a show.

We eat with ardor—your devotees—feeling never wary,
In spite that later evening comes, ensuing dysentery.

**Henry's Tacos / 11401 Moorpark Street / Studio City / 818.769.0343**

smack on Sinatra" sign being taken down. When she told us her dad took it to his house for safekeeping, we casually asked if we could have it. There was a moment of silence, and she didn't blink, but the question in her eyes was clear as day: "Say, weren't you the guys who came in here all fucked up about fifteen years ago and peed in the ficus?"

No ma'am. Never been here before. Check, please.

Seriously, Casa de Pizza is one of those old-school mom-and-pop pizza parlors that once populated the Great Plains as far as the eye could see, then died off in the Great Olive Garden Plague of the eighties and the Macaroni Grill Black Death of the following decade. Now, like radioactive renegades hiding in a wasteland far from the sheltered safety of the fortress mall, the last few survivors continue to churn out pizza and Italian food the only way they know how: the right way.

Hey, we just wrote the treatment for a new series on the CW!

## HAVING SEX WITH THE WHOLE FAMILY AT

# UWINK

uWink
6100 Topanga Canyon
Boulevard
Westfield Promenade
Woodland Hills
818.992.1100
www.uwink.com
(also open in Hollywood)

*Bring your own Purell.*

We're not sure whether uWink heralds the dawn of a new dining experience or the end of civilization as we know it.

Lacking the manic "Hey look, I'm a big kid!" bullshit of mega-pub chain Dave & Buster's, uWink is kind of like a sedate Chuck E. Cheese for grown-up button-mashers. That's no coincidence, since uWink's high tech "dining entertainment experience" is the brain-child of Nolan Bushnell, the founder of Chuck E. Cheese, Atari, and the first electronic arcade game, Pong. Those credentials alone moistened our Hanes before we ever set foot in the place.

It makes perfect sense that the first uWink is located in a mall in the San Fernando Valley, its vast sprawl having spawned more computer and console gamers than any other suburban incuba-tor in the world. UWink's combination of comfort food, booze, and interactive gaming isn't a unique concept, but its delivery is. Upon first entering the place, one is immediately struck by the discernible lack of testosterone so often found in establishments that combine alcohol, food, and friendly competition. Though the noise level is well above that of a Trappist monastery, it is decid-edly lower than that of a frat house during rush week. The walls are bare; artwork as well as group games are projected on them.

Clean, simple tables are outfitted with touch-screen monitors encased in brushed steel housings.

These monitors are the heart and soul of uWink. On them, you order your food and drinks, play an endless variety of games, and pay your bill. The only time you have to deal with another human (other than those in your party) is when your food is served. Or so it seems. Halfway through our uWink experience, it dawned on us that we weren't the first to have our hands all over those screens that day. We did not see waiters wiping down monitors after each service, nor were bottles of hand sanitizer provided on the table. When the first order of finger food arrived, we suddenly felt an intimate connection with everyone else who had pawed the monitors that day. We excused ourselves to wash our filthy mitts.

Despite the slim possibility of contracting the Ebola virus from a contaminated touch screen, the concept behind uWink is noble, at least in theory. Our first round of drinks arrived moments after we ordered. The appetizers were also delivered promptly. It was only when it came to our entrées that the seamless interface between man and machine went horribly awry. While some plates made it from the kitchen to our table, others apparently were lost like so much corrupted data on a failing hard drive. In our party of eight, the lucky ones were finishing their delicious Korean skirt steaks while others were just being served their less-than-stellar fish tacos.

This kind of gaffe in service may be tolerated by those who tend to be mesmerized by computer games, i.e., adult geeks and spoiled children accustomed to playing their PSP at the dinner table. However, for civilized folks, senior citizens, and Luddites, uWink can easily become an exercise in confusion and frustration. Even those who know their way around a computer may find themselves short on patience when the system fails to function the way it should—so just imagine how a hungry diabetic octogenarian would feel.

When it came to playing the games (for which you earn credits when you order your food), we fared only slightly better. While there are many entertaining diversions designed for individual play, only two accommodate multiple players. One of these was "Truth or Dare," which started out by asking us to simulate our favorite sexual act with the person to our left. More appalling than the fact that we were having dinner with our children, parents, and grandparents, was the game's disclaimer that it was suitable for ages fifteen and up. Fifteen? Really? We find it slightly disturbing that kids who can't even drive are expected to have a favorite sexual act other than masturbation, but who are we kidding? We live in an age when twelve-year-olds pimp themselves on MySpace and YouTube with all the subtlety of a Reeperbahn whore, which would also explain why the junior high schoolers at the next table were so deft at pantomiming scenes from *Salo: The 120 Days of Sodom*.

For those who put consistent service and human interaction low on the totem pole, and who enjoy coming into contact with someone else's bacteria while being forced to simulate oral sex on your grandmother, uWink is a great place to nosh, drink, and play mediocre computer games. Sure, you can just as easily do that at home, but the fact that you can also make a good cup of joe in the comfort of your own kitchen hasn't put a dent in Starbucks.

All kidding aside, if uWink offers us a glimpse as to what's in store for America's future, we should all be speaking Mandarin in no time.

*Cào nǐ zǔzōng shíbā dài!*

## GETTING SLOPPY AT

# DR. HOGLY WOGLY'S

## TYLER TEXAS BBQ

Dr. Hogly Wogly's
Tyler Texas BBQ
8136 Sepulveda Boulevard
Panorama City
818.782.2480

Roman Productos
Religiosos
8148 Sepulveda Boulevard
Panorama City
818.908.3637

Deep within the bowels of the San Fernando Valley, in an unassuming building in the heart of the ironically named Panorama City, tucked along an unattractive stretch of Sepulveda sometimes known as a destination for streetwalkers and their clientele, Dr. Hogly Wogly pimps the sweetest flesh on the block. Sure, it's a dirty business, but those in the know who prefer them young and tender are on a first-name basis with the Doc. You gotta thing for babies? He's got 'em.

That's right. Baby back pork ribs.

On the other hand, there are those who swear by his beef brisket. That's cool. Hogly Wogly swings both ways and even does the chicken thing, dishing up some of the best Texas barbecue in the

## OUT 'n' ABOUT

# WHAT'S A WEINIE WITHOUT A BUN?

On principle alone, we would endorse Weinie Bakery because of its name, so imagine our delight when we discovered a treasure trove of uniquely delicious pastries inside. The Taiwanese-style bakery serves up a variety of traditional treats, including homemade baozi stuffed with your choice of meat and/or vegetable fillings, red bean and plain mantou, and dessert cakes that are neither too sweet nor too filling. Best of all, Weinie serves up something called a Hot Dog Bun, which looks like a hot dog–studded Danish, sans the frosting. Freakin' genius! Similar creations include the Tuna Salad Bun and the Ham & Cheese Bun, both of which are also available in "Mini" bite-sized versions. Though the rolls with taro, red bean, onions, and other time-honored ingredients are excellent, we can't help but be impressed with the why-didn't-I-think-of-that ingenuity of the Hog Dog Bun and its cohorts. This is the kind of melting-pot experience that makes us proud to be Americans, goddamit.

**Weinie Bakery / 9250 Reseda Blvd / Northridge / 818.886.7331**

Southland. Now, we'll be the first to admit that barbecue is one of those topics that, like religion, engenders passionate debate—and that makes sense when you think about it, because for true believers, barbecue *is* a religion.

We've heard some local arbiters of taste scoff at the notion that Dr. Hogly Wogly's Tyler Texas BBQ serves *real* Texas barbecue, and we would have to say yes, this is true; the restaurant is located in California. But seeing as one of your humble authors hails from the Lone Star State, we'd like to think that when it comes to barbecue we actually know our asses from a hole in the ground (*hint: it's a little easier to sink a putt into the latter*).

First of all, not all Texas barbecue is created equal. There are regional styles within the state, and two different rib joints in the same city might serve completely disparate recipes. That said, Texas barbecue is the real deal, so don't even think about mentioning what passes for 'cue in Memphis, Kansas City, North Carolina, and other pretenders to the throne. (Despite our obvious elitism, check out the Missouri style Bear Pit Bar-B-Q, also in this chapter.)

*What have you been smoking?*

Not to be confused with the barbecue grill in your backyard, real barbecue is more about smoke than fire. But the sad truth is that many barbecue joints in Los Angeles don't even own a smoker. They cut corners and save time by boiling the meat first, coating it in barbecue sauce, and then baking it until it resembles the real thing. *Boiling?* Anyone who peddles this crap as real barbecue deserves a lynching, which, like Dubya, is another Lone Star tradition that Texans should be less than proud of.

Like most Texas barbecue, Hogly Wogly's smokes its meat for hours and hours over burning wood in a brick pit, and then serves it "dry," i.e., *au naturel,* and not slathered in barbecue sauce. To do otherwise borders on heresy and is considered strictly for rank amateurs and other non-Texans. Don't let the word "dry" fool you, though—at Hogly Wogly's, the meat is marinated and basted in a thin, liquidy "secret sauce" that makes it orgasmically moist. Once served, it's up to you whether or not to ruin a plate of perfectly good 'cue by drowning it in sauce. That said, Doc's concoctions—the hot one in particular—has caused us to dabble in a little saucery from time to time. Call it a guilty pleasure.

If a barbecue restaurant boasts slick interior design and an

unmistakable corporate vibe—the heinous Wood Ranch comes to mind—then expect the fare to be about as authentic as the decor. Formica countertops and clean silverware are all the ambiance a good barbecue place needs, though we certainly won't deduct points for bad Western paintings and cheesy wagon wheel chandeliers as long as they're old, yellowed, and dusty. The dining room is relatively small at Hogly Wogly's—a lot of the property is taken up by the kitchen and that infernal smoke pit—so you can expect a wait on some nights and weekends, but it's worth it. Though the side dishes (we prefer the collard greens at Phillips' Barbecue on Crenshaw) are nothing to get frothy about, they certainly suffice in a no-nonsense kind of way.

When you leave Hogly Wogly's your belly will be full—but if your spirit is still hungry, check out Roman Productos Religiosos next door. This tiny store sells a variety of talismans, saintly statuettes, and a slew of other religious paraphernalia. For a nominal fee they'll also cleanse your soul, but unfortunately, not your colon.

# FOUNTAIN COFFEE ROOM

Few structures in Los Angeles are more steeped in Tinseltown legend than the Beverly Hills Hotel. It's been a favorite trysting spot for A-list adulterers (Marilyn Monroe and Yves Montand steamed up bungalow #5, and Desi Arnaz loved many a "Lucy" here), and it's also served as a valued celebrity hideout (John Lennon and Yoko Ono locked themselves into bungalow #11 for a solid week). It's played host to the eccentricities of those too rich to question (Howard Hughes asked that room service perch his nightly roast beef sandwich orders in the branches of a tree just outside his favorite bungalow, #4), and set the scene for some of Hollywood's most volatile marriages (Elizabeth Taylor and Richard Burton played out a real-life *Who's Afraid of Virginia Woolf?* in bungalow #5, with a standing room service order of four bottles of vodka a day: two at breakfast, two at lunch). Celebrated drunks like W. C. Fields, Dean Martin, and Humphrey Bogart all have tied one on in the Polo Lounge bar.

In late 1992, the Beverly Hills Hotel closed its doors to undergo a $100 million restoration and remodeling. The moment the cyclone fencing went up around its twelve acres, many feared the famed landmark would be subject to the worst facelift in Beverly Hills history. Though the remodeling was limited mostly to the accommodations, there were numerous other changes that only we freaks for detail would ever notice.

Fountain Coffee Room
The Beverly Hills Hotel
9641 Sunset Boulevard
Beverly Hills
310.276.2251
www.thebeverlyhillshotel.com

# BASTURMA HARD DAY'S NIGHT

In case you never noticed it before, there aren't a lot of *basturma* (pronounced baw-stər-ma) shops around this town, and no, it's not Armenian for masturbation. Hey, admit it, you don't even know what basturma is, do you? Maybe that's because you're not man enough to handle it. Yeah, you heard me, tough guy. Basturma is the king of Armenian meats, an air-cured, super-spiced, garlic-packing delicacy that's about as delicate as a swift kick in the balls—but far more pleasurable. Still with us, champ? If that analogy doesn't fly, then let's put it in your terms: Basturma is an in-your-face cold cut that's so packed with flavor you'll have to borrow some taste buds just to get a *hint* of what it's like. And this isn't some industrial basturma, made in some faraway basturma plant and shipped in a plastic bag on the basturma express. Hell no! Harry Tashyan, proprietor of Sahag's, is a master basturma-ologist who gave up the good life being bombed by Israelis in Lebanon just to come here so he can make his delicious meats for you in the back of his tiny shop on Sunset. Standing proudly among his basturma and *sujjuk*— a savory little bastard of a sausage that'll stroll into your mouth and wrestle it into submission—Tashyan stands astride Hollywood's Little Armenia like a Colossus. Get your basturma or sujjuk prepared as a hot-pressed sandwich in the shop, buy it whole, or get it sliced to go. We like to get a wheelbarrow of it, thinly sliced, then dump it in a kiddie pool on a hot summer day and writhe around in it wearing only a pair of Speedos and protective goggles until we get high on the fumes. However you decide to enjoy it, be prepared to deal with garlic odor that is going to follow you around for days, attracting certain chicks the way Hai Karate cologne used to. Last time we ate at Sahag's, we ended up running down Sunset Boulevard with about fifty screaming Armenian women behind us, ready to tear our clothes off. It was just like the opening of *A Hard Day's Night*, except some of the ladies had wispy mustaches—which, in a weird way, was kind of hot.

This may be the very best basturma in the Western Hemisphere, but what would you know? You probably still eat pimiento loaf! Get to Sahag's Basturma and become a man, you pansy—and that means you too, ladies!

Sahag's Basturma / 5183 Sunset Boulevard / Little Armenia / Hollywood

The absence of the quaint downstairs drug store is sorely felt, as is the loss of Harry Winston Jewelers, which used to be located in the lobby (not that we ever shopped there), and the hotel's exterior, once washed with a timeless flamingo pink, was downgraded to a shade closer to that of a pencil eraser.

Fortunately, in spite of the extensive remodeling, the best spot in the entire hotel managed to slip by unaltered. Tucked away into a tiny asymmetrical nook just inside the curved stairway leading down from the lobby, sits the little-known Fountain Coffee Room. The classic 1949 design by architect Paul Williams is an unrivaled charmer evocative of a pharmacy soda fountain cross-pollinated with a dash of mid-century modern swank. A sweeping free-form black marble countertop lined with nineteen stools cuts through the center of the narrow room. Above, recessed lighting set into a streamlined stucco overhang runs the length of the counter. Some of the walls are plate glass, others are covered with the hotel's old trademark vintage wallpaper pattern of deep green banana leaves. Behind the counter, within arm's reach of your pink vinyl seat, a cook with a tall chef's hat serves up the food from a sparkling chrome grill, handing it off to chirpy waitresses in pink uniforms who maintain the impeccable service standards of the hotel's "nicer" eateries.

*Coffee shop chic.*

Fresh ingredients and fastidious preparation—to the extreme that grease is blotted from a bacon strip before it's placed onto your plate—may not do much to justify the prices or the parking fee, but the experience is worth the inordinate profit margin and the food is the best of its kind.

# LORD, LET ME GET TO THE PINK'S ORDER WINDOW BEFORE I DIE.

In the first edition of this book, we waxed poetic about Pink's, but now the honeymoon is over. It's not like we found a human finger in our chili (we didn't), or that the food has gone downhill (it hasn't), or that the prices have gone through the roof (they haven't). In fact, the problem isn't with Pink's at all, but with the patrons. There are just too damn many of them. What kind of dumbass drives all the way from Orange Country for a hot dog? Drop by Pink's on a Saturday night and take a gander.

You won't find quaint programatic architecture at the most popular hot dog stand in Los Angeles. Pink's doesn't have time for such nonsense: It's too busy feeding the ravenous hordes perpetually clamoring at the gate. If you want to purchase a hot dog at an oversized mock-up of a frankfurter nestled in its ubiquitous beige bun, you should have gone to Tail o' the Pup before it closed. If you're craving a decent dog and have a few hours to kill, then Pink's is for you.

The fare at Pink's is noteworthy, but hardly bizarre, and the place itself is the antithesis of obscure. What has us scratching our heads is the ungodly line that forms around the block for a hot dog that's certainly delicious, yet no better than that served at a dozen other wiener joints in the city. Yes, yes, Pink's is an L.A. tradition, it's the "hot dog to the stars," the chili is delicious, Orson Welles ate fifteen in one night, it's open until 3:00 AM on the weekends, blah, blah, blah . . . but when we spy a line, day or night, that's consistently longer than airport security, we can't help but question the sanity of the people standing in it. It's a fucking *hot dog*, people. Get over it.

(And if you think this is some kind of cheap ploy to thin the line so we don't have to stand in it, shame on you.)

Pink's / 709 North La Brea Avenue / Los Angeles / 323.931.4223

# FANNING THE FLAMES OF
# MARIA'S RAMADA

Maria's Ramada
1064 North Kingsley Drive
Hollywood
323.660.4463
www.mariasramada.com

Maria's has always seemed a bit misplaced to us. Belying its proximity to the headstones of Cecil B. De Mille, Carl "Alfalfa" Switzer, and Bugsy Siegel at the Hollywood Forever Cemetery, Maria's feels more like the sort of place you'd find along a dusty roadside near a sleepy Mexican border town—the restaurant you settle upon for lack of other options after having stopped for gas—or one of those of spots you venture into only because you've taken a wrong turn and need directions and a cold beer.

The food: excellent. The atmosphere: unparalleled. Restaurants without windows are always our first choice, but don't let the big dumpster next to the front entrance fool you, Maria's is really one of the best Mexican restaurants in town. It's also one of the few that gives its salsa—served in a stone mortar—enough heat. And if it's heat you're after, their complimentary bowl of jalapeño pickled vegetables are endowed with a faith-affirming fire by which—after eating all the jicama—we actually saw the Virgin Mary of Guadalupe appear in a tortilla chip. So what gives? Why doesn't Maria's enjoy the crowds of El Coyote?

*The diablo's in the details.*

How, after forty years in business, is Maria's still on the list of insider "secrets"? Beats the hell out of us, but at least we can always get a table.

Maria's interior astounds—to the extreme that one wonders if this wasn't the product of a credentialed set dresser, or if their decorator (perhaps Maria herself?) got exactly what she was aiming for by making the most of a minimal design budget. Like a mini-shanty town lit with the tawdry glow from miles of Christmas lights, the dining room is a maze of expertly handmade booths slapped together from of old boards, corrugated tin, and salvaged tree

branches—laden with sombreros, silk flowers, plastic produce, and crudely woven God's Eyes. Maria's is cozy. It's an environment that says, *"Bienvenido,* stay a while, *Amigo,* and burn yourself a new asshole."

The Latino playlist on the Seeburg Disc-o-theque in the corner, the cheap beer, and the superlative molé are but a few of the extras that put Maria's on our map of musts. Maybe it's the *mañana* mindset, but we always wonder if our server hasn't taken a siesta or been stabbed in the kitchen (or maybe it's just that we're always really hungry when we come here). No matter; the chips, salsa, pickled vegetables, and hearty lentil soup will keep you pacified quite nicely, and their food is always worth the wait. Uh . . . *Olé!*

## DINING INFERNO AT

# BAHOOKA RIBS AND GROG

Bahooka Ribs and Grog
4501 North Rosemead
Boulevard
Rosemead
818.285.1241
www.geocities.com/
bahookarestaurant

Now that Kelbo's, Sam's Polynesian, and Trader Vic's have all been scuttled, Rosemead is the final frontier of South Seas dining, home to the last of the great remaining and much-cherished 1960s pseudo-Polynesian restaurants in the Greater L.A. area.

Journey with us to Bahooka, a comfortably chaotic labyrinth of aquariums, tiki gods, plastic parrots, and miscellaneous shipwreck flotsam—a hyper-surrealistic South Pacific wonderland right in our own backyard. The dimly lit booths and alcoves are nearly private enough to have sex in—although this is not recommended—and with over a hundred fluorescent fish tanks bubbling away, it's the closest you can come to having dinner on the old "Submarine Voyage" ride at Disneyland.

In addition to its standing as the last of the greats, Bahooka is famous for three important things: (1) its ribs, the portion of which is so large it's almost unnerving to see that much animal on your plate; (2) Rufus, the bulimic vegan pacu fish holding court in the reception area; and (3) our favorite waitress in the whole wide world, Go Go (that's really her name, swear to God).

Not only is Go Go a complete doll, she can garnish a Polynesian cocktail like nobody's business. And when Go Go's

# DON'T THEY SELL BLEACHING CREAM FOR THIS?

"You got any *money*?" a voice calls from below a cinderblock wall as we approach Dale's Donuts in Compton. We pretend we're deaf and blind; when there are donuts to be had, we stop for no one. With the scent of sugary fried dough leading our way, we continue on our course. "HEY!" his volume increases, "I said, you got *any MONEY*?" he cries again, as an empty Big Gulp hurled from his location flies toward us with alarming accuracy, grazing an ear.

Dale's might make for a gritty scene, but in Los Angeles elephantine donuts constitute important historic architecture, and none should be overlooked. Originally one of the Wendell's Big DoNut shop chains of the early 1950s, Dale's is one of five surviving locations. Although one of them—Bellflower Bagel—has been revamped into a healthier empty calorie alternative, the rest still make good on their twenty-two-foot promise, with Randy's and Kindle's workin' it 24/7.

**Dale's Donuts / 15904 South Atlantic Avenue / Compton**
**Bellflower Bagels / 17025 Bellflower Boulevard / Bellflower**
**Randy's Donuts / 805 West Manchester Boulevard / Inglewood**
**Kindle's Donuts / 10003 South Normandie Avenue / Los Angeles**
**Donut King II / 15032 South Western Avenue / Gardena**
**The Donut Hole / 15300 East Amar Road / La Puente**

in the mood to garnish, stand back. She can pile a whole fruit stand on the edge of a highball. But most importantly, Go Go sets it all on fire. Go Go has actually served water and coffee on fire, bless her heart. But her talent for pyromaniacal cocktail garnishing hardly ends with beverages. She's the only waitress we know of who can make a side order of fries look like a Singapore Sling. Go Go has even set our Jell-O ablaze. Go Go is the pearl of Rosemead's oyster, bringing fun fun fun, Polynesian style, wherever she goes. You should have her autograph your copy of *L.A. Bizarro* while you're there. She's a star.

*Go Go: girl on fire*

However, we do need to offer a disclaimer here on Go Go's behalf. Evidently, with the success of *L.A. Bizarro's* first edition, Go Go became the most requested waitress at Bahooka, and with her new-found notoriety came many requests for ignition. Please understand that while, yes, Go Go is fabulous, sometimes she's just too busy to set your world on fire, especially on weekends when the joint jumps. Conflagrated cocktail fans please take note.

That said, we strongly encourage you to request Go Go as your waitress, tell her we sent you, and tip big. Seriously. Don't embarrass us.

After you've paid your check (and included a generous tip), make a polite request that Go Go show you Bahooka's famous bulimic fish, Rufus. He's almost thirty years old, is so large that he barely has room to turn around in his tank, and he chomps down carrot

sticks like a rabid dog. Unfortunately, there's a limit to the number of carrot-eating fish performances Go Go can give in one evening, since Rufus tends to regurgitate his veggies once he's had more than his fill. So if Go Go is unable to meet your request, please understand, and come back another time.

If you want to bring a little of the magic home with you, it should also be noted that Bahooka bottles and sells their own tropical drink mixes and salad dressing, and you'll also find T-shirts, hoodies, and their custom-designed fortieth-anniversary tiki mug available at the merch counter.

## SAVORING THE SEPARATE REALITY OF
# DEAR JOHN'S

**Dear John's**
**11208 Culver Boulevard**
**Culver City**
**310.397.0276**

Frog's legs, a cracking fire, and a Dean Martin tribute, all under one roof? In Culver City?

To say that Dear John's is merely a steakhouse would be a disservice, because it's so much more than a place to eat beef. It's so much more than a place to eat. It's so much more than a place.

The restaurant's name references not spurned servicemen, but the original owner, John, who had changed his last name from the awkwardly Eastern European "Hlivyak" to the more palatably Hollywood "Harlowe" prior to pursuing a career in movies. A busy working actor—but nary scoring more than a single speaking role—he hailed Brando's Mark Antony, rexed with a young

Marilyn, hoofed it with Jayne Mansfield, and soaked his trunks alongside Esther Williams, among other Grauman's-worthy names who peppered his lengthy resumé. But in 1965, he quickly turned his focus from third-rung film work to steak and cocktails in the form of Dear John's. And thank God he did.

Although the restaurant has changed hands to a non-John, the intimate, dimly lit, and windowless dining room—redolent with what seemed to be fumes escaping from the gas-fueled fireplace occupying the red brick hearth—hasn't changed much since its Johnson-era opening. To one side of the room patrons nestle into precisely the sort of tufted vinyl booths one would expect from a restaurant that serves shrimp Louie. On the other, eighteen stools line the bar, ready for warming beneath a glittered, chocolate-brown, cottage cheese ceiling. At first glance— particularly before your eyes adjust to the absence of light—Dear John's appears to reach almost Chasen's-caliber aspirations, with blood-red tablecloths, monogrammed menus, and glistening cutlery placed upon decoratively folded napkins. But the devil is in the details, and upon closer inspection we discern that while the table dressing is crisply pressed, all the silverware patterns are mismatched, as are most of the well-worn chairs. And although we noted no telltale signs whatsoever of any links to organized crime, Dear John's *feels* like the kind of place where an unluckily seated diner might be inadvertently gunned down in a mob dispute gone awry.

A perusal of the menu over a double Bombay on the rocks was intermittently punctuated by the ear-piercing audio feedback from the mic test taking place in a darkened corner. Stationed alongside the piano bar beneath a tattered George Nelson bubble lamp, our evening's entertainment—a one-man tribute to Dean Martin—was getting underway. The performer, another John, surname of Greenwood, the very same who was playing Dear John's twenty five years ago, was having a little trouble calibrating his sound equipment, momentarily silencing both the bar patrons and the jovial atmosphere of the dining room with tonal flourishes akin to a Cold War defense siren. After a fifteen-minute mic test that sent us into a state of hysterics, we couldn't wait to see what he could do with "That's Amore."

As our counterfeit Dino took to the floor, weaving his way though the dining room, peppering his playlist with tried-and-true patter ("I've got so much gas I could drive to Phoenix") and road-tested one liners ("The Bible told me to love thy neighbor, so I did— and my wife left me") diners are presented with those awkward moments that never seem to get addressed in etiquette handbooks. Like, for instance, when a

*I've got so much gas I could drive to Phoenix.*

# HOW SWEDE IT IS

Next time you're shopping for a Krämsp or Gløɾfnab at Ikea, take a break and park your buns at perhaps the finest eating establishment in Los Angeles—if not the entire world: the Ikea Restaurant and Café. Seriously, how many furniture stores have a clean, modern cafeteria that will serve you a plate of eight billion Swedish meatballs smothered in heart-stopping gravy with boiled red potatoes and a giant glop of sweet sticky lingonberries on the side, all for less than the price of a Croissanwich? Go to an Ethan Allen showroom and demand penne pasta with Alfredo sauce for ninety-nine cents and see how long it takes them to call the police. Does Pier 1 Imports serve your kid "chicken dinosaurs?" We think not. Sure, dinosaurs are extinct, but that doesn't stop Ikea from cookin' 'em up just for the little ones. The Swedes have a standard of living and life expectancy rate that kicks our ass, and we suspect the Ikea Restaurant and Café has something to do with it. The last time we were there, they offered a complete prime rib dinner for about a nickel. That means a typical family of twenty can gorge themselves on beef for about a dollar and then pass out in the bedding section. Okay, maybe we're exaggerating about the price, but trust us when we tell you that taking a catnap in a bin of Fältvädd pillow protectors with a belly full of steer is sheer ecstasy. And this place is not just an affordable family restaurant: It's also the most romantic spot in the southland. Is there anything that can bring a couple closer together than standing side by side, "accidentally" bumping their trays together as they move down the line? Is there a gesture more touching than bussing your lover's dirty plates? Whether you're on a first date or celebrating your fiftieth wedding anniversary, take your loved one to the Ikea Restaurant and Café and you'll definitely be getting some that evening—especially if you buy a couch. Single? No worries. When you're finished with your apple glazed salmon you can go downstairs to Ikea's Swedish food market, buy a dozen bags of frozen meatballs, go home, and keep stuffing yourself until you throw up all over your Sklümpft. Life is good.

**Ikea Restaurant and Café / 600 North San Fernando Boulevard / Burbank / 818.842.4532 / www.ikea.com**

# JUST AROUND THE CORNER FROM TIM'S FAMOUS CLAM & DURIAN HOT DOGS

In a town full of spotlight hogs, even fast food needs a gimmick.

Howard's Famous Bacon & Avocado Burgers / 11127 Venice Boulevard / Culver City / 310.838.9111

live entertainer performs "Innamorata" with his hand on your shoulder as you're trying to pull crab meat from its shell, are you supposed to stop what you're doing and look the performer in the eye? Or, seeing that you're here to eat, is it the entertainer's responsibility to negotiate around the etiquette conundrum of tableside performance?

Evidently the bar patrons—the only reminder to be had in Dear John's that, yes, we are in Culver City—weren't wrestling with such issues. With half the crowd looking like they'd arrived too early for the Super Bowl, and the other half looking like they'd been farting into the same bar stool since the days frog's legs were *de rigueur*, the live entertainment wasn't even enough cause to draw their gaze away from the X Games being broadcast sans audio. The bar also played host to our chefs, who seemed to spend as much time there as they did in the kitchen (though this was not reflected in the timely delivery of our meal), and even our ersatz Rat Packer took swigs from his beer between verses, ignoring his own performance.

The cheapness of Dear John's is only figurative; their vegetable platter is fifteen bucks and the lobster tail plate comes in at sixty. However, with anachronistic entrées like liver and onions, shrimp Louie, and a beef dip sandwich, with walls lined in celebrity 8 × 10s (only celebrities named John), and with live entertainment, mature waitresses, and tottering inebriates, you won't hear us complaining. While it's likely you'll end up parting with more cash than anticipated, you just can't put a price on the Dear John's experience.

A trip to the men's room, disappointingly, saw no twist on the John theme.

## ENJOYING THE ULTIMATE BLIND DATE AT

# OPAQUE

Opaque
2020 Wilshire Blvd
Santa Monica
310.546.7619
www.darkdining.com

As America's answer to a culinary movement that sprouted up across Europe in the past decade, Opaque offers "dining in the dark." We're not talking about mood lighting here, people; this is a restaurant that serves its fare in *total fucking darkness*. The theory behind the experience is deceptively simple: By depriving diners of their sense of sight, other senses—including taste—are heightened. The degree to which that's true will depend on the individual, but other than supercharged taste buds, one can easily surmise a few other benefits to dining in the dark:

1) ENDURING DULLNESS: Go ahead, close your eyes. You don't have to look like you care what your dinner partner(s) is saying. A simple "uh-huh" now and then will lead them to believe you're actually listening.

2) AURAL VOYEURISM: We found that dining in pitch blackness lends itself to eavesdropping; so much so that we spent more time listening to the conversations at other tables than bothering to engage in our own.

3) RUDENESS: No one can see your terrible table manners. Eat with your hands, pick your nose, make faces at your date, flip off the other tables—no one will know. Well, almost no one. Be aware that, for security reasons, there may be some degree of night-vision surveillance at the restaurant—we like to picture

Ted Levine from *Silence of the Lambs* roaming among the tables—so while the thought of eating dinner with your pants around your ankles in a crowded restaurant is understandably inviting, we would advise against it.

4) AVOID PUBLIC HUMILIATION: This is the perfect place to take someone you're embarrassed to be seen with in public, like an Ann Coulter or Kevin Federline.

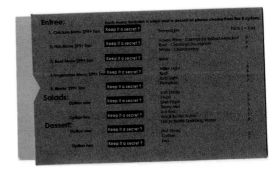

Those not schooled in Braille needn't worry about reading the menu at Opaque. Diners order their meals in the well-lit lobby area, and can choose from a *prix fixe* menu of beef, chicken, fish, or vegetarian entrées. Prefer surprises? Choose the *"Keep it a secret"* option from the menu and live dangerously. Once a selection has been made, you will be introduced to your legally-blind waitperson, who will then ask you to turn off your phones, take off anything that emits light (like a wristwatch or a Secret Squirrel decoder ring, or a uranium pendant), and put your hand on his/her shoulder before leading your party into the dining area like a slow-mo conga line. From that point on, you're in the dark, and completely at the mercy of your server. Fortunately, they are a kind-hearted lot.

Opaque's *table d'hôte* menu exists for more than just the sake of simplicity. Total darkness makes for some sloppy eating and prohibits the prompt bussing of tables, so the restaurant only allows one seating per table per night. While driving up the price of a meal, this policy ensures diners that they will not be sitting on someone else's misplaced pat of butter. Or worse. (See VH1's *Rock of Love*, season 2, episode 6 for more details.)

Once seated, we found the spatial disorientation to be oddly intoxicating, like being naked in public. Groping for the bread basket was a newfound odyssey. The sound of our water being poured proved to be an auditory revelation. The thrill of poking our eyes out while trying to eat our salads had us giddy with excitement. And cutting meat in the dark? *Fugeddaboutit!* Even if the food had been mediocre, the adrenaline rush alone would have been worth the price of admission.

But the food was *great*. We're not sure how much of it had to do our palates being enhanced by the darkness, but who cares? How often do you have the occasion to spend ten minutes speculating as to exactly what that delicious crunchy thing in the salad was? The beef "hangar steak," despite conjuring the frightful image of Joan Crawford looking over our shoulders, was incredibly tender and tasty. And though one of us is an avowed cheesecake hater, eating it in the dark made it not only tolerable, but

*Where the stars come not to be seen.*

downright delicious. Does this mean we'd be raving about a dog turd had it been presented to us on a plate? That all depends on how it's prepared.

Cheap scat humor aside, eating in the dark succeeded in forcing us to actually pay attention to what was going into our mouths. And once there, the food tended to linger longer than usual. We savored each bite, mulled over the combinations of tastes, and generally carried on like a couple of yahoos who'd never tasted feta cheese before.

We were not only pleasantly surprised by the quality of Opaque's cuisine, but also by the warmth of the service. Our waiter, Michael, had a soothing demeanor, was always prompt with the chow, and got bonus points for serenading us with "Blue Moon" on the trumpet. Suck on that, singing waiters!

Unless you camp out in the lobby, celebrity spotting is understandably difficult at Opaque. In fact, the restaurant is the only high-profile "can't-see-and-can't-be-seen" establishment we can think of. Notable patrons have run the gamut from transitory A-lister Mekhi Phifer to *Married with Children* gnome David Faustino to demented presidential has-run H. Ross Perot. If there are celebs at your seating, you will have to rely on senses other than sight to pick them out of the gloom. This is harder than it seems: we could have sworn we smelled Larry King, but it turned out to be the pesto-crusted chicken.

## GETTING ALL THAIED UP AT THE ORIGINAL

# TOI

Toi
7505 ½ Sunset Boulevard
323.874.8062
Los Angeles
www.toirockinthaifood.com

One of the advantages of writing a book like *L.A. Bizarro* is having the opportunity to supplement our chapters with an occasional biased rave for a longtime favorite haunt—but does a joint like Toi meet the criteria of an *L.A. Bizarro* entry? Is Toi on par with the Lawrence Welk Museum, anal bleaching, or the Easter show at the Crystal Cathedral? The truth is we've never really established a criteria for *L.A. Bizarro* entries, which is really convenient in a case like this. By definition, the word "bizarre" is actually rather vague, simply qualifying as anything strange or unconventional "as to cause interest or amusement"—which leaves L.A. wide open for our interpretation, because it's never taken much to amuse us. Hell, we like *F Troop*.

We may dig the outré, adore the depraved, and wax lyrical over the perverse, but that doesn't mean a nice friendly place can't make it onto these pages too. We love the Apple Pan just like everyone else, and couldn't even begin to count the number of times we staggered out the doors of Musso & Frank half-cocked. Gems of that ilk have their place here as well, especially since so many were kissed by the wrecking ball or subjected to a Mel's Diner makeover in recent years. Having watched more than a few decades come and go in Los Angeles has been sobering to say the least, and has allowed us the perspective to anoint a new wave of L.A. institutions. By that standard, certainly, Toi may take its place at the front of the line.

Like any good institution, Toi captures an era in Los Angeles (the eighties) and a spirit (rock 'n' roll), and stays true to its product (hearty Thai cooking), seeing no reason for facelifts, upgrades, or apologies—with a customer experience of unfailing consistency. Years could pass between visits, and upon your return you'll be digging into the same steaming heap of crab fried rice you came to know and love in 1986, served quickly, by a staff so attentive, adorable, and genuinely kind that the weaker among us need to restrain ourselves from licking them.

Upon first encountering a place like Toi one might expect an experience overwrought with attitude. A restaurant referring to its cuisine as "rock 'n' roll Thai," with a decidedly rock 'n' roll staff and a crudely rendered rock 'n' roll decor located smack in the middle of Sunset Boulevard's guitar shop district might induce heaves from uninformed elitists. It's markedly devoid of attitude, however, and it's got the comfort of a well-worn motorcycle jacket to boot. Occupying two old storefronts joined at the hip, Toi's interior nods a bit toward a hybrid of downtown's old Al's Bar and the original Duke's at the Tropicana, its tall, cracked walls and high ceilings haphazardly plastered with concert posters, album covers, and musical miscellany. Creatures of papier-mâché hang here and there, and fucked-up thrift shop lamps and colored bulbs light the dark space with an additional glow from vintage music videos running on random TV screens. It's broken-in and comfortable, no fuss, like the basement where a really good garage band might rehearse. You'd half-expect your server to offer a bong hit with your Thai iced tea—whether you're there with six friends or nestled into a corner table on your own, it feels like that. Like the fun places in Hollywood used to feel. And they're open till 4:00 AM, seven days a week.

No haute Thai to be had here, no candy-ass portions. Toi will stuff your gut like a truck stop diner with an impressive variety of seafood, curries, soups, salads, and noodle and rice dishes— and a genus of vegetarian specialties every bit as tasty as the face-bearing fare (their eggplant, pumpkin, and tofu entrée is a celebrated favorite). You'll find a no-nonsense treatment of the

*This place rocks.*

standards: grilled, fried, charbroiled and seasoned with the chili, lime juice, lemongrass, basil leaves, and coconut milk of the Thai you've come to know, liberally livened with the sublime. Thrill to their crispy honey duck or sweat it out over the *pad kra prao*; their menu of over forty entrées ensures return visits, and if you're able to stray from your tried-and-true favorites you could easily spend a very pleasing and obsessive-compulsive year eating your way though them all. With an unbeatable $6 lunch special and free delivery for agoraphobes, there's little reason to eat anything else.

Toi earns its success without banking on the reputation of a celebrity clientele or luring customers as the momentary go-to spot of an up-and-coming neighborhood. It's withstood the fickle spotlight of the restaurant scene by simply staying true to its original vision. With its pink neon illuminating the path through the dark and often misleading jungle of L.A. eateries, Toi is always there for us. Even if we sample the charms of another, Toi will take us back and hold us tight to its bosom; and there we'll find comfort alongside those same crappy thrift shop lamps, underneath the same rock posters, gorging ourselves with the same hearty food we've known and loved for decades— delivered to our table personally, posthaste, by that same lickable staff.

## GOING NATIVE AT
# SAFARI ROOM

**Safari Room**
**15426 Devonshire Street**
**Mission Hills**
**818.893.9768**

Safari Room is one of L.A.'s last great undiscovered restaurant-lounges from the 1950s, and if it were located in Los Angeles proper, it would be packed nightly with Bettie Page haircuts, pierced lips, and porkpie hats. Fortunately, it's hidden at the far end of the San Fernando Valley, where the only tats you may see are on the forearms of older gentlemen, and usually spell out "MOM" or "USMC" in faded letters. The crowd here is often older, mellowed, and well-preserved—much like the place itself.

Tucked into a nondescript patch of commercial storefronts along Devonshire Street in Mission Hills, Safari Room is easy to miss, so look for the dancing witch doctor on the sign that rises twenty feet above the white, low-slung building. Though the adjacent parking lot can get crowded on weekend nights, there's always plenty of additional parking in the back and on the street. And it's all free!

Step inside Safari Room and you're immediately impressed by the authenticity of its old-school charm. Unlike so many establishments that are overeager to parlay their retro roots, Safari Room doesn't try to be hip. It just is.

Inside the door, visitors are greeted by a display of spears, giant tortoise shells, and tribal masks. With the bar on one side of the long, rectangular room, and the dining area on the other, the restaurant is divided almost equally down the

middle by a row of circular tuck 'n' roll booths with faux cheetah endcaps. The well-polished bar is backed by wood paneling and an impressive collection of carved masks, shields, spears, guns, hats, animal skins, and other safari-motifed accouterments—some of which date back to the restaurant's inception. The rest of the walls, including those in the dining room, are constructed of rough-hewn brick that shines with numerous coats of glossy white paint. Framed por-traits of lions, leopards, and other big cats round out the African theme.

Behind the bar you'll usually find Karen, who's been pour-ing drinks at Safari Room for more than twenty years. She and chef Saul are now the co-owners, having bought the place from Jim and Jeri Gentry, who also once owned the erstwhile Fin & Feather over on San Fernando Road. While it's not uncommon for longtime employees to buy out retiring owners, Karen and Saul's motive for doing so is one of the reasons that Safari Room has maintained its time-capsule charm. "We bought it because we wanted to make sure that nothing changed in here," said Karen, as she wiped down the bar. "We didn't want someone else com-ing in here and turning it into something it isn't."

Amen to that, sister.

Stroll into Safari Room on a Friday or Saturday evening and you're likely to encounter a full house. While it attracts a some-what diverse array of clientele from the area—we've seen every-thing from suburban families to biker couples to middle-aged white-collar types—many of Safari Room's patrons are of the AARP variety, which means they tend to eat early and then hit the hay. In other words, if you're going for dinner, get there before 10:00 PM (and it helps to make a reservation).

And by all means, make it a point to have dinner at Safari Room. Although the bar is indeed sizeable and drinks are poured with a generous hand, it's the cocktail-era menu of comfort food

and the attentive service in the dining room that keep us coming back for more. The waitstaff consists of seasoned professionals who are veterans at the art of ingratiating themselves without being unctuous. They're called "career waiters," and are a refreshing change of pace from the transient, bored college students and aspiring reality-show contestants who fill most of L.A.'s food service ranks.

Before you even have a chance to order your drinks, a complimentary plate of crudités arrives at the table.

*The natives are restless; it must be bingo night.*

Munching a celery stalk, you'll peruse a menu that's packed with reliable throwbacks to a simpler time in America's culinary history, a flavorful stroll down memory lane for anyone who associates the word *fusion* with nuclear power rather than nouvelle cuisine. And considering the quality of the food, the prices are extremely reasonable.

For starters, we're particularly fond of the homemade New England clam chowder, the clam strips, and the shrimp cocktail—which contains crustaceans actually cooked on the premises and not thawed from a bag. For the main course, if you're in the mood for liver and onions, you can't do better than Safari Room's offering. When was the last time you saw old-fashioned short ribs on a menu? The prime rib is top-drawer and amply proportioned, and the steaks are all tasty and tender, but we find ourselves oddly enamored with Safari Room's take on an old favorite that's all but disappeared from restaurant menus: chopped steak with mushrooms and onions. We always say we're too stuffed for dessert, but we have it anyway.

Safari Room deserves special recognition for not blasting music so loudly that we can't talk to the person next to us without spitting flecks of food on their face. Bonus points are awarded for not playing hip-hop while we're trying to eat—or any other time, for that matter. The only 50 Cent you're going to find around here are a couple of quarters on the bar.

The bottom line is that Safari Room is one of the best of its (dying) breed. Like the prostitute who refuses to kiss in order to keep one small shred of her honor, we were tempted to keep this time warp to ourselves. On the other hand, considering the speed with which these kinds of establishments are being co-opted by trendy restaurateurs or disappearing altogether, we felt we had no choice but to share our treasure with you, dear reader, because we know we can trust you not to fuck it up.

Right?

## MAULING OUR APPETITES AT

# THE BEAR PIT BAR-B-Q

Standing outside of The Bear Pit Bar-B-Q, looking up at their exquisite vintage sign that promises "Missouri style" barbecue, we can't help but ask ourselves a question: Where the hell is Missouri again?

Like Iowa and Indiana, Missouri is one of those states you completely forget even exists until an election year when pundits try to be cute by pronouncing it "Missour-*uh*." Ask us where it is, and we'll tell you it's kind of in the middle and somewhere to the right. Right?

Located in Mission Hills just north of the 118, The Bear Pit has been around for more than fifty years—and it shows. In the 1950s, the original owner, Ben Baier, opened a small walk-up, take-out joint called "The Baier Pit" on Sepulveda Boulevard. Soon he was doing so well that he teamed up with a guy named Don Carrow, who would later go on to open the Carrow's restaurant chain. Together they added the dining room that encloses the original walk-up (you can still see the roof of that first building when you're sitting in the front dining room). After Baier died in the early sixties, the restaurant was sold with the stipulation that the Baier family name would be removed. Thus, The *Bear* Pit was born, and the new owner, Ruben Gordon, soon erected the giant neon sign out front that glows brightly to this day.

Inside, wagon-wheel chandeliers hang from the ceiling and the floor is covered with sawdust. Ancient Pabst and Hamm's beer signs recall a time when American brew was marketed with bucolic backlit images of fields and streams. Most noteworthy, however, are the bears frolicking across the walls, painted decades ago by moonlighting Disney artists (or so the story goes). They've never been repainted, at least not from scratch. When it's time for the interior to get

The Bear Pit Bar-B-Q
10825 Sepulveda Boulevard
Mission Hills
818.365.2509
www.bearpitbbq.com

*Where the hell is Missouri again?*

# RAMEN? I HARDLY KNOW HIM!

Have you ever gone to a food court and suddenly felt a pang of empathy for psychopaths who flip out and shoot everybody in sight and save the last bullet for themselves? The food court inside the Mitsuwa Marketplace on Centinela won't make you feel that way. For starters, Santouka has the best ramen in the city, hands down—the spicy miso with special pork is like God in a bowl. Second, the hamburger steak combo platter (with *gyoza*, shrimp, and *daikon* salad) at China Table Tokyo Hanten is a guilty pleasure that everyone should experience once before they die (finish everything on the plate and that may be sooner than you expect). Third, the cubbyhole of a store called Trendy has some of the coolest Japanese junk this side of Little Tokyo, including anime figurines that are hotter than any porn star we've ever seen. Lastly, Mitsuwa Marketplace is the greatest grocery store on the planet.

Food Court at Mitsuwa Marketplace / 3760 South Centinela Avenue / Los Angeles / 310.398.2113

a fresh coat, the bears are strictly off-limits, though they may receive an occasional touch-up from a specialist.

The "Missouri Style" barbecue is better than what most chains have to offer, and its sauce-heavy approach to 'cue will most likely appeal to a middle-American palate, i.e., white, hard-working folks whose idea of culinary adventure is indulging in the occasional Filet-O-Fish sandwich.

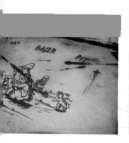

# CANADIAN CAFE

We Americans think we're so clever with our chili cheese fries, but our neighbors to the north are just as capable as we are of inducing arteriosclerosis via a gooey, wet conglomeration of potatoes, cheese, and brown muck. The culinary oddity known as *poutine* (pronounced poo-teen) may sound like your average adolescent scat site, but in fact it is uniquely Canadian. Then again, so is Céline Dion, but of the two, poutine is the one less likely to make you vomit.

Located amidst the tree-lined splendor of Monrovia's Old Town shopping district (a relatively undiscovered assemblage of mom-and-pop shops), the Canadian Cafe is a haven for Canuck ex-pats and domestic poutine aficionados alike. The Canada-centric decor is simple—maps, flags, travel posters, hockey gear, etc., and the menu, other than touting poutine, Canadian fish and chips, Canadian peameal bacon cheeseburgers, and a few other native dishes, is nothing to write home about—unless your home is currently suffering through a famine.

But oh, that poutine. The messy dish was born in rural Quebec in the late 1950s and became a national staple almost overnight. The ubiquitous concoction is served everywhere in Canada, from local pubs to school cafeterias to fast food chains like McDonald's and Burger King, and though plenty of variations on the poutine theme can be found in its homeland, the recipe served at the Canadian Cafe is the real deal: homestyle fries, layered with Québécois cheddar cheese curds, and smothered in piping hot gravy. The gravy partially melts the cheese, the cheese sticks to the fries, and all three congeal into a mass that tastes much better than it looks.

Without getting into a debate on what makes a good poutine gravy—which can easily be as contentious as arguing whether Doug Henning or Rich Little is the more annoying Canadian export—we'd say that the sauce at Canadian Cafe is sufficiently flavorful to pass muster. According to those who actually give a

Canadian Cafe
125 E. Colorado Boulevard
Monrovia
626.303.2303

*Freedom fries are for pussies.*

shit, the real secret to good poutine is all in the curds. Think of them as the building blocks of cheese, the first by-product of the curdling process, which are then pressed together and aged to create the blocks of cheese we know and love. The curds alone have a distinctly salty taste and springy feel—often described as a "squeak"—but must be consumed within a day or so lest they completely lose their flavor. Compare cheese curds with the heinous creation known as American cheese, which enjoys a shelf-life somewhere in the neighborhood of an eon, and you may begin to understand why the world *really* hates us.

That said, if you think "Canadian cuisine" is an oxymoron, you're probably right. When the signature dish of the country that occupies 41 percent of the North American continent is basically fries with cottage cheese and brown gravy, what kind of message does that send to the rest of the world? Worse, what does it say about someone who will drive all the way to Monrovia to revel in the questionable adventure that is Canadian food?

That's a question you'll have to answer yourself.

## A REVERIE IN TOMATO SAUCE AT THE ORIGINAL

# VINCE'S HOUSE OF SPAGHETTI

We'd guess that the day people got excited about spaghetti passed long ago. Apparently not, Vince's is quick to demonstrate. There are lots of people who get excited about spaghetti. Real excited. We don't just mean sploshers either.

If you venture into the saucy world of Vince's—and you damn well should—don't waste your time with any location but the original in Ontario. Owned and operated by the same family since 1945, it's everything you'd want a spaghetti house to be. And on a Friday or Saturday night, it's at full throttle, pulsating with all that spaghetti is and can ever be.

You can smell the sauce as soon as you step out of your car, and when hit with the anachronistic blur of green vinyl, red gingham, wood paneling, and polished terrazzo immediately upon entering, it will be unequivocally clear that the quarter tank of gas you burned to get here was not in vain. An idiosyncratic lighting scheme that was probably installed sometime before Nixon's resignation bathes Vince's expansive series of dining rooms in an abrasive yet strangely calming glow, bringing to mind some of the less-popular New York subway stations. And the claim that Vince's serves "over 15,000 miles of spaghetti a year" almost makes our nipples hard.

A refreshingly simple menu basically—but not exclusively— offers either spaghetti or mostaccioli served with tomato sauce, tomato sauce with meatballs, or tomato meat sauce. The food itself is pleasingly mundane, completing a

Vince's House of Spaghetti
1206 West Holt Boulevard
Ontario
909.986.7074
www.vincesspaghetti.net

## Get your carb on!

delicate but perfect balance between location and ambience; one has to search far and wide to enjoy a meal this dull, and Vince's House of Spaghetti pays off as one of the few restaurants in Los Angeles County that is 100 percent exactly what it is. The fact that dinner is wheeled to your table on a cart, that the beverage menu features buttermilk, and that the dessert list includes rainbow sherbet bumps Vince's precariously close to the top of our list. Plus there's a parmesan shaker on every table, so there's none of that "Would you like some fresh grated parmesan?" bullshit. Pour it the fuck on.

It is actually possible to stuff yourself for less than ten dollars. "Vince's Dinner" includes minestrone soup, salad, and a garlic or cheese roll (their "exclusive taste sensation"), puffy as a brand new bedroom slipper. And one thing Vince's knows is their spaghetti—a heaping platterful—cooked al dente, and not wanting of sauce. Add extra carbs with draft beer, even champagne, and a remarkably extensive wine list for a place where the most expensive dinner caps out at $11.95.

The Vince's staff runs like a well-oiled machine (including our secretary-hot waitress, but we digress) and they'll also serve up a bitchin' Vince's Spaghetti T-shirt upon request, a steal at only ten bucks.

And if you do happen to be a splosher you can get an extra dinner order to go, and no one will be the wiser.

## WAITING FOR EVELYN MULWRAY AT

# CHOP SUEY CAFE & LOUNGE

Chop Suey Cafe & Lounge
351 East First Street
Los Angeles
213.617.9990
www.chopsueycafeandlounge.
com

The Chop Suey Cafe & Lounge was originally called Far East, even though the words CHOP SUEY are about ten times bigger on the original neon sign out front, which dates back to 1935. Confused? Back when Chinese immigrants were charmingly referred to as Chinamen, Chop Suey was the popular Anglicized notion of what Chinese food should be. In other words, no self-respecting Chinaman would touch the stuff with a ten-foot pole. As was often the case with signage in those days, the type of food served at a restaurant (in this case, Chop Suey) took precedence over its name (Far East), thus the disproportionate relationship between the two on the sign, and the reason why so many round-eyes called the place "Chop Suey" instead of "Far East."

Still with us? Structural damage forced the building to close after the '94 quake. Seven years later, when the original owners, the Mar family, donated the earthquake-damaged building to the Little Tokyo Service Center, they did so with the caveat that the "Far East" name would not be used by whoever bought the place. But when the building became part of the National Historic Registry, the sign out front could not be changed or removed. So, despite the fact that it still says "Far East" out front, the new proprietors were forced to officially adopt "Chop Suey" as their moniker, which, again, is what a lot of people called the place anyway. Jesus Christ, that was complicated.

Despite the fact that the menu has been "updated" and an urban oasis has been added in the adjacent "alley" next to the original restaurant, the neon sign and original dining room area remain virtually unaltered. Even so, the ambiance has changed. In its heyday, walking into the Far East was like walking into another world. This was not a restaurant where people came to be seen, but to hide. The tall wooden booths held the secrets of hushed conversations and clandestine rendezvous. The place

**OUT 'n' ABOUT**

# A SAFE HARBOR FOR CHICKENS

Fried chicken is a lot like porn. Everyone loves it, but no one wants to admit it. And a health-conscious burg like Los Angeles makes this uncomfortable situation even worse. In fact, at this very moment, Rob Reiner is probably spear-heading a movement to tax the crap out of fried chicken, or to force people to stand outside if they want to eat Buffalo Wings. Are you tired of feeling guilty about fried chicken? At Slavko's Harbor Poultry, they understand. They feel your pain. They'll sell you some of the best fried chicken in town without looking at you sideways. They'll make you feel whole again.

Fuck Rob Reiner.

Slavko's Harbor Poultry / 1224 South Pacific Avenue / San Pedro / 310.832.8171

*We take our coffee like we take our movies. Noir.*

could be packed, but you'd never see another customer; only dark figures in shadowy stalls, their cigarette smoke billowing in the sparse shafts of light that made it through the front windows. The narrow passage between the booths, the darkness of the ancient wood, the aura of mystery . . . these all gave the place its signature *noir* vibe—in fact, it's rumored that Raymond Chandler came here to write, and scenes from *Farewell, My Lovely* and *Chinatown* were shot here.

Unfortunately, the high, broad panels that make the wooden booths so private are also removable. The last time we visited, the new owners had opted to take most of them down to make the room open and airy—which totally killed the old-school feel. Who wants to conduct an illicit affair or discuss a hit job out in the open? Not us, that's for sure. Fortunately, the panels can be just as easily replaced, a move we would strongly recommend to those with the power to do so.

Panels or not, Chop Suey is an L.A. icon, so if you want to know what passed for a real fake Chinese joint in 1930s Los Angeles, this is it—and it's a dwindling breed. As for the food, some of the old signature dishes are still on the menu, and we recommend you stick to those rather than the "Asian Burger." If we have to explain why, then go ahead and order the burger. You deserve it.

## LIFE IS LIKE A BOX OF MARKETING EXECUTIVES AT

# BUBBA GUMP SHRIMP CO.

Bubba Gump Shrimp Co.
1000 Universal Studios
Boulevard, Suite 114
Universal City
818.753.4867
www.bubbagump.com

Of all the mysteries that abound on this planet, perhaps the most troubling is the allure of the theme restaurant. Where did we go wrong along the timeline of gastronomic history such that good food, good service, and good ambience were no longer enough? When did our ravenous appetite for constant amusement supersede the sensual imperative of our taste buds? How did we become so jaded and unimaginative that we could only enjoy dining in one mini-Disneyland after another, surrounded by faux memorabilia and heinous bric-a-brac? Exactly when did we become the United States of ADD?

Los Angeles is certainly not alone in its embrace of themed monstrosities. God knows that good Americans in the heartland love prefab crap as much as we do, if not more. And when they come here to visit, they have great expectations. The first Hard Rock Café in the U.S. opened here, its popularity launching the odious chain around the world. Planet Hollywood followed suit, albeit not as successfully. Americans expect spectacle from Los Angeles, and we deliver it, usually with nauseating results.

It wasn't always the case that themed restaurants were soulless corporate concoctions. Trader Vic's and Don the Beachcomber were two of the granddaddies of this trend, and their Polynesian food and South Pacific motif provided exotic, gee-whiz thrills for countless postwar Americans. In the ensuing years, the evolutionary process gave birth to everything from El Torito to P.F. Chang's, each one reeking with a contrived authenticity born of focus groups and carefully controlled by marketing wizards and interior designers. The trend is not limited to ethnic eateries, of course, with chains like TGI Friday's being the most egregious violators of the sin of the well-placed tchotchke. There is also the case of the themed historical atrocity, best exemplified by the surge of faux 1950s diners that owe their existence to a naïve American hindsight that sees that decade as a sparkling, idyllic utopia as long as you were not or never had been a member of the Communist Party. It's hard to pick which is more emetic, eating at Johnny Rockets or watching a rerun of *Happy Days*, but at least you don't have to leave your home to suffer through the latter.

To us, however, the most baffling theme bistro of all is Bubba Gump Shrimp Co., a chain of eateries based on the movie *Forrest Gump*. Repeat: *Forrest Gump*. We could understand dining spinoffs of gloriously food-obsessive films like *Big Night* or *Tampopo*, but . . . *Forrest Gump*? Why, God, why? Of all the movies to transmogrify into an eating experience, what callow cabal of investors had the temerity to take an overrated, annoying, saccharine movie and turn it into an overrated, annoying, saccharine fish shack? Considering the sheer malevolence involved in hatching such a diabolical scheme, we were certain that the Illuminati, the Freemasons, and perhaps even the Log Cabin Republicans were somehow behind Bubba Gump, but the credit actually goes to Viacom Consumer Products. Congratulations, jerk-offs.

As we all surely remember in *Forrest Gump*, Forrest becomes a shrimper (that is to say, a fisherman, not a toe sucker), because

Is that a crustacean in your pocket or did Jenny give you crabs?

his buddy, Bubba Blue, delivers a heartfelt paean to the tasty *traif*: "Shrimp is the fruit of the sea. You can barbecue it, boil it, broil it, bake it, sauté it. There's, um, shrimp kebabs, shrimp creole, shrimp gumbo, pan-fried, deep-fried, stir-fried. There's pineapple shrimp and lemon shrimp, coconut shrimp, pepper shrimp, shrimp soup, shrimp stew, shrimp salad, shrimp and potatoes, shrimp burger, shrimp sandwich. . . . That's about it."

Well, we can think of a few more ways to prepare shrimp, but why quibble? From that unassuming side of dialogue—immortalized in giant neon letters outside the restaurant—has sprung a dining dynasty that now stretches from Kuala Lampur to New York City, and which, despite its very name, can't seem to cook the crustacean to save its life. Oh, the irony.

Out of purely morbid curiosity, we visited what we assumed would be the flagship establishment of the Bubba Gump chain at the Universal CityWalk, seeing that *Forrest Gump* was a Paramount release.

If, by way of example, we assume that Clifton's is the zenith of L.A. theme restaurants, then Bubba Gump is the nadir. While a movie like *The Godfather* surely inspired countless eponymous bistros with slogans like "I'm gonna make you a pizza you can't refuse," Bubba Gump is, as far as we know, the first corporate restaurant chain based on a motion picture property. Though never a franchise, Alan Hale's Lobster Barrel, which sprang from the loins of *Gilligan's Island* and once held court on La Cienega's restaurant row, is perhaps Bubba Gump's closest small-screen progenitor. That culinary barnacle has long since been scraped from L.A.'s hull, but you can read more about it in our *Lost Strangeles* chapter.

Located smack-dab in the center of CityWalk, getting to Bubba Gump is an adventure in itself. You can choose to pay top dollar for so-called "preferred parking" (which Bubba does not validate), but we recommend you use general parking in one of CityWalk's far-flung lots so you can walk off the lard that will already be making its way to your ass soon after you finish your meal. Bubba Gump graciously validates the first hour of parking for free, but it's $5 for the next hour and $2.50 for every half hour thereafter, so be prepared to either stuff your face and run, or pay through the nose.

Walking to the restaurant entails navigating through the treacherous sea of humanoids who amble through the CityWalk promenade like tree sloths on Nyquil. Dazed by the unrelenting torrent of visual and aural diarrhea (oversized signage, bright lights, buzzing neon, loud music) and slowed by the mix of churros and cheese pretzels churning in their duodenums, this hapless mix of turistas and locals is no match for the countless come-ons that urge them to buy things they neither need nor can afford. When trapped behind a slow-moving herd, we discovered that shouting "Allahu akbar!" will spread the stunned cattle like a *Hustler* centerfold.

When you finally reach your destination, you will find yourself in the massive quarters that once housed the Gladstone's 4 Fish. If you were ever unimpressed with their chow, brace yourself: Bubba Gump proudly lowers the bar when it comes to mediocrity.

You will first notice the change in decor. Gladstone's mishmash of nautical nonsense has been meticulously replaced with Bubba Gump's mishmash of nautical nonsense. The place looks like the Disneyfied aftermath of a hurricane: Imagine a giant shrimp boat that's been washed up on an old swamp shack, if swamp shacks were festooned with photos of Gary Sinise and Robin Wright Penn rather than seagull droppings.

Bubba Gump has all kinds of precious, cutesy touches that worked our gag reflex before the meal even arrived—so many, in fact, that it is difficult to pick our favorite. The menu also bears numerous stills from the movie, and is written in an "aw, shucks" style that bears the fingerprints of many a clever copywriter. Thirsty? Kick off your polio braces and try the "Run Forrest Run." Feeling naughty? Take a sip of "Jenny's Favorite," which, surprisingly, contained neither heroin nor a used condom. In the mood for a sandwich? Bite into the "Run Chicken Run" (are you beginning to see a pattern here?). Feeling gluttonous? Indulge yourself in "Boat Trash" or the "'I'm Stuffed' Shrimp." And for dessert, we heartily recommend "George Wallace's Segregation Sundae (with real Oreo bits)" or "The Arthur Bremmer Surprise," which comes topped with a lit M-80.

Okay, we made up those last two.

But seriously, with so many selections to choose from, we decided to keep it simple and ordered the peel 'n' eat shrimp, a shrimp cocktail, and some fried shrimp. After all, Bubba Gump is practically a temple to shrimp, and those are three of the most basic preparations. Who could screw that up? Surely not Bubba.

While waiting for our food to arrive, we took delight in the signage placed on each table letting the staff know that you need attention and you need it *now*. A blue metal sign that reads "Run Forrest Run" indicates that you are satisfied for the time being, even though the oft-repeated line from the movie relates to the hair-raising ordeal of a young, crippled idiot savant trying to outrun a blood-crazed gang of future Klansmen. Flip the sign and you have "Stop Forrest Stop" emblazoned on red metal, indicating that you would like to speak to one of the friendly staff members, perhaps to request an air-sickness bag.

Run, Forrest, Stop! Halt, Forrest, Go! Sit! Stay! Rollover! Fetch! As if waiters don't already deal with enough abuse, this device ups the potential for humiliation to new and exciting heights. Yet, despite its inherent cruelty, the contraption turned out to be utterly spurious. We thought we would have fun flipping the damn thing and timing the staff's response, but none ever appeared. Then, much to our chagrin, the food arrived. And here's where we must make a confession: As much as we loathe the very notion behind the contrivance of Bubba Gump, deep down we really wanted it to be good. We fantasized about the best shrimp we'd ever eaten. We wanted to walk out of there and tell the world we are all wrong about Bubba, and that beneath its crass commercialism it was *the* place to go for a plate of dee-licious shrimpies. We wished more than anything that we were about to discover a diamond in a mound of dung.

Digging into our dinners, our naiveté came back to bite us on the ass. Or, as Forrest would say, "Stupid is as stupid does." The peel 'n' eat shrimp weren't worth the effort of peeling, much less eating. Like the fried shrimp, they were small, overcooked, mealy, and bland. The shrimp cocktail fared no better. Our giddy anticipation quashed, the mood at the table became as joyless as a polio ward. To be sure, the Bubba Gump experience could not have been less enjoyable if Tom Hanks himself had climbed onto our table and taken a dump on it. Then again, we would at least have had something to tell our grandchildren.

Stop, Forrest, Stop! And take this crap from our table!

We sent our meals back and declined to investigate the kitchen's repertoire any further. Looking around at the other diners who seemed to be enjoying themselves even though they were missing *Dancing with the Stars*, we wondered aloud if the problem might not be with Bubba Gump, but with us. Could it be that we were incapable of knowing a good thing when it was right in front of us? Were we nothing more than effete snobs who labored under the mistaken belief that we were somehow better than Bubba Gump? Were we, to put it bluntly, *assholes*? The answer was clear.

*Nah.*

## BLOCKING OUR BOWELS WITH A LITTLE BIT O' BRAZIL AT

# GAUCHOS VILLAGE

Take the romantic ideal of Joao and Astrud and wipe it from your mind. And forget any tropical notions of Brazil-induced aphrodesia, because after you pay your check you'll probably be too constipated to have intercourse. Gauchos Village is a Brazilian escape of another kind. One of body glitter and thumping disco, of fatty meats and salad bars, of conga lines and plasma screens.

Of all the food trends to sweep the nation, Brazilian *churrascaria*—the colon-cramming carnivorous gorgefest spreading like shingles throughout the midsection of Greater L.A.—seems tailor-made for American translation. While there are many churrascaria establishments clogging arteries across Los Angeles County, Gauchos Village ups the ante—and although any restaurant that decorates with mannequins gets extra stars in our book, the Brazilian meat orgy is ratcheted up here in an exhaustive assault on all five senses, as well as some you didn't know you had.

It was from cosmopolitan Glendale that we departed for our night in Rio, where Carnaval never stops, it seems, at least until your table is needed for the next dinner seating. A long granite bar trims a cavernous Brazilian-themed dining room featuring a decor representing both gaucho life and soccer, accented with department store mannequins in Carnaval finery stationed above diners on high platforms. Sumptuous banquet seating makes use of every square foot, while a curiously small stage occupies a far corner, barely large enough to hold the percussion, much less the mostly naked, marabou feather–headdressed dancers we'd been promised.

No sooner than our anemic *caipirinha* was delivered to our table by a gaily costumed gaucho were we treated to the pounding beat of a contemporary twist on the classic "Brazil," cueing only three Carnaval dancers—Brazilianly tanned, flesh tight, and breasts of questionable origin—possessing all the qualities that read "sexy" in Brazil but "whorish" in America, to take the stage. With their reproductive crevices concealed by a strategically nestled sequined string, each made the most of an abbreviated

Gauchos Village
411 North Brand Boulevard
Glendale
818.550.1430
www.gauchosvillage.com

*Carne-vile!*

performance juncture, like body glitter–smeared angels dancing on the head of a pin. It was a gambol that appeared more likely fueled by strong Brazilian coffee than formal training, but since we've never gyrated in a G-string under a five-foot feathered headdress—at least not in public—who are we to judge? Clearly these were the sort of distinctions that eluded the crowd, reeling as the dancers took the floor and worked the room, a conga line soon trailing behind.

With a flip of our tabletop indicator, it was *espeto corrido*, the non-stop delivery of meat, meat, meat, sliced right from the skewer and onto your plate. Resilient ribs and a tensile top sirloin were followed by an elastic lamb, but not before a pimply pork sausage was paired with a gummy filet . . . and the meat goes on. While negotiating around the gristle with a steak knife and a set of tongs, a hazy and confusing montage of topless float queens, costumed midgets, synchronized wheelchair brigades, and banana-hammocked man-meat played out in Carnaval coverage from the streets of Brazil, running on no less than five giant plasma screens to the deafening score of the floorshow. Although there really isn't any opportune moment for a mostly naked feather-and-body-glittered dancer to thrash in the face of a diner wrestling a string of bacon fat from the back of his throat, Gauchos Village never loses sight of the Lent in relentless. With the urgency of Carnaval—standing in the shadow of the impending forty-day period of fasting and abstinence—there just isn't time to pick and choose those meaty moments as you'd like.

But as promptly as our evening commenced, it seemed, it was over. Our feathered friends dashed to the dark recesses of backstage as quickly as the flan slid past our tongue. The plates were cleared and our check delivered, as the streets of Brazil and the bare-breasted parade honeys vanished from the TV screens, in our case, due to a DVD glitch: THE DISK IS DIRTY – THE DISK IS DIRTY flashed in sync from all five screens, almost mocking our meat-induced reverie. And to add insult to injury, our gauchos—for whom just moments before we were the center of their meat-focused attention—efficiently set to work turning tables for the next seating, reminding us in this microcosm of Roman Catholic tradition, that even the merriment of Carnaval—especially the merriment of Carnaval—must come to an end.

Gauchos Village claims their food is "authentic." If that is in fact the case, we're canceling our flight to Rio. The one-sentence review from a fellow diner: "The carrots were good. On par with Brotman Medical Center."

THE DISK IS DIRTY – THE DISK IS DIRTY – THE DISK IS DIRTY.

Excellent. If all this meat ever passes though our lower intestine, we'll be back.

## COMPROMISING A FINE-TUNED PALATE FOR UNPARALLELED AMBIENCE AT

# RAE'S

It's so refreshing to know that there are still some crappy vintage diners within L.A. proper that haven't been revamped into something "fun." If you favor comfort food of the truck stop variety and you've got a penchant for romantic decay, there's a robin's-egg blue vinyl booth waiting for you at Rae's.

Yes, it's been featured in countless movies, and yes, the Department of Health gave it an "A." It's also true that Rae's won a *Los Angeles* magazine "Best Of" title in 2003, but that doesn't mean that the clam chowder doesn't separate or that their dinner salad won't be served soaking in a pool of cold water mottled with oily ranch. But nonetheless—virtually untouched since it opened in 1958—Rae's is a must-visit Santa Monica institution.

With an interior paint job akin to an underfunded state-run mental health facility, a countertop experience that might best be described as "tactile," and a loyal clientele who call to mind the phrase "Checks Cashed Here," Rae's oozes the sort of charm that's become nearly extinct with L.A.'s continual nip-and-tuck gentrification. Its comprehensive bill of fare leaves no stone unturned—but many words misspelled—and the service gets high marks, always. And the prices: a filet mignon dinner for $10.50? You do the math.

Shirt and shoes required. Taste buds, not so much.

Rae's
2901 Pico Boulevard
Santa Monica
310.828.7937

ACTUAL QUOTE OVERHEARD FROM AN ADJACENT BOOTH: *(window-rattling belch) "... I don't want to get all up in there and smell your stinky."*

# I'LL PUT $500 ON BLOATED DISCOMFORT TO WIN

*And they're off! First out of the gate is Ambrosia Salad, followed closely by Candied Yams from Hell, with Grandma's Putrid Green Beans in third. In the middle of the pack, it's Overcooked Turkey, followed by My Old Virginny Ham, Seafood Warrior, and Soggy Stuffing trailing far behind. Still at the gate is Cranberry Jelly, just turning in circles. At the halfway mark, Candied Yams from Hell holds the lead with Overcooked Turkey on his tail, but—hold the phone! There are two NEW horses on the track! I can't quite make out the names ... it looks like ... yes, it's ... Bloated Discomfort waddling towards the finish line with ... Tryptophan Overdose not far behind ... Bloated Discomfort is trying to come on strong, unbuttoning its pants*

*and loosening its belt, while it looks like Tryptophan Overdose is laying down in the middle of track and ... yes ... falling asleep! Bloated Discomfort is stumbling towards the finish and it looks like— wait just a minute, folks! What's this?! Overcooked Turkey and My Old Virginny Ham have dropped off the radar, and now there's another contender who's come out of nowhere! Goodness gracious, it's Unwanted Leftovers! Unwanted Leftovers is closing the gap! Bloated Discomfort is falling back, Unwanted Leftovers and Bloated Discomfort are neck and neck! It's Bloated Discomfort, Unwanted Leftovers ... Bloated ... Unwanted ... Bloated ... and the winner is ... Holy cow! It's*

*SALMONELLA SURPRISE by a nose! Nobody saw that coming! Oh, what an upset! Oh, the humanity! Oh, the diarrhea!*

If this holiday scenario sounds at all familiar, you may want to try the Thanksgiving buffet at Hollywood Park's Turf Club. You won't have to cook, the food is delicious, and there's no mess to clean up afterwards. A racetrack may seem like an odd place to enjoy Thanksgiving, but if you'd rather spend this special day with horses rather than a bunch of horses' asses, what have you got to lose?

Hollywood Park's Annual Thanksgiving Day Brunch / 1050 South Prairie Avenue
Inglewood / 310.419.1500 / www.hollywoodpark.com

## SIPHONED LIKE A HUMAN SLURPEE AT THE

# TOTAL HEALTH CONNECTION

Rysia Musnicki is a diminutive, keenly focused, bright-faced woman with a heavy Polish accent and a strong handshake. Blond by choice. One might guess her age at somewhere around the threshold of a barely-legal retiree—and a spunky one at that—though her life's trajectory would indicate otherwise, having originally emigrated to the United States to escape World War II. Her fountain of youth, it seems, is one of plastic tubing and pressure gauges, and her own juvenescence might be the best possible endorsement she could hope for in her business. "I get to work from this wonderful view," she says, her arm sweeping past the windows wrapping her fourteenth floor office, revealing a southeast panorama of Greater L.A., " . . . and I get to kick the shit out of people. Life doesn't get much better than this."

If Los Angeles had a royal court of colon hydrotherapy, surely Rysia Musnicki would be wearing a crown. As founder of the Total Health Connection, Rysia touts forty-plus years as a holistic health practitioner who specializes in getting way up in your stuff.

Whether or not colon hydrotherapy actually produces specific measurable benefits is debatable. Technically it's simply a

The Total Health Connection
6200 Wilshire Boulevard,
#1410
Los Angeles
323.934.0011
thetotalhealthconnection.com

*Shit happens.* method by which waste is transported from the colon with water. Naysayers claim the waste in question is that of time and money, likening colon hydrotherapy to ear candling, chakra alignment, and the Ouija board, and insisting that the process may even be detrimental depending on the individual. Others will swear by a regular laundering of their large intestine, with claims of diminished love handles, increased energy, clarity of mind, and a peaches-and-cream complexion. So really, who can say? Personally, we'd ear candle our asses on a Ouija board for diminished love handles and clarity of mind, so we're in Camp Rysia.

Were it not for the hygienic equipment, the fluorescent lighting, and the general whiteness that typifies a medical building, Musnicki's office isn't necessarily what one might expect of a facility in which shit is sucked from your ass through a flexible plastic tube. Little shrines dot the room, decorated with crystals and statuettes nodding to her path as a "Polish Buddhist." Family photos line the shelves and a number of prodigious pothos plants climb the walls, on which are hung Rysia's own impressionist works on canvas.

The client experience is simple enough, almost anticlimactic. After slipping into an examination gown and taking your place upon the hydrotherapy table, Rysia runs "virgins" through a brief procedural chat and addresses questions. Her approach is no-nonsense—save the occasional toilet humor—but she's quick to put those who aren't accustomed to having things slipped into their asses by Polish Buddhists at ease. Taking her place at the control board of a contraption reminiscent of the transducer in *The Rocky Horror Picture Show*, Rysia conducts her sessions almost as if she has two brains: one which can wax lyrical about

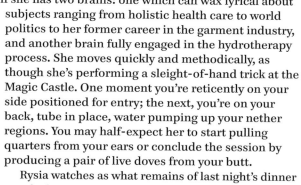

subjects ranging from holistic health care to world politics to her former career in the garment industry, and another brain fully engaged in the hydrotherapy process. She moves quickly and methodically, as though she's performing a sleight-of-hand trick at the Magic Castle. One moment you're reticently on your side positioned for entry; the next, you're on your back, tube in place, water pumping up your nether regions. You may half-expect her to start pulling quarters from your ears or conclude the session by producing a pair of live doves from your butt.

Rysia watches as what remains of last night's dinner travels through the transparent tubing and past the window of the transducer, thinking out loud. "I see you like fish and tomatoes," she'll remark, reminding you of your evening at Casa Vega, bringing a little old-world charm to her hydrotherapy sessions by reading your feces like tea leaves and the abdominal region like a crystal ball. "You're withholding emotion here,"

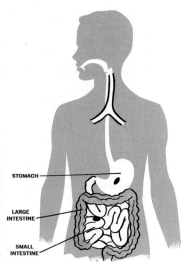

STOMACH

LARGE INTESTINE

SMALL INTESTINE

she says, manipulating a spot below the ribs with a smooth stone and working through the tensed muscle for her net result. "See. I create emotional release," she states with certainty, like a magician who correctly guessed the card we plucked from the deck. Sure enough, the clear tubes flush with fulvous gravy, and all that pent-up emotion is seemingly sucked from your innards with the effectiveness of a wet-dry shop vac. Oftentimes she'll make snap assessments regarding lifelong dietary habits or familial relationships with such accuracy that you might begin to wonder if she's been secretly going through your trash, which in fact, she sort of is.

Following the session (which lasts the better part of an hour), Rysia pulls the tubes and directs you to a bathroom adjacent to her office. Here you rest upon her throne and allow gravity to complete your session, which may take longer than one might think. It's amazing what the human body can hold—and even more amazing how much of it Rysia can release.

What the hydrotherapy ads don't tell you, however, is that it's virtually impossible for a first-timer to achieve a squeaky-clean colon with just one initial visit. And at nearly $100 a session (first visits are usually offered at a lower rate), that's a lot of money to spend on poop. But to the credit of Total Health Connection, there was no hard sell. Although an appointment scheduled for the next day was encouraged (plus four visits thereafter, as well as a bottle of Chinese herbs ready for purchase at the front counter), evidently Rysia walks the Buddhist walk. "You don't have to do anything I say if you don't want to," she says earnestly, with a genuine transparency not unlike the hydrotherapy tubing, "and if you don't, I will love you anyway."

You can say what you want about some holistic practitioners out there, but Rysia Musnicki is not—unsurprisingly—full of shit.

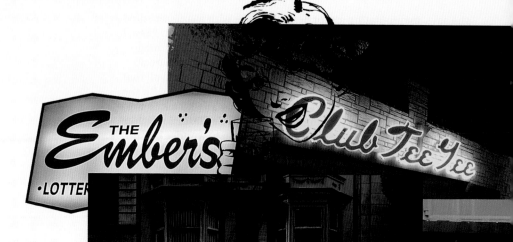

DIPSOMANIA

CHAPTER
№ 2

## WHERE DRUNKS AND DARTS MAKE HAPPY BEDFELLOWS:

# TONGA HUT

Tonga Hut
12808 Victory Boulevard
North Hollywood
818.769.0708
www.tongahut.com

Through the end of the last millennium, the Tonga Hut sat quietly on the dusty edge of Victory Boulevard, its façade resembling a neglected antiquity that nature had slowly reclaimed. Inside, its barroom was a well-shrouded relic of the late 1950s, obscured by layers of neon beer signage, pennants, and promotional mirrors—its three-tiered waterfall still intact, but bone-dry, and its tikis present but unnoticed. For decades, the Tonga Hut sat like a sunken pirate ship quietly resting on the ocean floor, undisturbed, cloaked with silt and covered with barnacles—host to a different sort of life than was originally intended perhaps, but still loaded with treasure. All the Tonga Hut needed was someone with a strong crane to pull the thing back up to the surface and give it a good scrub.

That day came just a few years ago when the Tonga Hut changed hands. The silt was cleared and the barnacles scraped. Repairs and restoration followed, revealing what remained of its former glory. The fountains flow once more, the candlelit booths beckon, and the TV screen stays warm with jungle movies, surf films, and sundry B-exotica rather than sporting events. The drink list is now peppered with the Polynesian, featuring the likes of the Rhumboogie and the Tonga Lei. You can almost see the Hut's massive *moai* figures cracking smiles in deference to the long-anticipated reinvention.

But make no mistake: A precious sixties ultra-lounge overrun with tiki geeks this is not. And if you want the fine-tuned cocktails of the Tiki-Ti, then go to the Tiki-Ti—that's what they're famous for. Called a dive bar by some and a tiki bar by others, the Tonga Hut is truly neither. You'll no sooner find junkies pissing their barstools than you will the slickness of a Trader Vic's; this is not a refurbished time capsule nor a refuge for the down-and-out. The Tonga Hut found its happy medium by taking the best of what it was, what it later became, and what it's now content to be. It has cultivated the kind of individual identity that only comes with a long, hard life—and with the passing of a torch to those who care. Remember the Atomic Cafe or the original Duke's at the Tropicana? Of course you don't. But it feels kinda like that.

There is no elitism among the Tonga Hut libations. One-dollar Pabst Blue Ribbon (on Monday nights) and wine share the bill

*"Victory Boulevard ... WE LOVE IT!"*
—RANDY NEWMAN, "I LOVE L.A."

with Blue Hawaiians and Zombies. Drawing both NoHo hipsters for whom the Hut is a local treasure and crusty regulars for whom alcohol is a major food group, the Tonga Hut cross-pollinates to great success. The Hut has hosted art shows, trivia nights, live DJs, and special events—and boasts a jukebox that tiki geeks, barflies, and local area drunks can all get equally excited about. The Tonga Hut is *truly* exotic.

You want the perfect Mai Tai? Book a flight to Bora Bora and shut the fuck up. The Tonga Hut offers free-and-easy parking, stiff drinks, *and* vintage Polynesian decor—bars this good don't grow on trees, especially in North Hollywood. Tag this one an L.A. institution.

## ART APPRECIATION AT
# EMBER'S LOUNGE

Another sixties strip mall, another bar, and more surprises. Even Santa Fe Springs, one of the many why-would-anyone-choose-to-live-here suburbs of Los Angeles, is rife with treasure. And how wonderful that Ember's Lounge offers an opportunity to tell someone, with a straight face, that you actually traveled east of Downey to go drink in a bar for the artwork.

Smallish, with a pool table in the back, lotto, and a digital jukebox, Ember's is a simple enough place: perfunctory red vinyl stools, brown Formica, and salty snacks. We wouldn't have pegged Ember's as a thinking man's saloon, but we eyewitnessed the not-scary clientele seriously engage in a game of *Jeopardy* broadcast from TVs at either end of the bar, and scoring so astonishingly well that we actually considered going back to school for a minute—but downed another shot instead.

But there's more reason than *Jeopardy* and beef jerky to make the trek out to Santa Fe Springs. Ember's serves double duty for hard-drinking culture vultures, as it's the home to what is arguably the finest work by artist Frank Bowers.

Ember's has a House of Satan theme, and Bowers's large-scale 1963 paintings depict a delightfully elegant hell, an R-rated inferno of wanton she-devils in black lace lingerie cavorting

Ember's Lounge
11332 East Washington Boulevard
Santa Fe Springs
562.699.4138

*Aloha from hell.*

among skivvied shirtless hunks. With names like "One Foot in Hell" and "Mixed Up Vixen," we see dudes in white tux jackets remaining cool despite the flames licking their elbows and the temptation from topless cheesecake babes wagging their tails in service to Lucifer, who looks on. This is exactly the hell we've fantasized about: an adults-only Hell, where flames don't hurt, flogging is fun, and hogtieing a nubile beauty simply means "I like you!" In this hell, vintage lingerie, boxer shorts, birthday suits, and tux jackets are all in keeping with the dress code—and all Satan wants is for you to have a damned good time.

Bowers's style is at its loosest here in Ember's, like a little bit of Lempicka cross-pollinated with a whole lot of pulp sexploitation. The artist didn't always work with a satanic theme, however. A native Californian, Bowers was a respected and accomplished mural painter whose commissions of the 1930s included the Federal Art Project and the Fruit Growers Exchange. Diehard enthusiasts can explore the other side of Frank Bowers with a mural he did for The Man hanging inside South Gate's City Hall.

Sadly, Bowers passed away at age fifty-nine, just a year after completing his work for Ember's. And for his sake, we can only hope he went straight to the hell he so marvelously envisioned. Thank the gods for this half-century-old Silver Lake institution.

## GETTING SHITFACED, POLYNESIAN STYLE, AT THE

# TIKI-TI

**Tiki-Ti**
**4427 Sunset Boulevard**
**Los Angeles**
**323.669.9381**
**www.tiki-ti.com**

*Dr. Funk is in the house.*

Though small in stature, the Tiki-Ti remains a steadfast giant among the shrinking number of pseudo-Polynesian cocktail haunts once liberally scattered across L.A. County. The place might be overrun with the decidedly hip—and you're likely to wait in line on weekend nights—but its eighty-plus signature libations never fail to thrill. Special bonus: the opportunity to light up and feel like you're in a *real* bar (the Tiki-Ti is owner-operated and therefore exempt from smoking restrictions) while sipping your way through an Uga Booga, a Princess Pupuli, or a Dr. Funk amidst the Ti's inimitable milieu.

Imbibers take heed: The fruity concoctions of the Tiki-Ti are notorious for packing a sucker punch. If you're not careful you'll get knocked on your ass faster than you can say "designated driver."

# DYING OVER THE MARGARITAS AT
# EL COYOTE MEXICAN CAFÉ

We're not sure where the rumor started, but it is said that on the evening of August 8, 1969, a very pregnant Sharon Tate—aka Mrs. Roman Polanski—and a small group friends enjoyed dinner and drinks at El Coyote before returning to her Bel-Air mansion for a nightcap, a little grass, and a surprise visit from the Manson family. This isn't meant to imply that you will also be shot, stabbed, and beaten to death by LSD-crazed hippies if you patronize El Coyote, but if you drink too many of their famously potent margaritas you'll wish you had.

We are fond of El Coyote in the same way we enjoy *Hee Haw*: It's unwaveringly formulaic, overwrought with cliché, and packaged with the sort of garishness that borders on the surreal. Allegedly the margaritas are so strong because the food is so bad that you need to get stinking drunk just to stomach it—but that philosophy makes about as much sense as poking out your eyeballs to avoid watching *Project Runway*. Yes, the margaritas are indeed powerful, but they also have the distinctive aftertaste of Mexican tap water left to fester in the Tijuana sun. Downing a dozen to get through a plate of heavy, greasy gringomex is nothing more than surefire way to buy a round-trip meal ticket. We know. We've taken the trip.

Spewing one's *machaca con huevos* on the sidewalk out front, it's easy to see where El Coyote's interior designers got their inspiration. Mismatched wrought-iron accessories, bad art on the walls, and chandeliers made from crushed glass and tile all combine to make the mess on your combo platter look like a post-impressionist masterpiece by comparison. We can't honestly say we like El Torito's décor any better. With few exceptions (Maria's Ramada comes immediately to mind), Mexican restaurants all look the same. El Coyote is just bigger, louder, and filled with more *yanqui* hipsters.

Honestly, while we understand the historical significance of El Coyote (it's been around since 1931), longevity is never a substitute for quality. The food sucks and the margaritas are overrated, but given the long wait for a table, we can only assume one of two things: People are idiots or we have our heads up our asses.

El Coyote Mexican Café
7312 Beverly Boulevard
Los Angeles
323.939.2255
www.elcoyotecafe.com

*I'll have the vomit omelette to go.*

If you're an idiot, we're guessing that you'll probably go with the latter.

El Coyote is another one of those long-running L.A. *traditions* (God, we're growing to hate that word) that, unlike poor Sharon Tate and her ill-fated entourage, refuses to die.

*Salud!*

# VENICE ROOM

Venice Room
2428 South Garfield
Avenue
Monterey Park
323.722.3075

*Half the price, twice the gilt.*

*Overheard at the Venice Room:*
*Man: You remind me of Uma Thurman. . . .*
*Woman: . . . You mean when she's green?*

A Venetian-themed cocktail lounge packed with Latinos in a predominantly Chinese community? Cosmopolitan credentials, cheap drinks, and an untouched 1957 decor keeps the Venice Room at the top of our list for barflies willing to go the extra mile for atmosphere.

Any place that brings us the magic of Venice with a moonlit scene of the Grand Canal rendered in day-glo paint and livened with the aid of black lights behind a bar of gold gilt gets our asses out to Monterey Park for sure. Ratchet up the Venice Room's high-style mix with mirrored walls, tufted booths, and its red, metallic gold, and black paisley wallpaper, and you've got an environment rivaling the romance of Piazza San Marcos—without the pigeon poo.

The Venice Room delivers on ambience with flying colors—with an assist from the benign bunch of locals warming its stools—but it's the no-frills, do-it-yourself steak dinner that keeps Venice Room aficionados coming back for more. In a

spotless adjacent dining room lined with cozy black vinyl booths, a simple gas grill transforms an evening of cocktails and psychedelic art appreciation into an indoor barbeque, where—for a mere fourteen bucks—patrons not only season their own New York strip, they grill it as well. So if you're the sort who orders steak "pink inside, between rare and medium but not too done and closer to rare but not bleeding," then have at it and save a chef some grief. There is no menu, and a salad of iceberg lettuce and a Parker House roll is all you'll find with respect to "sides," but if you're going to start complaining you can go wait in the car—where you'll be kept under surveillance via the live feed from the parking lot security cameras, broadcast on a large black-and-white monitor behind the bar. Maybe it's a Monterey Park thing, but the community gets a little touchy around the issue of parked cars. If they're not being monitored on closed-circuit TV, they're restricted up the rear-view by the signs on the street. If you drive a "public nuisance vehicle"—and who hasn't at some point in their life—you'd best grill your steak elsewhere, buddy.

Still, what's not to love? If this place were in Silver Lake, there'd be a line out the door.

## OFF WE GO, INTO THE WILD BLUE BATHROOM AT

# 94TH AERO SQUADRON

This granddaddy of theme restaurants has been around for decades and is just one of many owned by the Specialty Restaurants Corporation out of Anaheim (yes, it sounds like a Scientology front organization, but it's not). Judging by the quality of the food, we believe the longevity of the 94th is most likely predicated on its theme-park decor, its propinquity to the Van Nuys airport runway, and its wide selection of stiff drinks.

Strange but true: many pilots enjoy alcoholic beverages.

In fact, it's so important that pilots not be denied booze immediately before or following a flight that 94th Aero Squadron reserves a prime table just for them, right in front of the bar's main window, which looks out onto the runway. And even if there isn't a pilot in sight, the table is still off-limits. Not only is there a permanent sign on the table to wave off all non-flyers, but if you take a seat there, be prepared to show your pilot's license or get the boot. Staffers told us tales of more than one pilot who went into a tailspin over a civilian sitting at the table.

Built in the style of an early-twentieth-century-French-farm-house-cum-airstrip, the restaurant's design suggests a collaborative effort between Martha Stewart and Manfred Von Richthofen. The multitude of props from both World Wars gives the dining room a decidedly Disneyesque quality, while outside there's a

94th Aero Squadron
16320 Raymer Street
Van Nuys
818.994.7437
www.the94thaerosquadron.com/VanNuys

*Reliving World War I with a bad case of crabs.*

large patio with a number of fire pits, hanging lights, and, for that romantic touch, barbed wire.

We took a table in front of a huge bay window just as the sun was beginning to set, and ordered a few cocktails while admiring the view. To soak up the alcohol we decided to take advantage of the King Crab Cocktail Special so prominently advertised on the table display. While it seemed like a good idea at the moment, the cocktail's pungent bouquet heralded its arrival before it even got to our table. We would have assumed that due to its proximity to an airport runway, 94th Aero Squadron might fly regular sorties to Alaska to pluck its crab straight from the Aleutian waters. Oh, how wrong we were.

Cobbled together from what must have been the previous night's leftovers of the King Crab Cocktail Special from the King Crab Platter the night before that, our crabmeat tasted like it had indeed just been flown in, all right—via time machine from the trenches of Verdun. A quarter of a million soldiers died in that horrific battle alone, but we're fairly certain that one of the things they *weren't* fighting over was a bounty of fresh Alaskan seafood. When we informed the waitress of the crab's putridity, her reply was, "Oh. Okay." She removed the noxious crustacean meat with nary a hint of truculence, yet left it on our bill.

Perhaps that's how things were done back in the Kaiser's day, but we weren't about to stand for that kind of insouciance. So we stood up—and that's when we were struck by what Ted Nugent might describe as a severe case of Crab Scratch Fever. Whatever had made it to our stomachs had suddenly been cleared for takeoff, forcing us to make an emergency landing in the restroom, where we promptly cashed in our round-trip meal tickets. Interestingly, the crab tasted no different coming up as it did going down.

We'd guess that not everything on the menu is an emetic, but we were in no mood to find out that evening. Years before, if memory serves us correctly, we found the French onion soup to be palatable; even so, we think 94th Aero Squadron is far better suited to drinking than dining. We wholeheartedly recommend it as an unforgettable alternative to wherever it is you usually go to get drunk. You'll be hailed as a genius when you forego that tired, repetitive pub crawl of the same old pseudo-dives and instead bring your friends to one of the few seventies institutions overlooked by the Hipster Retronaissance.

And, hokey as it may seem, there's something awe-inspiring about watching what amounts to a midsize car with wings as it rolls down a runway, slips the surly bonds of Earth, and, quite literally, disappears into the sunset. There are no jetliners at the Van Nuys airport, and though the occasional Learjet will blow by, what you mostly get are little one-engine underwing jobs, amazingly cheap-looking Cessnas and Pipers that, because of their flimsiness, seem even more incredible when they take off before your very eyes. Even on such a small scale—or perhaps because of it—the miracle of flight is just that . . . and a stiff cocktail or two only enhances the wonder of it all. If we can get all worked up about the wild blue yonder just sitting at the bar, we can only imagine how inspired all those drunk pilots must feel as they buzz skyward, gazing down with pity on us earthbound peons choking down bad crab meat while they try to spot topless sunbathers and marijuana gardens.

You'll see a lot of weird shit at any given bar in Hollywood on a Saturday night, but we're fairly certain you won't see planes taking off and landing. And since the staff at the 94th can't recall any recent crashes, the potential for witnessing a tragedy—always a good conversation starter—might just be in your favor as well.

Formosa Cafe
7156 Santa Monica Boulevard
Hollywood
323.850.9050
www.formosacafe.com

## FLOGGING THE PAST AT
# FORMOSA CAFE

In recent years, the Formosa Cafe has tried hard to dispel its reputation for ho-hum food, going so far as to bring in a former Spago chef to spruce up the chow. Even so, don't start getting ideas about this being anything other than a vintage watering hole. We can't tell if the food got better or if the drinks just got stronger, but if you need to put something on your stomach to soak up the overpriced cocktails, ordering from the menu certainly beats going out back and foraging through the Dumpster (seriously, we've tried it). And while you could certainly do worse in Hollywood than what the Formosa serves, if you're looking for sustenance rather than inebriation, you may want to do yourself a favor and dine elsewhere. When the Formosa's own Web site admits that "most people just stop by for pre-dinner or after-hours drinks," well, what does that tell you?

Like most ancient Hollywood establishments—this one has been around since 1924 or 1925 or 1939 depending on whom you talk to—the Formosa is dark, intimate, and so fraught with alcoholic history that its vibe alone may get you intoxicated. What started long ago as a trolley car diner has expanded over the years into a still-cramped-but-cozy institution that has served as an auxiliary commissary for what began as United Artists studios across the street. Countless movie stars, rock gods, and mere

# ...AND THE HORSE YOU RODE IN ON

In the early to mid-twentieth century, the British pub—or at least our Americanized notion of it—inspired more local restaurateurs and bar owners than any other kind of ethnic bodega we can think of. There's no telling what prompted the mass Anglophilia that swept the nation during those decades, and we're grateful that the HMS Bounty is still around; unfortunately, the Tally-Ho, the Bull 'n' Bush, and Tail o' the Cock are gone forever, but their names still titillate. The White Horse Inn has also been ushered into the pages of history, but the shuttered building still stands, adjacent to what may very well be the rudest liquor store in Reseda. When we asked the proprietors if they knew what fate had befallen the venerable pub next door, they looked at us like we weren't speaking English. Adding a little volume and slowly enunciating each syllable, we posed the question again, this time in their native tongue: "When did White Horse go bye-bye?" We punctuated our query with a brisk horsey pantomime, once around the Funyuns display. This time they understood exactly what we were saying, and told us, in no uncertain terms, to get the fuck out of their store if we weren't going to buy anything. Hmm? Was this the kind of sales tactic that would prompt us to purchase a cheap butane lighter in the shape of a naked, decapitated woman (press one of her boobs and flames shoot out the other nipple)? As much as we were tempted, we knew we would find the same lighter, or perhaps a better one, at another liquor store, where we would not be treated like a couple of Kim Jong Il's dorky white lackeys (as if he would ever have dorky white lackeys). The White Horse was a fine place in its time, especially by Reseda's standards, and we enjoyed sucking up its cheap, dated ambiance along with a few stale ales. We're not on a first-name basis with God or anything like that, but we know that if She has any sense of justice, She'll make sure the White Horse Inn is delicately razed by a single lightning bolt . . . and a BevMo is erected in its place.

**The White Horse Inn** / **Corner of Roscoe Boulevard and White Oak Avenue (former address)** / Reseda mortals have drunk themselves to oblivion here, and if these walls could talk they would probably throw up on you first.

That said, we tend to be unimpressed with the "Movie Stars Ate Here" shtick. Who really gives a rat's ass which booth Marilyn Monroe and Clark Cable sat in between takes of *The Misfits*? Does it really matter that Sinatra ate chicken chow mein here the day after he won his Oscar? Why should we care if Bono comes in here every few years? We want our drinks *now*, goddammit!

We find it far more compelling that for a time, the Formosa was a gathering place for gangsters. This is where Lana Turner and donkey-dicked wiseguy Johnny Stompanato often wined and dined until Turner's teenaged daughter shivved the thug in self-defense. Bugsy Siegel was a Formosa habitué before he ate lead, and mobster Mickey Cohen hid his dirty money in a floor safe that's still there, right next to one of the booths. The so-called "Star Dining Car" section (the back room built from a trolley car) once hosted a prosperous bookie operation, where stars from across the street would come to pay off their debts or collect their winnings. We like to imagine deadbeats being hauled outside by their collars to have the snot beaten out of them, but the only parking lot violence we could uncover was when Shannen Doherty smashed a bottle over some guy's head and got two years probation. *Yawn*.

*Try the Shannen Doherty Special.*

The fact that the Formosa bills itself as "a staple for the young Hollywood set" should be a warning sign for any self-respecting Angeleno, but we have to give the place props for its signature green neon sign, and for enduring a 1991 effort to turn the relic into a parking lot. Yes, the Formosa is more cliché than bizarre, but we have a soft spot for survivors . . . even Shannen Doherty.

## AN EXERCISE IN STRIATION AT THE
# ZEBRA ROOM

Any shitty little bar in a 1960s-era strip mall that opens for business at 6:00 AM is enough to get us all anxious and sweaty, so just imagine the squirrelly dampness induced by the prospect of the Zebra Room.

Zebra Room
20930 Hawthorne
Boulevard
Torrance
310.371.2092

With a façade of black-and-white-striped decorative cinder block just yards from the edge of Hawthorne Boulevard in exotic Torrance, it seemed that the odds for a successful payoff were good. Although we should know better by now, we remain glass-is-half-full guys, always aiming high and reaching for the stars, even in Torrance. The Zebra Room, we thought, would be one of our greatest discoveries, a den of superlative Zebraness enjoyed only by a select community of South Bay alcoholics who feel the need to start drinking before most of us have gotten out of bed. Zebra-print tufted booths, we imagined, with zebra-skin barstools. Black-and-white-striped linoleum, prancing mosaic zebras in relief backlit behind the bar, and a gold-vein-mirrored ceiling. We expected the zebra upholstery might be cigarette burned and the linoleum in need of a good strip and polish, but it would be the apogee of hard-drinking zebradom, ripe for the sort of exploitation we live for.

After years of passing the Zebra Room en route to places of greater importance, the day had come to venture inside and experience the wild, wild, black-and-white world we'd been banking on. On an early Saturday evening, we pulled into the lot, cameras surreptitiously tucked. But before we could reach for the door, however, we smelled something. A rotting gin-soaked corpse? Fresh roadkill on hot pavement? A two-dollar whore after a long workweek? But it wasn't just the scent, is was the sound. That unmistakable sound we've heard so many times before. The sound of the shitfaced who've got nothing left to live for, wasting night after night in a place where they can feed the addiction that will slowly destroy their lives, one long day at a time. In general, drunk people tend to be loud, but this group could be heard from the street, through walls of decorative cinder block, competing with the heavy metal that nearly shook the Zebra Room's unzebra-like door from its hinges.

The Zebra Room smelled and sounded like a place where someone could get hurt, real bad.

Opting for a kinder, gentler experience we backed away, saving the Zebra Room for the AM hours. Surely the drunks showing up well before lunchtime would be too weak to throw punches. So as the sun rose over Torrance, we approached the Zebra Room once again. But before we could reach for the door, however, it flew open, and a crusty-looking Caucasian male, aged approximately sixty years, with a face that did a fair job of demonstrating the long-term effects of cigarette smoking and excessive alcohol consumption emerged only long enough to toss a lit butt toward the parking lot. Momentarily destabilized by the invasive sunlight, he retreated back into the Room. Cool, we thought. Evidently the Zebra Room allows smoking. We love bars that bend zoning laws.

Eagerly, we entered. Turning the corner we glimpsed a row of late mid-century Danish Modern–inspired ceiling fixtures lighting the bar. A great first impression, certainly, but trumped by a conversation we fortunately stepped into late, shouted at drunken decibel: " . . . *shut the fuck up bitch, I don't need to hear*

<h1>What's black and white and shitfaced all over?</h1>

*that shit from a nigger, don't fuckin' say shit to me, just shut the fuck up ya fuckin' bitch. . . . "*

Without making eye contact but with enough time to ascertain that our zebra-skin fantasies proved to be pure folly, we high-tailed it out.

The Zebra Room. How tragically ironic.

## DRINKING OURSELVES TO DEATH AT
# MUSSO & FRANK

Before Generation Hip ushered in a cocktail-lounge renaissance that made classic drinks ubiquitous in Los Angeles (the only "Cosmopolitan" that chicks knew in the eighties was the one they bought at the checkout stand), it was tough to find a good dry martini in this town. When overtaken by *the thirst,* there were two places in Hollywood to quench it: the now-defunct Nickodell Restaurant on Melrose (also noted for its heavenly chopped liver), and Musso & Frank Grill, still very much alive and kicking.

Unfortunately, the same cannot be said for William Faulkner, who accelerated his journey to the grave by way of the sanitarium at Musso & Frank's bar. We can't blame him. Any Pulitzer and Nobel Prize–winning author subjected to the indignities of Hollywood would have done the same. "Great story, Bill, but instead of a rural Southern town, can you make it take place on a submarine?" Faulkner was not the only writer of talent to enjoy a drink or two at the self-proclaimed "Oldest Restaurant in Hollywood." At one time or another, the bar played host to F. Scott Fitzgerald, Raymond Chandler, Dorothy Parker, Dashiell Hammett, Thomas Wolfe, Erskine Caldwell, Lillian Hellman, William Saroyan, Christopher Isherwood, John O'Hara, Heinrich and Thomas Mann (also a Nobel laureate), and even Charles Bukowski, once he could afford it. At the other end of spectrum: us. Fortunately, Musso & Frank does not discriminate based on talent.

Why are we so crazy about the martinis at Musso & Frank? To answer that, one must ask another question: What differentiates a great martini from a good one? The formula for the king of cocktails is deceptively simple, consisting of gin (*not* vodka, thank you very much), a touch of vermouth (enough to coat the ice cubes is plenty), and the highest quality garnish, be it olive, lemon peel, or onion (in which case the

Musso & Frank Grill
6667 Hollywood Boulevard
Hollywood
323.467.7788

## We'll have what the Nobel laureate is having . . .

drink is called a Gibson). With so few ingredients, the onus for distinction is placed squarely on their quality, combined with the ceremony involved in the cocktail's presentation. Musso & Frank acquits itself admirably when it comes to stocking an abundance of premium gins (we prefer Boodle's) but more than *what* they put into the drink, it's *how* they put it in front of you. Whether you prefer your martini shaken or stirred (Bond says shaken, we say stirred), the bartender (we like Manny) will mix it and then pour half of the elixir into that most perfect of vessels, the martini glass, and the other half into a tiny chilled carafe. Ask nicely, and he'll even stick the carafe in a little bowl of ice to keep it frosty.

If you want some old-school fare to accompany your old-school drink, may we suggest you take your liquid lunch to the next level with a bowl of chilled jellied consommé? We happen to think the two make a perfect pair, even if we've never won a Nobel Prize.

## YOU DON'T HAVE TO PLAY POLO TO GET HAMMERED AT

# THE POLO LOUNGE

The Polo Lounge
9641 Sunset Boulevard
Beverly Hills
310.276.2251
www.thebeverlyhillshotel.com

When we first moved to Los Angeles, we thought one had to be of a certain celebrity status to get hammered at The Polo Lounge at the Beverly Hills Hotel. Then, one summer afternoon, we summoned up the courage to stroll right in and order a beer. Much to our amazement, no one gave us a sideways glance. No one made us sit in the corner. No one asked us, in no uncertain terms, to leave. As the place filled up, our table remained our own personal fiefdom, despite the fact that a number of important-looking people were standing uncomfortably by the bar. Emboldened, we swore we would give up our seats for no man, with the possible exception of Bea Arthur.

Our paranoia about being treated like second-class citizens in Beverly Hills was not unfounded. Once, after an uncomfortably long wait at Kate Mantilini, we were on our way to being seated at a booth when our hostess was frantically waved back to the front of the restaurant by the maître d'. She left us standing in the middle of the restaurant where we were soon mistaken for busboys by angry patrons who shook their empty bread baskets at us and demanded to have their tables cleared. Hostess and maître d' conferred, glancing our way, and it was clear that the two titans of the food service industry were discussing our fate. The hostess rushed back and explained without the slightest hint of shame that "our" table was no longer ours. We'd have to wait for another one because someone special had just arrived and he had to be seated *immediately*. "I'm sure you'll understand," she said breathlessly, "Judge Reinhold is here."

Had we been asked to give up our table for, say, Judge Judy or Judge Wapner or even Judge Ito, we might have felt a twinge of magnanimity. But Judge Reinhold? Was she fucking kidding? Our ire took her aback. She was obviously accustomed to dealing with hungry plebeians who lived for the day when they could graciously give up their table to the star of *My Brother the Pig*, but that was not us, sister. This is not to cast aspersions on Judge Reinhold. He jerked off to Phoebe Cates's perfect rack in *Fast Times at Ridgemont High*, so he seems like a nice enough guy. No, our problem is not with celebrities themselves, but with the unctuous toadies who cater to them at our expense. That was the kind of snotty bullshit we expected at The Polo Lounge; instead we got it at a place known for its nouvelle meatloaf. Go figure.

We've since made up with Kate (only because she grills a mean trout), and Judge still enjoys steady work as a character actor, but our hat remains doffed to The Polo Lounge for always making us feel welcome even if we didn't play second fiddle to Eddie Murphy in an overrated movie franchise from the eighties. There we know we can rub cocktail olives with the rich and famous without suffering the incalculable humiliation that comes from being forced to give up our table and sit in the corner behind a potted plant whenever Efrem Zimbalist, Jr. walks in.

*Where they dare to serve even those who aren't Judge Reinhold.*

## THREE SHEETS TO THE WIND AT
# THE HMS BOUNTY

Appointed in a dense walnut-and-leather decor and punctuated by the occasional authentic brass porthole or ship's lantern, The HMS Bounty gives one the feeling of being safe and snug in the bowels of a galleon captained by Mickey Spillane. Like its neighbors the Brass Monkey, the Prince, and Taylor's Steakhouse, The HMS Bounty has in the past decade gone from being one of L.A.'s best-kept secrets to one of its most popular vintage bars. But we don't hold that against it since The Bounty was practically our living room back in the day (one of us lived at the adjacent Gaylord Apartments, which has a door to The Bounty in its lobby).

**The HMS Bounty**
3357 Wilshire Boulevard
Los Angeles
213.385.7275

# IS THAT A BOTTLE OF THUNDERBIRD IN YOUR POCKET OR ARE YOU JUST HAPPY TO SEE ME?

The first time we saw you, you crazy clown, we fell in love. We stopped and stared and tried to take you all in . . . but we couldn't. You were twinkling like a star, so bright and full of life—bigger than life, in fact. And that smile. Your magic, tragic smile. But our love could never be. We're just a couple of kids from the right side of the tracks, and you're a giant neon liquor store sign in the shape of a clown.

This mammoth, argon-fired, glass-and-steel Pierrot is more than just a sign, however. It's an icon for that primordial party animal in us all, the one that likes to strap on the red rubber nose every now and then and get downright stinkin' silly.

Next time you're in this blighted patch of NoHo—perhaps paying a visit to the clown-happy California Institute for Abnormal Arts just down the street—be sure to stop by and pay your respects.

Circus Liquor / 5600 Vineland Avenue / North Hollywood / 818.769.1500

And we're well aware that the surrounding area has also changed since then, not always for the better. When the first edition of this book was published in 1997, the Ambassador Hotel was shuttered but still standing, the once prestigious Wilshire District was in decline, and The Brown Derby was relegated to sitting on top of a mini-mall built in its former location. Gordon "Gordie" Fields, the man who launched The HMS Bounty in 1962, was still the managing partner of the bar, and had seen it through good times and bad. (His son, onetime local celeb and founder of Posh Boy Records, Robbie Fields, also looked after the place for a time.)

Cut to today: The Ambassador has been leveled to make way for another LAUSD boondoggle, Mid-Wilshire and Koreatown have mind-melded into one gloriously iconoclastic district, and The Brown Derby still sits sadly on top of a mini-mall, waiting for someone to put a bullet through its headband. We figure it's all a wash, except for the loss of Gordie, who passed away in 1998, a year after *L.A. Bizarro* came out.

We don't honestly know if he ever got the chance to read our fond paean to The Bounty, but we hope he did, if for no other reason than it may have given him hope. Despite the fact that in the mid-nineties local mags like *Los Angeles* and *L.A. Weekly* had written up The Bounty as one of the city's best "dives" (we wouldn't put it in that category), Gordie was still pouring his own money into the place as fast as he was pouring drinks. When we last spoke with him in 1996, keeping the doors open was no longer a business decision for Gordie, but a matter of pride: This was his home and he was damned if he was going to lock up his favorite hangout. These were grim times, as Gordie wrestled with everything from downsizing the menu to slashing food prices 60 percent to accommodate the influx of low-rent clientele (like us) who had replaced all the ten-martini lunchers who had kept The Bounty afloat in its heyday. And boy, did it ever have a heyday.

*What do you mean you're out of bullshot?*

Prior to 1962, The HMS Bounty wasn't The HMS Bounty. It was called "Dale's Secret Harbor." Then along came Gordon, who stepped in and "Bounty-ized" the place, changing the name and adding the placard out front that promises "Food and Grog" as well as brass portholes and other items nautical. Another of Gordon's improvements was the dim amber lighting, which, as he once told us, "makes ladies look younger and have less wrinkles." The trick worked. In the 1960s, a stampede of young, single professional women moved closer to their jobs in the bustling Wilshire District—they had their pick of the many newly constructed apartments between Third and Sixth Streets—and that's when The Bounty became *the* pick-up bar in Los Angeles. Gordie's amber lighting was so effective that, when combined with a few stiff double martinis, a man could easily leave the bar with Brigitte Bardot only to wake up in the morning with Rose Marie.

The Bounty was also a *huge* success as a power lunch spot for all the ad agencies and law firms that flocked to Mid-Wilshire in the sixties, culminating in the construction of the towering Equitable building in 1969, just a block to the west. From Monday to Friday, for more than two decades, lunchtime at the bar was packed with suits, many of whom would then return for cocktail hour (an American tradition that has sadly been replaced by 12-step meetings). Sufficiently lubed, patrons could easily find The Bounty too packed to permit a relaxing supper, and would

# CATCH A
# FALLING STAR

Celebs frequent Gil Turner's because of its convenient location. Plebs go there to see celebrities buying alcohol. We like it for its great neon sign, and because we could always buy booze there when we were underage. Of course, that was a *long* time ago and the store wouldn't dream of doing that now, but it *will* sell liquor to one of the Olsen twins, which is almost as scandalous.

Gil Turner's Fine Wines and Spirits / 9101 West Sunset Boulevard / West Hollywood / 310.652.1000 / www.gilturners.com

repair to the Bull 'n' Bush around the corner (also co-owned and managed by Gordie), The Brown Derby next door, the Cove, The Windsor, or Taylor's Steak House for a sumptuous dinner. Call it a hunch, but it must have been a great time to be alive; it's certainly an era that we pine for.

Businessmen and politicos from downtown weren't the only heavy hitters to make The Bounty their home away from home. When the Ambassador was still across the street, black performers headlining at the Cocoanut Grove were not allowed to eat or drink in public at the nightclub or the hotel, so superstars like Duke Ellington and Sarah Vaughan (she could put away an entire bottle of Martel in an afternoon, according to Gordie) regularly came to The Bounty to play. Another notorious boozer, Jack Webb of *Dragnet* fame, held court here in a corner booth on Monday nights in the early seventies. Whenever the New York Yankees were in town, Gordie could always count on Yogi Berra, Mickey "What Liver?" Mantle, and their thirsty teammates to knock a few bottles of booze out of the park. When Winston Churchill stayed across the street at the Ambassador, it was in The Bounty that he chose to partake in his ritual of a nightcap and cigar.

Despite The Bounty's rep for hosting celebrities and nobility, it was also a favorite hangout for some of L.A.'s most powerful bookies. Before the age of the cell phone, the pay phones in the back of The Bounty were ringing constantly, and big wheels would often have a phone brought to their table in order to do business. Keep in mind that this was also the age of the professional waiter, guys who were definitely *not* aspiring actors, but who had been around the block a few times and were always working some new angle to supplement their income—perhaps to open a place of their own. Their sense of duty to their patrons engendered a kind of loyalty that is rarely seen today, and there were plenty of businessman who would only sit at the table of their favorite waiter—some of whom were very accommodating when it came to bookmaking, and who would take the fall for it later.

Jumping back to the present, we're happy to report that The HMS Bounty is enjoying something of a heyday once again, even if Churchill, Webb, and Ellington are no longer warming their buns there. As much as we whine about the locust-like destruction that follows the path of über-hipsters, we're glad that a fresh generation has discovered The HMS Bounty, and that the new owner, Ramon Castaneda, a longtime protégé of Gordie's who has been with The Bounty since the day it opened, decided not to change it one bit. Gordie would be proud.

Unlike so many old bars that enjoy a renaissance, The Bounty has refused to let its newfound popularity go to its head. It's still a dark, intimate, almost claustrophobic watering hole bereft of self-conscious pretension or "hey-look-at-me-I'm-hip-now" attitude. Maybe that's because The Bounty has seen its share of glory days as well as dark days, which is always a humbling experience. If we had to pick a bar from which to learn our life lessons, it would be this one.

## THOSE AREN'T THE WAVES YOU HEAR CRASHING:

# DETOX, MALIBU STYLE

Gourmet meals prepared by a Cordon Bleu chef. Massage therapy. Yoga and Pilates classes. Shopping excursions. Hiking, surfing, kayaking, and bird-watching. A private room with a view of the ocean. No, this isn't the newest all-inclusive Cancun resort: It's rehab, Malibu style.

Leave it to Los Angeles to take the serious business of sobering up and accessorize it with shopping trips and your own personal Pilates instructor. The popularity of celebrity-attended

Malibu Rehabs
Various locations
Malibu

detox mansions with names like Promises, Passages, Renaissance, Malibu Horizons, and Stone Eagle Retreat have created a boom for dozens of similar facilities that have sprung up in the town whose name is now equally associated with rehab as it is with movie stars. This red-carpet treatment has even been given its own sobriquet—"The Malibu Rehab Model"—which is not to be confused with Malibu Barbie, Malibu Ken, Malibu Skipper, or any of their Malibu friends.

Drug and alcohol treatment has become a lucrative business, and the over-the-top pampering at many of the Malibu centers has raised eyebrows in what was once a stodgy, solemn industry. Checking into a traditional rehab facility like the respected Betty Ford Center—which costs about half as much as Malibu's big names—still means serious business. You won't find an on-site Chinese herbalist or "adventure director" at Betty Ford, and while the Rancho Mirage campus is nothing to sneeze at, don't waste your time looking for the "decadent closet space" as advertised by one Malibu rehab. If you're more concerned about the size of your closet than getting sober, crack open the Rémy and order another eight ball. You're not ready to get sober.

*Get three detoxes and the fourth is on us.*

Traditionally viewed as a liberal, live-and-let-live bunch, Malibu citizens have become increasingly concerned about their tony enclave being thought of as the destination for privileged speed freaks, drunkards, and pill-poppers. It's not that they mind the concept of getting sober, but please, not in their backyard. Then again, these are the same folks who have also banned plastic bags at grocery stores and smoking on beaches, so maybe they're not that easygoing after all.

Still, it seems to us that much of the griping—not just from Malibu residents, but from anyone with a hard-on for coddled addicts—smacks of jealousy and (dare we say it?) resentment. If the rich and famous can afford the finest booze and drugs, why should they be forced to scrimp when it comes time to get off them? Hard-liners will tell you that's simply not how it's done, that addiction is a disease and the only valid treatment entails austerity, some degree of suffering, and acceptance of a higher power. This has more to do with AA's puritanical roots than any basis in scientific fact, however, and some Malibu centers, like Passages, are bucking the "incurable disease" model by viewing addiction as a symptom of an underlying problem—and then selling a "cure."

Competition is fierce among the many rehabs that dot the wealthy coastal village, and bragging rights over who has the highest success rate is a constant refrain. For the most part, however, whether one goes through rehab in Malibu or Monrovia, attends meetings in Beverly Hills or Bell Gardens, or simply toughs it out on their own, the chances for staying sober are equally grim. Given those odds—and an unlimited bank account—we'd much prefer to spend thirty days in a gorgeous mansion with five other fabulous addicts, eating Veal Oscar and enjoying shiatsu massages, than endure lockdown in a mental institution where whackjobs in hospital gowns extinguish cigarettes on their thighs and attempt to make collect calls to the moon on the battered pay phone (full disclosure: we're not making that up). We'd rather have a group hug with Lindsay and Britney than . . . just about anyone, and if we're going to be forced to recite the Lord's Prayer, having Andy Dick and Mel Gibson standing right next to us will certainly take some of the sting out of forgiving those who have trespassed against us.

If you're solvent and have a drug or alcohol problem, or just want a good excuse to get away from your job and family for a month, tell your valet to pack your bags and have the chauffeur warm up the Bentley. You're going to Malibu! But be forewarned: Despite scuffling over who has the biggest success rate, none of the facilities offers a money-back guarantee. You may be taking your sobriety one day at a time, but your treatment center will most likely want your full payment up front. And if after a day or two you decide that sober living isn't your bag, you're free to go—but your money stays. Apparently, in Malibu not only are you powerless against your addiction, but the rehabs are also powerless to prorate.

# WHEN IS A DIVE BAR NOT A

# DIVE BAR?

## IN WHICH TO ASSAY THE MEANING OF A DIVE BAR, THE AUTHORS FREQUENT NUMEROUS ESTABLISHMENTS AND END UP WITH VOMIT ON THEIR SHOES

What is a dive bar? At one time it referred to a squalid, dismal, and often dangerous drinkery frequented by "regulars" (aka alcoholics) in order to tie one on, pick a fight, sob inconsolably, and, if one was lucky, get a gumjob from a man or woman who looked like William Frawley. Dive bars did not have karaoke. Dive bars did not serve mojitos. Dive bars did not have security guards or velvet ropes. Dive bars were not self-conscious about their precious retro decor. Dive bars were not popular, glamorous, trendy, or hip, nor were they frequented by anyone to whom those same adjectives would apply.

Dive bars were . . . dive bars, for Christ's sake. Like the Hard Rock. No, not *that* one.

For many years there was a bar in the worst part of downtown's Skid Row called Hard Rock Café, and it was already an ominous shithole in 1969 when it turned up on the back of the Doors' *Morrison Hotel* album. By the mid-eighties, we'd venture to say it was one of the most dangerous bars in all of downtown—no small feat when one considers that the bar sat directly across the street from the huge windowless LAPD fortress on Sixth and Wall streets. The Hard Rock was a human roach motel where the bottom of society's barrel came to drink when they had stolen or begged or sold their bodies for enough change to buy a shot of cheap booze. Inside it was dark and grimy and smelled of every human bodily fluid imaginable. Your hands stuck to the bar and your back felt conspicuously exposed. The grim silence of men drinking themselves to death was occasionally punctured by violent confrontations and staccato outbursts of demented screaming. Outside, the equivalent of human cow patties were spattered on the urine-soaked sidewalk where filth-encrusted bums suffering from the DTs ranted and stomped and flailed their arms. Fistfights, stabbings, and shootings at the Hard Rock were the social equivalent of shaking hands, so much so that the cops tried to ignore the mayhem as much as possible. It was not a bar where you went to have fun: It was a bar where you went to die. Not even we could find something redeeming in its wretched decay, and that, in our opinion, was what made it the quintessential dive bar.

Now, of course, dive bars are as cute and cuddly and collectible as Beanie Babies once were. No longer a bastion of solitude for the serious drinker who simply seeks a dark, semi-peaceful place to pursue liquid oblivion, dive bars have become funtime destinations to be plotted on a map for an evening of recreational drinking and driving. Upbeat and lively young professionals who want to pretend they're slumming it while meeting other upbeat and lively young professionals have so many destinations to choose from that they must organize an evening of coordinated bar-hopping en masse with the aid of a social networking site. What happened to the good old days when a *pub crawl* was what a drunkard did when walking upright was no longer an option?

When did it all go south? Some would say that the meaning of "dive bar" began to change with the dawn of the Great Ironic Revolution, which in turn was heralded by the arrival of punk rock. If you flash back to the late seventies (or what you imagine they were like), it's hard to envision Bee Gees fans seeking out the worst bars in town, whereas punks were drawn to dives like hungry bugs to the yellow porch light of rebellion. Urban rebels fanned out to find seedy watering holes, cafés, and nightclubs that did not cater to the polyester singles scene, nor to disco dreck and heavy metal mutants—places like the Hong Kong and Madame Wong's in Chinatown; Frolic Room, Seven Seas, and Cathay de Grande in Hollywood; Club 88 and the Music Machine on the Westside; and Al's Bar, the Atomic Cafe, and Gorky's downtown—and in doing so made them at first trendy, then popular, and finally, abhorrent.

The undiscovered cocktail lounge where one can drink with the locals in an irony-free atmosphere is now something of an endangered species in this town (in case you haven't heard, the gods stopped making vintage bars). If your favorite secret barroom has not already been overrun by strangers from the other side of town, it's probably

**DIVE BAR HAIKU NO. I**
*Booze makes me happy*
*I'm not an alcoholic*
*How did I get here?*

been torn down or, worse, purchased by a savvy impresario who, like a plastic surgeon, nips, tucks, plumps, and shapes the once sagging establishment into a perfect parody of its former self (hello Golden Gopher, Alibi Room, Saints & Sinners, et al.).

If we sound a bit disillusioned by it all, well, perhaps we are . . . and maybe that's our collective guilty conscience speaking because we've infiltrated a few unspoiled watering holes in our time, and now our karma is paying dividends. We know we doth protest too much, but as the late George Carlin once said, "Scratch any cynic, and you'll find a disappointed idealist." However, our shallow cynicism is balanced by what can only be described as our boundless faith in man's ability to adapt and, yes, *evolve*. Los Angeles will eventually run out of pre–Reagan era taverns one day, but it won't matter. By then, some future trendsetter will already have his eye on something so passé that it's prime for hipsploitation. Something like, say, an international chain of beer and burger palaces that once homogenized the notion of cool and stole the Hard Rock Café's name. If there's one thing we know to be true, it is this: what's shit today is chic tomorrow, and vice versa.

That said, there are always a few enduring classics that will be exceptions to the rule. We've tried to mention a few of them in this chapter and in the list below, a mixed bag of bars both familiar and obscure. Don't look for any rhyme or reason as to why we picked one bar and left another out. We're sure we've missed some good ones and touted some losers, but we're human, after all, especially when we're drunk. And quite frankly, all dive bars start to look the same after you've been to a hundred and twenty. We've tried to pick bars we love and bars we hate, bars you know and bars you don't (hopefully), bars for those who live in dread of not being part of the scene, and bars for those who are trying to escape it. We have attempted, to the best of our ability, to be equal opportunity curmudgeons.

So, to all of you, we tip our martini glasses and ask, without the slightest hint of facetiousness, "Who's paying?"

# FROLIC ROOM

Let's just go ahead and get this over with: the great thing about trends is that they're trendy. In other words, there will come a day when the clientele at the Frolic won't get on your nerves. Maybe that day is today, because the place attracts a diverse crowd, or maybe that day will never come. But we will always give the Frolic Room props for having the best name and the best sign of any bar in the city, plus bonus points for not succumbing to the desire to go all cutesy and redecorate (sorry, Boardner's, you blew it).

6245 Hollywood Boulevard / Los Angeles / 323.462.5890

# THE BLUE ROOM

After an orgy of Swedish meatballs and couch shopping at Ikea, bathe yourself in the azure ambience of the Blue Room, which obviously takes its name seriously (give your eyeballs a few minutes to adjust to the blue lighting and you'll be just fine). This ancient lounge still has many of its original fixtures, both human and inanimate, including vintage condom dispensers in the sparkling clean, fastidiously tiled restrooms. (In our humble opinion, a condom machine in the ladies' room says more about how our culture has changed than anything we've read from Susan Faludi.) Speaking of vintage, it must have been MILF night when we went, because there were a number of hungry cougars seductively sucking on cigarettes on the back veranda and eyeballing anything with a Y chromosome. Inside, there's usually plenty of elbow room, and the digital jukebox is neither loud nor discriminating; we endured a wide and annoying variety of hip-hop, heavy metal, and country-and-western hits.

916 South San Fernando Boulevard / Burbank / 323.849.2779

# THE LIQUID ZOO

The Liquid Zoo sounds like it would be a great title for a German pee-pee bestiality movie, which may explain why the name of this bar appealed to us so much. Then we went inside and we liked it even more, in the same disturbing way that something like glue huffing can strike your fancy; you wouldn't want to make a habit out of it, but you may not be able to help yourself. If we had to pick one word to describe this bar it would have to be "total-fucking-downer," even though the bartender is a total sweetheart. The last time we were there we sat by a regular who, by the look on his face, wanted kill us the moment we walked in. He was a husky guy, already well into his cups when he started talking about how everyone at the Zoo is like a big family and how one of the other regulars had died and how he used to sit right down there and how everyone at

the Zoo is like a big family and how important it is to have friends and how life is really short and how everyone at the Zoo is like a big family . . . and by the end of his rant it was obvious that he wanted to kill us even more because we couldn't hide the fact that we were hopelessly uninterested in becoming a part of his big family. We ignored him and hoped he'd go away but that was just wishful thinking since he was the only other customer in the place. As annoying as that sounds, we'd rather be locked in a broom closet with that loser than anyone who owns a fedora and isn't old enough to be on Medicare. Yes, the Liquid Zoo is a total shithole, but if that's what you're looking for, you can't find a better shithole than this.

7214 Sepulveda Boulevard / Van Nuys / 818.997.3818

# BAR SINISTER

If Mary Shelley is your idea of a goth superstar and your definition of industrial music begins and ends with Throbbing Gristle, you might want to skip Bar Sinister. On the other hand, if you head upstairs to the place they call "Purgatory," you will find a well-stocked chamber of horrors that may satisfy your as-yet-undiscovered need to sip a cocktail while watching someone get flogged. There's no telling whether you'll catch a high-schooler with a fake ID getting her first taste of leather or a pasty hedge fund manager trying to compensate for being a scumbag all day, but those are the breaks. Not surprisingly, it's also loud and crowded in Purgatory. Those who prefer to leisurely enjoy the sights and sounds of torture without having to endure a bowel-loosening bass line or incessant jostling by hopped-up wannabe embalmers who take their fashion cues from *The Nightmare Before Christmas* will be happier at any number of private S & M clubs around town. But if you're the nightclubby kind of BDSM fan, or a curious gawker, or just looking to shock your friends who are visiting from Boise, then bourbon and a ball gag at Bar Sinister might be right up your . . . alley.

1652 North Cherokee Avenue / Los Angeles / 323.769.7070 / www.barsinister.net

# BILLINGSLEY'S RESTAURANT

If you're like us, you easily tire of the fresh sea air and vain-glorious citizens of Venice, Santa Monica, and other snazzy beach communities. Whenever we're forced to head that way (say, for a trip to the addictive Santouka Ramen

**DIVE BAR HAIKU NO.3**
*I just took a leak*
*Without even getting up*
*My shoes are soggy*

in the Mitsuwa Marketplace on Centinela), we always need a drink or two just to deal with all the happy people. Ever since Bob Burns closed down, Billingsley's has become one of our first choices (the other is Dear John's) for an old-school bar attached to an old-school restaurant that's west of the 405. The last time we were there, a young couple wandered in by mistake, were amused by the big bubbly aquarium for about five minutes, then decided they didn't "get" the place and left. Guess they didn't like the idea of drinking with people who look like their grandparents, but we do.

11326 West Pico Boulevard / Los Angeles / 310.477.1426

# BLARNEY COVE

Any dive next to a mental health facility has to be good. See if you can tell the difference between the patrons and the escapees from next door. We can't.

22105 Roscoe Boulevard / Canoga Park / 818.716.0321

# THE CANBY

We used to drink at a dive called Weber's Place when it was a good spot to meet Valley girls who were no longer girls and seemed destined for either rehab or a starring role in the next highly anticipated installment of *Trailer Trash Gang Bang Choad Mongers*. Then, ironically, the bar was bought by a porn movie location company, renovated, and reborn as a place where Valley girls who were no longer girls and who had once seemed destined for either rehab or a starring role in the next highly anticipated installment of *Trailer Trash Gang Bang Choad Mongers* donned bikinis and rubbed their groins on poles in order to make dollar bills magically appear in their panties. It didn't work. The high-ceilinged, airy bar changed hands once again and was transformed into a respectable R&B joint with live entertainment and a pretty decent kitchen (try the catfish). So why the hell is this entry called "The Canby?" Because Weber's no longer qualifies as a dive bar; it's too goddam nice. But The Canby, which sits directly across the street, is still a dive, in the best sense of the word. For a few decades it was a glorious sleazehole called "Sneaky Pete's," but new management changed the name to "The Canby" a few years ago as a tribute to the iconoclastic film critic from the *New York Times*, the late Vincent Canby. No? Okay, we have no idea why they changed the name, and the only

**DIVE BAR HAIKU NO.4**

*She looked good last night*
*In the darkness of the bar*
*Oh god, I have crabs*

clue we have as to what a Canby might be is the drawing of what appears to be a fox dressed in equestrian regalia as depicted on their sign. Whatever. The name has changed but fortunately not much else has been altered at this dark little drinkery that's apparently not quite retro enough to attract the Young and the Groovy. That means it's usually filled with locals who may cast a suspicious eye your way when you first enter, but we found the natives to be exceptionally friendly once we let them sniff our butts—which in itself was not an unsavory experience.

19309 Vanowen Street / Reseda / 818.996.4195

## BROADWAY BAR

We have never taken joy in being trapped in a crowded bar. Unlike, say, the Tokyo subway system, where one has no choice but to be crushed together with strangers, we choose to go to taverns where we can enjoy a modicum of personal space and conduct conversations without our faces being dappled with saliva. The two floors of Broadway Bar give us plenty of the elbow room we seek while never sacrificing intimacy, and the high ceiling is a welcome change of pace in this sort of venue. With the exception of certain Vegas casino bars, we've always enjoyed drinking in the round, and the circular bar at Broadway is a dramatic centerpiece that accommodates visual flirting from multiple angles. Broadway Bar rounds out our Cedd Moses revival trio (it's a love-hate thing, obviously). Like its aforementioned siblings, Broadway has been gussied up to appeal to gentrified alcoholics and other pseudo-dive cognoscenti, yet it eschews guest lists, velvet ropes, and cover charges. When we consider some of the fly-by-night crapholes out there that have confused themselves with Studio 54, we have to give Moses (with the exception of his "private" club Doheny) props for putting elitism on the back burner.

830 South Broadway / Los Angeles / 213.614.9909 / www.thebroadwaybar.net

## SCHOONERVILLE

Unlike the many small, dark, skeevy dives in this end of the Valley. Schoonerville is a large, semi-lit, skeevy dive that serves a variety of draft beers in very large frozen goblets called schooners. But we still can't figure out why they call it Schoonerville.

8901 De Soto Avenue / Canoga Park / 818.718.1404

# BAR 107

Any bar with a Heileman's Old Style Beer sign out front that reads *Ollie's Sport Shop, Live Bait and Tackle* but that's really called something else (like Bar 107) is all right by us. Think of it as the great-grandson of Al's Bar, only without a peephole into the girls' toilet.

107 West Fourth Street / Los Angeles / 213.625.7382

# BONA VISTA LOUNGE

Revolving lounges are not only rarities these days, but they're so unhip that they don't even appeal to hipsters who go out of their way to frequent places they think are unhip enough to be hip. There was a time when a revolving lounge was actually an attraction—LAX and the Holiday Inn in Hollywood both had them—but for now it's just an anachronistic oddity to be enjoyed until it becomes hip again—which, in Los Angeles, was probably yesterday.

404 South Figueroa Street / Los Angeles / 213.624.1000

# SUNNY'S SALOON

Unlike its namesake, Sunny's is a totally depressing bikini bar in an even more depressing strip mall behind the old Wonder Bread outlet store on DeSoto. This is the heart of porn valley and there's a high school nearby, but that doesn't mean the bikini dancers are always hot or young. Go figure. If you strike out at Sunny's—and you will—you can always go cruise the teens looking for trouble at the Carl's Jr. next door. Sleaze doesn't get any better than this.

20922 Lassen Street / Chatsworth / 818.998.6178

# GOLDEN NUGGET

Your living room is bigger than this easy-to-miss dive in Simi Valley, a conservative burg known for its melanin-challenged populace, plentiful pre-planned communities, and an abundance of retired cops and firemen who apparently like to start drinking shortly after sunrise. Simi is notoriously niggardly when it comes to doling out liquor licenses, and Golden Nugget can only pour beer and wine, mostly to sincere drinkers whose tattoos are old enough to collect Social Security. The place sees more action during the day than in the evening, which says a lot about life in Prop 8–lovin' Simi Valley. You figure it out. The last time we

were there on a Saturday night we were alone except for a retired fireman and the bartender, who kept talking about some biker who used to come in there all the time and get into fights and may or may not have killed someone. All we know is that we love the place since no trendster in his right mind is going to drive here from WeHo. That's why we feel fairly safe in writing about it without fucking it up for the locals, but we've been wrong before.

4435 Cochran Street / Simi Valley / 805.583.9715

# THE TAP ROOM AT SHATTO 39

There is perhaps no greater pleasure in life than dropping some blotter with a couple of good-looking Ivy League coeds, donning formal wear, and going bowling at 4:00 AM at Shatto 39 Lanes. We're a little too old for that now, and Shatto 39 is no longer a 24/7 operation, but it's open 'til 3:00 AM on most nights, which just means you need to get started earlier. Those not into hallucinogenic tuxedo-and-prom-dress bowling can still get their freak on at the Tap Room, which, like the rest of the place, is right out of a Jetsons-era time warp. As far as we're concerned, there's nothing quite like the atmosphere of a bar in a bowling alley, as long as it's a *real* bar in a *real* bowling alley and not some born-again dive like Mr. T's, or even worse, the upscale afterbirth of Lucky Strike Lanes. But hey, if either of those float your boat, we won't miss you at the Tap Room.

3255 West 4th Street / Los Angeles / 213.385.9475 / www.shatto39lanes.com

# CANOGA PARK BOWL

The rednecks and Latinos who frequent this twenty-four-hour bowling alley don't exactly mingle, but they don't stab each other to death, either. We've always had a soft spot in our hearts for fleshy *cholas* who wear too much makeup; you'll usually find a few here, along with their boyfriends, who *will* stab you to death if you're not careful. So be careful. And no, you're not having an acid flashback—that's really the carpet.

20122 Vanowen Street / Winnetka / 818.340.5190

# CANTER'S KIBBITZ ROOM

Jews are not known as having a genetic predisposition towards alcoholism (that would be the Irish, thank you very much), so there's something especially perverse about

this vintage bar in L.A.'s most famous deli. It looks like neither has ever been remodeled—that's a good thing—and Canter's twenty-four-hour dining rooms have always drawn an eclectic late-night crowd, so it's only natural that the bar would get its share of local color as well. We think it may have become a bit too colorful, unfortunately, since we can remember the days when you could always find a seat. The addition of live musical acts in the early nineties raised the bar's *shem* a few notches, and we have to admit we liked the *platz* more when we didn't have to *shrayen* over the loud *muzik*, for crying out loud. But the *yungelayt* like to do the rock 'n' roll, so who are we to *kvetsh* about the whole *simkhe*?

419 North Fairfax Avenue / Los Angeles / 323-651-2030

# TATTLE TALE ROOM

Does every dive bar in Los Angeles now sport a condom dispenser in the ladies' room? Just as our parents can recall a time when men opened doors for ladies, we still remember when guys paid for their own rubbers. Now men are usually too busy thinking of ways to talk women into bareback sex, which explains the need for a condom machine in the gal's head. Like the Frolic Room, the Tattle Tale has a great name and great sign, and though it's been semi-discovered in recent years, it's still no Boardner's, thank Christ. They used to sell a T-shirt that read "Tattle Tale: A Disgusting Place to Meet," but apparently their self-effacing humor has waned as the slogan is curiously absent on the current offering, replaced by the comparatively tepid image of a champagne glass and Hawaiian lei. Yawn. During the week, Tattle Tale has a relatively low HAF (Hipster Annoyance Factor) that rises slightly on weekends when club kids are apparently seized by the urge to pretend they're slumming it. That, combined with the aforementioned condom dispenser in the women's room, means that you can probably find someone here who will have sex with you. Then again, the same can be said of the Greyhound bus station.

5401 South Sepulveda Boulevard / Culver City / 310.390.2489

# CLUB TEE GEE

Club Tee Gee has garnered quite a following for a number of reasons, not the least of which is the owners who, if they take to you, treat you like one of the family. They'll also

yell at you like one of the family if you act like an asshole. That may be great for some, but for us it's the last thing we need. We go to bars to get *away* from our families, not to find new ones. Fortunately, Betty doesn't know us from Adam and leaves us alone, and that suits us fine since the décor, vibe, and cheap drinks in this dive are just about perfect. Young 'uns and old-schoolers mix well here, especially on the weekends when age comes before beauty on both sides of the bar.

3210 Glendale Boulevard / Los Angeles / 323.669.9631

# YE RUSTIC INN

Defying Webster as to the conventional definition of what "rustic" means, Ye Rustic Inn is anything but pastoral. As long as you're not expecting some kind of romanticized notion of what an English pub should be, you probably won't be disappointed by this place, which has been around since 1971. And if it happens to be filled with regulars and you don't feel like getting into an argument with someone about "their" seat, you can always go across the street to the Drawing Room, which is also usually bereft of those wishing to "make the scene," if you dig.

1831 Hillhurst Avenue / Los Angeles / 323.662.5757

# THE DRAWING ROOM

We fucking hate karaoke. The Drawing Room does not have karaoke, so right there it already gets high marks. 'Nuff said.

1800 Hillhurst Avenue / Los Angeles / 323.665.0135

# SEVEN GRAND

This self-conscious manly man's bar (again from Cedd Moses) is so manly that it's almost unmanly if you think about it too hard. From the dead stuffed animals on the walls to the rolling library ladder that allows access to the sky-high shelves of premium booze behind the black walnut bar, this place is designed to look like it would have appealed to Hemingway, but it's hard to say whether Papa would have preferred to drink at Musso's with Faulkner—even though he hated his guts—before being caught dead in a neo-dive like this, or if he was just enough of a self-possessed blowhard to revel in its Scotch-and-cigar manliness, which, as we have previously noted, is extremely manly. In fact, every perfectly planned prop at

Seven Grand is so rife with macho hyperbole that it sometimes comes off as parody of a *Cosmo* expose ("The Truth About Where Manly Men Drink!"), and seems less aimed at dudes and more towards gullible gals who are moistened by the notion they've penetrated the inner sanctum of the male mystique. In that way, Seven Grand serves its purpose as a decoy, drawing attention away from the far sleazier things that constitute What Men Like.

515 West Seventh Street / 2nd Floor / Los Angeles / 213.817.5321 / www.sevengrand.la

## HANK'S BAR

Thanks to Staples/Nokia and whatever else they're building to make downtown more like Univiral Shittywalk, a lot of existing downtown businesses have cleaned up their act in hopes of grabbing some of that gentrified action. Located in the less-than-tony Stillwell Hotel, Hank's didn't need to change a damn thing since it's always been a "safe" place to drink in an area that traditionally has a disproportionate share of dangerous watering holes.

840 South Grand Avenue / Los Angeles / 213.623.7718

## CHANCES

Don't let the Ma-and-Pa-Kettle façade of this deep Valley dive fool you. You'll certainly find the occasional Mountain Dew redneck in here, but it's mostly populated by neighborhood locals who, surprisingly, are friendlier than the average alcoholic. We like the suggestive sleaziness of the name, too, as in "If I go home with this person, what are my *Chances* of getting herpes?"

20160 Roscoe Boulevard / Winnetka / 818.458.6937

## GOLDEN GOPHER

What kind of drug do you have to be on to envision a golden gopher? Is it a veiled sexual reference? Does it have political overtones? Apparently not—it's just a light brown mammal, but we'll always believe there's more to it than that. This is one of the most well-preserved and, dare we say, *elegant* downtown dives that doesn't really qualify as a dive, mainly because of its makeover by the Pied Piper of downtown über-impresarios, Cedd Moses. Though the neon signage out front is stunning, the clientele tends to get on our nerves, perhaps due to *Esquire*'s 2007

**DIVE BAR HAIKU NO.6**
*The urinal cake*
*Though it may be round and pink*
*Is not really cake*

anointment of it as one of the best bars in America. Of course, we realize we're old and cranky and probably not helping the situation by writing about it. On the plus side, the Golden Gopher has had its liquor license since Teddy Roosevelt was in office, which means you can also buy booze to go. So if you don't like the crowd, get a six-pack and bail. Here's mud in your eye.

417 West Eighth Street / Los Angeles / 213.614.8001 / www.goldengopherbar.com

# FOXFIRE ROOM

This is the bar in the movie *Magnolia* where William H. Macy (as Quiz Kid Donnie Smith) has the hots for the beefy bartender with braces, and where Henry Gibson (as a character impossibly named Thurston Howell) tells Macy, "It's dangerous to confuse children with angels." That alone should be reason enough to have a few drinks at the Foxfire Room, but when you add the occasional presence of a young and excessively groovy crowd, what more could you ask for?

12516 Magnolia Boulevard / North Hollywood / 818.766.1344

# CHIMNEYSWEEP

Years ago, when we were regulars at the "Sweep" after doing comedy shows just down the street at the L.A. Connection—the Kmart of improv clubs—we'd have done a spit take if anyone had suggested that there would someday be a line to get into the place and a doorman out front. "What next? Valet parking at Der Wienerschnitzel?" we would have derisively snorted. Well, the joke is on us, and on anyone else stupid enough to wait in line for a bar, much less a bar in the Valley. And before you accuse us of being Valley snobs, know this: When we lived in North Hollywood it was the armpit of San Fernando, a sad, sprawling, no man's land of forgotten mom-and-pop shops and vintage treasures like Phil's Diner and the Palomino. It was so beautifully hideous and tragically unhip that it deserved a sardonic nickname. Never would we have imagined that our little joke, "NoHo," would catch on, just as we would have assumed that the Sweep would forever remain an undiscovered gem where we could always find a seat on a Friday night. Back in the day, they even put one of our favorite songs on the jukebox, which was no small feat considering it was an obscure Elvis Costello tune and the jukebox was the kind that still played 45s. They also played along with our youthful binge drinking, allowing us to create a drink called a "Taco," which was a draft beer, a bloody mary, and another draft beer, placed on the table in that order, and downed immediately in succession by a single drinker. Instead of charging for three drinks, they chalked up each Taco as one premium drink order. That engendered a lot of love between us, but if we were to try it now, they'd look at us like we're crazy . . . assuming we ever made it through the line.

4354 Woodman Avenue / Sherman Oaks / 818.783.3348

## STOVEPIPER

It is a perversity of nature to separate drinking and smoking—especially in a dive bar—and there's nothing sadder than the sight of a bunch of smokers standing outside of the Stovepiper sucking down cigarettes. They should be inside the Stovepiper, sitting at the bar, sucking down cigarettes. Just because the Stovepiper used to let you smoke in the bar doesn't mean they still do—that would be against the law—and just because it's been a while since we've seen a group of smokers huddled out front like lepers doesn't mean they're all inside lighting up. Whether or not you smoke, you will love the unspoiled splendor of the Stovepiper's low-rent ambience, and, of course, the cheap, strong drinks. In a nutshell, the Stovepiper still is what the Chimneysweep used to be. Go there before it isn't.

19563 Parthenia Street / Northridge / 818.886.2526

## HOP LOUIE

A Chinatown institution that is known for its rudeness to roundeyes. We can't say we blame them.

950 Mei Ling Way / Los Angeles / 213.628.4244

## TAYLOR'S STEAK HOUSE

We have nothing funny to say about the bar at Taylor's Steak House. It's everything we think a bar should be— dark, clean, and almost reverentially quiet—which is why we saved the best for last. A class act in a crass town.

3361 West Eighth Street / Los Angeles / 213.382.8449

**DIVE BAR HAIKU NO.7**
*Comfort can be found
In the smell of Naugahyde
And a toothless hag*

RARE
PORCELAIN PORTRAIT
BUST OF
ELVIS
VALUED @ $600.00
(made in 1977)

ELVIS
1935-1977

Agua Espiritual
de Tapa Voca

Legítima Agua Espiritual
de Tapa Voca

30 Days

60 Days        90 Days        60 Days

6 Month        9 Month        6 Month

All Program

# CONSPICUOUS CONSUMPTION

## GETTING A SCAM AND CHEESE TO GO AT

# MATT & TONY'S

## SUBMARINE SANDWICHES AND MISSION HILLS

# PSYCHIC

Matt & Tony's Submarine
Sandwiches
10710 Sepulveda Boulevard
Mission Hills
818.365.2310

Mission Hills Psychic
10712 Sepulveda Boulevard
Mission Hills
818.838.1128

How many times have you thought to yourself, "Hey, I could really go for a sub sandwich and a glimpse into the future?" When we get the urge for some capicola with clairvoyance on the side, we head straight to Mission Hills.

Matt & Tony's Subs and Mission Hills Psychic sit cheek by jowl on Sepulveda Boulevard in the shadow of the Ronald Reagan (118) Freeway. Other than the wall that divides the two buildings, they share no affiliation—at least on the surface. Matt & Tony's is a popular hole-in-the-wall sandwich shop favored by locals and characterized by its overstuffed subs and surly staff. When we attempted to follow up on a few facts about the history of their fine establishment (we used to eat at Matt & Tony's years ago when it was located on the other side of the Valley), the employee we spoke with was so incredibly rude we could only assume he had confused "We want to include Matt & Tony's in our bestselling guidebook" with "We want to sodomize your grandmother with an eggplant and then force her to buy a timeshare in Death Valley." We're not sure if he was an owner, manager or what—he hung up on us before we could find out.

Whoever he was, we'd be lying if we said we weren't disappointed that his display of bad form dampened our enthusiasm for Matt & Tony's. Even though we share the same given names, it only takes one turd in the punchbowl to ruin a party—and it proves that you can't put a price tag on courtesy, especially when you're looking a gift horse in the mouth. Other than civility, Matt & Tony's can also be sometimes short on seating, which, if you can afford to part with about $40, is one reason to take your sandwich next door to Mission Hills Psychic. There you will have your future foretold by a guy named—we're not shitting you here—Tony. Do you see a pattern emerging?

After a tenuous exchange through the screen security door—he actually seemed suspicious that someone wanted their cards read—we stood outside for about ten minutes while Tony presumably tidied up the place. That seemed a little odd; shouldn't a psychic have known we were coming? We snapped a few pictures of the building's sign and tattered awning that flaunts "Love Spells, Candles, Incense, Oils."

"I'm sorry, you can't take pictures," came Tony's voice through the door. Really? Says who? Taking pictures of public signage is, in fact, perfectly legal, but we decided not to argue about it since we had yet to discover what fate had in store for us.

Inside, the reading room was decorated in early Spartan: recliner, television set, small table, deck of tarot cards. Tony, a full-sized, soft-spoken man, seemed slightly uncomfortable with our presence, but still did his best to make us feel at home. Before we got into the heavy stuff, we told Tony we were working on a book, and asked if he knew anything about the brutal turf war that was being waged between two Gypsy families who control most of the psychic business in Orange County. He assured us he had no idea what we were talking about, and said that he had inherited his "gift" from his grandmother. "It skipped a generation," Tony explained. He then described the two kinds of tarot card readings he offered, and we chose the deluxe model that promised more details and allowed us to ask some personal questions at the end. He also asked if we wanted to hear only positive information or the negative stuff, too. We told him we'd prefer to hear *only* the bad news, but Tony said that wasn't an option.

*Capicola with provolone? You read my mind!*

Before he started the reading, Tony told us to take out the cash and put it next to us on the table. The way he said it made it seem like it was an essential part of the reading, but we knew he just didn't want to get stiffed. We asked him if we could take notes. "I'm sorry, you can't do that," he said. (Without notes, we were forced to call back a few months later to check our facts. Yes, Tony remembered our session, but the line mysteriously went dead when we asked about the different kinds of read-

ings he offered and how much they cost. Numerous attempts to call back went straight to his voicemail. Apparently there's more of a connection with Matt & Tony's than we realized, at least when it comes to their preferred method of dealing with inquisitive writers.)

Once he started laying down the tarot cards, it became clear we were sailing into familiar waters. "You're a good person, but people don't treat you so well," he said, obviously familiar with our previous publisher. "You've had your heart broken a few times, haven't you?" Well, yes—we're

in our forties and haven't always been fat and/or bald. "You're not really fulfilling your dreams and negativity is holding you back." Holy shit, is it *that* obvious?

When you're being spoon-fed this kind of twaddle, fifteen minutes can seem like an eternity, but eventually it came time to ask our three magic questions.

"Who's going to win the presidential election?"

"I can only answer questions that have to do with you."

"Okay. When am I going to die?"

He looked down at the cards.

"You are going to live a long and happy life."

"Really? Is that going to start any time soon?"

"All I can tell you is that I see a great deal of happiness in your future. You have one more question."

"Is the new edition of *L.A. Bizarro* going to be success?"

Again, he glanced down at the cards. He looked up and smiled.

"Yes. The cards tell me that your new book is going to be very, very popular."

Hot damn. Now *this* is a psychic we can believe in.

## ENJOYING A SOBER MOMENT AT
# MY 12 STEP STORE

My 12 Step Store
8730-B Santa Monica
Boulevard
West Hollywood
818.623.1702
www.my12stepstore.com

Once upon a time, the very notion of being on the wagon in West Hollywood made about as much sense as teetotaling your way down Bourbon Street. Now that it's far more hip to be sober than shitfaced—and your chances of getting laid are better, too—we're surprised that there aren't more chic boutiques like My 12 Step Store to cater to all the beautiful people in the Program. That's not to imply that all recovering alcoholics and drug addicts aren't beautiful—they most certainly are. It's just doubtful than an AA bookstore in Pacoima is going to carry tight whites with "Sober" emblazoned across the buns. It also goes to show just how much West Hollywood has changed; never before have so many gays been this straight.

My 12 Step Store is impressive for a variety of reasons, not the least of which is its prominent location on Santa Monica

## OUT '*n*' ABOUT
# PISTOL PACKIN' PATTY

California has produced some notorious heiresses, but few have lived more sensationally than Patty Hearst. Even Tori Spelling and Paris Hilton have never been pardoned by a United States president, and a cloying reality show or home made porn video can't stand up against the exploits of William Randolph's infamous granddaughter. Patty showed the world what separates a real heiress from the amateurs with a full-on carbine-totin' bank heist, during her year-and-a-half-long tenure as urban guerilla and celebrated member of the Symbionese Liberation Army. Tori and Paris, take note.

On May 16, 1974, only a month after Hearst's ECU on the Hibernia Bank security cameras and while still on the lam, she and two comrades hit Mel's Sporting Goods at the corner of Imperial and Crenshaw for a little retail therapy. After fellow SLA members Bill and Emily Harris finalized $31 in legitimate purchases, a tussle ensued, reportedly over a pair of purloined gym socks. Eagle-eyed Hearst, keeping watch from a Volkswagen van parked across the street, fired a few shots from a .38 caliber handgun in lieu of a coupon for their five-finger discount. Her blasts shattered the storefront windows and allowed for the Harris's quick exit (presumably with the gym socks in tow). They made yet another miraculous getaway and continued to remain on the FBI's most wanted list for another sixteen months, before finally being arrested in September of '75.

Mel's closed in 1979, the building has since been bulldozed, and the corner is now home to a Burlington Coat Factory and a "No Prostitution Zone." Nonetheless, the intersection of Imperial and Crenshaw is there to remind us that long before Patty Hearst secured a lifelong career as a John Waters contract player, she was an abducted teenage heiress terrorizing the working classes of El Segundo from a VW bus. And she was a damn good shot, too.

**Mel's Sporting Goods / 11425 Crenshaw (former address) / Inglewood**

*They can do their own inventory, thank you very much.*

Boulevard, the decidedly un-somber decor and upbeat and empathetic staff (if you catch our drift), and its diverse inventory of books, gifts, and Twelve Step paraphernalia that would give even Otis the Drunk pause to reconsider his lifestyle. Other than the aforementioned underwear, the store also stocks a variety of hip and humorous shirts with slogans like "Don't blame me, I went to rehab," "Sober Brat," "Got twelve?" as well as Home Depot and American Airlines logos cleverly tweaked to send a sober message.

This cheery apparel, along with the many sobriety chips available for recovery groups ranging from Narcotics Anonymous to Crystal Meth Anonymous, heralds a new age for the Twelve Step revolution, once solely dominated by AA members who would have frowned on anything lighthearted, and who felt that addiction to alcohol was different (or, as was often implied by their dry drunk rants, somehow better) than addiction to any other substance. Unfortunately, there are still old-timers and young hard-liners who espouse such intolerance, but no matter what kind of meeting(s) you attend, you'll find the right chips and medallions here to celebrate sobriety of all shapes and sizes, and books to get you on the right path whether your weakness is OxyContin or Oreos.

And for that special breed of predatory scumbag who lacks any conscience whatsoever (i.e., single males) this is where you can pick up your own five-year sober chip without ever having to hold hands and say the Lord's Prayer. Buy a few books, learn the lingo, then casually whip out your chip in grocery stores, coffee shops, *even Twelve Step meetings* in order to take advantage of vulnerable, trusting young women trying to straighten out their lives and get sober after being fucked over by someone just like you. Recent divorcées and unscrupulous cougars can also stalk and kill plenty of fresh young prey with this surefire method.

But seriously, folks, getting sober can be a life-or-death proposition, and AA was never intended to be a social club or a dating service. Unfortunately, for many, that's what it has become, not because of an inherent flaw in the program, but because of the inherent flaws in human nature. People gravitate to power and sex even when they're fighting for their lives. While we cringe at the thought of someone using a fake chip to get laid, the sad truth is that such tactics are no worse than the infamous "thirteenth step," when even the most pious friends of Bill W. knowingly take sexual advantage of vulnerable newcomers. There's an old saying in the program that goes, "There's a slip under every skirt," but we'd have to amend that with " . . . and in every 'Sober' pair of briefs, as well."

# KEEPING IT REAL AT
# DAPPER CADAVER

A disemboweled human torso lies prostrate on a worktable, as the midday sunlight dances through the windows and hits a shelf lined with specimen jars, allowing their contents—daiphinized rat skeletons, fetal chicks, human lungs, and sheep's eyeballs— to glisten softly against the brushed-steel medical cabinetry. Utilitarian baker's racks jammed with plastic tubs labeled "hands," "skulls," and "legs & feet" are piled high with their respective—and bloody—contents, while morbid antiquities, roadkill, biological models, rotting skeletons, and "toe pinchers" (that's coffin lingo), are found packed into every available corner, or in some cases, hanging from metal hooks.

Such is the scene at Dapper Cadaver, movieland's *mercado* of the macabre. Not all its wares are real, of course—this is a prop business after all—but were it not for owner B. J. Winslow's strict "no human remains" policy, one might wonder.

Among prop houses, fabrication studios, and retail stores, Dapper Cadaver is a rarity, not only because it happens to be all three, but also because it's the industry's only prop shop specializing in death, biological oddities, gore, and laboratory equipment—*and* it's open to the public. Located beside the Bob Hope Airport, and rating as one of the more scintillating spots along San Fernando Road, Dapper Cadaver's approach to its business is unique among such studios. Except for the fact that its front windows might feature a rotting corpse on an autopsy table or a fetal pig specimen floating in a jar of formaldehyde, Dapper Cadaver presents just like any other independently owned business hanging their shingle on a busy Sun Valley sidewalk.

The customer experience is a privileged one, like gaining access to a working prop department of a major studio, but fashioned with a merchandising aesthetic akin to one of those *Saw* movies. You're welcome to look with your hands and you're likely to catch a Dapper Cadaver artist in action, putting the finishing touches on a mutilated corpse or decayed mummy. Set against oxblood walls, Winslow's antique autopsy equipment, collection of tribal weapons, taxidermy, and variety of animal skulls give Dapper Cadaver the air of a museum, while items like the snaggletoothed killer clown, human organ Jell-O molds, and comic tombstones add the morbid irreverence of Halloween. An accommodating staff is happy to answer questions (without revealing trade secrets) and show you the goods, the likes of which have earned them credits on *Dexter*, *Nip/Tuck*, *Bones*,

Dapper Cadaver
7572 San Fernando Road
Los Angeles
818.771.0818
www.dappercadaver.com

*Two realistic rotting heads are better than one.*

*Pirates of the Caribbean II*, and *Law & Order*, in addition to music videos, IMAX films, soap operas, even Broadway musicals—and, yes, a *Saw* movie. Winslow is also quite proud of his original-recipe stage blood, which he asserts is "the tastiest in the business."

You'll certainly find no shortage of filmland souvenirs in L.A.'s many schlock shops, but why settle for a James Dean com-

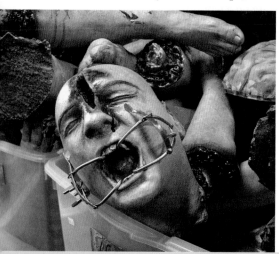

memorative plate or a plastic Oscar statuette when you can go home with a Dapper Cadaver original? All the Marilyn Monroe coffee mugs in the world couldn't hold a candle to a two-headed human fetus, a realistic rotting head, or a severed limb that may have actually been featured in you favorite crime show or horror movie. Dapper Cadaver may deal in the fake, but their fake is the real deal.

# I'LL BE THE GUY IN THE LAST STALL, SLATHERED IN ASTROGLIDE AND WEARING THE MERV GRIFFIN MASK

We love this place, even though they told us not to take photos (what, someone might steal their gorilla mask design?). Not only is the neon sign outside Grade-A vintage, but inside they have every conceivable costume and mask known to man, including Merv Griffin—at least we think it's Merv, but it may be Regis. It's hard to tell them apart with their clothes on. It doesn't matter—whoever came up with the name "Beautilities" deserves a star on Hollywood Boulevard.

**Robinson Beautilities / 12320 Venice Boulevard / Los Angeles / 310.398.5757**

# GALCO'S SODA POP STOP

It used to be that when you'd receive a dinner party invitation, a quick trip to your local wine seller for a nice bottle of something that didn't look too cheap was enough to fulfill your obligation as the gracious guest. But now it seems that practically everyone in L.A. is a recovering alcoholic, and arriving with a perfunctory bottle of wine is like dropping a ticking time bomb into the lap of some hosts. What was once a well-mannered gesture can now be an egregious faux pas, with the potential to send your wagon-riding host skidding back down the craggy slope of addiction.

You can skip these land mines of dinner party etiquette by heading to Galco's, where you can find hundreds of varieties of arcane bottled sodas. A case of twelve will only set you back about the same as a good bottle of French red (and will serve many more guests), and how much cooler to surprise your teeto-taling host with Galco's faux woodgrain cardboard crate, packed with a hand selected variety of the obscure and exotic, in bottles so cool they may put an end to recycling.

The selection is dizzying, with over forty varieties of root beer alone. A single visit might yield a bottle of extra-hot ginger beer from Jamaica, a creamy peach Nesbitt's, a sugar cane cola, or a deep pink "Leninade" with a label bearing a hammer and sickle. They offer contemporary sodas infused with lavender, rhubarb, lemongrass and kumquat, along with a handful of the temptingly esoteric, like a delicate cucumber, an aromatic rose water, and a dandelion and burdock brew.

John Nese is Galco's crown prince of carbonation, for whom Galco's Market had been a family business for over a century, keeping this Highland Park location since the mid-fifties. In his one-man effort to keep soft drink behemoths like PepsiCo and the Coca-Cola Company from wiping out the lesser-knowns like Kickapoo Joy Juice and Faygo Redpop, John decided to devote a section of Galco's to some of his unsung favorites sometime around 1995, even hitting up independent bottlers to reproduce old recipes. Now the aisles are almost exclusively devoted to bubbly

Galco's Soda Pop Stop
5702 York Boulevard
Highland Park
323.255.7115
www.sodapopstop.com

*Hitting the bottle.*

CANDY FOR 85¢

beverages you've either never heard of or completely forgotten about. While stocking his shelves, John is quick to make suggestions, pointing out an exotic new arrival, and sharing distinctions among seemingly identical sodas with the knowledge and enthusiasm of a fine wine merchant.

If you can't get your fill of sugar on the soda shelves, roll your cart over to what used to be Galco's produce section, where Chic-o-Sticks and Charleston Chews are stocked chockablock with other throwbacks like Chase's Cherry Mash, wax bottled Nik-L-Nips, Old Faithful Bars, or Idaho Spud peanut clusters. They're also one of the few-and-far-between retailers still offering the longstanding perennial favorite, bubble gum cigarettes (can we get an amen for the company that still produces bubble gum cigarettes?!).

Galco's may be a haven for candy freaks and purveyors of pop, but they offer beverages of the fermented variety too. There's a fine assortment of beer and wine, with picks nearly as arcane as their soda selection. But just try to make an exit without at least one bottle of soda or an Abba-Zaba. Just try.

## PERUSING THE CELEBRITY SKIN AT

# BABY JANE OF HOLLYWOOD

Baby Jane of Hollywood
The French Market Place
7985 Santa Monica
Boulevard, Suite 104
West Hollywood
213.848.7080
www.babyjane.net

Despite the number of entertainment memorabilia shops pimpling the face of Tinseltown, just where might a fan go to score an 8 × 10 glossy of *Hogan's Heroes* bad boy Bob Crane getting his dick sucked? Britney going commando? Paris Hilton's saddlebagged cameltoe or Davy Jones's asshole? At Baby Jane, the fun never stops.

The West Hollywood shop specializes in the private parts of public figures, and because their clientele is primarily gay, the stock is heavy on celebrity schlong. Virtually every scandal shot you've ever heard about or seen ruined with "censored" bars is in the tabloids Baby Jane has for sale, and then some. From early shots of Yul Brynner, Victor Mature and Steve Reeves, to current shots of Eminem, Colin Farrell, and the late Heath Ledger, when he was alive. They deal in naked dames too, although the selection is considerably less impressive.

Infamous purveyors of arcane celebriana, it was the '94 earthquake that put Baby Jane on the map. In the wake of the Northridge tremblor, fans could purchase the shattered remains of housewares and floor tiles from their fave star's home, beautifully mounted, titled and numbered. Celebrity underwear has also done well in this West Hollywood shop, and owner Roy Windham archives his favorites. Among his most prized: Schwarzenegger's jockstrap ("padded for continuity") and Madonna's panties. Not available for sniffing, so don't ask.

Baby Jane's is also beefcake headquarters, with dozens of black-and-white "physique" shots from the fifties, including one of a young Jack La Lanne sans the red stretch bodysuit. The collection is the most comprehensive in town (favorite pick: a porcine Marlon Brando in his underwear). From Hank Aaron to Chesty Morgan, take time to dig and you'll likely find it.

*Hollywood's best undressed list.*

## GOING TO PEN HEAVEN AT

# KINOKUNIYA BOOKSTORE

Kinokuniya Bookstore
123 Astronaut East Onizuka
Street
Los Angeles
213.687.4480
www.kinokuniya.com

*Write on!*

Ridley Scott's overhyped opus *Blade Runner* foresaw a futuristic Los Angeles that looked a lot more like Tokyo than the glorified Tijuana it has become. And while animated billboards have begun to spring up around the city, we've yet to see the pouting face of a geisha selling beer on the side of giant dirigible as it lumbers silently overhead. Maybe next year.

To be a true Angeleno hipster, it's *de rigueur* to have some sort of appreciation for—if not an absolute obsession with—Japanese culture. It can be argued that Angelenos singlehandedly put sushi on the nation's culinary map by exporting our insatiable appetite for what was once an obscure and expensive delicacy to the rest of the lower forty-eight. Now it appears we're doing the same for kushiyaki bars, ramen joints, and izakayas. Oh goody, you exclaim.

Manga, anime, Sanrio—these pop Japanese exports have all become part of our lexicon, and locals with even the slightest pen fetish will confess to having a special place in their hearts for Japanese writing instruments. If any culture truly connects with the visual and tactile thrill of the pen, it's the Japanese. We have our own personal favorites we can't buy at Staples— refillable Sailor brush pens, Pentel Aquash watercolor markers, high-end

Namiki retractables—and we like to stay on top of the latest Nipponese offerings by paying regular visits to Kinokuniya bookstores. We're particularly fond of the San Francisco store, but locally we'll settle for the Little Tokyo location, on the second floor of a mini-mall just across from the odd-looking memorial to Challenger astronaut Ellison Onizuka.

You don't have to read Japanese to enjoy what Kinokuniya has to offer. Besides plenty of manga and books in English, the store also boasts a

# WHAT KIND OF MILEAGE DOES IT GET?

We could easily write some academic bullshit about this eyesore being a programmatic tribute to L.A.'s car culture, but the fact of the matter is that it's just plain fucking hideous . . . in a beautiful kind of way.

**Cadillac-Shaped Building / 19611 Ventura Boulevard / Tarzana**

decent selection of imported CDs, assorted office gadgets and cartoon geegaws, and an impressive magazine section. Whereas child molesters may salivate over the catalogs for Japanese schoolgirl uniforms, we do our drooling in the stationery section, where the dizzying array of offbeat journals, bookbags, sumi accoutrements, and of course, writing instruments make our hearts go pitter-pat. Whether you're looking for a disposable fountain pen, a double-tipped sumi brush, or a hard-to-find Tombow refill, Kinokuniya has it—and so much more. Even if you're not a confirmed pen freak, you'll find yourself rapidly becoming one as you stare in awe at more colors and styles than you ever thought possible.

A word of warning, however. Kinokuniya is evidently more than just a bookstore, and quite possibly doubles as either a hub for international spies or a repository for classified information. While the staff at Kinokuniya tends to be cheerfully accommodating, they can turn ugly *real fast* the moment you brandish a camera. Apparently confusing a row of disposable pens with the mainframe computer room at CIA headquarters in Langley, one employee angrily yelled, "No pictures! No pictures!" Their disposition grew darker as we tried to explain that we were merely capturing the breathtaking majesty of their Pilot Rollerball selection for our popular book, and were not going to sell the photos to Israeli spies. This did not go over well, and it became clear that the store uses the same employment agency as Matt & Tony's Subs. It has been said that the pen is mightier than the sword, but apparently the camera has them both trumped at Kinokuniya.

# ADVENTURE IN POSTCARDS

**Adventure in Postcards**
**8423 Foothill Boulevard**
**Sunland**
**818.352.5663**

Making the trek out to Sunland is an adventure in itself, but if you came home with a lurid color postcard of L.A.'s long-defunct Zamboanga South Sea Nite Club ("Home of the Tailless Monkeys"), or an autographed photo of Wayne Newton, wouldn't the trip be worth it?

"Insane Asylums," "Swastikas," "Outhouses," and "Amish, Mennonite, and Shaker" are but a few of the arcane and meticulously sorted categories you'll find among thousands of postcards—many dating from the turn of the century—crammed into boxes for easy tabletop perusing. You'll also find the obvious: headings for each state, famous cities, foreign countries, animals,

food, hotels, et al., but don't pass over the binder of cards titled "Ethnic and Macabre" or the collection of autographed celebrity photos and correspondence (featuring the likes of Dom DeLuise, Isabelle Sanford, Bob Barker, and Vincent Price).

Owner Lee Brown used to deal exclusively in depression-era glass, but seeing that she was "so close to the fault line," she figured merchandise that didn't shatter into a million sharp pieces when it fell to the ground might be a safer bet. She made the shift into the postcard biz over thirty years ago, keeping this Sunland shop for nearly twenty. Lee knows her stock well, and aside from being sweet as pie, she maintains the most extensive, varied, and reasonably priced collection in Southern California. Thousands of cards are priced at twenty-five cents, most range from $1 to $5. Although the collection is postcard-heavy, the store carries most any kind of vintage paper matter: luggage and travel stickers, matchbooks, playing cards, tourist pamphlets, and the like. Look deeper into the corners and you'll spot swizzle sticks, political buttons and God knows what else.

From kitty cats to cannibalism, Bozo the Clown to Hindu cremations, this little gold mine covers it all—and with its hit-and-miss hours of operation (call first), far-flung location, and the thrill of the dig, Adventure in Postcards is treasure hunting at its best.

*Wish you were here.*

# COTTER CHURCH SUPPLIES

Want to start your own church? Get better service in restaurants? Lure a teenage runaway into your van? Everything you need to get the job done effectively is available at Cotter Church Supplies, where shopping is literally a religious experience.

Who can honestly say they've never fantasized from time to time about being a Catholic priest? At Cotter, your fantasy becomes reality. You'll be squealing *Hosanna!* as you shuffle through racks of albs, chasubles, copes, baptismal gowns and funeral palls— completing your sanctified ensemble with a genuine pastoral kit or handheld thurible. Unfortunately, there are no dressing rooms.

Cotter Church Supplies
1701 James M. Wood Boulevard
Los Angeles
213.385.3366
www.cotters.com

*Shop, shop, shopping at heaven's door.*

Next time you and your partner engage in some erotic role-playing, give the "clergyman and the altar boy" game new realism with genuine raiment courtesy of Cotter. There's nothing quite like slipping your hand beneath the hem of an authentic altar boy cassock or choir robe, and here you'll find an ungodly selection. For the detail-oriented, Cotter also sells that unmistakably churchy-smelling incense, as well as processional crucifixes and pew torches. Communion tables, three-foot altar candles, and *prie dieu* kneelers suddenly take on provocative new possibilities.

For the secular, Cotter's holy water bottles in the shape of the Virgin Mary of Guadalupe make great travel containers for shampoo, baptismal fonts are perfect for paper clips, and the wooden last rites crucifix kit with the sliding lid functions beautifully as a stash box for the coffee table. Liven up tired hors d'oeuvres by serving pimento loaf on host wafers, available in bulk. A gallon jug of cheap sacramental wine always makes a good gift, and with an EMERGENCY CLERGY ON CALL dashboard placard you can thumb your nose at street cleaning fines, tow-away zones, and valet parking attendants. It's just that easy.

One look at a few of Cotter's price tags and you'll understand why churches are so insistent about passing those collection plates. Oh, and they sell collection plates, too.

## BRINGING THE DUNGEON OUT OF THE CLOSET WITH SONNY BLACK

# DUNGEON FURNITURE

Sonny Black
Dungeon Furniture
5128 Venice Boulevard
Los Angeles
323.939.BDSM
www.dungeonfurniture.com

When considering the sort of character who builds dungeon furniture for a living, one might conjure the image of a potbellied, craggy-faced leather daddy with a handlebar moustache and a power drill, his arms blurred with biker tattoos that long since faded to indigo, his fingers stained with nicotine, and a workday's worth of sawdust caught in a thick tuft of graying chest hair pushing from beneath the well-worn neck of a stained white tank. But those stereotypes no longer hold. The BDSM torch, in many respects, has been passed. The once dark world of S & M has a bright new face, and there is perhaps no better example than Sonny Black.

Sonny is no more in step with the hardened leathermasters of yesteryear than the Osmonds were with Janis Joplin. He's never so much as smoked a cigarette, much less taken a drink or experimented with drugs, and were he a little younger he wouldn't be entirely out of place modeling an ironic rock tee and a pair of Vans on the pages of an Urban Outfitters catalog. Ironic, then, that this genial guy whose toothy smile and fastidiously spiked hair exudes all the wholesomeness of Christian rock is the same dude responsible for—among other original designs—the GS Combo Deluxe, the gothly sleek freestanding black toilet seat designed to facilitate an in-your-face delivery to the eager mouth of a hungry submissive.

The matters of caging, restraining, and sundry torture have been Sonny's business for over ten years, building top-notch apparatuses and various accoutrements for professional dungeons, kink balls, celebrity clients, and private playrooms around the world. His studio is like the Design Within Reach for sadists: Working more or less within the traditional style of fetish equipage, he creates tight pieces with sleek lines and fine-tuned details, uses the best materials he can get his naughty hands on, and assembles his finished product with solid, thrash-resistant construction. Once you're buckled into a Sonny Black piece, you're there until you beg your way out.

His business grew from necessity. After building a few simple pieces for the play parties he'd host at his downtown loft in the nineties, his work caught the eye of a professional dominatrix looking to upgrade. Word spread, commissions followed. Now, having seamlessly dovetailed his personal affinity for the BDSM scene with his background in carpentry, welding, design, and sales, he's known internationally as the go-to guy for fun-loving perverts with a penchant for punishment.

Black dismantled the showroom of his 2000-square-foot studio after discovering word-of-mouth referrals and Web sales were enough to move the goods, but he's always happy to meet with potential clients in person and allow them to see the work firsthand. Prices vary widely; a chrome-plated spreader bar goes for about $30, and the most substantial furnishings cap off at about $3000. His line of tried-and-true bestsellers is joined by frequent new designs, some of which are multifunctional (his doggie-style bondage bench breaks down to an innocuous coffee table), and for deviants whose proclivities can't be satisfied with Black's standard fare, he's always up for a challenge, receiving raves from slaves with disposable income glad to have blown a prodigious wad on a custom job.

*"The dungeon is the new hot tub."*

—TABOO MAGAZINE

Evidently no corner of commerce is safe from branding these days, to the extreme that even the dungeon is now subject to name recognition and celebrity endorsement. You'd think a matter like the designer of your bondage bench would be an incidental if not absurd detail for someone about to be trussed like a turkey and buggered with a prosthetic, but the status game knows no boundaries. Like the Louis Vuitton of kink, Sonny Black fosters a loyal clientele—whip burns on their asses, cuff marks on their ankles, and Sonny's logo on their spanking horse.

## GETTING WHACK-HAPPY IN THE
# PIÑATA DISTRICT

The Piñata District
Olympic Blvd. between Kohler
and Central Avenue
Los Angeles

God damn those Mexicans. It's bad enough that they come here illegally and steal all the good jobs, but now they're pirating intellectual properties from the likes of mom-and-pop corporations like Disney, Pixar, the Cartoon Network, and Hanna-Barbera Productions—with the sale of *counterfeit piñatas* no less! Thank God this blasphemous free-for-all was curtailed in 2005 through a concerted effort by which said corporations whacked these piñata anarchists with a copyright and trademark infringement lawsuit. And who can blame them? Today, yes, maybe it's only piñatas sold from an independently owned market, but tomorrow? Who's to say these people won't start their own television network, film corporation, cruise line, or uranium enrichment program?

It was our now-infamous piñata district in downtown Los Angeles that stirred the interest of undercover investigators. Like a bright pink gladiola pushing through cracked asphalt, a vibrant strip of warehouse *piñaterías* bustles amid the industrial grayness of Olympic Boulevard and Central Avenue. In a circus of colored foils and curly streamers you'll find aisles stacked sky-high with a goldmine of party goods and bulk candy from both sides of the border. Double Bubble and Tootsie Pops share the shelves with guava and tamarind confections, alongside Mexican novelties, bins of tropical produce, and a whole lot of other stuff.

If you're in the market for a piñata—and why shouldn't you be—these warehouse shops offer more than an inexpensive means to an end: They continue

# POSITIVELY FABULOUS!

Out of the Closet has locations in Northern and Southern California where resourceful shoppers can pick up incredible deals on all kinds of used stuff, but at these two locations in Los Angeles, customers can also get something for nothing: an HIV test. It's quick, it's easy, and it only takes about twenty minutes. Yes, there are other free HIV testing facilities in the city, but we seriously doubt you can show us one where you can also pick up a vintage Frito Bandito T-shirt or a stuffed armadillo on the way out. Certified counselors perform the tests daily between 3:00 and 7:00 PM, proving you really can't put a pricetag on peace of mind.

**Out of the Closet (Hollywood) / 6210 West Sunset Blvd / Los Angeles / 323.467.6811**
**Out of the Closet (West Hollywood) / 8224 Santa Monica Boulevard /**
**West Hollywood / 323.848.9760**

a rich, fascinating and centuries-old tradition. The Spiderman, Dora the Explorer, and Sponge Bob varieties we've come to know actually evolved from the pre-Columbian rain rituals and year-end celebrations honoring the Aztec war god. The Mayans added the string and the blindfold—because Mayans obviously have more fun—and the rest came by way of Spanish missionaries who just couldn't leave well enough alone. As they have so many times throughout history, Christians dry-humped a pagan tradition and thereby spun the simple pleasures of the piñata into an endeavor overwrought with the biblical. The "traditional" piñata of the seven-pointed star—that being the Native American-Spanish hybrid—came to represent the seven deadly sins (one of which is greed, *hello Disney*). The practice of the blindfold was reinvented as a symbol of religious faith, and the club with which the piñata is beaten signified virtue and the Christian fight against evil. The candy and sundry whatnot: the rewards of walking a righteous path. Yeah, whatever.

*Beat it.*

Should piñata-makers have to rely on the likes of trademarked characters to stay in business? Certainly not. Can an innocent tradition loosen its foot from this litigious trap? Absolutely. Cut counterfeit piñata demand by hitting the corporate bullies where it hurts; wean kids off the likes of Disney and Pixar altogether, we say. Tell your children that watching *The Little Mermaid* will make their fingernails rot with a painful fungus. They'll believe you—kids are gullible, and if they put up a fight, well, then maybe they just don't get a birthday party, how about that? Who's calling the shots here anyway? Children are easy to frighten, and fear is an effective tool; if it worked for the Bush administration, it can work for the birthday party of a first-grader. Besides, L.A.'s piñata vendors probably get pretty tired of cranking out the same-old same-old year after year. You're not shackled to Disney. Why go for an Ariel or a Pocahontas when your birthday girl could opt instead for something like, say, Ann Coulter? Maybe she won't hold as much candy, but wouldn't you love to see Ann hanging by a rope while a bunch of sugar-crazed kids beat the shit out of her with a wooden club? We sure would.

## THE ALLURING LUNACY OF THE MAN, THE MYTH, AND THE LEGEND THAT IS

# CHICKEN BOY

Chicken Boy and the
Chicken Boy Souvenir Stand
Future Studio
5558 North Figueroa Street
Highland Park
323.254.4565
www.chickenboy.com
www.nelaart.com
www.arroyoartscollective.org

Behind every bright young performer you'll find a pushy stage parent standing in the wings, prodding their little darling into the spotlight. Sacrifice is the name of that game. The life of a stage parent is not an easy road, and few can balance their roles as loving father *and* pimp daddy with the finesse of a Joe Jackson. Beating the bejeezus out of a twelve-year-old because he hasn't committed his lines to memory or nailed that dance step might seem a bit extreme for some, but spare the rod and you spoil the performer. Heck, without such leadership would Michael get to enjoy his fabulous life of vanity surgery and long Saudi Arabian vacations? Where would Tito be today? It's all about trade-offs. What would a "normal" childhood have offered Judy Garland that a childhood of pills and fourteen-hour studio workdays couldn't? Tatum O'Neil may whine about the years she was subject to neglect and psychological cruelty, but she got an Oscar out of the deal, so boo hoo hoo. Would Ashlee and Jessica Simpson have garnered the same ink if dad hadn't hawked scandal shots to the tabloids? What about those great *Home Alone* movies? *The Donny and Marie Show*? Christ, do you think the skies just opened up one day and God *handed* us the Cowsills?!

*Diff'rent Strokes*: one success story after another. And from all of them, every single one, you can draw a straight line to a pushy stage parent who cared enough to put their own needs aside to focus on the career of a youngster who would have otherwise grown up to be a big fat nobody.

Certainly Chicken Boy is no exception. He hasn't been beaten or psychologically abused—save for the few years he was locked into a storage facility—but every bit of his success is due to the selfless toiling and fierce determination of his pushy stage mother, Amy Inouye.

Just so you don't think Amy's got some kind of genetic disorder, it should be noted that she did not deliver Chicken Boy vaginally. In fact, they share no blood relation. He was abandoned by his real parents on top of a downtown Los Angeles fried chicken restaurant on the corner of Broadway and Fourth Street, and "rescued" by Inouye—with the aid of sundry cohorts—during the wee hours of a spring morning in 1984. Pretty much any mom can drag her kid from one audition to another, but it takes a special parent with a special kind of commitment to dismantle a half-ton steel and fiberglass poultry-headed orphan and drag him off the roof of a downtown restaurant without the aid of a crane. Not to mention the task of bringing him home and acclimating Chicken Boy to his new life. Just imagine the stares they must have received the first time she took him to shop for new school clothes.

## The boy is back in town.

Saddled with sole parenting duties while holding down a full-time job as a busy graphic designer was a daunting prospect for Inouye, so she did her best to find the Boy a good home. The Smithsonian passed, as did the Museum of Contemporary Art. It seemed that Chicken Boy had the face that only a mother could love, so, as a single mom with few options, Amy beheaded him. She put his googly-eyed noggin' on display in her studio, stashed the rest of him into storage facilities around Greater L.A., and quickly set to work developing a sensational product line.

Pretty soon the image of that chicken was on T-shirts, hats, watches, and mugs. Toothpick holders, snow domes, panties, and postcards. She merchandised the beak off that Boy, creating a following that became almost cult-like in its adoration—and the media was all over it. International coverage followed: the *New York Times*, *Esquire*, *Marie Claire*, *Details*, *Newsweek*, the *Evening Standard*, and countless others. The years of Inouye's judicious career moves and Colonel Tom Parker-esque management savvy had finally paid off. Chicken Boy was more than a star: Chicken Boy was an icon.

Although both Amy and Chicken Boy were enjoying the merchandising projects and the media coverage,

# WHAT WAS MEL GIBSON THINKING?

The stars don't make a move without stopping here first.
Trust us on this one.

**Hollywood Psychic (Reader to the Stars) / 1467 Tamarind Avenue / Hollywood / 323.469.7380**

there was the non-negotiable issue of his height to consider. At twenty-two feet, talk shows and personal appearances proved difficult, and the ceiling of her design studio wouldn't allow for more than his head. But his public couldn't get enough. They adored their Chicken Boy socks, key chains, and the floaty pens bearing his image and the slogan "Too Tall to Live, Too Weird to Die," but without the Boy himself to witness—and worship—it all began to feel like an artfully packaged tease. Until the fall of 2006.

It was then that Inouye moved her design studio to Figueroa Street in Highland Park, and the roof of her new building became the perfect stage for the one-note talent of her feather-headed hybrid—who had now become known internationally as "The Statue of Liberty of Los Angeles." After years of applying for permits and raising funds, the Boy took his place in the sun once again—for the first time in over two decades—all twenty-two feet of him, bucket held high, ever Sphinx-like, and without looking a day older.

Amy's managed Chicken Boy's way through nearly twenty-five years in show business, and he's survived. He hasn't snorted his fortune away, nor are there any embarrassing photos of him circulating on the Internet. He gets to choose his own projects, and he's never been subjected to bad publicity. Chicken Boy has played the game and won. Some may call Amy an unrelenting taskmaster, some might accuse her of flagrant exploitation, some might even claim Chicken Boy's success has been at the expense of a "normal" life—but they've made all the same accusations about Teri Shields, and, except for that marriage to Andre, Brooke turned out okay.

In the old-school tradition, Chicken Boy always leaves his public wanting more. And more you can have: Chicken Boy's new permanent home is atop Future Studio, and its Chicken Boy Souvenir Stand is open to the public, evenings, for the

NELAart's Second Saturday Gallery Night on the second Saturday of each month (and by appointment). The building also houses an informal art gallery featuring individual and group shows in cooperation with the Arroyo Arts Collective. Never tiring of adding new twists to the product line, Inouye has expanded into Chicken Boy sock monkeys and statuettes, and keeps the souvenir stand well stocked with a judiciously edited jumble of kitschy gift goods, functional art objects, and one-of-a-kind reinvented vintage lamps, all of which are subject to Inouye's discerning eye and singular style.

It could certainly be said that Los Angeles is a necropolis for well-intended careers gone wrong. Too often stage parents are left with blood on their hands after once promising careers hiccupped and took an unexpected nosedive with a network cancellation, poor box-office numbers, or a difficult adolescence that turned an effervescent child into a teenaged werewolf. In spite of those odds, Chicken Boy is quick to demonstrate that not every career at the hands of a pushy stage parent ends with a crash and burn or an E! *True Hollywood Story*. Some endure without incident.

For tourists hunting for the ultimate L.A. souvenir, or for locals exploring their own backyard, Chicken Boy gives us something in which we can all take pride.

## A DESULTORY QUEST THROUGH THE STUPEFYING WARES OF

# ROMADI'S

If you love a good flea market but can't bear the thought of rising any earlier than 10:30 AM on a Sunday morning, there's good news in the heart of Hollywood: the queer and curious world of Romadi's.

Romadi's
6630 Hollywood Boulevard
Hollywood
323.467.5560

No need to wait until the whatever-eth Sunday of the month to dig through the exotic, arcane, perversely decorative whatnot and cast-off miscellany of decades past: Romadi's is open daily. Though this emporium of the odd doesn't rival the scale of the Rose Bowl, you're likely to find just as diverse a jumble, albeit an undiscerning jumble because Mr. Romadi doesn't edit. "Anything that someone might buy" seems to be the order of the day here, and "anything I haven't gotten around to tossing" would classify the debris piled into boxes and shoved under tables. Shopping at Romadi's feels like nosing through the basement of your friend's pervy uncle, the one who decorates with African art, wears a pinky ring, and never married.

*Support your local salvia salesman.*

Do you love Jesus? Do you love butt plugs? Does vintage taxidermy send you into a covetous meltdown? Your wish is Romadi's command. Shellacked sea turtles sit atop showcases filled with sundry religious iconography, opposite the battery-operated sex toys, cock rings, and adult gags which line the walls behind the front counter—along with pothead novelties, character bongs, and sheesha pipes. The motorized trays of Romadi's jewelry case are akin to a lost-and-found heaven, replete with estate pieces, dated ephemera (remember the "Oh Shit!" necklaces of the seventies?), the ethnic, and the ecclesiastical, all scattered among delicate gold chains, grandma brooches, and silver pendants set

with semiprecious stones. Seashells are big here too—for whatever reason—and there are several shelves lined with recycled food jars in dozens of different varieties.

Vintage smut is nearly as abundant as the selection of wicker baskets and the motel room–style landscapes in oil. Need the April 1976 issue of *Oui* to complete your collection? You're likely to find it here—as well as other second-rate men's pubs of the eighties like *High Society*, *Club International*, and *Velvet*. But don't go pointing a sexist finger; you'll find lesbian titles like *On Our Backs*, random *Playgirl* centerfolds, and a whole box devoted to off-brand gay fare squeezed into Romadi's racks of pre-owned pornography. Secondhand home appliances and used books have their place here too, so if you're in the market for an old television set, a Time-Life hardcover on elephants, or a first edition of *Mommie Dearest*, look no further.

Judging from the dust collected on the surface of the plastic bags covering their heads, it doesn't look like the keepsake dolls are getting much action—and the abalone art isn't exactly flying out the door either. The dream catchers sure are pretty, but whether or not they'll ever find a permanent home is anyone's guess—and it's no matter. This is the beauty of Romadi's. There is no urgency to move out one season's unsold inventory to make way for the next. There's no clearance table, no dump-bin of the deeply discounted, and no after-Christmas sale here. What doesn't sell just gets buried, adding another layer—and additional intrigue—for the next intrepid shopper digging for the thing they didn't know they wanted.

# DANCING WITH DEMONS AT THE

# HARRY BLITZSTEIN

## MUSEUM OF ART

Hungry for culture? The Wilshire/Fairfax area is a veritable feed bin. You've got dinosaur remains and hot tar at the Page, a hootenanny of the hand-rendered at the Craft and Folk Art Museum, and if you can look past LACMA's botched facelift you'll discover Ancient Egyptian antiquities, German Expressionism, and overpriced concessions in addition to many exciting special exhibitions. And then closer to the corner of Fairfax there's some dollhouse place and that car museum too.

Even better, a jaunt further north up Fairfax puts you cheek-by-jowl with Canter's Deli and what's left of the neighborhood's once thriving Jewish community. And even better than that, right across the street you'll hit what is arguably the best culture klatch within a fifty-block radius of Miracle Mile: the Harry Blitzstein Museum of Art.

Harry Blitzstein not only owns and curates the museum—which occupies the former sites of the Fair Shoe Shop and Moe's Meat Market—but he's also its sole artist. Furthermore, as a youth, Blitzstein worked at the shoe store, which was owned and operated by his father from 1956 to 1984 (he never worked at the meat market, however). Don't let the word "museum" mislead you, though: There isn't an admission fee or any established hours (it generally opens by "twilight" or by appointment), and the work on display is very much for sale. Like many of his paintings, the museum was more or less an experiment. Its doors weren't initially opened to the public and the storefront simply served as an exhibition showcase so Harry could "see what kind of a response I'd get."

Blitzstein is an affable, light-hearted, wiry septuagenarian for whom the term "senior" would be absurdly ill-fitting. He earned an M.F.A. in painting in 1964 and has several one-man exhibitions on his resumé, but considers his work "outsider art" and credits influences like *Snow White and the Seven Dwarves*, Kafka, Bosch, and Leonard Cohen. It might prove difficult to draw a straight line from one of Harry's influences to another, but the disparity is

Harry Blitzstein
Museum of Art
428 North Fairfax Avenue
Los Angeles
323.852.4830
www.blitzstein.com

*An art scene without the "scene."*

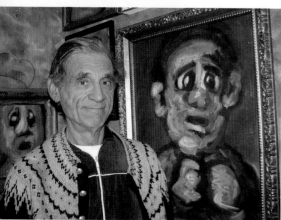

somehow synergized by his vision and his talent; once a viewer makes an acquaintance with his work—and with Harry—it all seems to makes perfect sense.

"If a painting doesn't have eyes or something that depicts the soul, and if it doesn't have humor or pathos, it just doesn't click for me," he says. As a student in the sixties, he was searching for "beauty and mysticism," but toward the close of the decade—during the war—he claims "demons started popping out, and it was like opening a floodgate. They were pretty horrifying and at the same time hilarious," he confesses. "I was just trying to be as crazy as possible." The war changed a lot for Blitztein, who served in the army from 1961 to 1963. "I couldn't stand painting beautiful things when the world was in such turmoil. . . . I wanted to paint truth."

Walls stretching nearly two stories are alive with the visions dancing in Blitzstein's head. Simple shapeless blobs with happy faces hopping jigs across a smeared foreground hold court with pensive dogs and giddy-looking birds. In contrast, deceptively crude characters in apparent fits of maniacal ecstasy, madness, or evil leer from the loft above, barely contained by their gilded frames. Other subjects reveal themselves through the grain in a piece of plywood or a minimally transformed found object. The same figures are seen scribbled across the concrete floors and climbing the brick and mortar in the back, like the cell walls of someone whose been held in solitary with a Sharpie marker. An unbridled liveliness pervades all of it, as does great spirit in its execution, and an oddly cheerful warmth to the work that Frances Bacon called "too grotesque."

Most refreshingly, visitors will not be met with the egotistical conceit that typifies so many L.A. artists. Harry Blitzstein is not here to make sure you know how fabulous he is, nor will he pontificate over the "message" as do many didactic docents further down the street. Instead, he claims his work is "the opposite of cool," greets strangers like old friends, welcomes reaction, and demonstrates genuine interest in what others see, feel, and relate to in his work—and what they might have to say about it all.

Ironic that as this stretch of Fairfax slowly gentrifies into a self-conscious culture scene—and with all the arts opportunities to be had just a few blocks south on Wilshire—it's only Harry Blitzstein who's giving the district any real soul. His eponymous museum allows us to experience art unencumbered, and provides us with the rare opportunity to get up close and personal with a true L.A. artist.

# FARMACIA Y BOTANICA MILLION DOLLAR

Religion has figured as notably into L.A. culture as frozen yogurt, road rage, and third-rate family comedies. Temples, mosques, churches, and synagogues are as prevalent across the Greater L.A. landscape as Pilates studios and laser hair-removal centers, leaving pious Angelenos with no shortage of places to tune in and turn on to one or more of the world's five major faiths. Then there are the less recognized beliefs, the ones you don't hear celebrities talking about on *Oprah*. Santería, the colorful mutt of Nigerian ancestry, is certainly one among them that keeps a lower profile. You won't see politicians lying about their faith in Santería to get votes the way Christians do, nor will you find animal sacrifice ceremonies packed with Hollywood A-listers like a class at the Kabbalah Centre.

While Santería may not have celebrity spokespeople like the Church of Scientology, it does boast a sensational history; its path to the United States was a long, tortured, and complicated one. Its nature-centered West African traditions traversed the Atlantic by way of the slaves sold to Caribbean sugar plantations. After Christian proselytization, Catholic saints began to integrate with the original Nigerian beliefs, and as the religion traveled to Cuba, then later to the States, it joined hands with Haitian voodoo, Latin America and Central Africa practices, and other influences—even the ancient Egyptian pantheon has made it into the contemporary mix. In the process, Santería grew into

Farmacia Y Botanica
Million Dollar
301 South Broadway
Los Angeles
213.687.3688

*Is that a Nigerian talisman in your pocket, or are you just happy to see me?*

# WHEN IS A DRUG NOT A DRUG?

Your worries are over. At last, after years of research, ethical drugs are finally available to the public. Get yours today.

**Ethical Drugs / 254 North Western Ave / Los Angeles / 323.467.2101**

an exotic pastiche of beliefs, practices, and traditions passed through storytelling and ceremony from one generation to the next, one culture to another: criminalized, celebrated in secret, disguised for preservation, and, centuries later, defended in the courtroom (what with those animal sacrifices and all). Even today, Santería refuses to remain static.

In addition to its compelling history, Santería makes for great shopping. We challenge you to visit Farmacia y Botanica Million Dollar—a veritable Santería superstore—without dropping some cash. Although it looks much like a traditional drug store from the street, inside you'll find Pepto-Bismol, Sucrets, and Cold-Eeze, among voodoo dolls, protective amulets, pussy-magnet soap, curative candles, and dozens of bad-whatever-be-gone aerosol sprays and powders—and so very much more. For non–Santería-practicing Anglos, a foray through Farmacia y Botanica Million

Dollar (so named because of its placement within the historic Million Dollar Theater block) is almost as baffling as walking the aisles of a Vietnamese market, but for a shop catering to such a specific demographic you'll find the staff quite accommodating to the outsider. And though Spanish is the language spoken here, you won't get attitude for not being as bilingual as they are.

We'd love to see Santería become the hot new faith-based trend in Hollywood. Wouldn't it be great to see Madonna chopping the head off a chicken in a slaughter ritual on the pages of *People* magazine? We could watch Miley and Billy Ray trance-dancing and channeling deities on E! Even Oprah could get in on the action. She could feature a spread in her magazine on one of those celebrity-chef-catered over-the-top wedding receptions where a famous couple like her and Gayle make a commitment in a Santería friendship ceremony wearing designer gowns. Of course, they'd have to find something for Steadman to do, like fill all the swag bags with cool stuff from Farmacia y Botanica Million Dollar.

GETTING OUR EARS LOWERED AT

# JOHN'S TAPO ST. BARBER SHOP

1969: The ubiquitous barbershop—purveyor of flat-tops, crew cuts, fades, and other clipper-induced styles—seemed like it was becoming an endangered species. Not only had those haircuts fallen out of fashion, to be replaced by the far groovier blow-dried, feathered, hair-sprayed, helmet-head look—but the shops themselves and the white-shirted men who manned the chairs were also considered passé. It was a time in America when women were demanding to be treated like men, and men were demanding to be pampered like women. Check out the fashions of the late sixties and early seventies and you'll see that long before the term metrosexual entered the vernacular, hetero men were declaring their own kind of swishy independence by carrying clutch purses, donning caftans and billowy scarves, and going to salons where they too could be hovered over like little princes. This was the antithesis of the no-frills, no-nonsense barbershop,

John's Tapo Street
Barber Shop
2100 Tapo Street
Simi Valley
805.526.8679

and the man who neutered America's barbershop poles, almost singlehandedly, was named Jay Sebring.

Murder buffs will recognize Jay's name as one of the unfortunate victims of the Manson family, butchered with Sharon Tate and three others in the early hours of August 9, 1969, in Tate and Roman Polanski's Bel Air home. By then, Sebring (born Thomas John Kummer) was well known among Hollywood elite as *the* stylist to the stars, having created the "natural look" made famous by clients like Steve McQueen, Jim Morrison, and Warren Beatty (who would later appropriate Sebring's persona for the movie *Shampoo*). At the time of his death, Sebring had successful

shops in West Hollywood, San Francisco, New York, and London, and his own line of hair care products for men. His empire would continue to grow, spawning countless imitators, and though the brand has lost its luster over the years, Sebring International still sells hair products and trains stylists in the Sebring Method.

2009: In Los Angeles, the trend has come full circle with self-conscious hip barbershops like Floyd's 99 on Melrose and Shorty's on Fairfax, which are to cutting hair what Forty Deuce is to stripping. That's cool, we get it, and if you want to pay a little more for the retro-modern, just-off-Melrose, scenester-haircut "experience," then knock yourself out, champy. We still prefer old school to faux-ld school, and there are plenty of barbershops to fit that bill in Los Angeles and the Valley, but our favorite is in Simi Valley.

Hidden in the corner of one of Simi's least robust strip malls, John's Tapo Street Barber Shop is about as far away from the studied coolness of Floyd's 99 as it is from Sebring International's dated frou-frou methods. The owner, a laid-back, friendly guy named John Couracous, runs a traditional barbershop that offers the usual selection of straight-ahead haircuts at very reasonable prices. If you want your hair washed you can do it yourself before you come in, and there are plenty of Vietnamese nail shops in the area that will be happy to give you a manicure; this place cuts hair, pure and simple. John might put K-Earth on the radio, but not so loudly that you can't have a conversation, and the Pabst Blue Ribbon painting that's been on the wall for years was hung without a hint of conceit. This lack of pretention, along with the good haircuts and better prices, is why we've kept coming back to John's since it opened back in 2004. Any business that can survive in a location that shitty has got to be doing something right. And one of the many things that John has done

# COME FOR THE POCKY, STAY FOR THE SPAM ROLL

There's nothing quite like this space-age convenience store with a name that sounds disturbingly like "famine." And with two exclamation marks, no less. Do they know something that we don't?

**Famima!! / Various locations around Los Angeles**

right is bring in a guy named Sal every Thursday and Friday to help out with the pre-weekend crowd.

Now, before we go any further, you have to understand that even though Salvatore Orefice is an old pro with the shears, haircutting isn't his main gig anymore. It's more like an old habit, one he indulges just to get out of the house every week so, as he puts it, he "can be with the people." Not that he considers himself royalty or anything—in fact you probably won't meet a more humble guy than Sal—but his heart is in his writing, and writers, at least the obsessive kind, tend to not get out much. Over the years he's dabbled in a few genres, scribbling out a couple of successful plays that made it to the stage in Hollywood, the occasional *Power Rangers* script, and now he's working on a screenplay. That's hardly a unique resumé in this town, but what does set Sal apart from the crowd is the autobiography he published back in 2007 about his adventures traveling around the country as the hairstylist for a musical performer who went by the name of Elvis Presley. You may have heard of him.

*Haircuts fit for the King.*

Traveling with Elvis on the road, or hanging out the sets of cinematic turds like *Harum Scarum*, Sal was as much as a confidante as he was an employee, perhaps because he never fell into the sycophantic rut in which many of the King's inner circle found themselves. And of course, he was good at what he did.

As implied by the title of his book, *Tripping with the King and Others*, Presley wasn't Sal's only high-profile client, and to the author's credit, what could have been a tawdry tell-all is more like a self-effacing slice of Hollywood history that came and went all too quickly. More amazingly, he treats his subjects with equal deference, whether he's writing about *Hollywood Squares* regular Jan Murray or the King of Rock 'n' Roll. And that's not as easy as it sounds.

Written in a breezy but über-smart hybrid patois of beatnik and flower child, the self-published paperback details Sal's high times as one of the hottest stylists in Hollywood during the sixties and seventies, when locking the doors and blowing a joint in between clients (or with the clients) wasn't unusual, and when everyone from Sam Cooke to Sterling Hayden sought out his skills. But the star of the book, other than Presley, is Sal's best friend and coworker, Jay Sebring, who in many ways is a more interesting character than anyone else Sal holds the mirror up to.

After working off-and-on with Sebring, Sal opened his own shop on Melrose, "The Iron Flute," with his best friend's blessings. There he serviced his own crowd of celebrity regulars who ran the gamut from novelty (Alan Sherman) to nobility (David Geffen), all before *Shampoo* and John Peters cemented the rep of the hairstylist as a powerful cog in the Hollywood machine.

Things were going well when Sebring popped in one day to announce he was going to open an international chain of charm schools for men—and wanted his Sal to help him run the business. The next morning, as Sal was mulling over the endless possibilities that this new partnership might bring, he heard on the radio that Sebring had been murdered.

Maybe that was a catalyst, maybe not, but Sal eventually grew tired of the scene and moved up to Big Sur to get away from L.A.'s materialism—a Zen Buddhist riff runs throughout the book—and to do a lot of nothing (as those who move to Big Sur are wont to do). Then, when the money ran out, he moved back down to Los Angeles to get back on the hamster wheel. Then back up to Big Sur, and back down again. Rinse and repeat.

Over time, the desire to cut hair and the urge to write became inversely proportional, which brings us back to Simi Valley. We didn't know a goddamn thing about Sal when we first sat down in his chair, nor the next time, nor the time after that. In fact, it wasn't until he asked us what we were working on that he mentioned he was writing a book, too. And then, almost in passing, he mentioned Elvis. At first, we thought he was pulling our leg, or maybe just full of shit. We imagine he's not the first barber in the world to claim to have cut Elvis's hair. We forgot all about it until the book came out, and then we were suddenly dumbfounded. We would say that having one's hair cut in a tiny barbershop in Simi Valley by Elvis Presley's former stylist is akin to sitting in a diner outside Bakersfield and seeing Paul Prudhomme in the kitchen, or taking a taxi in Hemet and seeing the name Mario Andretti on the cabbie's placard—but even these

# KILLER SHOES, MAN!

Remember when you had to shoot someone and pry the shoes off his still-warm feet just to get a decent pair of Air Jordans? Now, thanks to RIF Los Angeles, those golden days are back again! RIF is the Spartan yet upscale sister boutique of Tokyo's L.A. Avenue—one of the world's first sneaker consignment stores—and offers both consignment and "buyback" options that will undoubtedly make anyone who wears nice sneakers a prime target for gang members, crackheads, car owners, and anyone else in need of a quick buck.

Looking for a pair of Nike Dunk Undefeated Ballistics in black/grey? RIF has a brand-new pair in the box, and they'll only set you back $12,000. Out of your price range? For a little over $500 you can walk around looking like a total dick in your red, white, and blue Nike Air Max Kelly high-tops (the box is damaged, sorry). Are you more into high-priced irony? How about a pair of Vans Simpsons sneaks by Gary Panter for $300? They're hideous *and* cool at the same time!

And RIF doesn't stop at sneakers—they can help you out with obscure collectable caps and sportswear, too. Hey, why just watch the assholes on *Entourage* when you can actually pretend to *be* one of them? Just be sure to wear an adult diaper before you go shopping because you'll likely shit your pants when you see the $900 price tag on a pair of Supreme Neighborhood jeans.

Of course, these bargains will be long gone by the time you read this, but don't let that discourage you from seeing what's new at the store. Then again, if you'd rather stay home and save the gas, you can just burn a stack of twenties instead.

**RIF Los Angeles / 334-A East Second Street / Los Angeles / 213.617.0252 / www.rif.la**

analogies seem piddling by comparison. After all, other than his hips and lips, Elvis's look was defined by his hair. And in Elvis's darkest hour, when his hair was in the shitter—Sal described it as "a damp clump of black spinach"—it was Salvatore Orefice who brought it back from the abyss. From then on, he was the only human Elvis trusted with his hair. And that's one thing we'll always have in common with the King.

# PRESSING THE FLESH

# CHAPTER 4

# DESPERATELY SEEKING RON JEREMY AT

# PORN STAR KARAOKE

With all the gang bangs, blow bangs, DPs, ATMs, POVs, double-anals, three-ways, reverse cowgirls, pile drivers, facials, and bukkakes thrust upon them, Lord knows that porn stars just don't get enough attention. It's no wonder, then, that come Tuesday evening, many a siren of the soggy screen has been known to grab her hemorrhoid donut and head out to Sardo's in Burbank for an evening of dipsomaniacal dissonance. For the past six years, at this humble strip-mall bar located just spitting distance from Warner Bros. studios, Porn Star Karaoke has been a weekly phenomenon that's proven to be as much an industry gathering as it is an opportunity for professional fornicators to serenade their adoring, tone-deaf fans.

And these are not just your typical, oft-maligned, Y-chromosomed wanker fans, either. Porn Star Karaoke proves once and for all that smut isn't just a man's game. Lots of ladies show up for Porn Star Karaoke, as we discovered before we even set foot in the bar. We were standing on the sidewalk in front of the club when a carload of trailer parkettes rolled up in a battered old Nissan. The driver flagged us over.

"Hey! Is Ron here yet?" she asked in a voice exquisitely sculpted by Kools and crystal meth.

"Ron?"

"Ron Jeremy. You know, *the Hedgehog*. Is he here yet?"

"No idea."

"Well, is he coming tonight?"

"Couldn't say."

"I bet you he's coming tonight." She said, her cruel, gap-toothed maw peeling into a grin. "I bet you he's coming all over the place!" The whole car erupted in a Bakersfieldian cackle, then lurched into the night.

Touché, madam. *Touché.*

Sardo's is not a very big place, or at least it doesn't seem that way when it's impossibly crowded. The crush at the bar is as thick as a Cincinnati Who concert, and getting there can be a slow, painful exercise in unintentional frottage. We wedged ourselves into the human wall and turned out attention to the stage, where a twentysomething guy was doing an impression of Flea doing an impression of someone who really has to go to the bathroom. We had no idea what song he was singing, not because it was an obscure selection, but because *we didn't care*. This was *Porn Star* Karaoke, after all, so where were the porn stars, goddammit? Not to be sexist—and with all due respect to the hillbilly ginches in the parking lot—but when we think of porn stars, we think of *vagina*. If we wanted to watch dudes grab their crotches while belting out Toto's greatest hits we could have stayed home and watched *American Idol*. And then shot ourselves.

The chatter was so loud that it almost drowned out the karaoke. No one was paying attention to the Mark Wahlberg clone onstage because the real show was at the tables, where jaded, silicone-plumped MILFs provided poignant counterpoint to fresh-faced hopefuls with stars in their eyes and traces of seminal fluid in their hair. Bulimics and belle beefers alike comingled in the aisles, while an older gentleman with too much jewelry and not enough buttons on his shirt scanned the room like a jackal looking for a fresh carcass. Another guy sported a toupee so hideously greasy, it looked like one of the girls had just given birth to a stuffed beaver on top of his head.

Last but not least there were the gawkers. From overly-tatted hipstas to balding endomorphic onanists, we witnessed a wide selection of voyeurs who'd come to watch a human train wreck set to the soundtrack of their feeble lives. It wasn't quite a donkey show, but on a slow Tuesday night in Burbank it would have to do.

Finally, the song ended . . . and much to our chagrin, the chump passed the mic to yet *another* dude who was still not Ron Jeremy. Though it seemed obvious to us that no one in the place was there to bask in the glory of an all-u-can-sing sausagefest, the show had to go on . . . unfortunately. We glazed over as the next wannabe cranked up his mojo, clutched the mic to his chest, closed his eyes, and literally *kicked* out the jams. What a dick.

*Follow the bouncing bazongas.*

We stepped outside for a breath of fresh air and to look for the inbred Hedgehog fan, but she was nowhere in sight. That's when we spied up-and-cummer sex star Sunny Lane, pert and perky and not looking a day over eleventh grade. She was all smiles when we said hello and asked how her parents were doing. You see, unlike most starlets who either hide their careers from their folks or do everything they can to rub it in their faces, Sunny has a healthy relationship with her peeps. She has to: They're her managers. So far, she'd come through for them with flying colors, and had recently snagged a lucrative gig as the "contract girl" for the giant strip club chain, Déjà Vu.

Sunny was stoked about that, but not about getting in front of the mic. "I have to save my energy," she said, "because I'm going out on the road next week." No shit, sister. The last thing you need is a vaginal aneurysm trying to hit the high note from that shitty Whitney Houston song (at least they all sound shitty to us, so take your pick). A girl has to take care of herself, especially if she's about to embark on a non-stop dance tour through some of the Deep South's more charming gentleman's clubs. As any exotic dancer will tell you: You haven't been tipped until you've been tipped by Boss Hogg.

We walked back inside and were astounded to find a real live porn star belting out . . . well, not really belting out, but . . . *delivering* a song. It was the lovely Monica Mayhem, and she graced us

OUT '*n*' ABOUT

# THE HOUSE THAT TITS BUILT

Russ Meyer. He was a legend in his own time—the inimitable auteur who built a career on cleavage, the one-man movie studio responsible for the influential classics *Faster, Pussycat, Kill! Kill!*; *Beyond the Valley of the Dolls*; and *Mondo Topless*. Meyer purchased this Hollywood Hills house (uncannily breast-like with its bullet-bra roofline) in the late 1970s for the production of what would be his last completed film, *Beneath the Valley of the Ultravixens*. The house figures prominently into many of the Ultravixens exteriors—as did some of the neighborhood's adjoining streets—and was briefly featured as an interior in the film's opening sequence. The house also served as Meyer's personal residence, editing bay, and center of operations for RM Films International until his death in 2004 at age eighty-two.

**Russ Meyer's House / 3121 Arrowhead Drive / Los Angeles**

with her rendition of . . . Christ, does it really matter? She's a porn star. She's singing karaoke. End of story. Can we go home?

In the end, Porn Star Karaoke turned out to be less interesting than we thought it would be, but the reader should keep in mind that we are on a first-name basis with more than a few starlets and have worked in the industry. Getting excited about Porn Star Karaoke would be akin to a gynecologist getting jazzed about a tap-dancing pap smear. So if you're not completely jaded like us, and thrill to the thought of listening to "Jagged Little Pill" as rendered by a woman whose likeness you may or may not have jacked off to, you probably won't be disappointed. The only reason we were let down was the fact that Sardo's karaoke library is some 40,000 titles strong—including a number of children's classics we would have paid good money to have heard sung by a world-class fellatrix—yet none of the evening's would-be divas had the artistic integrity to stand up there and belt out "Pop Goes the Weasel." Hell, anyone can sing "Like a Virgin," but to take "Wee Willie Winkie" and make it your own . . . now *that's* talent.

## SEEING SOUNDS AND HEARING COLORS AT THE

# MADONNA INN

Oh, the fickle finger of fate. It can prod a Georges Marciano toward a Vickie Lynn Hogan and send a misguided Texan down a slippery slope of catastrophe. It can tempt a bunch of acid-tripping lunatics up to Cielo Drive and spawn a bestseller. It can fly a pair of facelifted magicians to the apex of Vegas entertainment, and destroy the act in an instant between the jaws of a punch-drunk white tiger.

But fate isn't always a malcontent, and the partnerships it generates needn't always end with an accidental drug overdose or a fur-flying bloodbath. Often fate will put its fickle finger in a place that leaves you feeling really good, and sometimes it'll even move that finger around a little in such a way that you might gasp and bite your lip. Sometimes fateful partnerships flower, fruit, and feed the world with their juicy yield. What else but that special magic could have given us the inspired teams of Salvador and Gala Dalí, Buck Owens and Roy Clark, Masters and Johnson, or Shields and Yarnell? Alex and Phyllis Madonna are one of those dynamic partnerships, and the Madonna Inn is their juicy yield.

The Madonna Inn
100 Madonna Road
San Luis Obispo
800.543.9666
805.543.3000
www.madonnainn.com

There are a lot of hotels up and down California's coast that can offer first-class amenities, but only one can provide an environment on which your brain can actually chew. The flocked fleur-de-lis, crushed velveteen, glitter-flecked cottage cheese, and the Madonna's fearless amalgamation of patterns might be enough to induce a seizure in the unsuspecting epileptic, but every square inch is an adventure in color, texture, and motif, pushing the envelope, challenging preconceived notions, and creating new standards by which all hotels should be measured. Vertiginous vaulted ceilings, walls of stacked rock, and carpets in pleasing plaids climb, rise, and crawl among styles spanning from colonial to safari to 1960s contemporary. Amid a blissfully muzzy palette of eye-watering candy-apple red and radioactive robin's-egg blue you'll enjoy a liberal use of gilded cherubs and sparkling candelabras. Dizzying shades of blistering pinks and abusive fuchsias are met with Louis XIV furnishings and massive Palos Verdes flagstone. Electric kelly green and blinding canary yellow are peppered with raucous florals and miles of gold swag chain, demonstrating that what happens in Vegas may have actually happened in San Luis Obispo first.

It could very well be said that the Madonna Inn is to interior design what fusion cuisine is to food, but unlike the wasabi-infused follies of the nineties, the Madonna interiors endure, head held high. Rather than coming off like a tawdry flight of fancy taking a desperate stab at the next road-weary traveler, the Madonna Inn stands confidently against the ever-changing winds of boutique hotel trends with no apologies, as solid as the stone supporting many of its walls. The Madonna Inn is here to stay.

Alex Madonna is the mastermind behind the architectural design and construction—it was his idea to make each room different from the next ("... that way we can't make the same mistake twice"). His wife Phyllis was saddled with the task of creating the interiors of the inn's 109 rooms, two restaurants, and common areas, without any prior decorating experience. Pulling zebra fur, flying cherubs, and filigree woodwork from her bottomless toolbox, Phyllis—an accomplished accordion player—has in fact created, defined, and mastered a design aesthetic entirely her own. Rooms with enticing names like "Jungle Rock," "Cloud Nine," "Ren Dez Vouz" (three adjoining rooms named "Ren," "Dez" and "Vouz"), and "Barrel of Fun" are the fruits of her God-given talent, each one forcing guests to view the world through her advantaged lens.

The Madonna Inn opened its doors on Christmas Eve of 1958 with a total of twelve rooms, and invited its first round of visitors to stay free of charge. By 1960, the inn had tripled in size, and construction soon began on the main building and restaurants. Today the inn is a veritable Madonnaland, featuring a coffee shop (with pink sugar at every table), a ballroom (live music through the week), several gift boutiques, a sprawling waterfall-fed pool, state-of-the-art gym, and gourmet food and wine shop—none of which have been denied the peerless Madonna Inn milieu.

## Inn-credible!

The Gold Rush Room is their formal steakhouse, done entirely in bright reds and pinks, with a marble balustrade from Hearst Castle and a twenty-eight-foot gold "tree" dripping with gilded grapes, cherubs, and twinkling candelabras as its central lighting scheme. Circular pink vinyl booths (vinyl is a popular material at the Madonna Inn) are girded with potted faux cherry blossoms and ferns, all strung with thousands of glimmering white lights. A doll way too big to be cute sways back and forth on a mechanical swing hanging from the oak branches above the cashier's stand, and her costume changes with each holiday. Adjacent to the dining room is the ultra-plush lobby and Silver Bar, with its pink vinyl heart-shaped chairs and white marble cocktail tables positioned around a monstrous flagstone fireplace (prehistoric bones jutting from the adjoining masonry). Don't miss the downstairs men's room just off the wine cellar, celebrated for the cascading rock waterfall urinal, which in itself has justified many a visit.

The Inn's backyard location to Los Angeles lends itself well to lost-weekend logistics, and when you book your stay at the Madonna Inn, do it right. While every room packs a punch, it's the larger suites that will bring you to your knees. Many of these rooms boast sizable sitting areas or separate living rooms, fireplaces, and private balconies with panoramic views of the pastoral San Luis Obispo countryside. These suites are also ideal for partner-swapping and group action if that's your bag, as many are multiply bedded, and the famed stone grotto waterfall showers are large enough to accommodate several oversexed adults.

Don't make the mistake of showing up without a reservation with the intention of scoring a popular suite like the Caveman Room. The best rooms—especially the Caveman—can get booked up months in advance. Be specific about what you want (a rock waterfall shower is very important) and do your homework; all the rooms are pictured on their Web site. There's a photo album featuring all 109 rooms available at the reservations desk for your perusal in case you should decide to upgrade once you've arrived, and if you're staying more than one night it's perfectly acceptable to ask for a different room each night to get the most out of your visit.

A stay at the Madonna Inn is always over too soon, but look at it this way: With 109 different rooms you won't be at a loss for weekend plans for at least the next two years, even more if you serial date. So don't waste any more time. Your new home-away-from-home is calling your name.

## NO MORE RING AROUND THE COLON WITH

# ANAL BLEACHING

**Pink Cheeks**
14562 Ventura Boulevard
Sherman Oaks
818.906.8225
www.pinkcheeks.com

*Hello, friend. Is your butthole too dark? Are you bothered by unsightly pigmentation around your O-ring? Would you like to turn your browneye into a pinkeye? Well, thanks to the modern miracle of anal bleaching, you can now relive those carefree days when you'd walk down the street with a spring in your step and your head held high, knowing your bungus was sparkling fresh. That's right, in just a few short days, you'll start to see your shadowy stinkstar transform into the bright beautiful flower you've always wanted it to be!*

When we first heard about anal bleaching, we openly scoffed at the notion like a couple of stodgy British scientists in a fifties Hammer film. "What's that, Smedrick? You say you've discovered a way to reanimate the dead *and* give a tired old asshole a fresh pink pucker? Why, that's sheer poppycock!" Then, when a porn star actually showed us the results of the procedure on her own winker, up close and personal, we saw the light. In fact, we were almost blinded by it. And now we're here to spread the good word: anal bleaching really works!

Like penis lengthening and vaginal rejuvenation, anal bleaching is just another way to feel better about the ugly things God put inside your underwear. And the procedure is not only for porn stars and strippers. It's ideal for anyone who can't help but flash their butthole in public, as well as practitioners of the rusty trombone, and folks who just want to feel good about themselves . . . down there.

A number of salons now offer the procedure, but if you want to visit the place where it all started, then stop by Pink Cheeks in Sherman Oaks. Owner Cindy Esser-Thorin will be happy to explain to you why buttholes are dark in the first place, how they can get dingier over time, and how the anal bleaching procedure works. Hell, she's a veritable expert on anal aesthetics.

Originally, the entire process was done in the store, but now, other than the initial waxing of the anus, the process can be completed at home while watching *Dancing with the Stars*, thanks to Pink Cheek's easy application take-home kit. They also sell the kit over the Web, where they've found that over one-third of the sales are to men, many of them in Texas. Apparently, down in the heart of Texas, the stars at night do really shine big and bright.

Fun fact: The active ingredient in anal bleach, hydroquinone (4 percent), is commonly found in products used by African Americans to lighten skin tone. Once again, whitey has found a way to co-opt black culture and be an asshole about it.

*And in no time, your anus will be so white and shiny, you'll have to wear sunglasses just to wipe your butt! A brand-new asshole is the first step in creating a brand-new you, so what are you waiting for? Think of what a new pooper will do for your self-esteem! So come on, feel good about yourself again. Our anal operators are standing by, call now!*

*See you on the bright side of the moon.*

## OUT *'n'* ABOUT
# LEAVE YOUR WEDDING RING AT HOME

Park Motel / 12963 Ventura Boulevard / Studio City / 818.501.9292

# GRAND SPA

Grand Spa
2999 West 6th Street
Los Angeles
Men's Sauna:
213.380.8887
Women's Sauna:
213.380.8889
www.grandspala.com

Before we're held responsible for inadvertently polluting an unspoiled and virtually homogeneous Korean spa with a bunch of prurient-minded round-eyes (namely horny white American men and the markedly Eurotrashy, including men of the greater Mediterranean regions), we need to get a few things down on record.

Yes, there are beautiful Asian women working at Grand Spa, but they will not be providing you with a happy ending or a "full body" anything, so if you've got a bad case of yellow fever, take some aspirin. In addition, dudes on the prowl for some sweaty boy-on-boy action won't find it in the dark recesses of this sauna; spa doesn't stand for "stroking penises anonymously" (at 24 Hour Fitness perhaps, but not here) so keep your hands to yourself, leave the Koreans alone, and let the patrons of Grand Spa have their peace. Furthermore, there is no mixed bathing: Men are relegated to one facility and women to another, so those cruising for eye candy take note. Unless, of course, naked Korean businessmen are your thing, but even so, it's not polite to stare.

The pleasures of the flesh are of another variety at Grand Spa, which also houses a karaoke bar, a nightclub, a Korean restaurant, a gift shop, and an alfresco produce stand, all within a facility open twenty-four hours—with an admittance fee of $15. Take that, Beverly Hot Springs.

Although Grand Spa offers the standard extras (massage, wraps, facials, body scrubs, and the like), the main attraction here are the saunas and soaking pools—a radiantly-heated sanctuary to get naked, get wet, and sweat your guts out, with no apologies. The fun is making the rounds from the large, granite-tiled shower rooms (both traditional Korean and Western) to the saunas (one dry, one wet, both cooking), and through a series of three small pools (cold, warm, and hot salted) until your psyche is softened and your legs are ready to buckle. If they do, pull yourself up, dry off, grab a robe, and head to one of the sleeping rooms to catch a nap on a floor mat. Once you're feeling more alert, you can have dinner sent up from the restaurant downstairs and grab some chow without getting dressed, or settle into the TV room and watch Korean sitcoms on the plasma screen.

For about the same as you'd pay for three small cups of yogurt product at Pinkberry, you'll have virtually limitless access to Grand Spa's simple and immaculately tended facility, which

offers virtually everything one might need to clean up and dry off, right at hand. Piles of warm fluffy towels, cotton robes, and slippers are yours without extra fees, and if you're uptight about your genitals, there's a stack of boxers available too—just toss it all in the hampers on your way out. Toiletries are free—razors, shaving cream, shampoo, toothbrushes, and toothpaste—and the barber shop room is loaded with hair product and blow dryers should you be the sort who requires that sort of maintenance. Even little details like Q-tips aren't overlooked. These Koreans know where it's at.

*Sweatin' to the oldies.*

Aside from the incongruous oldies playing low on the sound system, the Grand Spa's greatest advantage is that it's one of the precious few sanctuaries in Los Angeles where one can rejuvenate both the body and the mind—by clearing L.A. from your mental environment altogether. There are no conversations about a screenplay option or a recent industry strike to spoil your time in the sauna, no posturing gym-dandies at the mirrors eyeing their abs in onanistic adoration, no celebrity name dropping or Bikram yoga bullshit. Just a lot of sweaty Koreans quietly powering down. And for our money, that in itself is an experience worth its premium.

# SIZE REALLY DOES MATTER AT

# BEVERLY HILLS

## SURGICAL SPECIALISTS AND

# LASER VAGINAL

## REJUVENATION INSTITUTE

Beverly Hills Surgical
Specialists
99 North La Cienega,
Suite 102
Beverly Hills
310.854.1600
www.beverlyhillssurgical.com

The Laser Vaginal
Rejuvenation Institute of
Los Angeles
9201 West Sunset Boulevard,
Suite 406
Los Angeles
310.859.9052
www.drmatlock.com

Once reserved for strippers and other attention whores, the boob job has blossomed into a convenient surgical pick-me-up for women of all stripes who seek to boost their self-esteem by forcing men to stare at their heaving fun-bags. Bulging, overinflated bazoos are becoming as common at a Sweet Sixteen party as they are at a senior citizen center, though at the latter there stands the very real possibility that someone copping a feel may very well be groping a colostomy bag that's reached peak capacity.

Ironically, there are many men who value small breasts over large ones, yet rare is the woman who actively seeks out dinky dicks.

This explains, in part, why men are so utterly consumed with the size of their cocks, regardless of how large they actually are. We know one woman who eventually dumped her donkey-dicked lover because, even after she provided a hundred assurances that, yes, his dong did hang down to his knees, he couldn't stop asking if she thought it was big enough. It was like *Long Dong Silver* meets *Monk*. And men have the gall to find "Does this make my ass look fat?" annoying?

Even so, the options for guys with feelings of penile inadequacy have been disappointingly superficial when compared to the immediacy of a few strategically-placed 600cc bags of silicone. Until recently, men with small packages had but a few choices to offset their deficiencies, the short list being rounded out by the customary overcompensation in musculature, clothing, choice of automobile, or all of the above. Until recently, penis enlargement surgeries—especially performed south of the border or in Thailand—produced results that would have horrified even John Merrick.

Since men are such fragile creatures, women have long been trained to tell us what we want to hear—that size doesn't really matter—but only a self-deluding schmuck is going to buy into that disinformation. You think we don't scan the cover of *Cosmo* at the checkout line? We only *pretend* to not know that all women are size queens, just like women pretend a boner the size of a Vienna sausage is good for anything other than a canapé and a laugh.

But there's good news, boys and girls! With the many exciting advances being made in the field of plastic surgery, not only are boobs rounder, chins bigger, noses smaller, and thighs less cheesier, but almost every body part can be plumped, trimmed, or reshaped exactly to one's exacting specifications. From calves to butts to pecs to chins, a variety of implants now brings us much closer to our perverted notion of the perfect physique. But all of these augmentations are child's play when compared to the holy grails of plastic surgery: penis enlargement and vaginal reduction. Whether you desire a tree snake between your legs or the va-jay-jay of a seventh-grade Filipina—and hey, who in Los Angeles doesn't?—these wet dreams are now within your grasp.

As professional authors, we get spam about penis enlargement every day of the week, and believe us when we say we've tried them all. In fact, our penises are so large now, we are prohibited by law to be within a hundred feet of playgrounds, churches, public swimming areas, and Cub Scout meetings. But perhaps you don't have the time to spend hours a day taking pills, applying exotic creams, or strapping on a dork-stretching contraption that looks better suited to an orthodontist's office. And that's where surgery comes in.

At Beverly Hills Surgical Specialists, they can make your dong longer in about an hour. Think about it—*that's less time than you'll spend in line at Pinks!* Give 'em another two hours—the average length of a Tom Cruise movie—and they'll widen your load as well. Not happy with your helmet? Got a little too much curve in your banana? Does your "turkey neck" (their term, not ours) bum you out? Or maybe your beanbag is just too damn big? Don't despair, my friend. At Beverly Hills Surgical Specialists, your groin grief is over.

On the other hand, your financial woes are probably just beginning. Penile perfection is not cheap. The lengthening process alone will set you back about $4500 for an extra inch or two (yes, results vary), and "The Grip" —required hardware for your post-op salami-stretching program—will run you another $290. It works like this: About one-half of the human wangus is hidden inside the body, attached to the pubic bone by a ligament. When the ligament is severed through a small, discreet incision at the base of the pubis, more of the chub-pack is allowed to hang outside the body. The downside is that without the support of the ligament, an erection may not point as skyward as it once did. It's all about compromise.

*Taint no big thing.*

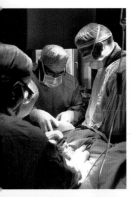

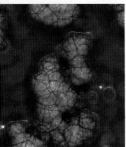

Penis widening costs about $8500—further proof that girth trumps length—and consists of a series of dermal-matrix grafts just below the skin. As far as we can tell, this process does not involve Keanu Reeves in any way. Think of it as wrapping a thin layer of extra flesh around the Slim Jim, enough to increase its circumference by up to one inch. If the lengthening and widening procedures are done at the same time—a common choice for most patients—the total cost is somewhere around $10,500. Maybe your little head also needs plumping, or perhaps you wish to put a hem on that sagging, elephantine grocery sack you call a scrotum. Are you afflicted with peno-scrotal webbing, that aforementioned "turkey neck" condition where ball sac and shaft share a little too much real estate? Worry not, my friend. All can be corrected . . . for a price. The bottom line is that there are a myriad of procedures you can undergo to put some extra funk in your junk, but even when you add them all up (and include a healthy tip for your anesthesiologist) it will still cost you less than a new Corvette. And you'll actually end up with a big dick rather than just driving around like one.

Speaking of big dicks, vaginas are apparently not as resilient as our sex ed teachers would have had us believe. Aging and childbirth are the biggest culprits for what is commonly referred to in the medical community as SBS or "Sloppy Beaver Syndrome," but we'd also like to think that all those surgically enhanced megacocks banging around out there are also in some small part to blame. Or maybe not, but the fact remains that an increasing number of women, in their relentless quest for eternal youth, are having their poozles trimmed, tweaked, tightened, and hermetically resealed. Anyone who's endured the ambiguously creepy *Dr. 90210* on E! already knows that the Laser Vaginal Rejuvenation Institute of Los Angeles is the place to go when it's time to get your yoni taken in.

Gals who regret losing their virginity to the first schmuck who paid them a compliment can now turn back the hands of time by restoring their hymens to factory-new condition though the miracle of hymenoplasty. Similarly, ladies who insisted on natural childbirth for their first dozen or so children can reduce or eliminate that annoying echo altogether through Laser Vaginal Rejuvenation® (LVR), which decreases the diameter of the cootch both inside and out, and also helps to enhance muscle tone and strength. As an added bonus, the one-hour procedure also strengthens the perineum, which is good news for those who plan to do heavy lifting with their taint. The overall result of LVR is the creation of more friction during intercourse, which in turn leads to heightened sexual gratification, which ultimately results in more cougars and MILFs prowling teen chat rooms and mall parking lots. The procedure costs somewhere in the neighborhood of $10,000, which is a small price to pay to

# JUST AROUND THE CORNER FROM COLLEGE AND SLUT

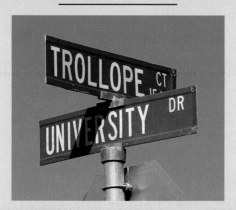

**Trollope Court and University Drive / Moorpark**

experience the sweet tenderness of losing your virginity all over again.

Cooter surgery is not only about improving pleasure. According to LVRILA's Web site, many women are unhappy with the appearance of their yum-yums, and when asked for an example of an aesthetically pleasing vulva, a majority chose the girls in *Playboy* as the standard bearers for the perfect quim (and we thought ladies only read *Playboy* for the articles). When asked what they *didn't* want their vulvas to resemble, the answer was a tie between Barbara Bush's face and a plate of haggis. Kennedy's autopsy photos came in a close second.

Though this newly created market for vaginal vanity has mortified many feminists, social critics, and anyone else who believes that the last thing women need is something else to make them feel insecure about their bodies, customers are apparently lining up to have their drapes redone via the miracle of Designer Laser Vaginoplasty®. At the skilled hands of Drs. Matlock and Simopoulous, the lauded snatch sculptors at LVRILA, even the most heinous bat cave can be transformed into a come-hither grotto of love.

As with penis augmentation, the options for DLV are numerous. Various forms of laser reduction surgery can reduce the size of the labia minora, plump the labia majora, remove fat from the mons pubis, trim excess skin along the sides of the clitoris, and rejuvenate an aging perineum. Sadly, unlike wines and cheeses, the taint apparently does not improve with age.

For purely sexual thrills, women can also enjoy G-Spot Amplification (aka the G-Shot), wherein an injection of special collagen into the G-spot area is said to increase arousal and gratification. Women can opt for a single dose at around $1860, or belly up for a double shot of the stuff for $2500. Regardless of how much is injected, the enhancement lasts about four months, or in college terms, approximately a hundred and fifty boyfriends.

Despite our glib posturing, we're thrilled that men and women in Los Angeles can now attain the kind of genitalia only previously available through airbrushed photography and Tom of Finland drawings. After all, the Beautiful People aren't really beautiful unless they're also beautiful *down there*. At last, we can all sleep at night knowing that inner beauty doesn't hold a candle to a resilient perineum.

## WHERE THE STREET SCENE UPSTAGES THE PINK:

# THE TIKI THEATER

The Tiki Theater
5462 Santa Monica Boulevard
Hollywood
323.462.0345

*"Santa Monica Boulevard . . . WE LOVE IT!"*
*—Randy Newman, "I Love L.A."*

Places this skeevy usually die a quicker death, but some Southlanders don't have the luxury of viewing smut within the privacy of their own homes, and like a Laundromat or a car wash, the Tiki Theater is their service center. Although live nude girls no longer gyrate here and the entertainment is now exclusively limited to video, the Tiki Theater is like the Musso & Frank of peep shows. It's one of the few left of its kind, a tried-and-true Hollywood institution. Although unlike Musso & Frank (but much like Angelyne's bids for public office) it's never going to receive the acknowledgement it so rightfully deserves.

*Keeping the "ease" in sleazy.*

Upon our approach to what might certainly be our last pilgrimage to the Tiki Theater, a woman about age twenty-four came running from the door of the building just east of the theater entrance. She was barefoot and wearing only a bra and some exercise pants. With her arms awkwardly folded over her chest, she dashed quickly around the corner of the building and disappeared into the alley. Lumbering down the stairs immediately after her was a guy of about the same age, built like an enormous water balloon, his oversized jeans hanging strategically off his fat ass, a fair sixteen inches below the waistband of his boxers. The woman's black shirt was wadded in his right hand.

"Yeah, bitch, *run!*" he shouted down the alley, "See how far you get!"

He tossed her shirt to the sidewalk in front of him. He waited half a moment, first looking west on Santa Monica Boulevard, then east, his body uncertain, his face slightly pensive. Then he waddled back upstairs.

A passing pedestrian saw the shirt in the middle of the sidewalk, stopped, picked the shirt up, and thoughtfully hung it over the side of a newspaper vending box. A few moments later a second passerby stopped, picked the shirt up, and held it out in front of him. He inspected it, his head tilted. After having made his quick assessment, the shirt was placed back on the vending box and he walked on. A third pedestrian grabbed the shirt off the box as he quickly passed, but lost his grasp, and the shirt fell once again to the sidewalk. He kept walking.

WE LOVE IT!

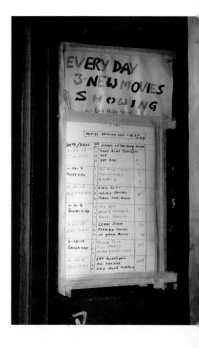

# WIGWAM VILLAGE MOTEL

In 1955 the marquee luring visitors to Wigwam Village, one of the more distinctive roadside motels built during the halcyon years of Route 66, read "Sleep in a Wigwam, Get More for Your Wampum." However, by the close of the twentieth century, Foothill Boulevard was a road far less traveled, and the slightly more desperate "Do It in a Teepee" was the catchphrase used by the Wigwam management to attract potential guests.

It seemed that the clientele to which Wigwam Village originally catered was long gone. There were no apple-cheeked American families on summer vacation frolicking among the rambling lawn hosting Wigwam's eighteen stucco teepees. The kidney-shaped pool had been drained, and served mostly as

Wigwam Village Motel
2728 Foothill Boulevard
(Route 66)
San Bernardino
909.875.3005
www.wigwammotel.com

*No reservations required.*

a receptacle for dead leaves. The grounds, once grassy green, were an arid wasteland uncannily evocative of the reservations issued to Native Americans by the United States Government (the Wigwam maintenance crew must have been scalped around the same time that the 10 Freeway offered an alternative high-speed route through San Bernardino). As for the teepees themselves, patches of mismatched paint had been slapped over graffiti, iron bars secured the tiny windows, and if there were a star rating system for squalor, this motel would have scored a perfect five.

The future of Wigwam Village however, is looking up. After changing ownership, the place is slowly beginning to look like its former self. The graffiti is gone, as are the bars over the windows, and the pool is now filled with water instead of San Bernardino's airborne litter. Wigwam Village is beginning to heal.

And for the record, it's no less fun to do it in a teepee.

## DROPPING OUR SOCKS AT

# RESEDA FOOT RELAXOLOGY

## AND CHECKING OUT THE FUNGUS AT NEW BANGLUCK MARKET

Reseda Foot Relaxology
7343 Reseda Boulevard
Reseda
818.996.5956

New Bangluck Market
7235 Reseda Boulevard
Reseda
818.708.0333

After the most incompetent administration in American history has left us with an economy about as robust as Dick Clark on two bottles of Nyquil and currency on par with Chuck E. Cheese game tokens, you're probably already familiar with the last notch on your belt. And unless you're in the oil or arms businesses, you've likely done away with unnecessary luxuries like food and medicine in order to keep your car full of that cheap gas we went to war for, just so you can drive to your low-paying job and then pick up a jumbo sack of Chinese tube socks at Wal-Mart on your way home.

Yet, despite these hardships, you're proud to be an American 'cause at least you know you're free . . . right? Damn straight! Just because the sun is rapidly setting on the American Empire doesn't mean that liberty-lovin' Americans like yourself don't deserve a little pampering now and then—even if you voted for

Shrub and company. If you have to dip into your IRA or your kid's college fund to pay for the indulgence, don't give it a second thought; once the United Corporations of America becomes a wholly-owned subsidiary of the Sino-Arabian Conglomerate, higher education and retirement will no longer be options anyway. So, while you still can, go ahead and splurge on a $25 one-hour massage.

No, that is not a typo.

If you didn't know any better, you might mistake Reseda Foot Relaxology for a La-Z-Boy showroom. Twelve ridiculously plush recliners with ottomans line the dimly lit communal room, which means you won't get much in the way of privacy here, but nor will you have to get naked in a room full of strangers. Life is all about trade-offs.

Technically speaking, you're paying for a foot massage, and while these folks will indeed work wonders on your feet, nary a body part goes unkneaded during almost sixty minutes of low-budget bliss. After rolling up your pant legs (we recommend wearing shorts and flip-flops for comfort and convenience), you'll take a seat on the ottoman for a relaxing foot soak in a wooden bucket filled with warm green tea. Though you may be tempted to drink it once you're done, we advise against it.

The soak lasts anywhere from five to fifteen minutes depending on how busy the place is. Friday and Saturday nights tend to be the most hectic, but even then the wait for a walk-in appointment is bearable, and you can always amuse yourself by gawking at the oddities next door (more on that in a moment). Open from 11:00 AM to 10:00 PM every day of week, there's bound to be a convenient time slot for you. They'll even give you a little card and stamp it each time you get a massage; after eight, you get one free.

*It's good for the sole.*

Once you've climbed into the recliner and your feet have been towel-dried, that's when the real fun begins. We're not sure where the friendly Vietnamese massage therapists get their training, and for twenty-five dollars, nor do we care. Each one seems to employ his or her own personal style, and as long as they don't cause us grievous bodily harm, we're fine with that. Besides rubbing our aching dogs, they dug in with gusto to work out the rest of our kinks—the ones in our muscles, at least—and had us turn over in the chair to get to our backs. There's even a hole in the chair's headrest for your face to fit in. The scalp massage brought back pleasant childhood memories; so much so that if they offered that alone for an hour, we'd be all over it. Along with a smile and a "thank you," that's their idea of a happy ending at Reseda Foot Relaxology, so don't get any bright ideas.

Despite its name, New Bangluck Market right next door does not offer hand jobs either, but you should check it out if only to savor its malodorous milieu. Once you get past the olfactory assault that greets you at the door, you'll find a wealth of items you'll never see at Von's: edible beef and pig blood, preserved duck eggs, shredded melon candy, fish sauce with whole anchovies, big ol' honkin' chunks of dried white fungus, and of course, everyone's favorite, pork meat loaf in an anchovy-flavored sauce wrapped in banana leaf. They also have wonderfully obscure fresh vegetables here, and the seafood department, with its live crabs, clams, and catfish (take one home as a pet!), is like visiting some kind of third-world aquarium. Heck, they'll even kill the creature of your choice and cook it for you right on the spot. Try getting *that* kind of service at Whole Foods, mofo!

If you're looking for an inexpensive way to impress *and* disgust a first date, or simply fall in love with your partner all over again, a romantic evening at Reseda Foot Relaxology and New Bangluck Market may just be the answer. And if not, rest assured that at the very least it will be an adventure worth telling someone else's grandchildren.

## KEEPING U CLOSE TO STDS: THE
# STUDS THEATER

Studs Theater (formerly the Tomkat, formerly the Pussycat)
7734 Santa Monica Boulevard
West Hollywood
323.656.6392

While the rest of L.A.'s adult movie theaters went under by the close of the twentieth century, the former Pussycat location on Santa Monica Boulevard remains a noteworthy exception.

The modest art deco building experienced a pornomorphosis in the early nineties, and the new management honored the Pussycat's dubious past while taking advantage of its West Hollywood location, just a hop, skip, and a cock ring from both the Pleasure Chest and the French Market. Having been reinvented as the Tomkat, the bill of fare remained triple-X, but this cat was sniffing up a different sort of ass.

True to his name, though, the Tomkat eventually moved on, and the last bastion of big-screen skin flicks changed hands once more. Screening the same smut but now calling itself Studs Theater, the establishment wasted no time cultivating a reputation as dubious as its predecessors. Two signs posted out front pay homage to the location's history, while also encouraging potential customers to explore the theater's "dark" and "cavernous" interior, which allegedly "shrouded" "private indiscretions" in decades past. Curious.

Regardless of the name changes or what might be taking place in its darker corners, 7734 Santa Monica is an important stop on any sightseeing tour for one primary reason: It's the Grauman's Chinese of skin flicks, a Pussycat-era holdover that is easily missed unless you're on foot. Featured in concrete along the theater's shallow forecourt are the prints of porn luminaries like Linda Lovelace, Harry Reems, and Marilyn Chambers. Even the munificent John Holmes is represented here, and seeing that Betty Grable put her leg in concrete for Sid Grauman, and Jimmy Durante his nose, we'd expect a little more from King Dong, who only saw fit to press his hands and the soles of his shoes into the Pussycat's wet cement—neither of which are particularly big, either. There goes that myth, but good.

Nevertheless, seems like there's plenty of cock to be had on this sleepy side of WeHo. Whether you want to get in touch with porn's past, or get touched in the dark, Studs Theater seems to offer a little something for everyone.

*Louse shampoo and a large popcorn, please!*

## CATCHING UP WITH THE HOROSCOPE AND HORSE-HUNG TRANNY ESCORTS OF THE

# L.A. X . . . PRESS

As we watch Hollywood become Universal CityWalked with aggressive sanitization and corporate co-opting, we find ourselves pining for our Hollywood of yesteryear. Not the one of Garbo, Gable, or MGM musicals, but the Hollywood of porno theaters, head shops, and dive bars. Where teenaged runaways were chewed up and spit out like sunflower seeds. Where Hollywood Boulevard was a shopper's paradise—for aspiring hair bands, cross-dressers, and sundry sex workers. Where you were far more likely to find a wig shop or a ladies shoe store specializing in sizes eleven-plus than you were a Victoria's Secret. It was a Hollywood that didn't know Banana Republic jeans, unless they were pushed down around the ankles of a twenty-dollar john who managed to find a private place to park. Sure, there were the eager tourists who came sniffing 'round Grauman's and dropped a little cash on car-wash-caliber novelties from the adjacent T-shirt stands and souvenir shops, but further beyond the forecourt of Grauman's, the tourist foot traffic waned. The stars on the Walk of Fame grew dingier and dirtier on the blocks stretching eastward, their pink terrazzo serving as dependable daybeds for the down and out. The only time Hollywood looked worse was at Christmas, when lackluster garlands snaked around streetlights

L.A. X . . . Press
Distributed throughout
Greater L.A.
www.hollywoodlaxpress.com

and arched over the boulevard in a futile attempt to kick up residual stardust. Like garish makeup on an old woman, the dressing only served to highlight what it was trying to hide. Settling into Hollywood's sagging skin and crawling up its lip lines, it sadly punctuated a long and very rough life, subject to the fickle nature of the city over which it once reigned supreme.

For better or worse, Hollywood Boulevard was our 42nd Street, and just like New York's onetime epicenter of sleaze, it's taking the same path. Its dubious garishness has been replaced with a different sort of dubious garishness, and revamped into a circus of digestible family fun. That's why we treasure the *L.A. X . . . Press*. As one of Southern California's most widely distributed free weekly periodicals, *LAXP* is quick to remind us of the *other* Hollywood, the one forced further underground in recent years. Like beacons of sleaze, its iconic red and white distribution boxes stand on virtually every corner, almost as if to say *"Hey! Hollywood isn't that cleaned-up, there are still plenty of ways to see live nude girls, take an erotic enema, or hook up with a he-devil in heels!"*

We can hear you now: "My days of tranny hookups and erotic enemas were over in the nineties." Perhaps. But don't be too quick to dismiss all of *L.A. X . . . Press*'s content as pay-for-play personals. Their coverage of world news alone is worth the shame of being seen pulling a copy from a corner box. "COLUMBUS CARRIED SYPHILLIS FROM NEW WORLD, EUROPEAN STUDY SUGGESTS" and "TIGER ESCAPES ZOO, KILLS 1 PERSON" aren't headlines you're likely to see garnering much ink in *USA Today,* but such fodder is business as usual for the *XP.* Following suit, their local-interest coverage is boiled down to its most salient, going right for the jugular with civic corruption, brutal murders, and natural disaster. *People* magazine might waste pages with celebrity puff, but the *XP* is your source for stories like "WILL SMITH ANGRY OVER HITLER COMMENT" or which was the latest A-lister to get thrown into—or released from—jail.

Pet adoptions, horoscopes, and the "Party Joke of the Week" round out the *XP* content along with the randomly-featured "Hollywood 24 Hours List," assuring us that there is indeed a community supporting fast food joints, towing services, sex shops, and Laundromats through the wee hours. Wikipedia-sourced celebrity featurettes will catch you up with the likes of Kim Kardashian and Shannen Doherty, while superfluous adult film profiles are padded with superfluous trivia (" . . . After her split from porn director Seymore Butts, she had a tattoo with his name turned into a dolphin."). "Life in the Fast Lane by

Wild-Man Bill" gives the *XP* a personal voice, and although it's unclear exactly how fast Bill's lane actually is, we love how he'll wax poetic over circus freaks one week, and guide readers with gentle encouragement like the Norman Vincent Peale of sexual liberation the next. Sports, scandal, comics, perfunctory film reviews—and you thought the *L.A. X . . . Press* was only for the depraved.

Certainly, there's plenty here for the depraved as well. The *XP* hasn't been rolling its presses since 1972 because people love horoscopes. Seems that you can't throw a stone in any direction without hitting a happy-ending massage therapist in this town, and those in search of a summer job may find an interesting new path in the *XP*'s "Help Wanted:" section. And if you're looking to fill your dance card, look no further than their "Specialties" pages, where a bevy of "fully functional" ladies tease suitors with bikini shots and boast measurements like "36D-26-34, and 9 inches."

For information junkies who just can't get enough, the *L.A. X . . . Press* is a worthwhile ride though a Los Angeles subculture you just don't find walking the streets anymore. Don't miss out: visit a distribution box today.

*The massage is the medium.*

## NOTING THE CONSPICUOUS LACK OF GLORY HOLES AT

# FREDDY AND EDDY

Our unwavering affinity for the old-fashioned adult bookstore is much akin to our love for skeevy dive bars and ancient cafeterias: they are dying breeds, each imbued with a unique, often appalling charm. Decades ago, in one of our first peep show booth experiences on Sunset Boulevard, we were so callow that we had no idea why there was a small hole in the wall. We just wanted to watch a porn loop. Moments later, when an engorged glans peeked through the opening like the swollen snout of a tentative anteater, we were so startled that we impulsively administered a full-force karate chop to the errant wang. The ungodly howls and commotion that emanated from the booth next door signaled that it was a good time to make a hasty exit. We have not been

Freddy and Eddy
12613 Venice Boulevard
Los Angeles
310.915.0380
www.freddyandeddy.com

# The cleanest dirty bookstore in town.

able to play Whack-A-Mole since.

The glory holes, the sticky floors, the bright fluorescent lights, the creepy cruisers, the zombie staff, the cheap vibrators that broke the moment you brought them home, the frightening butt plugs bigger than Paul Lynde's head, and, of course, the movies, magazines, and pulp novels with titles like *Granny Bangers*, *Golden Shower Chicken Slave*, and *Amber, The Lesbian Queefer* (we did not make those up)—these are all things you will *not* find at Freddy and Eddy.

Conversely, the pimply-faced stooge behind the counter at Le Sex Shoppe never offered us cappuccino, much less asked us if we wanted cinnamon on it. But we're getting ahead of ourselves. . . .

When we first heard about Freddy and Eddy, we have to confess that we assumed it was a gay sex shop. Freddy. Eddy. Duh, right? But as we soon found out, Freddy and Eddy are not two dudes, but merely the fictitious representations of Ian and Alicia Denchasy, the happily married couple (and proud parents of one) who gave up their previous careers (schoolteacher and attorney, respectively) to jump-start their own sex life by improving those of other couples, straight and gay alike. Not surprisingly, they've geared their business towards couples of all sexual persuasions, branding their store a place "Where couples can come." (Come. Get it? *Come*.) Singles (and their money) are, of course, welcome, but the Denchasys will be the first to recommend a competitor if they feel a client is barking up the wrong dildo or looking for a product they feel doesn't fall into the category of "sexual health."

Beyond the brilliant concept of opening a sex store in order to expand their own erotic repertoire, the Denchasy's also made the conscious decision not to sell sex toys, adult novelties, or porn. Eschewing those monikers, their self-described "sexual health boutique" peddles "sexual health products" and "sexual health entertainment": vibrators, dildos, butt plugs, lubes, whips, handcuffs, ball-gags, blindfolds, and DVDs with titles like *The 69th Sense* and *Blacklight Beauty*. You know, *sexual health products* (wink wink).

Even though we don't refer to the gentlemen who pick up our trash every Thursday as "sanitation engineers," we get what the Denchasys are doing. It is not just clever wordplay that separates their low-key store from the traditional not-so-clean, well-lit sex shops that have come to define the adult bookstore stereotype (and now that the priapic dinosaurs are dying off, we miss them already). From the free espresso to the New Age hominess to the sexual health parking available in the rear, every little detail of the Freddy & Eddy experience is meant to mitigate sexual embarrassment by making the customer feel as comfortable and welcome as possible. This is a good thing, since Americans are still the most inhibited, repressed, sexually screwed-up hypocrites on the face of the earth and often need to be coddled into understanding that there is nothing shameful about pursuing their God-given right to an orgasm—even on the West Side.

Entering the store is like walking into the hip, Ikea-appointed home of a slightly oversexed couple who've obviously worked through most of their *issues* and would like you to have as much fun in bed as they do. Lurid colored walls complement the more muted couches and chairs that greet you when you come through the front door. In the room to the right, in what used to be a bar called "The Place," are the bulk of the products, tastefully arranged in a mishmash of homey cabinets and Swedish Modern shelves. The narrow hallway that leads to the small fetish room is lined with books and a few DVDs that the Denchasys not only sell, but also loan out for *free* on the honor system. Yes, you read that correctly. Try going to Hustler Hollywood and telling them you just want to borrow *Barely Legal 17* for a week or so.

On the other hand, the clerks at Hustler Hollywood won't ask you if your girlfriend knows that you want to buy her a vibrator, or if your boyfriend is cool with the notion of being on the receiving end of a strap-on. At Freddy and Eddy, they want to know such things, not because they're busybodies, but because they believe that an ill-conceived sex toy surprise can do as much damage to a relationship as good. Accordingly, they've been known on occasion to send a customer home empty-handed, suggesting they have a talk with their partner, or better yet, bring him/her/it back to the store. Admittedly, this anti-sales technique is not for customers who just want to buy a butt plug without playing Twenty Questions, but F & E tends to attract the less furtive, more open-minded patrons who don't mind having a discourse on cunnilingus or sexual dysfunction with perfect strangers. Return customers—and there are plenty—do not remain strangers for long. Indeed, F & E regulars pop in and out of the store like neighbors in a sitcom, grabbing a toy or some lube and strolling out with a "Love you!" or "Put it on my tab!" If Dr. Ruth and the cast of *Three's Company* had opened a sex toy emporium in Hooterville, its howdy-neighbor hominess might have been something like this.

It's that personal touch that makes Freddy and Eddy unique—bizarre, one might even say—in a city already known for its Pleasure Chests and Babelands, Kikis and Cocos, Rough Trades and Stockrooms. To their considerable credit, the Denchasys manage to pull off this touchy-feely feat without seeming like obnoxious sexual know-it-alls or sleazy swingers with a not-so-hidden agenda. Anyone willing to take risks to fight for just a little more sexual freedom for all of us is okay in our book; their decision to step out from behind the cutesy Freddy and Eddy personas they've so carefully cultivated and put their real names and faces out there for the world to see is an incredibly ballsy move. Freddy and Eddy is not just a labor of lust, but of love, a testament to the Denchasy's commitment to change the world one sexual health product at a time, albeit *sans* glory holes. Drop in and let Ian whip you up a free cappuccino while Alicia shows you their whip selection, and find out for yourself.

## COMING INTO OUR OWN AT

# WORLD MODELING

## AGENCY

World Modeling Agency
4523 Van Nuys Boulevard
Sherman Oaks
818.986.4316
www.worldmodeling.com

The San Fernando Valley is famous for many dubious achievements, not the least of which is its rep as the nation's capital of porn production. While the Internet has allowed anyone in the world to compete on the global market as long as they can get their hands on a camera, a computer, and some genitals, the Valley is still home to the majority of the players in the X-rated industry, and is a veritable incubator for porn fodder, i.e., fresh meat.

And during the golden years of porn's heyday, no one fed the industry more new flesh than the Farmer John of porn agents, Mr. Jim South of World Modeling Agency. A pompadoured, mustachioed gentleman with a slick Southern drawl that betrays his Texas roots (his dad was the assistant chief of the Dallas Police Department), South was once the de facto king of the nudie agents before he decided to hang up his spurs back in 2006 after thirty long years of slinging snatch. Competition from the Web and young upstart agents made it harder and harder for South to turn a profit, even though there were more girls entering the business than ever before. Gone were the days of the true porn superstar, when a handful of quality clients kept South solvent: beauties like Christy Canyon and Ginger Lynn, original suicide girls Savannah and Shauna Grant, and most famously, an underage Traci Lords, who duped South, the industry, and even the

U.S. government into believing she was old enough to be fornicating on film. In those days, a beautiful porn starlet was worth her weight in blow—and the blow got spread around. Now, even an average-looking smut queen—the kind who stars in a twenty-one-guy creampie then disappears—tends to be more attractive than the hottest contestant on *America's Next Top Model*. Throw in the fact that looking and behaving like a streetwalker is now standard operating procedure for certain mega-celebs; overt sluttiness will get you your own reality show rather than ostracized; and that any girl with a Webcam and a lock on her door can become an international sex superstar while Mom and Dad are watching *Dancing with the Stars* in the next room; and, well, it's easy to see how an old-school porn agent might be a bit of an anachronism.

But showbiz is in the blood, as they say, and South couldn't stay out of the business. When he reopened World Modeling less than a year after shuttering the place, he promised to limit the number of performers he represents—but we're not sure that's going to help him. Having seen a steady decline in his clients prior to his early retirement, South lost the rest when he decided to close shop. After being out of the loop so many months, and with his former clients now being repped by newer and shinier agencies like L.A. Direct Models, he has his work cut out for him. In many ways, South is like an X-rated version of Mike Ovitz. Both were once puppet masters who are now striving to make a comeback, and though Ovitz may appear to have the more difficult task ahead of him in a town that is fickle at best when it comes to granting second chances (Paul Reubens, anyone?), just scrolling through the talent on the World Modeling Web site shows just how fucked South might be. Perusing his current stable of, uh, talent, is akin to going through CAA's client roster and finding out their biggest clients are now Tova Borgnine, Jared from the Subway sandwich commercials, and Baby Shamu. Grim, very grim.

*Have you ever considered a high-paying career in the exciting world of pornographic entertainment?*

But we're rooting for South (who has teamed with his son, Jim, Jr.) if only because he's a good ol' boy as well as an XXX relic this town can't afford to lose. His "cattle calls" were the stuff of couch-stained legend, and his office was the nexus of the porn industry. Within the faux wood-paneled walls of World Modeling there's no telling how many angry fathers, brothers, and boyfriends threatened to kill him; how many naked nymphets pranced on the balcony to the chagrin of motorists on Van Nuys; how many lines of blow were snorted off freshly-waxed pudenda; how many corny stage names were invented; how many dreams were fulfilled; how many lives ruined; how many boners induced; how many marriages destroyed; how many tears shed; how many loads blown; how many boxes of Kleenex consumed.

The numbers stagger the mind.

# CRUISIN' FOR A BRUISIN' AT

# LADY HILLARY'S DOMINION

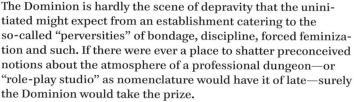

Lady Hillary's Dominion
(Address provided upon
session confirmation)
Los Angeles
310.204.6777
310.559.7111
www.dominionsm.com

The Dominion is hardly the scene of depravity that the unini-tiated might expect from an establishment catering to the so-called "perversities" of bondage, discipline, forced feminiza-tion and such. If there were ever a place to shatter preconceived notions about the atmosphere of a professional dungeon—or "role-play studio" as nomenclature would have it of late—surely the Dominion would take the prize.

When a patron disappears behind the security gate of Lady Hillary's discreet Tudor, they're given the sort of respect usually reserved for attorney-client privilege, or that of a pharmacist filling an embarrassing prescription. The climate here is profes-sional, friendly, non-threatening, and genuinely relaxed. In fact, the shame and stigma generally associated with such a service is so completely lifted that were it not for the paddles, hoods, whips, gags, and cuffs hanging from the tool racks lining the hall behind the front desk, booking an appointment for a session at the Dominion isn't too unlike scheduling a back wax and facial at an exclusive day spa, only a lot sexier. You will find no cotton-smocked aesthetician in the Dominion's decidedly sumptuous parlor. Instead, a towering raven-haired vixen sheathed in black latex might be the one to receive you for your pre-session inter-view, amid purple walls, glowing candles, and Victorian-inspired furnishings, in a comfortable room that might even be consid-ered "homey" if you grew up in a classy French cathouse.

However, if it's a whore you're looking for, call an escort agency: The goings-on at the Dominion are legal and completely legit. They keep a strict "no penetration" rule here and staff members will not offer a "release" (nor is it appropriate to ask for one). But if you're interested in spending some quality time with a well-trained domme or sub who'll indulge your power-play fantasy—or some other fetishy predilection which the last eight people you dated didn't share or appreciate—the Dominion will do you right.

Hearts tend to beat a little faster in Lady Hillary's elaborately appointed rooms, and for many clients, the décor alone is cause for titillation; the sight of a stately worship throne, the texture of a black rubber floor beneath your feet, or the mere suggestion of a wrought-iron suspension bar swinging from a vaulted ceiling may in itself encourage weakness in the knees. No two rooms are alike, and all are styled with the dramatic flair and theatrical bent that Dominion clients have come to expect. "The Vault," "The Enclosure," and "The Powder Puff Room" are among the studio's six private spaces, each one offering a variation on the theme and nodding towards different specialties. "Lady Hillary's Chamber" features a silver-studded stock secured at the foot of a large bed covered in crushed velvet. Opposite, a sturdy leather sling hangs suspended in a dark corner by heavy steel chains, lit from above by the glow of deep red light. Downstairs, a barred holding cell occupies a portion of a room appointed with walls of brushed aluminum, a chrome interrogation chair, and a gleaming metallic table-topped bondage cage as its centerpiece. Elsewhere, gothic sconces, burning candles, spanking horses, and leather cushions provide a client with another sort of headspace, and traditional pieces like a St. Andrew's Cross may even leave old-schoolers feeling a sense of nostalgia. The spirit of the studio is further reflected in the artwork hanging from many of its walls. The black-and-white fetish photography celebrates BDSM earnestly, while a sense of irony is evident in the collection of vintage exploitation movie posters. Elements like tiger skin carpets or leopard throw pillows add a naughty playfulness. Little of the Dominion's attention to detail is lost on the client, with a privileged perspective provided by large, strategically positioned mirrors.

"I explain this as a sensual and erotic experience, but without the sex," says Lady Hillary, an affable straight-talker with over twenty years in L.A.'s BDSM scene. "This is a mind fuck—there's no penetration, no fluids exchanged—but if someone knows how to fuck with your mind, you can leave here feeling like you've had sex." This is exactly why she takes the training of her staff so seriously, and demands integrity in their demeanor. They're to observe studio protocol whenever a client is present in the lobby: Submissives take their places on floor pillows, dominants stand. Almost like a finishing school for the leather-and-latex set, Lady Hillary runs a tight and meticulous ship, with each hire subject to her exacting standards and exhaustive quality control. She also prides herself on passionate, skilled, and experienced personnel, requiring that each of them earn their position on the Dominion talent roster by effectively proving their abilities through a stringent probationary period. All aspiring (but inexperienced) dominants are first hired as submissives, demonstrating the studio's attention

*"A lot of men think that some bitch is going to greet them at the door, pull them by the hair, lock them in a room, shove uncomfortable things up their butt and send them on their way. That's not what happens here."*

—LADY HILLARY

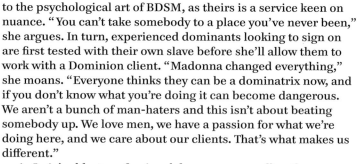

to the psychological art of BDSM, as theirs is a service keen on nuance. "You can't take somebody to a place you've never been," she argues. In turn, experienced dominants looking to sign on are first tested with their own slave before she'll allow them to work with a Dominion client. "Madonna changed everything," she moans. "Everyone thinks they can be a dominatrix now, and if you don't know what you're doing it can become dangerous. We aren't a bunch of man-haters and this isn't about beating somebody up. We love men, we have a passion for what we're doing here, and we care about our clients. That's what makes us different."

As L.A.'s oldest professional dungeon—as well as the only female-owned and -operated fetish studio in town—the Dominion boasts a bevy of over thirty dominants, submissives, and switches, from the young and nubile, to the seasoned and mature ("Some of our older clients feel a little pervy booking a session with a really young girl," she explains). Up for a sportier scene? Lady Hillary's competitive wrestlers—"Women," she assures, "who can kick butt"—are at your service. Although she's seen a decline in wrestling requests in recent years (as fetish trends often come and go like bell-bottoms) her girls are more than ready to hit the mat. "These ladies know what they're doing— they know all the holds and things . . . and they *need to*," she stresses, "because the guys who are into that can kick butt too!"

Newcomers are encouraged to visit the Web site, which

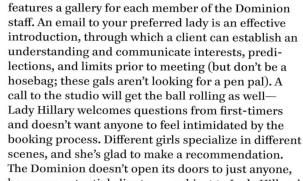

features a gallery for each member of the Dominion staff. An email to your preferred lady is an effective introduction, through which a client can establish an understanding and communicate interests, predilections, and limits prior to meeting (but don't be a hosebag; these gals aren't looking for a pen pal). A call to the studio will get the ball rolling as well— Lady Hillary welcomes questions from first-timers and doesn't want anyone to feel intimidated by the booking process. Different girls specialize in different scenes, and she's glad to make a recommendation. The Dominion doesn't open its doors to just anyone, however; potential clients are subject to Lady Hillary's subtle but discerning screening process too. Her talent as a keen judge of character ensures that trouble is rare, and if a client is even suspected of having hit the bar, the bong, or the slopes prior to their arrival, they won't make it past the front desk. Period.

Sessions run about $200 an hour, $100 for the half, and about $300 for an hour session with two dommes. Rates vary for submissives, "heavy sessions" (in which a sub would consent to caning for instance), and other services like fantasy or competitive wrestling. A straight room rental—which includes use of the Dominion's custom-built stocks, cages, tables, and all the accompanying gear—can be had for those who've got the playmate but not the place, at about $150 an hour. They accept all major credit cards, with discretion given to your billing statement—earning miles has never been this fun!

It should also be noted that the clients seeking the services offered by the Dominion are by no means limited to men: Women frequent the studio, as do couples. With a thirty-year history and a stellar rep, the Dominion has fostered a large, loyal, international, and even multi-generational clientele ("We have father and son clients that don't know the other comes here," she chuckles), some making visits to a favored domme with weekly regularity. The studio also gets their share of lunch-hour walk-ins just like a hair salon. "We've got eighty-year-old guys who've been coming here since we opened," Lady Hillary says, barely audible over the incessant ringing of two phone lines and the ding from an incoming client waiting at the Dominion security gate. "If I had to stop advertising today, we'd be fine."

Furthermore, the Dominion is seemingly impervious to the economic slumps that might send another luxury service, like a dog psychic or a life coach, due south—quite the contrary, in fact. While others tighten belts, the Dominion ladies are lashing theirs over the hindquarters of a despondent real estate developer or harried investment banker: ball-gagged, hog-tied, and anxious to decompress. "When there's a recession, people tend to get stressed out and frustrated . . . and that's exactly when they need their asses spanked," Lady Hillary asserts with the air of a seasoned shrink offering a routine diagnosis. "It makes them feel better."

## BLOWING IT ALL SKY HIGH AT THE

# BONAVENTURE HOTEL ELEVATORS

Long, long ago, in the olden days of the seventies, screenwriters and art directors conveniently envisioned the future as a bright, shiny, Buck Rogers kind of place that looked a lot like the Bonaventure Hotel. How convenient. With its mirrored cylindrical towers and angular concrete ramps, the hotel was the perfect

The Bonaventure Hotel
Elevators
404 South Figueroa Street
Los Angeles

location for not only many cheesy sci-fi epics (*Logan's Run* and the original *Battlestar Galactica* were shot here before construction was even completed in 1977), but for everything from cheesy romantic comedies (*Forget Paris*) to cheesy dramas (*In the Line of Fire*) to cheesy action flicks (*Die Hard*). In *True Lies*, Arnold Schwarzenegger rides a horse through the lobby and into one of the twelve glass elevators that zoom up and down the exterior of the structure, and it's certainly true that the glass lifts are among the most memorable aspects of the Bonaventure's design, but not always for the reasons that location scouts might choose them for.

Though the Bonaventure certainly gets its share of tourists and families, the hotel also caters regularly to conventiongoers, businessmen, and—with the gentrification of downtown—white, middle-class cheaters. It's no secret that conventions are hotbeds for out-of-town lust, businessmen have been known to enjoy a hooker now and again, and cheaters aren't there to play pinochle. Ride the hotel's glass elevators long enough, and you may well get a glimpse of exactly what we're talking about. We wouldn't be telling you if we hadn't seen it with our own voyeuristic eyes.

## Going down!

Even without the prospect of witnessing an illicit act, the Bonaventure's elevators are great fun. From the lobby, they shoot up through the interior of the six-floor atrium and burst through the ceiling to reveal a breathtaking view of L.A.'s multi-hued smoggy skyline. As they scale the Bonaventure's thirty-five stories, they also offer direct views into many of the adjacent rooms. Given the fact that most guests are savvy enough to know about drapes, the odds of glimpsing anything truly perverse are usually a long shot, but some folks forget, don't realize, or simply don't care that there are elevators whizzing past their windows.

The best time for spotting fornicators is when the sun has gone down and the lights are on in the rooms. Lulled into the false sense of security that comes with being so many floors above the busy street, the guests tend to relax and let their hair down, have a few drinks, and slip into something comfy . . . or nothing at all. Some stand at the tinted glass and gaze out at the city, letting their hands roam where they will. Others, feeling frisky and adventurous, are inspired to seduce partners or rendezvous with secret lovers, and then there are those who have no other choice but to call an escort service. Forty-five minutes later, and BAM! You're in the elevator, watching a fat, middle-aged guy in a fez and black nylon socks receive a cappuccino enema from what appears to be a transgendered Puerto Rican dwarf nurse wearing a strap-on as big as a leg of lamb. Or maybe not. Sometimes you can't be sure what you just saw, because Bonavoyeurism is all about brief glimpses, not lingering gawks. It's not as if you can stop the elevator anywhere and just soak up the sights—especially if there are other passengers who don't share your interest in the mating habits of Iowa insurance salesmen. You have to take it as it comes, so to speak. Maybe on your next pass you'll catch the dwarf smoking a cigarette in the non-smoking room and using the drapes to wipe up, or maybe the room will be mysteriously empty. You never know, and that's what makes it so . . . magical.

Of course, you may spend hours, even days riding the elevators and never see even a hint of impropriety. It's all a matter or patience, timing, and luck—like fishing. That's why we recommend that you make yourself some sandwiches, pack a cooler of beer, grab a folding chair, and, of course, a pair of binoculars. Then stake your spot in one of the glass elevators and start punching buttons. You may never glimpse more than someone's pay-per-view porn channel, but we guarantee you'll have a great time until you're forcibly ejected from the elevator by burly security guards, turned over to the LAPD, then beaten and sodomized within an inch of your life.

After all, let's face it: every pleasure has its price.

# LUCHA VAVOOM

Time and again, science has categorically proven that the three most effective methods to relieve stress are:

1) Sex
2) Drinking
3) Throwing midgets around

Oh yeah, and laughing is supposed to help, too.

Take the esoteric art forms of Mexican masked wrestling, burlesque stripping, and stand-up comedy, throw in a couple of well-stocked bars, and stick it all into the most beautiful vintage theater in Los Angeles, and you have the ingredients for Lucha VaVoom. Sure, the sex is vicarious, and so is the midget bashing, but those things will only get you into trouble anyway. Best to simply enjoy a cocktail, sit back, and let the pros handle the rest. You know the hoary cliché about "the most fun you can have with your clothes on?" This is it, folks. Second, of course, to reading this book.

Let's start with the venue. The Mayan Theater has been our favorite classic movie house ever since it started showing porn back in the seventies and was featured with the Ramones in

Lucha VaVoom
The Mayan Theater
1044 South Hill Street
Los Angeles
www.luchavavoom.com

Roger Corman's *Rock 'n' Roll High School*. Of course, its history goes well beyond that, and of all the city's famous themed theaters—the Chinese, the Egyptian—the Mayan is the most impressive, with a poignant history to accompany its beauty. The incredible detail found in the carved war gods, feathered serpents, celestial symbols, and hieroglyphs of the building's exterior and interior are a reflection of the original designer's obsession with pre-Columbian art. Francisco Cornejo worked in tandem with the architectural firm of Morgan, Walls and Clements to create the Mayan Revival masterpiece, which is perhaps the architects' greatest work after their art deco opus, the aqua-tiled Wiltern Theater. They also built the El Capitan, now commandeered by Disney for its own performances.

When it first opened, the Mayan had a seating capacity just shy of 1500, and though it enjoyed some years as a stage theater and then a first-run movie house, it eventually went the way of many downtown institutions and drifted into seediness. By the seventies it was showing porno movies, some of which were shot

in the theater's basement. In 1977 it was divided into a triplex (still showing porn) and though that may have seemed like the last nail in the Mayan's coffin, it was made whole again in 1990 and now enjoys a second life as part of the downtown renaissance and a designated historical cultural monument. We can't think of a more perfect venue for Mexican wrestling.

Those unfamiliar with the long, dignified history of *lucha libre* have a lot to look forward to. More graceful, theatrical, and humorous than its troglodytic American cousin, Mexican wrestling is not just about the outrageous masks and the costumes (though they certainly make the sport more enjoyable). Just as in the States, the wrestlers (*luchadores*) are divided into *rudos* (bad guys who break the rules) and *técnicos* (good guys who follow them), but these fighters are far more acrobatic and rely on more airborne maneuvers than their gringo counterparts. Whereas most American wrestlers seem to be popped out of the same hulking, neckless, steroid-infused

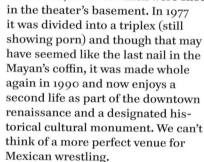

brute mold, luchadores come in all shapes and sizes—from tiny wrestlers like "The Minis" (we favor *El Cabrito*, the baby goat, and his diminutive compatriot "Little Chicken"), to beefy he-men like *Toro Rojo* and *Ultimo Guerrero*; from svelte hotties like "Crybaby" and "The Poubelle Twins," to the flamboyantly effeminate switch-hitter "Cassandro," who has played both sides of the good/evil coin. Our personal favorite? *Chupacabra*, of course. The green, spiny wrestler

based on the Mexican folk monster has a charm all his own, although "Dirty Sanchez," with his skid-marked underwear and gargantuan merkin, gives the goatsucker a run for his money. Along with perennial crowd pleasers like "The Crazy Chickens," every show also features special guests from Mexico (like Blue Demon Jr.) and maybe even a new character or two.

And then there are the strippers—or "Buxotics" as Lucha VaVoom likes to call them. Revitalized by Dita Von Teese and the Velvet Hammer, popularized by Ivan Kane's Forty Deuce, and now a regular part of the hipster circuit, burlesque performers are not to be confused with "gentleman's club" strippers. The job requirement for the former demands a modicum of creativity; the other, genitalia. Thus, owing more to the theater and less to the gynecologist's chair, burlesque dancers rely on elaborate costumes, props, and above all, a sense of fun to successfully build to that climactic moment when they finally reveal less than what Janet Jackson showed at the Superbowl.

Over the years, in her alter ego role as Lucha VaVoom headliner "Ursulina," Rita D'Albert has taken off more clothes than most women will ever put on. Rita (who cofounded the show with her partner, Liz Fairbairn) is what one might call a new traditionalist; she trades in the classics while adding modern twists to her sophisticated strip routines. She is not alone in her creative talents. Lucy Fur is a virtuoso of the tasseled pasties; once she gets them spinning, she's been known to generate enough wind current to affect climate change—and to cool off the back row of the mezzanine, too. Lola La Cereza's matador act will have you yelling "Olé!," and Michelle L'Amour's balloon dance is as arousing as it is inspiring. Some of the acts go beyond the call of duty and are literally jaw-dropping. The Wau Wau Twins disrobe while performing flawless acrobatics twenty feet above the stage and without a net. Some of the sexiest chicks

*Pasties, midgets, and a guy who sucks goats.*

# A LITTLE BIT OF VEGAS IN DOWNTOWN L.A.

If you've got an itch to get hitched, you don't have to drive all the way to Sin City to have a McWedding—just head downtown to the Guadalupe Wedding Chapel and say "I do." Choose from a variety of civil, "religious," and Catholic weddings, as well as five—count 'em, *five*—wedding chapels that all look pretty much the same (although we have to admit that the trompe l'œil ceiling and Virgin Mary altar in Chapel Numero Cinco are muy fabuloso). Don't have time to deal with the Hall of Records? No problem! Thanks to Guadalupe's on-site notaries, couples can drop in on a whim and make a commitment that will last forever—or at least until they sober up. Though the chapel has no particular aversion to broken glass or people dancing in circles, a traditional Jewish wedding is not included on its menu, and BYOR (Bring Your Own Rabbi) is not kosher at Guadalupe. But Jews who can do without a *chuppah* and who are willing to settle for one blessing rather than seven are welcome at the Guadalupe Wedding Chapel—as are Log Cabin Republicans, Rastafarians, and dwarves. Hell, these folks will marry just about any couple as long as they're both human and over eighteen. Reservations are accepted, but not necessary. *Mazel tov!*

The Guadalupe Wedding Chapel / 237 South Broadway Street / Los Angeles / 213.628.0551 / www.guadalupewedding.com

on the stage aren't even chicks. Karis looks so hot and does so many amazing tricks with a bevy of hula hoops that by the time she reveals that she's a he, you're too distracted to fully grapple with your sexual confusion. Likewise, Roky Roulette—who is all dude from the get-go, so bring the ladies—manages to bounce around on a customized hobbyhorse pogo stick for his entire routine, which looks like a hell of workout. Whether he's dressed as a cowboy or Louis XVI, Roky whips off his regalia while narrowly missing the six-foot drop off the edge of the stage. If we are going to be forced to watch men take off their clothes and bare their asses, this is how we prefer to do it.

Frankly, with that much wrestling and burlesque talent onstage, the comedians interspersed to round out the show and tie it all together aren't just spurious overkill, they're also kind of annoying. Even with the relentless chucklebug nattering (and persistent plugs for the show's sponsor, *El Jimador* tequila) Lucha VaVoom is one of three good reasons to live in Los Angeles.

We're still working on the other two.

## MAKING A BEA LINE FOR

# GOLDEN GALS GONE WILD

We think Lenora Claire is the kind of gal Russ Meyer would have liked, which pretty much means we worship the ground she walks on. Okay, maybe *worship* is overdoing it, but, well, let's just say we're big fans. The alabaster skin, the fiery red hair, the cleavage from hell—those assets alone are enough to leave us smitten, but when you add sassy and savvy to the mix, well, *fuggedaboutit*, sistah!

Lenora is the beauty and the brains behind Golden Gals Gone Wild, perhaps the greatest art show the city of Los Angeles has every seen (with the possible exception of Mark Mothersbaugh's Peek-A-Boo Room show at La Luz de Jesus in 1998). Inspired by the now infamous nude oil painting of Bea Arthur by Chris Zimmerman (which she purchased for a mere $110), Claire set out to curate a show for which she would assemble a "crack" team of artists to create what one might loosely term "erotic" works of art based on the defunct TV show *Golden Girls*. The end results ranged from the redneck wet dream of Rue McClanahan in a Confederate flag bikini (*schwing!*), to Betty White in neo-Nazi S & M regalia (*double schwing!*), to a pair of underwear with a cartoon of Bea Arthur's face on the crotch (*off-the-charts schwing!*). The latter also conveniently doubles as a contraceptive device since no one is going near your junk with Bea Arthur glaring out from between your legs. Personally, we found the nude painting of Estelle Getty splaying herself in true *Hustler* style to be in poor

Lenora Claire's "Golden Gals Gone Wild"
www.lenoraclaire.com

World of Wonder
Storefront Gallery
6650 Hollywood Boulevard
Hollywood
323.603-6300
www.wow-storefront-gallery.
wowtv.tv.

taste—until we noticed that she was sitting on a giant hot dog in a bun. Now *that's* tasteful!

Speaking of tasteful . . . the soulless, grinning macaque known as Joe Francis somehow got the notion that his highbrow *Girls Gone Wild* series was being exploited by Claire's show. No stranger to exploitation himself, Francis—from the comfort of his jail cell—made sure a cease-and-desist order was issued, which was promptly ignored. Are we the only ones who find it ironic that neither CBS, Disney/Touchstone, the producers of *Golden Girls*, nor the stars of the show found it necessary to take legal action against Claire's playful exhibit, while the man who makes his living by exploiting inebriated, barely-legal, spring-break retards felt that *he* was the one being violated by nude paintings of Bea Arthur?

The show, which opened on August 11, 2007, and ran through the end of October, attracted the attention of national media. Among the more notable headlines was the one that ran in all caps across a double-page spread in that bastion of journalistic integrity, the *Globe*: GOLDEN GIRLS X-RATED SCANDAL. With that kind of press, it was surprising that neither LACMA nor MOCA failed to show interest in acquiring the works as part of their permanent collections. We can only assume they're overstocked on Hockneys. Most of the artwork was subsequently sold to private collectors, although a $6000 Swarovski crystal-studded walker has yet to find a home. We're betting Rupert Murdoch already owns one.

OUT 'n' ABOUT

# DOES HE DO CANINE?

IT'S THE LAW: *Any* depiction of a man posted in West Hollywood requires that he be overly muscled and nude—or at least wearing something so Lycra-snug that the line of his body remains unbroken—even on municipal signage.

West Hollywood Dog Shit Signs / All neighborhoods / West Hollywood

Claire followed up the success of Golden Gals with a holiday-themed jiggle-fest, the "Merry Titmas" show, which cleaved its way into the hearts of Angelenos with artwork that included a Nativity scene depicting the Virgin Mary as a Hooters waitress and Baby Jesus in a manger full of hot wings. Who knew the birth of Christ could be so delicious?

Both shows are but memories now, but the exhibit space in which they were held—World of Wonder Storefront Gallery—is still weaving its magic on Hollywood Boulevard. As for Ms. Claire, one can rest assured that she still has a few tricks left in her ample brassiere.

*Art for tart's sake.*

## ONE-STOP SHOPPING AT

# XPOSED, PRIVATE MOMENTS, WET SPOT, AND 2 AM

Taken individually, these four establishments—strip club, topless bar, adult bookstore, medical marijuana dispensary—are a dime a dozen in Los Angeles. Put them all together, practically under one roof, and they combine to represent the very pinnacle of man's hopes and dreams. We know of no other location in this fair city that combines booze, pot, porn, sex toys, and live nude women in the same place. Okay, maybe Bill Maher's house, but that doesn't count.

Let us begin in the parking lot, which alone is a feast for the senses. With the same majesty the Lighthouse of Alexandria undoubtedly once brought to the ancient Egyptian coastline, the sign for Xposed towers over an unremarkable stretch of Canoga Avenue, illuminating the smoggy night sky in neon blue hues. Beneath its Ionic pediment, a winsome blonde playfully lifts her blouse, exposing the bottom of her silicone-plumped breasts as if to say, "Look at me, I'm taking off my shirt." Bleached, plucked, and retouched to porn-approved perfection,

Xposed
8229 Canoga Avenue
Canoga Park
818.996.7616
www.xposedclub.com

Private Moments
8237 Canoga Avenue
818.446.0120

The Wet Spot
8237 Canoga Avenue
818.996.7616

2 AM Dispensary
8239 Canoga Avenue
818.264.0790

*You won't know if you're coming or going.*

two pouting starlets gaze out from the mammoth backlit photo that is the centerpiece of the sign. Their yearning eyes beckon working stiffs to come in and take a load off—or just drop one. "Full Nude" and "Full Bar" promise full pleasure in capital letters, and though the cryptic phrase "Rear Parking," seems to hint at yet another exotic service offered by the club, the neon words merely herald the parking that is available behind the building. Another large sign, this one to promote the porn/dildo/bong emporium called "Private Moments," intrigues with its sophisticated image of a woman in fuck-me pumps pulling her panties down around her ankles. Further back, above the entrance to the bar, "The Wet Spot" marquee promises "Live Entertainment, Full Bar, and Free Admission." One can only imagine how families must thrill to these lively images. As they pass by the bustling parking lot in their Dodge Caravans, parents will happily entertain questions like "Is there such a thing as half nude?" "Is that lady getting ready to go to the bathroom?" and "Isn't that the top of Aunt Sylvia's head bobbing up and down in that car?"

Inside, Xposed is a large, loud, unsoiled strip club with the *de rigueur* runway, poles, and booths for "special" dances. In fact, with twenty lap dance booths, bed booths, and something they call a "state-of-the-art hands-free peep-show booth," Xposed is all about the booths. They even promise "full nude, full contact bondage" booths in the near future, but apparently have no plans to build a "John Wilkes" Booth or "Shirley" Booth anytime soon.

The girls here, for the most part, are real and do not resemble the Stepford Sluts on the sign out front. That's a good thing, in our opinion. We'd rather see an assortment of dancers who prove that beauty comes in all shapes and sizes rather than an indistinguishable procession of cosmetically enhanced bimbos who can only be differentiated by their hair color, tramp stamps, and whether or not their assholes have been bleached.

Although topless bars in Los Angeles can obtain a license to legally serve booze, once the panties come off it's a different matter. So-called gentlemen's clubs that allow dancers to go all the way—like Xposed—are not allowed to pour anything stronger than Red Bull. But what's the fun of gawking at a gyno show when you're fully sober,

DAMES, DRINK, DOPE AND DILDOS!
**GANGWAY!**

## OUT *'n'* ABOUT
# A STAR IS PORN

Its streamline-moderne tower still catches eyes on Sunset Boulevard, and architecture buffs are well acquainted with the mélange of Mexican, Turkish, Italian, New England, and French elements to be had further along the corridors of designer Robert V. Derrah's 1936 oddity. However, few realize that Crossroads of the World is the Schwab's Drug Store of porn, being the site of adult entertainment's greatest discovery, John C. Holmes.

After retiring from his career as a forklift operator at a South Bay meatpacking warehouse, the prodigiously endowed twenty-five-year-old soon set his sights on a meatpacking career of another sort: one of stag films and porno rags. It was here in 1969 that an aspiring Johnny Wadd showed up for an open casting call looking to score some X-rated print work. He wasn't handsome or in particularly good shape, but his mutant penis opened doors leading to a long and prolific career in adult films. While starring in movies like *Pizza Girls*, *Saturday Night Beaver*, and *Eruption*, Holmes also kept busy with a myriad of part-time work. In an effort to avoid jail over a pandering arrest he served as a semi-professional squealer for the LAPD, helping to bust the very same industry that had been paying his bills. A noted pathological liar, he later hustled intermittently as a drug dealer, gigolo, and small-time thief, stole luggage from the LAX baggage claim, pimped his barely legal girlfriend, and perpetrated credit card fraud against the first of his two wives.

His most famous role, however, would be his special guest appearance in the brutal "Four-on-the-Floor" murders in the Hollywood hills, which would in turn become subject matter for the documentary *Wadd: The Life and Times of John C. Holmes* and the feature film *Wonderland*. After a little jail time, the granddaddy of porn jumped right back in the saddle, starring in several more features before dying of AIDS in 1988. And since he never bothered to share his HIV status with any of his co-stars, we might also add "deceitful murderer" to this hosemeister's impressive resumé. That's Hollywood!

**Crossroads of the World / 6671 Sunset Boulevard / Hollywood**

you ask? Exactly, says the L.A. City Council. Xposed's owner, a former Chippendale's dancer and porn performer who goes by the name of Brick Majors, found a brilliant way to throw off this wet blanket by opening a topless joint with a full bar adjacent to the main club. At the Wet Spot, patrons can get plastered, stare at titties, then stumble over to Xposed to remind themselves what the rest of the female anatomy looks like. Many of the same dancers at Xposed will come next door to do a topless routine on the Wet Spot's micro-stage, and if the patrons are

lucky, hang out and chat for a bit. Dancers and other employees can go back and forth through a side door, but customers must schlep an excruciating twenty or so feet from one entrance to the other. The Wet Spot also has a couple of pool tables, is less noisy than Xposed, and admission is free.

Not content to rest on these laurels, however, Majors opened Private Moments and 2 AM in 2008—two adjoining boutiques that take the Xposed experience to the next level . . . and the one beyond that, too. Private Moments sells sex toys, lingerie, porn, and smoking accessories in a clean, well-lit environment. Just steps away, across the driveway that leads to the Rear Parking, 2 AM dispenses the stuff you can put in the smoking accessories. If you have trouble finding it, just follow your nose. Perhaps this is not what most people have in mind when they think of a medical marijuana facility, but we're hoping that will change over time. We look forward to the day when medical marijuana shops are as common in airports, movie theaters, and sushi bars as they are at strip clubs.

Much of the landscape in this semi-industrial neighborhood has changed over the years. The Sizzler that once stood next door is long gone, but an enormous Costco sign competes for attention just across Canoga. Just a few blocks south, in the building where Flooky's Hot Dogs has changed hands a few times, the art department for one of the world's biggest porno companies used to churn out boxes and catalogs for 8mm Swedish Erotica loops. The surrounding area has traditionally been a bastion of body shops, mechanics, and low-rent apartments for immigrant workers. Little by little, gentrification is changing all that.

The establishments that once occupied the strip mall where Majors is building his empire of pleasure were exceedingly forgettable. Not anymore. The former stripper possesses an entrepreneurial spirit that has already enabled him to commandeer most of the real estate in the Xposed complex in order to create a kind of Disneyland for perverted Peter Pans and other Lost Boys. When he buys out the remaining liquor store and pizza parlor and turns them into a Thai massage parlor and Mexican pharmacy, we'll know the American dream has finally been fulfilled.

# KULTURESCHLOCK

# CRUISIN' FOR XEMU AT THE
# L. RON HUBBARD LIFE EXHIBITION

The L. Ron Hubbard Life
Exhibition
6331 Hollywood Boulevard,
Suite 100
Hollywood
323.960.3511

If you don't know about Scientology by now, you've probably been trapped in ice and stuffed in a volcano.

When this book was first published in 1997, we included an entry about our visit to the L. Ron Hubbard Life Exhibition, and went out of our way not to be excessively snarky lest we raise the ire of the church. What would they want with a couple of clowns like us, anyway? Chump change, right?

Nonetheless, shortly after the book's publication, someone who identified himself as a representative of the L. Ron Hubbard Life Exhibition called one of the authors at his unlisted home number (when pressed, he evaded questions about exactly how he got the number), in order to extend an invitation to meet at their offices so they could "provide us with more data." We politely declined the offer and told them in no uncertain terms never to call the number again. To their credit, they never did, but later we were contacted by an *L.A. Bizarro*–loving librarian who thought we'd be amused to know that the Church of Scientology had launched a phone and fax campaign targeting L.A.'s public libraries in an effort to remove *L.A. Bizarro* from their shelves. At the same time, in New York, some legal go-rounds ensued between our former publisher and COS attorneys who pushed for removal of the page in question from future printings (which the publishing company refused to do). Finally, a representative of the Church camped out in the lobby of the publisher's office every day for the better part of a week in an attempt to get some face time with any honcho who would speak to him. None did, and eventually he gave up and returned to the mothership.

Though our brief, tempered entry on L. Ron Hubbard's lovely museum was superfluff compared with what the *L.A. Times* and *Time* magazine were printing about the Church in the early nineties, we were apparently deemed just threatening enough to warrant what we can only assume is the equivalent of the Blue Plate Special when it comes to COS harassment. Since then, Tom Cruise has come out—about his religious convictions—and the Internet has supplanted print as the new battlefield for the hearts and minds of Scientologists and their opponents. In other words, if we weren't chump change then, we certainly are now.

For the update of this edition, we decided to take some fresh photos of the exterior of the L. Ron Hubbard Life Exhibition, and in doing so, got a reminder about just how suspicious and efficient the COS truly is. The museum sits on a section of Hollywood Boulevard trafficked by plenty of tourists, so we assumed that the COS staff would be somewhat blasé about the presence of shutterbugs on their sidewalk. Silly us. Though it took less than two minutes to park, get out, and snap a handful of photos of their quaint façade on Hollywood Boulevard, that was plenty of time to send their shock troops into action.

As we strolled up to the front of the Hubbard, we noticed a man in a pseudo-security jacket standing at the bus stop. He watched us intently, then pulled out a walkie-talkie and muttered something into it. A few moments later, two church members clad in matching light blue shirts and dark slacks walked by and gave us the eye, then disappeared into a nondescript building across the street. We took a few more photos, returned to the car, and as we pulled into traffic we witnessed the most amazing spectacle: One, two, three, four identically dressed church members (including the two we had just seen) emerged from the building next to the museum, somber-faced and swift of foot. It was obvious from their resolute strides that they were on an important mission: to confront us. Resembling an undead Geek Squad improvising a *Benny Hill* skit, the only thing needed to complete the scene would have been "Yakkity Sax" honking at full volume.

Alas, much to their chagrin we were already gone ... well, sort of. So wrapped up were they in their intruder alert, they failed to notice that we were sitting in a car at the stoplight, about ten feet from the curb, staring right at them. As we watched their animated conversation—which we like to imagine was chock-full of conspiracy theories as to our intentions and whereabouts—it was clear that these good people actually *live* for exactly this kind of confrontational moment. We may have vanished into thin air, but it seemed that we had also made their day.

But wait—was this déjà vu? Hadn't we encountered similar mistrust a few months earlier when we called to ask a few innocent questions about the book shop at their "Celebrity Centre" in Hollywood? The conversation went something like this:

"Good afternoon, Celebrity Centre."

"Hello, can you please tell me if you have a bookstore or gift shop there?"

"Yes ... but why do you want to know?"

"Just curious. What are the hours?"

"Why do you want to know the hours?"

"Because I'd like to come when it's open."

*Paging Mr. Thetan, Mr. Operating Thetan, please come to the white courtesy phone.*

"Yes, but why?"

"To see what kind of things you sell."

"What kind of things are you looking for?"

"I'm not sure. Books? Maybe E-meters? Do you sell those?"

Silence.

"Hello?"

"We don't sell those to the public," she said angrily. Then, "How do you know about E-meters?"

"I've read about them."

"Where?"

"Online."

"Where online? There's a lot of false information online."

"That's why I want to come down there. Go straight to the source, you know? Do I have to be a celebrity?"

"No. How did you find out about the Celebrity Centre?"

"You have a Web site. I'm looking at it right now."

"You're calling from another area code. Why would you come all the way down here?"

"Because . . . that's where you're located."

"What's your name?"

"Why do you want my name?"

"All right, then, where do you live?"

"Look, I just called to find out about the bookstore—"

"What are you hiding?"

"Thank you, ma'am. You've been very helpful."

*Click.*

Though Scientology boasts more than 3,200 churches, missions and groups in 154 countries, it's not surprising that Los Angeles has more Scientology and Dianetics centers than it does Pinkberrys. L. Ron Hubbard established the first Church

of Scientology here in 1954, and Hollywood is a major locus for Hubbard's billion-dollar brainchild and its numerous spin-offs, including the tony Manor Hotel and Celebrity Centre (we love that classy spelling), the "Big Blue Building" on Sunset, the Scientology building on Hollywood Boulevard, the Psychiatry: An Industry of Death Museum, the Citizens Commission on Human Rights, and the L. Ron Hubbard Life Exhibition, which opened in April of 1991 with the customary low-key, humble fanfare that marks any Scientology fête.

Skeptics say that the museum plays fast and loose with the facts of Hubbard's life; but skeptics also say man never landed on the moon and the Holocaust was a hoax, so who are we to question its legitimacy? Hell, we can't even prove El Ron is dead—at least not in the true sense of the word. Scientologists contend that the ruddy-faced sci-fi scribbler eventually reached such a state of enlightenment that he shuffled off this mortal coil because it had become a hindrance to his research—which we can only assume he now continues on the same astral plane occupied by Casper the Friendly Ghost and his friends. In this case, debating the meaning of "dead" with a Scientologist is a lot like debating Bill Clinton on what the meaning of the word "is" is.

If one thing can be said about the COS, they're certainly not cheap, at least when it comes to self-promotion. It's obvious that no expense was spared in putting together the Hubbard. Unlike the equally bombastic Psychiatry: An Industry of Death Museum at the nearby Citizens Commission on Human Rights, visitors at the Hubbard are not allowed to roam freely through the more than thirty multimedia presentations and displays (one of which includes the humble typewriter on which the Commodore, as Hubbard liked to be called, wrote the first edition of *Dianetics*). Appointments for the guided tour are encouraged, but walk-ins are also welcome. Depending on how inquisitive your group is—and how many people want to fiddle with the E-meter display—the tour can take anywhere from half an hour to ninety minutes.

This desire to personally usher you through the Hubbard appears to serve two purposes: (1) to keep an eye on you. Never known for its lax security measures, the COS has clamped down ever tighter in light of the war being waged against it by the group that calls itself Anonymous: There are more rent-a-cops lurking about than soldiers at the Tel Aviv airport. And (2) being a captive audience facilitates the museum's goal of deifying its founder. You will learn about El Ron and you will like it. No fast-forwarding.

The museum is packed with a wealth of images and artifacts from Hubbard's life, yet the man himself—on audio or video—is conspicuously absent from the exhibit until almost the end of the tour. Whether this is to maintain an air of mystery about Hubbard or to avoid exposing visitors to what some might call his overbearing demeanor, we can't be sure.

If you know anything about Scientology, you've probably formed an opinion. If you're a neophyte, the Hubbard will provide you with a pair of rose-colored glasses through which to view its fearless leader. Love him or hate him, Hubbard is an undeniably fascinating character whose impact on the cultural landscape of Los Angeles can't be underestimated. So what if the museum omits the less-than-legal escapades from El Ron's life? If you've ever spent a few yawn-filled hours down the street at Ripley's or the Wax Museum, then you owe it to yourself to drop by the Hubbard and see what real showmanship is all about. Yes, those crappy tourist traps can be guilty pleasures in their own right, but so can this lavish tribute to a man who is either the most important prophet since Jesus Christ or a twentieth-century snake oil salesman out to prove P. T. Barnum right. You decide.

## AN EXERCISE IN COMPETITIVE TEDIUM:

# MEDIEVAL TIMES VS. PIRATE'S DINNER ADVENTURE

Medieval Times Dinner and
Tournament
7662 Beach Boulevard
Buena Park
888.WE.JOUST
www.medievaltimes.com

Pirate's Dinner Adventure
7600 Beach Boulevard
Buena Park
866.439.2469
www.piratesdinneradventure.
com

In addition to an overcooked meal and a lot of overpriced tchotchkes, Medieval Times and Pirate's Dinner Adventure both offer a themed bout, where patrons are not only encouraged but in fact required to band together in blind solidarity for their assigned combatant, cued to cheer for this pirate or that, the green knight or the blue, all depending of course on the color-coded section in which you happen to be seated.

Aside from their respective themes, the two appear nearly identical with regard to their scale, business model, cuisine, performance spectacles, sales tactics, and historical liberties. But there are differences to consider before booking your evening of adventure, be it at sea or in the jousting arena. So we've decided to pit the two against one another, knights against pirates, one Buena Park behemoth against the other in a no-holds-barred, winner-take-all competition. Best of all, it will not be necessary for you to don a paper crown or buy a pirate bandana to partici-pate. We will, however, expect you to cheer when cued, so pay attention.

As your arbiters of culture, we'll declare our victor among these fight-focused family-friendly dinner establishments not by swords, cannon balls, jousting rods, or pistols, but by an arbitrary and unscientific evaluation of the unique properties that distin-guish each, using a simple point system.

You might be quick to assume that a medieval-themed din-ner attraction centered solely around a live jousting tournament may be somewhat of a rarity, but you'd be wrong. You can find

Medieval Times as far north as Toronto and as far south as Dallas, as far east as Lyndhurst, New Jersey, and as far west as our own backyard. So just in terms of real estate holdings alone Medieval Times already has a lead over Pirate's Dinner Adventure, which touts only two measly locations: one in Buena Park, the other in Orlando. However, pirate shit has really taken off over the past few years. In fact it's practically been a bull market of late, and if the stock exchange sold shares in disposable pop culture, we'd be on the horn to our broker right now. "Get us five hundred shares of pirate trend *posthaste*!" we'd bark, while keeping a close eye on Johnny Depp's next career move.

*Is that a vaginal pear in your pocket or are you just happy to see me?*

With both Pirate's Dinner Adventure and Medieval Times the adventure starts with a drive to the epicenter of Orange County themedom, Buena Park (-10 points for each). And with both, the magic begins as soon as you step through the doors, with a photo op in which you have no say. At Medieval Times, a costumed staff member beams "Welcome to our castle!" before slamming a paper crown on your head and seeing that you file into line for your medieval moment with the castle's king and queen, later delivered to you as a digital print in a paper frame should you produce the cash. At Pirate's Dinner Adventure, we were not given any costuming, paper or otherwise, and posed only with a single pirate aiming a flintlock pistol, who wasn't even wearing an eye patch (-5 points). At neither Medieval Times or Pirate's Dinner Adventure does anyone ever actually ask to take your picture; they simply blast a flashbulb in your face and return later to try and peddle some overpriced item bearing your startled mug.

Although our welcome at Pirate's Dinner Adventure left us somewhat underwhelmed, we were given a disclaimer forewarning us of stage explosions and atmospheric fog (+5 points), and the possibility of the "artists" interacting with "willing participants" (-10 points). Ushered into an elaborate seventeenth-century governor's mansion-cum-saloon, we were immediately treated to an "appetizer buffet" of cheese cubes, meat cubes, and crackers, plus a difficult-to-locate shrimp cocktail bar, as well as hot egg rolls—but only if you're quick enough to flag down a hostess. While the patrons outnumbered the cabaret-style seating nearly four to one, we did have access to a full bar with the option of a drink served in a crudely carved keepsake coconut shell fashioned to look like the head of a pirate (+4 points). However, once the town crier took the stage, delivering our tedious prologue to the preshow—and reminding us twice about the gift shop—a double Grey Goose on the rocks suddenly seemed more necessary than a fruity drink in a coconut. The vodka set us back $14.50, before tip, and was served in a disposable plastic cup (-5 points). A pirate adventure, indeed.

At Medieval Times, it's all about the jousting arena, which reeks faintly of horse piss (+10 points). The theater seating is in the round, at long tables, divided into six different color-coordinated sections which correspond with your color-coded crown: only the colorblind and those short on cash will have trouble at Medieval Times. Shortly after being seated, you're met with another blast from the castle's paparazzi, and much later in the evening you'll find yourself paying astronomical sums of money for these commemorative photos, just so that a picture of you wearing a Medieval Times paper crown doesn't fall into the wrong hands somewhere down the road. Anyone interested in pursuing a career in politics take note.

"Hi! My name is Greg, I'll be your slave tonight," chirps a teenaged food server in medieval costume. Though agile and well-trained, it should be noted that our slave never once begged for us to shit in his mouth, flog him with a cat-o'-nine-tails, or affix alligator clamps to his nipples. The services provided by the slaves at Medieval Times are limited to food, it seems, because Greg was not receptive to any of our suggestions, creative and consensual as they may have been. Being offered a slave of any gender is titillating nonetheless, particularly when it's an Orange County youth (+5 points). As the slaves began slinging forth steaming bowls of "Dragon Soup" from a large bucket, schlock hawkers peddling everything from souvenir pennants to electric roses pass your table, in an attempt to joust as much cash as possible from your pockets before the tournament begins. Your wallet never seems to get cold at Medieval Times.

At Pirate's Dinner Adventure we weren't provided with a slave but we were given "Rando," the resident town drunk, who plays off the town crier like a seventeenth-century warm-up comic (-15 points). Rando is also responsible for goading many of the aforementioned "willing participants" to take the stage (-10 points). Our word of advice for those who never asked for an ad hoc career in show business: should you be approached to take

the stage by Rando or any other artist on the Pirate's payroll, we found that simply looking them straight in the eye and deadpanning, "Please don't touch my rash" will ensure your immediate release from any performance duties for the rest of the evening.

To rousing music, dramatic lighting effects, and aerial acrobatics, we were introduced to the Royal Highness of something or other and given too much expository information concerning Captain Sebastian Black, a golden gypsy, a magic box, and an emerald-studded prosthetic or some such rot we were now too drunk to follow. But

# THE MOOSE THAT ROARED

For many of us who grew up in the sixties, Jay Ward was something of a living god. His weird sense of humor skewered popular culture, took cartoons to a brainier level, and brought us not only Rocky and Bullwinkle, but Sherman and Peabody, George of the Jungle, Super Chicken, and "Fractured Fairy Tales," among others. Alas, Ward's wacky gift shop, the Dudley Do-Right Emporium, with its once-familiar zigzag roofline, has gone the way of all things, having been transmogrified into the ubiquitous taco stand and parking lot. Just around the bend, in front of a dog grooming place that once housed Ward's offices, stands the statue of Bullwinkle J. Moose and Rocky the Flying Squirrel that was unveiled on September 24, 1961, to welcome *The Bullwinkle Show* to the NBC lineup. Next time you're in the neighborhood, stop by and pay homage to the agoraphobic genius without whom Spongebob Squarepants would never have been able to make obscure references to Man Ray.

**Bullwinkle Statue / 8218 Sunset Boulevard / Los Angeles**

to our great relief the preshow was finally underway, and amid cries that "We've been Shanghaied!" our pirates stormed the room. Swinging from ropes and climbing from the dark recesses of the saloon, they took the stage, popping pistols and filling the room with cap gun smell (+5 points). They captured the golden gypsy, dry humped the princess (+10 points), and then, after jokes about being a "captive audience," the real adventure began. The town crier instructed us to check the color of our "passports" before boarding the ship—but not before we were reminded once more about the gift shop—as we were funneled like cattle into our color-coded seating sections which smack of the Medieval Times template: raked, on three sides, at long counters, and with the very same novelty peddlers making the rounds (do we sense a parent corporation at work here?). At center stage was the deck of an elaborate pirate ship with a mast reaching a good four stories, centered in a sea of real water (+5 points). Soon after we were seated, our food was served from chafing carts by an adorable waitress who expressed sincere enthusiasm that anyone

was seated in her section (turnout was slim). "Food," however, is a relative term here, seeing that we're in a pirate-themed dinner show in Buena Park (-10 points).

Medieval Times has a preshow too, and evidently the Middle Ages have come a long way since the Middle Ages. Here, the black plague has been replaced with a psychedelic light show (+15 points), fluffing us good for our "evening of spectacular pageantry." The audience is treated to a second-rate LSD trip via the rousing colored spots and freaked-out light filters swirling across the dirt floor of the jousting arena and onto the faces of bedazzled audience members. After that, the preshow gets iffy unless you're into birds of prey; some chick brings out a falcon and has it fly around the arena before attacking a chunk of raw meat she's been swinging around on a leather strap. Some horses prance around and do fancy kicks in unnatural ways (+5 points). There's some kind of story going on and a lot of yammering between the king and the knights, but in spite of the jousting, the sword fights, and the stunts, nothing grabs the audience's attention like when a horse takes a big dump in the arena, which eventually gets stomped over by every other horse in the arena. But these are the days of the Spanish Inquisition, before vaudevillians had coined the phrase "never work with children or animals." Try eating dinner with your fingers as you see the rectum of an Andalusian stallion dilate and spill forth ten or fifteen pounds of road apples (+15 points). "*Slave, bring us another basted potato!*"

Though the "tournament" is staged much like a WWF wrestling match, the audience is either so young, so drunk, or so ignorant that they actually scream and cheer for "their" knight (who is also color-coded to your crown and seating assignment, just like the pirates up the street) throughout the competition. Full-grown adults actually leap from their chairs screaming "Go Blue Knight!!" and "Kill 'em Green!" as if there's really some question about who might win. Mind you, these are the same people who elect the leader of the free world. Medieval Times is not a good place to restore your faith in collective American IQ. Actually, the same could be said for much of Orange County.

Best to put your palate on shore leave before eating at Pirate's Dinner Adventure. While the free-flowing flat Coke was refreshing, our overcooked chicken, overcooked shrimp, and our overcooked pencil eraser–sized scallops served alongside our overcooked rice had us wondering why, if we were on a fucking ship, was good seafood so damn hard to come by?! Our salad dressing was served in a foil-capped plastic cup; peeling away the lid induced a pang of nostalgia for the days when airlines used to serve dinners exactly like this. The pirate show was fast-paced, peppered with song (-15 points), and hit occasional crescendos of the TV game show variety, with "willing" audience members (who at this point had actually been costumed, with more of their time spent working on the show than watching it) throwing bags of loot to crow's nest–perched pirates in a down-to-the-minute contest for something, and racing around the ship in electric-powered boats to be the first to reach somewhere or whatever. We just wanted to get the explosions and the atmospheric fog we'd been promised. Shortly there-after shirtless pirates took to the trampoline (there was a trampoline on deck), shifting the mood of the

performance from a family-friendly theme restaurant to some-thing more like an evening at Chippendale's. Our first indication that the evening was nearing its end came when our cute server slopped up a dish of low-grade ice cream drizzled with choco-late-flavored corn syrup paired with a gelatinous mess of apple pie filing littered with pieces of broken crust. Dessert (-5 points).

More aerial acrobatics, some pirate-tinged soft rock, and many rousing crescendos indicating that just maybe this show would soon be over proved false. Rifles were passed out to the youngest members of the audience (+10 points), cannon balls splashed the front rows (+5 points), wenches were traded like livestock, and the pirate captain actually hit a woman across the face (+5 points). Coffee was served. Finally, now feeling sea-weary and mentally exhausted—and our vodka having long since worn off—our evening of adventure concluded with Coffee-mate and the recitation of a pirate's oath before we were allowed to exit, to the strains of the Village People's "YMCA" (-15 points).

Medieval Times wastes no expense on dessert either. Right about the point in the performance where the victorious knight chooses his Queen of Love and Beauty or something like that (we stopped paying attention after the light show) your slave will serve dessert: a medieval Pop-Tart and the Kingdom's most burnt cup of coffee. The photo wenches then peddle the final portrait of the evening, plucking the last few bills from your exhausted wallet. After clearing the auditorium, guests are invited to the "Knight Club" for dancing and cocktails, and to meet "your" Knight in person. "Get an autograph from YOUR KNIGHT, take a picture with YOUR KNIGHT, do whatever you want to do with YOUR KNIGHT," the DJ keeps chanting like a mantra, and after spending as much money as you will undoubtedly have by that point you'll start feeling like that damn knight really does belong to you. As the club spins an odd assortment of tunes, from Blondie's "Call Me" to vintage polka numbers to "Funky Town,"

Teva-sandaled, fanny-packed tourists take to the dance floor and kids start dropping like flies on the blue vinyl booths. Meanwhile, the Knights have changed into their après-jousting attire and make themselves available at the bar, fluffing their long, rock 'n' roll hair like a bunch of tenth-century gigolos, eager to chat up the legal-aged PYTs on summer vacation. Later you can see these same girls engrossed in intimate conversation with their Knight, now in his street clothes, outside the employee entrance of the castle at the north side of the parking lot. Hot (+15 points).

You're also encouraged to spend lots of time in the Medieval Times gift shop, which is nearly as big as the arena and features a sword concession, Medieval Times DVDs, postcards, mugs, and ashtrays, plus all the standard vendibles you'd expect to find at the Renaissance Pleasure Faire: pewter miniatures, court jester hats, crystal balls, et al. The gift shop also gives you a privileged peek at the Medieval Times equine collection, caged on the other side of a plate glass window. You may also take a spin through their Museum of Torture. It's not free, of course, but you get a crash course in medieval S & M over an array of gadgets and equipment that even the Pleasure Chest doesn't stock, like the fallbret, the Judas cradle, and the rectal/vaginal pear (+15 points). Hang around that employee entrance and you just might find yourself a willing slave.

Upon our final exit from the Pirate's Dinner Adventure auditorium, however, the very same room that once played host to the Governor's Ball was now the loneliest of dance floors. Colored lights playing upon the empty parquet, thumping music calling—almost begging—for the patrons filing past, headed straight for the exit.

We saw no pirates scoring pussy in the parking lot, nor were they grabbing purses or stealing jewelry from Dinner Adventure patrons en route to their cars, which would have been more authentic. We'd expect some degree of randiness from a pirate and these blokes seemed downright flaccid (-10 points).

One final point to consider: the Pirate's Dinner Adventure's raven-haired wench kicked ass over Medieval Time's pasty queen (+15 for the pirates).

So, who's the real winner? Which relentlessly cloying Buena Park dinner destination gets the *L.A. Bizarro* crown? Will it be Medieval Times? The Pirate's Dinner Adventure? Cheer louder, we can't fucking hear you. And wave those goddamn flags.

Just like the combat staged at both establishments, there was never really any question about our outcome. The victor in *L.A. Bizarro*'s contest of theme tedium: Medieval Times!!! Cheer louder. And you're not leaving this auditorium until we say it's okay to go.

Medieval Times is sexier for sure, but it's not just because of the torture museum, the parking lot hookups, and the horse dung dumped over dinner. It's because the Medieval Times

# GO ASK ALICE

*Sung to the tune of the* Brady Bunch *theme*:

Here's the story,
Of a house named Brady,
That doesn't really have a top floor window.
The residents of which,
Don't want you gawking,
Leave them the hell alone.

**The Brady Bunch house / 11222 Dilling Street / Studio City**

public relations office—unbeknownst to our contest—answered our media inquiry within twenty-four hours, gave us lots of cool shots to use in this book, and offered us comp tickets anytime we wanted. We followed up at least twice with Pirate's Dinner Adventure, however, and they—perhaps wisely—never responded, thank you very much.

And on our stage, that's what a fair contest is all about.

## PAYING HOMAGE TO THE HARDEST WORKING WOMAN IN SHOW BUSINESS,

# ANGELYNE

She's the muse of the Southland, the undisputed enigma of Hollywood. She's the head-turning, eyebrow-raising target of both pathological adoration and merciless mudslinging. She's our only-in-Los Angeles phenomenon, Angelyne.

Her age, and the puzzling objectives of her longtime benefactor may remain Hollywood's two best-kept secrets. An elusive and ever-changing account of her past (including a driver's license bearing the improbable surname "L'lyne"), no less her present, keep the details of her real life lost in a murky mystery on par with the Lindbergh Baby.

Yeah, maybe she puts more than her fair share of greenhouse gases into the atmosphere, but to what better end? Angelyne is

Angelyne Fan Club
P.O. Box 3864
Beverly Hills, 90212
310.285.9399
www.angelynepink.com

everything wonderful about L.A.: She drives an ostentatious car, wears sunglasses indoors, uses lots of hair product, and sports a wardrobe that consists almost exclusively of spandex and vinyl. And how many other people accessorize with marabou during the day?

However, her work has been subject to gross misinterpretation, which has been the unfortunate downside of her twenty-five-plus-year career. People generally assume Angelyne aspires to be something while entirely missing what she is. Angelyne has only ever aspired to be Angelyne, and no one can deny that she's done an excellent job. Like a Christo with cleavage, she gives the Los Angeles landscape some color, a shot of whimsy, and a little mystique. In a city where we endure a relentless daily onslaught of in-our-face advertising, isn't it nothing short of a godsend to have a few billboards around town that aren't dictating unattainable standards in order to sell us a product we don't need? Angelyne is simply there to say hi and sprinkle her pixie dust. A harmless bit of cheesecake. A peroxided Betty Boopish pituitary case who cares enough to keep L.A. from taking itself too seriously.

Angelyne should be L.A.'s goodwill ambassador. She should be grand marshall of the Rose Parade. She should have a street named after her like L. Ron Hubbard. At the very least, the mayor should present her with a key to the city, because we can't imagine a Los Angeles without her.

# WHERE THE FANTASY AND FICUS COLLIDE:
## THE LOS ANGELES COUNTY
# ARBORETUM

Sometimes—oftentimes—the best places to be in L.A. are the places which allow you to forget that you're in this godforsaken city altogether. Were it not for the roar of the 210 Freeway audible from virtually every corner of its 127 acres, the Los Angeles County Arboretum in Arcadia could be one of those places.

If the Arboretum and Huntington Gardens were sisters, the Arboretum would be the sister who didn't marry as well. She lives close to the freeway. She's beautiful for sure—don't get us wrong—and we dig her jungle big time. Her hot, moist green-house smells divine, and she's also got nearly friendly peacocks and aggressive ducks roaming her grounds. Plus there's an out-of-this-world *Osmanthus Fragrans* growing next to her public restrooms that we just can't get enough of. Take a whiff when it's in bloom and tell us that we're wrong.

But the real star of the Arboretum, upstaging the carnivorous plants and the almost-approachable peacocks, is the Lilliputian Frenchman who immortalized the property in the opening sequence of the hit television show *Fantasy Island*. Perched in the bell tower of the Arboretum's turn-of-the-century Queen Anne cottage, Hervé Villechaize became an instant icon after forcing his underdeveloped lungs to give it their show business best when shouting *"The plane! The plane!"*

Never was there a more appropriate resident for Fantasy Island than Hervé. Standing only three feet eleven inches tall and pretty much unintelligible for the French accent, he came to New York from Europe on his own just barely out of his teens, taught himself English by watching television, and soon set his sights on an acting career. Born during the Nazi occupation, he was destined to be the next Lautrec, studying as a painter at the prestigious Beaux-Arts School in Paris. But after arriving in New York he traded his paint-brush for the footlights, and for the next decade or so played a variety of characters in avant-garde film and off-Broadway theater. His breakthrough role came as Nick Nack, the sidekick to Christopher Lee in the early seventies Bond film *The Man with the Golden Gun*, but it was four years later, 1978, that was to be the year of Hervé. As *Fantasy Island* first warmed television

Los Angeles County Arboretum and Botanic Garden
301 North Baldwin Avenue
Arcadia
626.821.3222
www.arboretum.org

## Viva Hervé!

screens across the country, Villechaize became an overnight sensation, a household name, a millionaire, and eventually a less-than-busy actor after being axed over a salary dispute. Appearances on *Hee Haw*, *The Larry Sanders Show*, and commercials for Dunkin' Donuts and Coors followed.

Trophy wives, security paranoia, handguns, horse ranches, and high living aren't perks reserved only for Hollywood stars of normal adult height. Hervé had it all. His North Hollywood home welcomed visitors with signs bearing the messages "Have Gun Will Shoot" and "If You're Here at Night, You'll Be Found Dead in the Morning." And the feisty Frenchman wasn't all talk, reportedly once holding his agent at gunpoint in a booth at a Los Angeles restaurant. He was also accused by his second (and last) wife of shoving her into a fireplace and firing a pistol in her direction. He also had his share of run-ins with the law, being arrested and fined in the eighties for bringing a loaded handgun into a hospital.

By the early nineties, the fantasy was nearly over. After decades of health complications, by age fifty Hervé was taking upwards of thirty different medications just to stay alive. Weighing a mere sixty pounds and with only one working lung, an enlarged heart, gallbladder trouble, gut-wrenching ulcers, gastritis, a spastic colon, rotting teeth, and a battle with pneumonia that nearly killed him, he secretly began making plans for a simple suicide.

After a night out with his five-foot-nine live-in girlfriend of four years (who sported a near life-sized Tattoo tattoo across her back as a tribute to her love), he returned home, waited for his inked-up miss to fall asleep, then quietly set to work. Hervé disconnected the phone lines, employed a cassette recorder to ensure there would be no question of foul play, grabbed two pillows to help muffle the gunfire (a little misguided perhaps, but thoughtful), and—as he stated in his tape-recorded farewell—stepped outside to the back patio because it would be "less messy" (the carpets had just been cleaned). He then managed to fire not one, but three shots from two guns (he had a backup, no less) into his own chest. This from a man who weighed only sixty pounds and could barely breathe.

Unfortunately, the results weren't as instantaneous as Hervé had hoped; his final words on the tape were "Well, I guess now I just wait. . . . "

He left his body to UCLA for dwarfism research, with orders to be cremated thereafter; he insisted upon no funeral, and requested that his ashes be scattered at sea. That's class. Ah, the French.

In a suicide note which was discovered shortly after he was pronounced dead at 4:00 AM on September 4, 1993, Hervé laid it down for anyone in doubt: "I love everybody. No one is to blame. I'm just tired of the struggle."

We hear ya, man.

## GETTING LOST IN THE SURREAL WORLD OF THE BOB BAKER

# MARIONETTE THEATER

Just because you've lost your baby teeth doesn't mean you're too old for a visit to the oldest operating marionette theater in the country. No, we're not talking about the Oval Office, we're talking about a good old-fashioned Bob Baker mental holiday.

You never know what you'll find tucked away under a freeway overpass or scattered on the outskirts of downtown Los Angeles. Sure, we've got disenfranchised youth, ethnic ghettos, and public parks teeming with the homeless. But we've also got slithering sequined serpents, talking birthday cakes, flying fluorescent witches, and self-plucking fiddles—singing a program of vintage show tunes and timeless novelty songs six days a week, no less.

In this converted warehouse, the Bob Baker Marionette Theater sets the scene for the happy childhood you never had. The walls are striped like a gaily wrapped birthday gift and draped generously with glittering garlands, hulking Mylar bows, supersized lollipops, and strands of twinkling lights. A rainbow of spotlights and motorized color wheels wash the otherwise dimly lit room with a dreamy, candy-coated glow, while orchestrated circus tunes play from the two large speakers positioned at either side of the stage topped with life-sized toy soldiers (the nice kind like at Christmas, not the ones that wear camo and torment detainees).

The center of the room is kept clear, with seating on three sides. Being *cabaret marionettes*, these puppets aren't limited to the confines of the boxed stage most people associate with puppet shows, and roam freely on the stage floor—with the aid of the puppeteer of course—working the room like a troupe of hungry lap dancers. Audience members are encouraged to get comfortable on the plush red carpet, and although there are folding chairs available for those with stiff hips, floor seating puts you at eye-level with the marionettes (some of which are as tall as four feet) and cheek-by-jowl with children young enough to be your own. The child-heavy audience is easier to take than one might expect, generally more delightful and better behaved than

Bob Baker Marionette
Theater
1345 West First Street
Los Angeles
213.250.9995
www.bobbakermarionettes.
com

most adults, and only once did we find it necessary to smack one upside the head.

Shows change seasonally and it's impossible to stumble upon a flop. With forty-plus years behind them, the productions are time-tested and airtight. The marionettes themselves are exquisite, some beautifully refurbished (many are as old as the theater), and do—in spite of your own disbelief—take on lives of their own.

After the curtain call, guests are invited into the event room for ice cream and refreshments, sorta like an afterparty without the rock stars, groupies, and free-flowing liquor. There's also a counter where you can purchase super-cool Bob Baker Marionette Theater patches and buttons, as well as hand puppets, marionettes, toys, and novelties.

If you're looking for a great place to take your child—or to get in touch with your inner child—but feel some degree of trepidation when presented with the idea of a puppet show, let the folks at the Bob Baker Marionette Theater tune you in, turn you on, and show you where it's at.

Because when you get right down to it, we're all puppets in one way or another, aren't we?

## SMILE, YOU'RE IN

# CAMERA OBSCURA!

Camera Obscura
Senior Recreation Center
Pacific Palisades Park
1450 Ocean Avenue
Santa Monica
310.458.8644

You young whippersnappers may be surprised by how many fun things there are to do at the Senior Recreation Center in Palisades Park—and we're not just talking about tinkling in your pants, either! Play a spirited game of canasta, work up a sweat on the shuffleboard court, or just drool yourself to sleep on one of the benches that overlook the Santa Monica beach. And if you're feeling particularly adventurous (and your goiter isn't acting up), turn in your driver's license for the key that opens the door to the Camera Obscura.

Located up a flight of stairs just inside the center, the Camera Obscura (Latin for "darkened chamber") is more than just a convenient make-out spot for octogenarians. It's a state-of-the-art entertainment center from the turn of the last century, a visual thrill unlike anything you've ever experienced— or *smelled*, for that matter, thanks to the proximity of the restrooms and an elderly population apparently hell-bent on eating asparagus three times a day. Okay, we're slightly exaggerating the odor, and the small, stuffy room is actually kind of romantic in a *Bridge on the River Kwai* hotbox kind of way, so don't let us scare you off. In fact, the center boasts some of friendliest oldsters just this side of the pearly gates, and we encourage you to bring the whole family so they can enjoy that rarest of opportunities, the chance to inter-act with real live senior citizens. Think of it as a human petting zoo where the animals wear hearing aids.

Great, you say, but what's a camera obscura? Glad you asked. Basically, the building functions as a giant pinhole camera, the principles of which were first observed by the Chinese philosopher Mozi and later elaborated on by Aristotle (the original, not the Onassis). The first camera obscura was built sometime around the tenth century by Arab scientist Abu Ali Al-Hasan Ibn al-Haitham, who would have been considered an Iraqi if the need to cobble together a puppet state in order to exploit its oil reserves had existed a thousand years ago. The term "camera obscura" was itself first coined by noted mathematician, astronomer, and donkey-punch enthusiast, Johannes Kepler, who built his own camera obscura in a tent. As tourist attractions, camerae obscurae were wildly popular around the globe in the late nineteenth and early twentieth centuries. Now it's just something to do for free that beats the hell out of watching anything with Dane Cook in it.

Though the mechanics on all camerae obscurae are essentially the same, the one in Santa Monica works something like this: On the roof, set over a small hole in the ceiling of the room, is a rotating metal turret that contains an angled mirror. An opening on the side of the turret allows light to hit the mirror, which then reflects the image downward through a convex lens onto the large white disk located on the floor of the room. The disk is also angled at 45 degrees, and placed at the proper focal length to receive the scene coming through the lens in crisp focus. In this case, the scene is a 360-degree view of Santa Monica, which the viewer can pan with the skipper's wheel mounted in front of the disk. You'll never find the bumper-to-bumper traffic on Ocean Boulevard as

*More fun than a barrel with a dead monkey in it.*

captivating as it is inside the Camera Obscura. Unfortunately, the effect doesn't work unless the room's lights are off, and overcast or rainy days will provide less than spectacular images. To spice up the experience on such gloomy days, we recommend hiding under the projection disk, then leaping out and screaming at the next set of unsuspecting suckers who walk in. Imagine the madcap laughs you'll share with perfect strangers!

As if to rain on the Camera Obscura's parade, a newer camera obscura was built in 2006 at the Griffith Park Observatory. We recommend boycotting it. We don't know who the hell those people think they are, but they should be content with their utterly mesmerizing cloud and spark chambers and leave the poor old Camera Obscura alone.

Other than the fact that the first Santa Monica Camera Obscura was built on the beach around 1900, and sometime later relocated to its current spot where it was given a facelift in 1955, that's basically it for Santa Monica's quaint tourist oddity . . . almost. We've saved the best for last: the sign on the outside of the building. The silhouette of the camera and tripod combined with the vintage script font is, in our humble opinions, one of L.A.'s greatest unappreciated works of art. It's as much of a joy to behold as the optical illusion within.

So pay a visit to one of L.A.'s most *obscure* (pun intended) tourist attractions, and on your way out, why not stop for a cup of tea and a few Celebrex with some of the seniors who frequent the center? Don't worry, they don't bite. They lost their teeth a long time ago.

## AN EVENING OF EXOTIC DANCING WITHOUT A POLE AT

# EL CID

El Cid
4212 West Sunset Boulevard
Hollywood
213.668.0318
www.elcidla.com

Just off the edge of a less savory stretch of Sunset Boulevard toward the new frontier of the exponentially gentrified Silver Lake, El Cid's austere façade may not immediately entice. Venture beneath the awning and down El Cid's oblique brick stairways, however, past the blooming flowers and trickling fountains of its sunken multi-leveled courtyard, and *aqui tienes!* There you are, right back in the 1500s, in the midst of "an authentic replica of a Sixteenth-century Spanish Tavern," or so their menu claims.

Should key terms like "replica," "Sixteenth-century," and "Spanish" send you into a cold sweat by inducing nasty flashbacks of Buena Park, rest assured that El Cid does not pick up where Medieval Times leaves off. You're in for anachronistic adventure nonetheless, though you will not be required to cheer for your favorite color-coded flamenco dancer or eat with your hands—nor will you be held prisoner for three-and-a-half hours.

The building housing the histrionic elegance of this restaurant and bar was, as the story goes, originally the site of an early movie studio built by D. W. Griffith at the turn of the last century, and later served as the screening location for his racist epic *Birth of a Nation*. El Cid had a second incarnation as a cabaret in the 1950s, and since 1961 exists as it is today: a dinner-and-flamenco thrill ride, five nights a week.

For whom doesn't the jackhammer rat-tat-tat of castanets, the stomping of heels, and the syncopated hand-claps by a troupe of feisty flamenco dancers inspire? You can opt out of dinner with a show-only price of $25 (and two-drink minimum), but if you've bothered to come all the way back to the sixteenth century, you might as well eat something, and the fusion menu features more than one might expect from an authentic replica of a Sixteenth-century Spanish Tavern. You can graze your way through clams, fried manchego, empanadas, or seared tuna with nearly twenty tapas selections, or choose from their entrée list, which, at an all-inclusive $35, is easily L.A.'s best bet for your dinner-and-entertainment buck.

If flamenco's not your bag, no reason to head elsewhere for an evening's entertainment. El Cid takes artistic liberties with its recreation of the sixteenth century, offering nights of burlesque, stand-up, and rockabilly, as well as "The Super Sexy Show" on first and third Thursdays.

You're in good company here. This little-celebrated Hollywood landmark has played host to an eclectic list of luminaries, from Leonard Nimoy to Marlon Brando. Bette, Lana, and even Raquel nibbled paella here, too; you'll probably work into this motley equation somewhere between David Bowie and Fonzie. Get there early and dig the scene; you'll want time for dinner and drinks, and you'll need to peruse the 8 × 10 glossies of El Cid's roster of performers posted in the lobby, peek into the curio cabinets filled with flamencoabilia, hang at the bar, and wander the balcony. Early arrival will also ensure a ringside table, but don't sit too close. The whipping of flamenco skirts and projectile perspiration could make for an unsavory experience if you're in the wrong line of trajectory. Or the best line of trajectory, depending on what you're into.

The timing of the flamenco show is impeccable: It lasts almost a full hour and concludes just when all that clicking and tapping starts to work your last raw nerve.

*Is that a pair of castanets in your pocket or are you just happy to see me?*

# SAVORING THE EXQUISITE
# PROPAGANDA OF THE
# NIXON AND REAGAN
# LIBRARIES

Richard Nixon Presidential
Library and Birthplace
18001 Yorba Linda Boulevard
Yorba Linda
714.993.3393
www.nixon.archives.gov
(National Archives)
nixonlibraryfoundation.org
(Nixon Library Foundation)

The Ronald Reagan
Presidential Library and
Center For Public Affairs
40 Presidential Drive
Simi Valley
805.522.8444
www.reaganlibrary.com

Politics is about luck and personality, and Richard Nixon was short on both. That's why, deep down, the poor bastard must have truly despised Ronald Reagan.

Both were Republicans who launched their political careers in California. Both built their reputations by imagining commies hiding under every bed in America. Both enjoyed landslide reelections into their second presidential terms. Both surrounded themselves with weasels who brought scandal to the White House—and that's where the similarities end because only one of them got away with it.

Whereas Nixon was an astute politician burdened with a perpetually sweaty upper lip and the aura of a necrophiliac embalmer, Reagan was a B-actor blessed with the golly-gee ability to deliver the most preposterous right-wing jingoism as if it were written by Eugene O'Neill. In SAT lingo, Iran-contra is to Watergate as rape is to jaywalking, yet it was Nixon who suffered the singular, ignominious shame of having to resign the presidency he had fought his entire life to attain, while Reagan bumbled his way to presidential glory by sleepwalking through history and always hitting his mark. In short, Reagan is the Teflon yin to Nixon's shit-magnet yang, which may explain why the Gipper ended up with a presidential library that in some ways makes Nixon's look like a Der Wienerschnitzel by comparison.

Separated by two county lines, the Nixon and Reagan libraries stand as architectural symbols of the men they enshrine. Despite being stuck in the ho-hum hinterland of the OC, the Nixon Library at first glance seems impressive enough for a president who was ridden out of Washington on a rail. After all, it has a big ol' helicopter, a self-effacing gift shop, and plenty of ample parking. Yet it's not until you've driven up the seemingly endless road that leads to Reagan's sprawling domain atop the Simi Hills that you begin to truly comprehend the difference between the legacies of these two presidents. With its Mission Revival architecture, sweeping vistas, and bigger-than-life exhibits, the Reagan

Library is at once casual and majestic, reeking a relaxed grandeur with effortless self-confidence. Much like Reagan himself, the place has a faint whiff of phoniness that's overshadowed by the onslaught of can-do bravado and all-American magnificence that greets you from the get-go. Likewise, the Nixon library tries hard to make you like it, but ultimately comes off as stiff, sterile, and slightly uncomfortable. Remind you of anybody?

"The Richard Nixon Presidential Library, Birthplace, Garden, Gravesite, Gift Shop, and Café" would be a more apt name for this all-encompassing tribute to our dead thirty-seventh president, located in fragrant Yorba Linda. For sixteen years the institution was run entirely by a private organization of friends and loyalists, the Nixon Library Foundation, making it the only presidential library to be operated without taxpayers' funds. At first blush that may seem a magnanimous gesture until one considers that it was also the only presidential library that contained no original presidential papers. A 1974 law ensured that Nixon's White House records would remain in Washington lest the former president be allowed the opportunity to destroy even more evidence of his wrongdoings. Without federal oversight, the privately funded library had little obligation to the whole truth and nothing but the truth, and was able to engage in the kind of hagiography that put other presidential libraries to shame, often sacrificing full disclosure in an effort to reshape Nixon's legacy. Indeed, the museum's first director, conservative wing nut Hugh Hewitt, made it clear that only Nixon-friendly researchers would be welcome at the library. He later changed his mind, presumably after someone pointed out that he was being a total asshole.

All that changed in 2006 when the facility agreed, somewhat reluctantly, to be operated in part by the National Archives, which also oversees eleven other presidential libraries. It was a move advocated by presidential daughter and Obama supporter Julie Nixon Eisenhower, who realized her father's library was anything but presidential without his White House papers— for good or ill. She succeeded in getting lawmakers to repeal the ban and to have the papers moved to the Nixon library, as long as the public was assured continued access to the records. Interestingly, the addition of these archives and the structure to house them marked the first time that taxpayers had to shell out for new construction at a presidential library prior to paying any of the operating expenses.

After extensive negotiations, the National Archives moved into the building in July 2007. So began the contentious relationship between the new nonpartisan occupants and the decidedly partisan Nixon Library Foundation, which still controls event space, the museum store and café, and the foundation's offices. In a clever strategic move, the National Archives obtained control of the hallways, but have yet to employ hall monitors. Touché!

*Are you now, or have you ever been, a member of our frequent commie-baiter program?*

(To get an idea of just how differently these two groups approach their subject matter, check out their Web sites at the URLs listed at the beginning of this entry.)

First on the National Archives' list of renovations was the Watergate exhibit, which, under the foundation's watch, portrayed the scandal that put an end to Nixon's presidency as an unfortunate glitch in an otherwise seamless political career. Under the curatorial auspices of the National Archives, the new improved version relies more on facts than wishful thinking. Ominously, the National Archives promises over the next several years to revise many more of the exhibits, transforming the Nixon library into a "nonpartisan, interactive, digital, and self-curated museum." In other words, Dick's legacy will probably not be as shiny as originally planned.

Even so, there's a lot to absorb at the nine-acre complex. After all, this is the site of Nixon's birthplace in 1913 and features the home in which he was born, as well as the final resting places for Nixon and First Lady Pat. As far as we can tell, Checkers the dog is not buried with them. For the sheer novelty factor, we can't decide which we like better: the allegedly authentic moon rock or the Sikorsky "Sea King" helicopter (aka "The Oval Office in the Sky") that whisked Nixon away from the White House for the last time on August 9, 1973.

Other than the men's room, the last stall of which features

a chinchilla-lined glory hole and a small brass plaque that reads "Donated by Friends of Larry Craig,"* we'd have to say our favorite part of the library is the gift shop, which possesses the same sense of humor that brought us the temporary exhibit of twenty-three never-before-seen gifts from Tricia Nixon's wedding, glibly entitled "But They Didn't Get a Blender." That was more than ten years ago, but the folks who run the concession obviously understand camp (the same cannot be said for whoever is responsible for the stodgy Reagan Library gift shop). Displaying a surprisingly hip grasp of our pop consumerist culture, the Nixon gift shop wisely chooses to merchandise the crap out of the famous picture of Nixon shaking hands with Elvis Presley. The fact that the drug-addled rock star visited Nixon because he wanted to be anointed as an honorary DEA narc is almost as stupefying as the fact that the photo is the most

*Okay, we made this part up.

requested document in the entire National Archives, beating out even the Bill of Rights and the Constitution. The gift shop offers not only an 8 × 10 glossy (black-and-white or color, framed or unframed) of the odd duo, but also a slew of items on which the image has been emblazoned, including scratchpads, mousepads, postcards, bookmarks, kitchen magnets, T-shirts, shot glasses, coffee mugs, picture frames, and toilet paper. Okay, not toilet paper, but we can dream, can't we?

Bowling also figures prominently into the gift shop's catalog (Nixon and his wife were avid fans of the sport and built an additional one-lane alley at the White House in 1969). You can pick up a gorgeous color 8 × 10 of Dick in mid-throw, or perhaps a T-shirt sporting the same image. We also went nuts over the selection of authentic vintage campaign buttons, and not just Nixon's; we snagged some Johnson and Kennedy beauties as well. Best of all, for only $5,999 (plus tax) you can purchase a replica of the Presidential Resolute Desk in all of its hideous splendor. This amazing piece of furniture is a duplicate of the original, fashioned from the timbers of the HMS Resolute and given to President Rutherford Hayes by Queen Victoria in 1879. It has been used by every president since then, with the exception of Johnson, Ford, and—*wait for it*—Nixon. Somehow, it all makes [expletive deleted] sense.

If for some reason you forget to buy your very own $6000 Presidential Resolute Desk when visiting the Nixon library, fret not; you can always pick one up at the Ronald Reagan Presidential Library and Center for Public Affairs, just sixty miles northwest of Yorba Linda in sumptuous Simi Valley.

As already mentioned, this monument to the Reagan years sits atop a summit that overlooks an endless cascade of golden rolling hills and tract after tract of cookie-cutter McMansions as far as the eye can see. On a clear day you can even make out the coastline of the Channel Islands, some twenty-five miles to the west, which means you can probably spot them once every few years. When it gets hot, the air is filled with the soothing sound of hundreds of baby rattlesnakes trying out their new tails. And we thought the "Poisonous Snake" warning signs posted around the grounds were about Karl Rove.

If Simi Valley seems to you like an odd home for America's favorite president, you're not alone; it wasn't Reagan's first choice, either. The plan originally called for the Reagan Library to be built at Stanford University in Palo Alto, but protests from both students and faculty forced the project to be scuttled. Reagan, for the record, went to Eureka College in northern Illinois, but Stanford is home to the conservative think tank, the Hoover Institution.

When the library's current home was proposed, that almost didn't get off the ground either. City officials for Simi Valley,

Thousand Oaks, and especially Moorpark were less than thrilled with the notion of the library sitting in the middle of a greenbelt that accounted for almost half of the one hundred acres donated to the library by real estate development company Blakeley-Swartz. The catch? The developer also wanted to build a 300-room hotel and conference center on 540 acres right next to the library site. When the three cities balked at the library being a magnet for further development in the greenbelt, plans for the hotel and conference center were dropped.

Construction began in 1988, and when it finally opened in November 1991, it was—like everything else about the Reagan administration—the biggest and most expensive presidential library ever built. Predictably, Bill Clinton's (library) would be even bigger; more predictably, the Reagans refused to be outdone, and snatched back the title in 2005 with the addition of the massive 90,000-square-foot Air Force One Pavilion. Outside of airport bathrooms, who knew the Republicans were such size queens?

That said, the gargantuan complex is made less imposing by its terra cotta–tiled rooftops, rough-hewn wooden beams, adobe walls, burbling fountains, and surrounding greenery, which all combine to convey a kind of laid-back, western dignity not unlike that of its progenitor. If the Reagan library could talk, it would be a sincere and humble giant that would never belittle its less-blessed cousin in Yorba Linda by saying something like "Nice helicopter, dickweed, but mine is newer! And check out Air Force One, chump. It's not a model—it's the real deal, and the pavilion it sits in is bigger than your entire campus! Oh, I'm sorry. I forgot that you have a moon rock. How much did you say that fake weighs? Well, check out my four-ton chunk of the Berlin Wall, shitheel. Yeah, I know you have one, too, but did your president single-handedly bring down the Evil Empire and save the free world from everlasting darkness? Of course he didn't—*he's a quitter!*" Of course, the Reagan library *can't* talk, but if it could, we all know it would never go down that road.

In fact, you can see the Reagan library's compassion in the eyes of the noble, bigger-than-life bronze sculpture of Richard Crenna that greets you at the museum's front doors. The full-body statue is supposed to resemble Reagan, but the two men can easily be confused: Not only are they both dead actors, but Crenna played Reagan in the 2001 made-for-TV epic, *The Day Reagan Was Shot.*

# MUSIC FOR MONGOLOIDS

Conspicuously chartreuse, Mutato Muzika is the creative banker for subversive Devo genius Mark Mothersbaugh. Though the color begs attention, please do not disturb the occupants unless you are a TV, movie, or commercial producer with sacks of cash.

**Mutato Muzika / 8760 Sunset Boulevard / Los Angeles / 310.360.0561**

It's spooky. Unfortunately, this isn't the first time that a Reagan sculpture hasn't looked like Reagan. The library used to have a bust of Reagan out front that was so comical it would have looked more at home at Disney's "Haunted Mansion." We have always assumed it was not the sculptor's intent to render the Great Communicator as a maniacal mutation of Howdy Doody, even though both were famous puppets who enjoyed dressing up like cowboys. The statue has since been moved to a less conspicuous spot under the rear portico, but if you have trouble finding it, ask anyone wearing an official blue sport coat to point you in the direction of "the hideous, grinning, scary Howdy Doody thing."

Moving past Richard Crenna and into the main lobby, be sure to take a look at the wall-to-wall list of the hundreds of sponsors and patrons whose kind donations, along with your tax dollars, made the mega-museum possible. For some reason, the folks in the blue jackets are not fond of flash photography, but if you hit the place late in the day when the sun is casting a warm glow across the walls of the lobby, you can get a really nice golden-hour shot of the Walt Disney Company, Johnson & Johnson, Korea Explosives Group, and many other fine companies who obviously believed in Reaganomics. And if you can't get your head around the basics of trickle-down theory, don't sweat it. Just through the glass doors, the rear lawn features an exhibit even a simpleton can appreciate. That's right, we're going to the Berlin Wall.

Having seen the wall in Berlin both before and after its fall, we can safely say that this is the cleanest piece of the Iron Curtain we've ever seen. The spray-painted graffiti of the butterfly, flower, and grass look almost a little *too* perfect, but who are we to argue with its authenticity? After all, it was Reagan who implored, "Mr. Gorbachev, tear down this wall," so it only makes sense that he gets the nicest piece of the pie, right? But while that worked out great for the people of Germany, you have to wonder what our world would be like today if Reagan had only demanded, "Mr. Gorbachev, tear down this *mall*." The implications are mind-boggling.

Down a short walkway, at the edge of the lawn, is the surprisingly humble grave of the costar of *Bedtime for Bonzo*. The circular concrete slab is fronted with a brass rail, and backed with a curved marble wall on which these words are inscribed:

*"I know in my heart that man is good, that what is right will always eventually triumph, that there is purpose and worth to each and every life."*

Wow. Whatever Reagan was on the day his speechwriters wrote that, we wanted some, too. Standing at his grave, we couldn't help but get a little misty thinking back to June 2004, when the weeklong orgy of coast-to-coast memorial services culminated in an historic traffic jam as Reagan was rolled into his final resting place at no more than ten miles an hour. The sun was just beginning to set when they finally got around to planting Dutch in the hot Simi dirt, and Nancy, after playing it up for the cameras for almost a week, appeared exhausted. As she stood on the hillside looking like a Margaret Keane waif in a Galanos skirt suit, her handsome, white-gloved Marine escort in tow, she looked relieved it was finally over. We were, too.

As we recalled that sober moment, an obese family of Midwestern tourists waddled up and leaned against the railing. They were huffing and puffing from having made the arduous 250-foot walk from the snack shop to pay their last respects. After about ten seconds of silent prayer, crew-cut dad sucked the last bit of liquid from his extra-large soda, then turned to his wheezing wife and crew-cut kid and solemnly announced, "You know, they're gonna have to tear up all that concrete and stuff when they dig him up."

What the fuck?? What do they know in Idaho or Iowa or Illinois that we don't know? Just who are "they," and why do "they" want to "dig him up?" Can't "they" just leave the man alone? Jesus, and we were just starting to buy into that whole "man is good" routine, too. Feeling that our world was about to come crumbling down around us, we needed a drink, and fast. Fortunately, the Reagan Country Café was there to save the day.

You may be as surprised as we were to learn that you can get hammered at the nation's largest presidential library. Despite the fact that Reagan was a lifelong teetotaler, the Reagan Country Café is the Gipper's answer to the Betty Ford Clinic. The hip eatery puts the Nixon coffee shop to shame not only with its

gourmet fare, but also with its wide
selection of beers and wines. That's
just as well; Nixon was notorious
for not being able to hold his liquor,
and was known to get mean and/
or weepy as he stumbled through
the White House in the wee hours.
Reagan Republicans and neocons,
on the other hand, are a jubilant lot
when they're inebriated. When not
wrestling their homosexual demons,
they can usually be found pulling
zany college pranks like disrupt-
ing Florida vote counts, outing CIA

agents, and torturing suspected terrorists. In fact, some would
say that the only difference between hazing and waterboarding
is that you don't get to join a frat when they finish with you at one
of our many secret prisons . . . but isn't Al Qaeda just an Animal
House for Islamofascists?

Considering the immensity of the Reagan library, you very well
may need to pound some Bud Lights and eat a few F-14 Fighter
Dogs (no joke), before venturing into its vastness. Besides the
replica of the Oval Office—a standard feature at any presidential
library—and a slew of temporary and permanent exhibits, there's
also the spectacle of Air Force One to keep you entertained for
at least fifteen minutes as you investigate the marvels of the customized Boeing 707 both inside and out, and wonder why it took
so long for the most powerful leader in the world to finally get rid
of this relic and order a couple of jumbo jets. There's also Marine
One, the president's mega-chopper; an F-14 Tomcat; some Secret
Service vehicles; and a bunch of other presidential toys, but
oddly enough, Sea-Doo One is nowhere to be found.

The most important aspect of any presidential museum,
however, is not the number of aircraft it has on display, nor how
many bad bronze likenesses dot the landscape, nor even the
official papers housed in the library itself. A presidential library
lives and dies by its gift shop, and though Reagan's is bigger
and fancier than Nixon's, here's an instance when we can definitely say that size doesn't matter. While Reagan's store has its
moments of irony—like a "Just Say No" refrigerator magnet—
it's got nothing on the Elvis/bowling motifs at Nixon's place.
Even though you can pick up a DVD called "Stand-Up Reagan"
featuring a selection of jokes and anecdotes told as only Dutch
could tell them ("We begin bombing in five minutes" is still our
personal fave, but probably not on the disc), that kind of shtick is
to be expected from a former actor. The Jelly Belly jelly beans, the
"Peace Through Strength" sportswear Reagan donned at Camp
David, even the Air Force One stewardess dolls . . . they're all

cute, but ultimately lack the self-effacing humor that makes the Nixon gift shop so marvelous.

Surrounded by shoppers who checked out the prices of White House china replicas and tried on faux bomber jackets, we found ourselves feeling very much alone and yet enraptured by the plasma TV on the wall. It played a DVD they sell in the store, a documentary called *Tribute to Ronald Reagan*, which was more honest about the fortieth president than anything else we had seen that day. It mentioned Reagan's lack of military service as the reason he so loved to play soldiers on the screen, and how he put his own theatrical spin on his salute; how his naiveté gave way to callow opportunism when, as president of the Screen Actors Guild, he showed his first anti-commie, anti-union political stripes; how his obsession with politics drove his first wife, Jane Wyman, to leave him (he is, as of this writing, still our only divorced president), and the spiritual devastation that ensued. In watching just ten minutes of the documentary, we realized that we didn't learn much about Reagan at all from his library, much less his eight years in office. Suddenly, he seemed very human, and almost tragically superficial. Where Nixon was spectacularly flawed—a brooding, intelligent, crass, cunning, and above all, paranoid man—Reagan was a consistently charismatic but shallow character, the kind Americans are obviously drawn to every few decades, the kind who probably buys into his own bullshit, which makes him so good at selling it. This is the glimmer of a reason that explains the successes of presidents like Reagan and Bush Jr., who manage to engender respect—at least for a time— while also displaying colossal incompetence and wreaking havoc on the country and people they have pledged to protect.

And this, at the end of the day, more than the size or the spectacle of their respective libraries, is the difference between Nixon and Reagan. Though he fought it tooth and nail, Nixon was

in a way liberated by the scandal for which he was forced to take responsibility. Reagan, on the other hand, got away with far worse crimes, at least as far as the general public is aware, and therefore the keepers of his legend feel no need to shine any lights on the shadows of his administration. As the Nixon library beefs up its Watergate exhibit, Iran-contra was removed from the Reagan library altogether, other than a brief mention in an orientation video.

And so we come full circle, with perhaps a better understanding of

# WHO'S YOUR DADDY?

We have yet to see a work of public art in Los Angeles besides Watts Towers and Angelyne that doesn't make us wince. As if the corner of La Brea and Hollywood didn't look bad enough before, in 1993 we were given the glorified hood ornament titled "Gateway." The artist responsible? Catherine Hardwicke. For what reason? To honor multi-ethnic women who appeared in film during Hollywood's golden era. Okay, then why—along with Dorothy Dandridge, Delores Del Rio, and Anna Mae Wong—does Mae West serve as one of the four pillars, and the ubiquitous Marilyn cap its spire?

**Gateway / La Brea Avenue at Hollywood Boulevard / Hollywood**

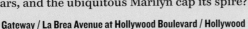

why Nixon must truly hate Reagan. While the cliché will always be to revile Nixon as a "crook," few are aware that the Reagan administration lied about never dealing with terrorists (they sold weapons to Iran and supported "Freedom Fighters" in Central America), told kiddies to Just Say No to Drugs (while getting the country hooked on cocaine to fund their covert wars), turned a blind eye to the HUD and Savings and Loan scandals, and stole credit from Gorbachev for the collapse of the Soviet Union (which could barely stand up on its own by the time the Berlin Wall came down).

Presidential libraries—left, right, or center—are not ware-houses for the facts, but holy places for true believers; they see no profit in peddling wholesale truths. When compared to Nixon, it doesn't take a visionary to see that it was Reagan and company who took us to the next nadir of the conservative movement, not some imagined summit. Nixon may have been a creep, but he couldn't hide his discomfort no matter how he tried. Reagan, on the other hand, was a cipher who got away with murder because he *could* hide whatever was under that grin, if there was anything at all.

Nixon left office in the worst possible way, forcing a smile and waving peace signs while the nation flipped him the bird. By the time Reagan left office, 138 of his administration officials had been convicted, indicted, or investigated for criminal violations or official misconduct. Soon, Reagan would remember none of it, not even his most glorious moments. And the more senile Reagan became, the less we were inclined to pin on him.

For a time there, it seemed almost impossible to imagine a conservative administration that could supersede the moral bankruptcy of the Nixon administration and the hypocrisy of the Reagan White House. Who would have imagined that President George W. Numbskull would bring back so many of Nixon and Reagan's neocon apostles (Rumsfeld, Cheney, Wolfowitz, Armitage, et al.) for an encore performance that would make Watergate and Iran-contra look like Christmas episodes of *The Love Boat*?

Looking back, past mountains of wasted money, hills of smoking wreckage, a smoldering economy, and endless piles of twisted bodies, all of which came to fruition in the first eight years of the new millennium, one almost has a sense of nostalgia for the Reagan era. So what if the seeds of conservative failure were planted there? Who cares if Reaganomics killed our economy? Just turn up the volume on "Don't Stop Believing" and cut us a few more fat rails.

## STAR FUCKING AT THE

# HOLLYWOOD WAX MUSEUM

Hollywood Wax Museum
6767 Hollywood Boulevard
Hollywood
213.462.8860
www.hollywoodwax.com

One of the crudest by-products of L.A.'s celebrity-obsessed culture is appropriately located right in the heart of Hollywood Boulevard. Although we've never actually created a list, the Hollywood Wax Museum should probably rate number one for sheer unadulterated absurdity and experiential emptiness.

The quality of the work represented at the Hollywood Wax Museum is hardly what you'd expect from a city whose chief industry is illusion, and scant care has been given to upkeep. Props are falling apart as quickly as they were slapped together and it would seem that light bulbs are burning out faster than they can be replaced. On any given day, George Washington may be absent his right hand, Franklin D. Roosevelt's nose may be stuffed with gum, and many of the Wax Museum's faces are as scratched up as yesterday's lottery tickets from the clawing of overzealous patrons. And with its sticky floors and stale air it's easy to forget that this is not, in fact, a private viewing booth in an adult bookstore.

With the sole exception of Michael Jackson, the likenesses among the museum's collection are hardly striking, looking a whole lot more like a gallery of celebrity impersonators and punch-drunk drag queens. Clearly the figures are not made of wax—just scratch one and you'll see for yourself—and most are pieced together from garden-variety department store mannequins.

Look for the hit-and-miss attention paid to male anatomical detail. Seems that some of these dudes could have choked Linda Lovelace, while others were suspiciously shortchanged. Patrick Swayze's got a cameltoe, and Burt Reynolds's crotch looks about as smooth as a Barbie doll's. Know the old real estate maxim, "location, location, location"? Seems just as pertinent in the business of celebrity effigies: Is that Elvis's manhood or is it a colostomy bag about ready to burst? Only the magic makers at the Wax Museum know for sure. Curious to know just how far the wax crafters take their work, we yanked down Michael J. Fox's jeans to determine what separates the men from the boys. Our discovery: a wad of tinfoil securely held in place with several pieces of duct tape, just like we do at home.

Remember the "USA for Africa" craze of the eighties? You'll surely never forget it after stumbling upon the museum's "We Are the World" diorama. Personally, we think it's super fucked-up that life-sized likenesses of Cindy Lauper, Lionel Richie, Elton John, David Bowie, and Willie Nelson (they all sang on "We Are the World," and lest you forgot, there's an endless audio loop to remind you) have been placed downstage of photo enlargements featuring real starving African children, but perhaps such cynicism is unwarranted considering the difference that music video made for the people of Africa.

Our favorite feature of the museum is the accessibility of most displays, save a fence or reasonably low barrier wall. You can hop right in as long as no one sees you, and take a few pictures. An electric eye protects some of the installations, but all they do is beep twice and there isn't enough staff on hand to do anything about it. Quick test for the photo bug: Wave your hand in front of the electric eye first; most of them are broken. If you don't hear a beep, hit your mark and make love to the camera, but be careful not to knock anything over. And if you're a big fan of someone in particular—like a super big fan who obsesses and writes scary letters and makes bomb threats to profess your undying love—you can dry hump your favorite star here and get it out of your system before you really hurt somebody. Just be sure to wipe up.

*Is that a wad of tinfoil in your pocket or are you just happy to see me?*

Intriguing footnote: Of all the celebrities on display, only three of them were deemed prominent enough to be featured in the museum twice—Sylvester Stallone, Arnold Schwarzenegger, and Jesus.

Displays change frequently, so visit often.

## SOUTH OF THE BORDER GENDER-BENDING AT

# THE PLAZA

The Plaza
739 North La Brea Avenue
Los Angeles
323.939.0703

*Is that a burrito in your dress, or are you just happy to see me?*

Anyone who ever paid a visit to the cross-dressing palace La Cage knows how excruciating a drag show can be. Barbra Streisand, Dionne Warwick, and Carol Channing already look like men in women's clothing, so what's the point, really?

At the Plaza you won't be subjected to an Adam's-appled Minnelli miming his way though "New York, New York," or a broad-shouldered Cher flogging a tune like "Gypsies, Tramps, and Thieves." In fact, you won't even hear any songs with English lyrics. The drag here comes from down Mexico way, and what's more, not all the breasts represented on the Plaza stage are made of foam rubber.

The Plaza performances are a little more lax than those of the garden variety drag show—no obnoxious emcee; no self-conscious, tongue-in-cheek irony; and half the fun is trying to distinguish the real chicks from the chicks with dicks. It's more like a homespun talent show for grown-ups, where drag perform-ers compete for best lip-sync, with the rest of the acts generously rounding out the bill for those who might not be so into watching a man in a dress pretend to belt a Latino pop ballad. They keep it real at the Plaza, and if your attention wanders from the stage, *no problema*, drink up, this isn't IMAX—although it can be equally overwhelming since the show is rarely limited to the confines of the stage. A pint-sized Latina covered in nary more than the Lycra equivalent of three tortilla chips may land in your lap, or you could come face-to-waist with a tableside performance from a seven-foot glamourpuss who brings to mind all the estrogen of Aaron Spelling's *Dynasty*.

While the Plaza audience is captive and loyal, it seems no one is having a better time than the would-be gals on stage. Our money says you're watching the same show these guys were performing in front of their bedroom mirrors at about age nine or ten, except now they've got real beaded gowns, passable wigs, and a stage mic instead of a hairbrush. Dripping with the fringe and feathers of their childhood fantasies, they give their best to an audience all too happy to indulge this evening of make-believe. Tucking a bill into a plunging neckline (or under the waistband of the rare dude who sees fit to perform as a dude) is a favorite Plaza pastime, so make sure your wallet is packed with a few extra singles. A kiss on the hand may be quite conti-nental, but when the entertainers work the floor, they're looking to recoup a little of the cash they put out earlier in the week for cosmetics, depilatory creams, and supportive undergarments.

Although the club is technically gay and almost exclusively Latino, you'll find a gringo-friendly crowd and a dance floor scattered with lip-locked heteros, big-boned dykes, and randy *rancheros* seemingly up for anything. Shows are offered twice nightly (10:15 and 12:00) Thursday through Monday for a mere $5 cover, and the Plaza is just a two-minute walk from Pink's. Where else within the greater L.A. area can one drink hard liquor, watch a man play dress-up, hold a mostly naked girl in their lap, *and* feel like they've left the country?

We mean, of course, without having to pay for a room.

## HANGING ON
## FORREST'S LAWN AT THE

# ACKERMANSION

NOTE: *Just before* L.A. Bizarro *went to press, we were saddened to learn that Forrest Ackerman had gone to join L. Ron Hubbard in that great sci-fi convention in the sky. We leave this record of our unforgettable afternoon with "Uncle Forry" as a heartfelt tribute. Forry is gone now, but if you drive by the Ackermansion, you can still sense that something (and someone) magical once lived within its walls.*

The Ackermansion
4511 Russell Avenue
Hollywood
323.666.6326

Long before it was chic to be a geek, Forrest J Ackerman was paving the way for an era when slobbering over sci-fi movies, collecting toy figurines, and dressing up at comic book conven-tions would get you laid instead of ostracized. When you think about it, that's a feat as impressive as putting a man on the moon.

He didn't look it, comfortably nestled into a plush La-Z-Boy that seemed to swallow his diminishing frame, but "Uncle Forry" (or just "Forry" as he was affectionately known) was bigger than life. Also dubbed "Mr. Science Fiction," the spry nonagenarian was probably the oldest living expert on all things sci-fi, having coined the phrase himself as a riff on *hi-fi* back in 1954. (Not everyone was a fan of the term, though: Harlan Ellison famously complained that "sci-fi" is a "hideous neologism . . . which sounds like two crickets fucking." Forry was none too fond of Ellison, either.) Forry was also famous for having donned the first "fan" costume at a sci-fi convention (The First World Science Convention in 1939), which pretty much made him the Patron Saint of All Geekdom.

As the creator, publisher, and editor of the defunct magazine *Famous Monsters of Filmland,* Forry practically invented the fanzine, and influenced a generation of artists from George Lucas to Gene Simmons. In his heyday, Ackerman helped establish the Los Angeles Science Fantasy society, was the self-labeled "illiterary" agent to such noteworthy cultural icons as Ed Wood, Jr. and L. Ron Hubbard, and formed a lifelong friendship with Ray Bradbury and Ray Harryhausen at the Los Angeles Science Fiction League, which met regularly at Clifton's Cafeteria. He also invented the character "Vampirella," had had well over

a hundred cameo appearances in movies, and was fluent in perhaps the most futile language on earth, Esperanto.

Through the years, Ackerman amassed the greatest private collection of sci-fi, fantasy, and monster movie memorabilia on earth, which he proudly displayed at the eponymous Ackermansion, his eighteen-room museum/home in Los Feliz. Cordial to a fault, the ultimate fan had always loved to share his treasure with other fans, so, beginning in 1951, he opened his door forty times a year to invite perfect strangers to enter, behold, and by all means touch his weird and won-

derful world. More than fifty thousand fans and admirers crossed his threshold until 2002, when he was forced to sell the Ackermansion and most of his collection. An ugly legal battle with a business partner had taken its toll, and though Ackerman won a judgment of $724,500 in civil court, he never collected. The defendant declared bankruptcy, leaving Forry holding the bag for over $200,000 in legal fees. In one of the greatest unpublicized tragedies Hollywood has ever seen, most of Ackerman's 300,000-plus item collection was sold off in a two-day glorified garage sale. Though he offered to *donate* the entire collection to the city of Los Angeles for a sci-fi museum, the mayor's office just couldn't get its act together. Nor did longtime fans with deep pockets, like Lucas and Steven Spielberg, step up to help their alleged hero. Instead, Forry sat on a folding chair outside the Ackermansion and watched the collection he had started at the age of nine systematically dismantled and carted off by fans who, understandably, wanted to own a piece of history. It was the end of an era, cruelly punctuated by a stroke and subsequent battle with a life-threatening illness.

*Hollywood's friendliest monster was also one heck of a guy.*

Couple these momentous setbacks with the death of his beloved wife during a carjacking in Italy, and any lesser monster would have hung up his cape. But, like so many of the characters from the movies he adores, Forrest J Ackerman would not be vanquished.

Which brings us back to that La-Z-Boy chair where Forry reclined, his legs kept warm by a fuzzy blanket adorned with dancing skeletons. It was a cool, wet Saturday morning in late 2008, and Mr. Science Fiction was still holding court for the faithful at his downsized digs, a humble yellow bungalow he calls the Ackermansion. Though the visiting hour was from 11:00 to 12:00 every Saturday morning, we arrived late and were still graciously beckoned inside the tidy 1911 Craftsman home.

Forry managed to hang on to some of his most prized possessions, and every nook and cranny of the modest home was packed with precious cargo like Bela Lugosi's Dracula cape and ring, the brontosaurus miniature from the original *King Kong*, Ray Harryhausen's shattered Capitol dome from *Earth vs. the Flying Saucers*, a full-scale replica of the robot "Maria" from *Metropolis*, Lon Chaney's top hat from *London After Midnight*, plaster life casts of all the horror greats, and so many other gems that it boggles the mind to think they represented only a tiny fraction of Ackerman's original collection. Though he'd had plenty of memorabilia ripped off by sticky-fingered visitors over the years, Forry urged us to explore every room in the tiny house, including his bedroom in which he kept a chair once owned by Lincoln. He didn't know us from Adam, and he was certainly not getting out of his chair, yet he encouraged us to touch everything, and by all means, ask questions. We can't think of a soul, including ourselves, who would be so trusting with their prized possessions, or so gracious when a clumsy oaf stepped on his pee bag. And though the collection is indeed impressive, it was Ackerman himself who was always the main attraction.

For a stroke victim well into his nineties, Forry was smarter, quicker, funnier, and had a better memory than someone a fraction of his age. Effusive and mischievous, he also had not lost his eye for the ladies. In between nonstop patter of corny one-liners, classic tales of Ray Bradbury and L. Ron Hubbard, and a flawlessly delivered monologue from *The Invisible Man*, Forry serenaded the only lady in the room with a heartfelt rendition of "April Showers." He may just have been the last Al Jolson fan this side of Leisure World.

On occasion we have been known to wax snarkily about the indomitable human spirit—often while taking a cheap shot at the elderly (after all, they're slow and defenseless)—but we'll be damned if Forrest Ackerman didn't put a couple of lumps in our throats with his lugubrious humor and infectious lust for life. If we could hope to be only half as hip at his age, we might rethink that suicide pact.

Whether or not you're a fan of sci-fi or monster movies, an hour spent with Uncle Forry was worth a lifetime of otherwise dull encounters. The sweetest monster in filmland would have welcomed you into his home with open arms, and trust us when we say you would never have forgotten him. We know we won't.

## LEARNING NEW WAYS TO TEABAG AT THE LOS ANGELES
# SHERIFF'S DEPT. MUSEUM

Los Angeles Sheriff's
Department Museum
11515 South Colima Road
Whittier
562.946.7859

What better way to honor the fine men and woman of the Los Angeles County Sheriff's Department than to establish a museum dedicated solely to its history and accomplishments? And what better way to ensure that absolutely no one ever visits the museum than to stick it in a godforsaken stretch of flatland and give it bankers' hours from Monday through Friday only? Maybe that's why you've never heard of the Los Angeles Sheriff's Department Museum (LASDM) . . . until now.

Located at the Sheriff's Training Academy in Whittier on what was once a high school campus, the museum and adjacent bookshop share the grounds with a number of the department's specialized bureaus including the Reserve Forces Bureau, Major Crimes Bureau, Family Crimes Bureau, and Narcotics Bureau. Accordingly, if your idea of a good time is to shoot some heroin, beat your spouse, and plot a terrorist attack, we advise you not to do it here.

Unless you're really into cops—and hey, who isn't?—the LASDM might not be the most exhilarating museum in Los Angeles, but it certainly contains some stuff you're unlikely to come across elsewhere: sawed-off shotgun? *Check*. Drug paraphernalia? *Check*. Gang gear? *Check*. Video of the fatal *Twilight Zone* helicopter accident? Uh . . . check?

The museum features a vintage Studebaker patrol car, a couple of helicopters, and lots of mannequins in various uniforms, but we were transfixed by the TV monitor that, at the touch of a button, plays a very worn-out, glitchy tape of disparate events, including the aforementioned outtake from the *Twilight Zone* movie in which Vic Morrow and two child actors are decapitated by a helicopter blade when a stunt goes awry. The long, lingering crane shot is interesting because, unlike most of the footage on the Web, it continues well after the chopper has crashed and shows crew members scurrying around in the water looking for the actors . . . or pieces of them. Some say that director John Landis, who allegedly yelled for the helicopter to go lower just prior to fatal crash, escaped justice when he was acquitted of involuntary manslaughter, but we think that being relegated to directing episodes of USA Channel's *Psych* seems fitting—if not excessive—punishment.

But wait, there's more! The tape continues with a hodge-podge of footage of the 1986 air disaster in which an Aeromexico DC-9 collided with a small plane and nosedived into a Cerritos neighborhood, followed by a sensationalistic "documentary" on the Manson Family, and then concludes with more disconnected footage of the 1970 riots in East L.A. By the end, we weren't sure if we had just witnessed a journalistic mess or avant-garde video art. Regardless, it seemed like the highlight of our trip—until we found the gift shop.

As with most bureaucratic endeavors, the gift shop's policies seemingly have no rhyme or reason. Civilians can buy T-shirts and other gear emblazoned with the Sheriff Department's logo, but a majority of the shop's most intriguing items—police batons, folding knives, trauma kits—aren't for sale to the public, even though civvies can buy them online or at many army-navy stores. Yet the gift shop will happily sell you a "slim jim" for unlocking any car door, or a KMA-628 license plate holder to let other cops know you're one of those assholes who thinks he can get out of a ticket by pretending to be associated with the Sheriff's Department.

Also of great interest is a handy little book called *Drug I.D. and Symptom Guide* which will not only teach the reader about the right way to do all kinds of drugs, but where to hide them, how to avoid looking fucked-up, and what slang terms like "Zany Bars," "White Girl," "Strawberry," "Robotrippin'," "Choking Game," "Thrusters," and "Nukin' the Coke" mean. As in, "I was already

*Excuse me, Officer, which way to the Nam June Paik installation?*

robotrippin' when I took a few zany bars to bring me down before I started nukin' the coke, and then some strawberry said she'd let me play the choking game if I would front her some thrusters." And that's just the tip of the iceberg. Did you know that "teabagging" refers to inserting a GHB-soaked tampon in your butt?

And all this time we thought it had something to do with Siegfried & Roy.

## TIME-TRAVELING WITH THE

# LOS ANGELES CONSERVANCY

## BROADWAY THEATRE DISTRICT TOUR

The Los Angeles Conservancy
523 West Sixth Street,
Suite 826
Los Angeles
213.623.2489
www.laconservancy.org

*Q: What do glory holes, the bible, and Mary Pickford have in common?*

Until recently, most Angelenos would have recoiled in horror at the prospect of exploring downtown Los Angeles on foot. Beginning in the 1960s and lasting well into the nineties, the once-bustling nerve center of our city had succumbed to a fast and seemingly irreversible decay. And while it was still a good place to score drugs, get stabbed, rub elbows with a Vietnam vet, or brush up on your foreign language skills, downtown offered little for those without a taste for inner-city adventure.

Make no mistake, downtown Los Angeles still offers plenty of reasons to recoil in horror, most notably the results from years of revitalization projects and new development. The McArtist Loft trend has hit, as have the precious cafés and self-consciously hip bars that would have died a painful but quick death had they opened just a decade ago; downtown L.A. is losing its charm. And fast.

However, one of the advantages of ambling downtown Los Angeles's streets is that you do feel like you're in a real city. Not a good city, and not even an American city per se, but an odd city-within-a-city unlike any in the country. It's indisputably cosmopolitan and unquestionably gritty, and it's got a *je ne sais quoi* that you just can't find elsewhere in the Southland. Downtown's street life is colorful and loud. The din from the audio-video stores and mega-arcades packed chockablock is matched only by the barkers in front of jewelry shops and the hard-sell street vendors peddling everything from marijuana leaf belt buckles and electroplated gold chains to live turtles and homegrown produce. On corners you might find a wheelchair-bound religious zealot screaming passages from the New Testament, or a nonreligious zealot standing on two healthy legs screaming just because he has a lot to get off his chest. Then of course there's downtown's historic architecture and some of Los Angeles's richest history— particularly that of our single most noteworthy export: movies.

The stretch of Broadway Street between Ninth and Third is the largest historic theater district in the world, listed on the National Register of Historic Places since 1979. Beginning with the nickelodeons and vaudeville houses of the early 1900s, Sid Grauman helped to establish Broadway as the city's theater center when he built the first of his hyper-sumptuous movie palaces here, the Million Dollar Theater, in 1918. By the early thirties there were a dozen major theaters operating on Broadway, but after Grauman opened the Chinese Theater on Hollywood Blvd. in the late twenties, the focus moved considerably west, thus putting the first nail in the coffin of downtown's theater district.

Amazingly, many of the original downtown movie palaces, the very same theaters originally built as vaudeville houses and later converted for films, are still open to this day showing first-run movies, albeit with Spanish subtitles. Some are closed, their futures uncertain.

The Los Angeles Conservancy is an organization dedicated to the preservation of what little architectural history Los Angeles has left. The Conservancy also gives us the only good reason to wake up early on a weekend with their series of Saturday morning walking tours. Their most popular of the walking tour series, often booked months in advance, is Broadway's theatre district.

The experience of the Conservancy tour is much like that of an urban archaeological dig. Among the crumbling and neglected ruins of downtown Broadway lies the most awe-inspiring theater architecture Los Angeles has to offer. To pass through the portals of these breathtaking movie palaces is to step into another time, a time that predates shopping mall cineplexes by nearly a century.

Harry Houdini and Sarah Bernhardt were among those who took the stage at the Palace Theater, built in 1911 as a showcase for the Orpheum vaudeville circuit. The Palace is the oldest of the remaining Broadway theaters and is one of several that originally featured live entertainment, later being converted to screen silent films, then eventually talkies. Remarkably, the Palace is still in operation. But all that glitters is not gold in the stately 2000-plus seat auditorium with its lavish French/Italian interior; its

original segregated balcony offsets the gilt. As with the Globe farther down the street, the segregated balconies of the theater district are a haunting reminder of a not-so-distant era in which it was perfectly acceptable to be mocked on stage in blackface, while access through theater's front entrance was prohibited for some Angelenos. Accessible only from the alley, the Palace's segregated seating was located in the second balcony no less, conveniently offering both the worst view and the stuffiest air.

Only three of the twelve theaters on Broadway remain open to the public. Some theaters have closed down altogether, while some have experienced an intriguing metamorphosis. The Globe Theater is possibly the most dramatic example. Opening in 1913 as the Morosco, it remained a successful theatrical venue until the Depression, when it was converted to a movie theater and renamed the Globe. Although it continued to run movies through the 1980s, it soon after mutated into a swap meet. It's been augmented almost beyond recognition, although the exterior still bears the old Globe marquee (behind which is the original Morosco sign). The raked theater floor has been leveled out with concrete and the interior of what was formerly the lobby now houses a cramped network of make-shift booths hawking the same wares found in Tijuana. At eye level, piles of underwear, baseball caps, and Mexican leather goods fill your field of vision, with all elements of the theater architecture conspicuously absent. Until you look up. Above the chaos of cut-rate wares, the gaping remains of the theater loom hidden in plain sight, four stories overhead. Gold-gilded box seats are positioned on each side of the proscenium arch, behind which hangs the original hand-painted asbestos curtain. The empty balcony reaches to the high corners of the ceiling, with the segregated portion still visible. In the far rear of the building, you can see what once was backstage, stacked with three stories of small dressing rooms, now like a mini vaudevillian ghost town. Just one of the many mind-boggling moments on your jaunt down Broadway.

Regardless of their specific architectural influences, it was a theme of opulence that prevailed, in a concerted effort to provide theatergoers with a place to completely lose touch with reality. The State Theater combines medieval, Spanish, Moorish, and Greek elements, with a large gold Buddha sitting atop the proscenium arch. Both live acts and film were offered here when it opened in 1921. It served as one of the early venues for Judy Garland while she was still Frances Gumm, decades before she would become immortalized by generations of female impersonators. And if the crinkling of candy wrappers or the smacking of popcorn during a movie drives you into a homicidal rage, you have the State to blame. It was the first theater to feature a snack concession, originally offered only for the kiddie matinees. It's still open as a movie theater today, showing first-run films subtitled in Spanish. The auditorium smells like urine.

The Orpheum Theater is one of Broadway's most spectacular, designed in the style of a Parisian opera house with heavy brocade drapery, tri-level box seats, and chandeliers that could crush an elephant into a bloody pulp. The Orpheum is the only Broadway theater with an operating pipe organ, still played by the Los Angeles Theater Organ Society between films on weekends. In its glory years, the Orpheum was host to the Marx Brothers, Gypsy Rose Lee, Sally Rand, Eddie Cantor, and Sophie Tucker among other vaudeville notables. Now the Orpheum is home to the homeless who frequently set up camp inside its tiled portico. It's a popular film location too, having appeared in everything from *Hart to Hart* to *Ed Wood*. What your tour guide may gloss over, but of historical note nonetheless, are the glory holes bored through the solid marble walls of the men's bathroom stalls—many of which have since been covered with steel plates or filled with concrete, so don't get any ideas.

The imposing Spanish Gothic Cathedral–style design of the United Artists Theater is markedly unlike the others on Broadway, and its cathedral design was not entirely without purpose. Mary Pickford and Douglas Fairbanks built the theater in 1927 with the intention of creating a veritable shrine to the motion picture as well as a showcase for their new venture, United Artists. Rudolph Valentino, John Barrymore, Norma Talmadge, Errol Flynn, and other movie actors from the period are featured in the elaborate murals on the walls inside the theater near the balcony. Crowning the auditorium high above, a dome lined with hanging crystals originally became animated when the theater was air-cooled, and the interior of the dome itself changes color depending on your vantage point. So who needs a movie!?

Like the State, the United Artists Theater morphed over time, coming by its glory holes honestly. Just a few decades after its star-studded opening, the Fairbanks's house of film worship would be running porno flicks, and soon after would serve as a *panaderia* that made use of the theater's large auditorium and lobby as the exhaust duct for its large ovens which eventually covered the ornate mirrors and frescos with a thick layer of soot. Stranger still, the UA's cathedral prophecy was eventually fulfilled, and it's now an honest-to-goodness church. The infamous Dr. Eugene Scott and his congregation have not only saved the theater from potential demolition, they have painstakingly worked to restore its architectural integrity. Integrity being the operative word here, as Dr. Scott has augmented the original frescoes with a little handiwork of his own, like his twist on Michelangelo's *The Creation of Adam*. Above one of the balcony exits, we see the hand of God passing Adam a cigar—Dr. Scott's trademark. An antique Bible display now replaces the popcorn counter, and among the Bibles encased behind glass is a 1631 edition containing the badly bungled commandment "Thall shalt commit adultery." Also featured is the "Wife Beater Bible" of 1545, which offers old-school advice to exasperated Christian husbands burdened by a surly spouse: " . . . beate the fear of God into her heade."

The Conservancy tour also provides an informed look at some of the other noteworthy buildings along Broadway, as well as the histories of the other theaters currently closed to the public. The Tower Theater, said to be one of the most outstanding, was the first to feature sound movies. The original stained glass window above the lobby features a design of celluloid filmstrips, still intact and visible. Look closely and you'll spot some of the original marquees running along the top of the structure's heavily ornamented façade, bearing the ghostly remains of the words "NEWS REELS."

The Los Angeles Theater is Broadway's French Baroque mothership. The lobby alone features sweeping marble stairways, bronze banisters, a tiered fountain dripping with crystals, and massive chandeliers suspended from vaulted ceilings. The level beneath the lobby once offered a restaurant, a smoking room with built-in cigarette lighters, a circus-themed children's playroom, cavernous marble restrooms (featuring sixteen individual marble vanities in the ladies' room), and a periscope set-up that projected the movie onto a smaller screen in an adult lounge so that you could socialize without missing too much of the film. That shiny Gehry thing can't compete.

The Los Angeles Conservancy hosts an annual event called Last Remaining Seats that resuscitates new life into aged theaters like the Los Angeles and the Orpheum. One of their most popular offerings is their silent film night, with a pipe organ and full orchestra providing a live score, and turnout is phenomenal. Film aficionados line up for blocks in anticipation of gaining entry into one of Broadway's forgotten wonders.

The Conservancy events are the best thing going for anyone interested in exploring the rich history and lost elegance of downtown Los Angeles, offering perhaps the only chance you'll have to see one of these historic theaters running an uncut classic film, seated with an audience civilized enough not to urinate in their seats or make use of the many glory holes down in the men's room.

## MULLING WIDTH VERSUS LENGTH AT THE WORLD'S

# LARGEST PAINTING

On the family tree of America's roadside attractions, you'll find no branch bearing the World's Largest Painting. It shares no kin with the World's Largest Tire in Dearborn, Michigan, or the World's Largest Pecan of Brunswick, Missouri. The World's Largest Painting is of a different ilk entirely. This is Forest Lawn, after all, the highfalutin cemetery/cultural center hybrid that specializes in making death dignified. And for all of Forest Lawn's very uncemetery-like special features, there is perhaps no bigger surprise than "The Crucifixion," the World's Largest Painting.

No love of Jesus is required in order to appreciate this monster. And it *is* large. Gigantic. Immense. Brobdingnagian. So big that Forest Lawn created a majestic eight-hundred-seat theater to allow for its viewing—and it's a good thing too, since catching sight of this behemoth while standing has induced symptoms likened to that of vertigo or anorexic euphoria, even among the secular. It's *that* huge. The accompanying automated sound-and-light show might be an exercise in overkill, but when you're in possession of the World's Largest Painting, there's no room for understatement.

One might guess that a painting of this scale (and to qualify the claim, it should be noted that "The Crucifixion" is a painting in the traditional sense, mounted on canvas, rather than a fresco) might have been a Forest Lawn commission: one of their tailor-made attractions like their Liberty Bell replica or the "Visit with Michelangelo" performances. But Forest Lawn window dressing it is not. The World's Largest Painting is, in fact, over a hundred years old and was actually, ironically enough, "lost" for almost four decades. It was created by the Polish artist Jan Styka, who

The Hall of the Crucifixion
Forest Lawn Memorial Park
1712 South Glendale Avenue
Glendale
800.204.3131
www.forestlawn.com

*Size matters.*

had originally unveiled the masterwork in Poland. After its debut in Warsaw, "The Crucifixion" went on tour and finally across the Atlantic with the plan to exhibit at the Louisiana Purchase Exposition of 1904. The poor guy carted the thing all the way from Eastern Europe only to discover that it was too big to mount at the Exposition venue. To make matters worse, unable to pay the duty on the painting before departing from the U.S., he had no option but to leave for Poland without it. He died twenty years later and never saw it again. And artists today think they have it rough.

In 1943, after some hunting, the powers that be at Forest Lawn located "The Crucifixion" in Chicago. After making the purchase, construction soon commenced on the Hall of the Crucifixion, a dedicated viewing gallery with plush theater seating, a fancy light show, and a monstrous motorized curtain—the draw of which teases spectators like a seasoned fan dancer, oh-so-slowly revealing all 195 feet of Styka's remarkable work. You'll forget you're even in a cemetery—and it's free. Can you say *cheap date*?

Morbid footnote: After he died, Styka was interred in Rome. Thirty or so years later, they dug him up. Apparently not satisfied with just the painting, Forest Lawn Memorial Park founder Hubert Eaton had made arrangements to bring Styka's remains to Glendale, where his well-traveled corpse now rests in Forest Lawn's Court of Honor—alongside Gutzon Borglum, the sculptor responsible for Mount Rushmore. Could Forest Lawn be working on assembling the World's Largest Collection of Dead Guys Who Created the World's Largest Works of Art?

Call for showtimes.

## VEGETABLE GARDENING FOR HITLER AT
# MURPHY RANCH

Murphy Ranch at
Rustic Canyon
Casale Road
Topanga State Park/
Brentwood

Let's pretend that the U.S. never entered World War II. And let's pretend that, try as they might, England wasn't able to make a go of it on their own and capitulated to Nazi rule. Then let's pretend that the U.S was next to fall, floundering without an administration to guide the way. Just where, in that state of chaos, might you guess California's new Nazi leadership would emerge?

You don't really need to guess and we're tired of pretending so we'll just tell you: Pacific Palisades.

This is not in reference to the infamous anti-Semitism once rife throughout the traditionally WASPy community of

Hancock Park and other enclaves that stretch to the coast, but to a real live Nazi compound: a community developed by a genuine German with a burning love for the Führer and plans to govern the West Coast after the certain defeat of England. The fifty-acre site was established in 1933 by the heir to a mining fortune, who was persuaded by a Nazi spy to invest over four million dollars to equip the ranch with its own water, power, and fuel stations. Behind a guarded iron gate, a community of over fifty residents farmed the land, cultivated their own food, and engaged in regular military drills, in effect making Murphy Ranch a self-sufficient Nazi compound, while a mere eight miles or so away Hollywood's elite were sipping cocktails at the Polo Lounge.

Personally, we harbor fantasies about turning the remains of Murphy Ranch into a historical reenactment attraction: the Murphy Ranch Theme Park and Dinner Adventure. We envision costumed tour guides portraying misguided fascists, speaking in heavy German accents and peppering their spiel with terse Teutonic phrases. They would go about their daily military drills and their vegetable gardening while sharing the good news about the impending New Order with disappointed tourists, who could have opted for a day at Universal Studios. It would be like Colonial Williamsburg meets *Hogan's Heroes*, complete with an admission turnstile, public restrooms, a snack concession, and barbed wire. The Department of Parks and Recreation doesn't see the potential in our proposal, however, and the site will probably be bulldozed once they pull the funding together.

In the meantime, take a hike though the lush, green hills of Rustic Canyon and see the remnants for yourself, which have evidently changed hands from the small community of National Socialist German Workers' Party members to an even smaller community of bored teens looking for a place to party. To reach the trailhead, take Capri Drive north off Sunset up to Amalfi, and park. Continue to follow Capri up to Casale, and turn left. Once you've entered Topanga State Park follow the hiking trail about a mile, and you'll reach the ornate wrought iron gates of the compound. Just to the right of the stone wall is an easy access point to enter the property. By following the road as it splits to the left, you'll pass the graffitied remains of the water and power facilities, and come to what's left of the garage and housing. Be sure to bring water for your hike—and a can of spray-paint if you want. You certainly wouldn't be the first.

Fortunately, the grand plan of Rustic Canyon's secret Nazi community was never realized. The spy who spearheaded the compound was arrested the day after the United States entered

*We got Nazis in them thar hills!*

World War II, and the Murphy Ranch residents' totalitarian dreams were dashed for more than fifty years, until the Bush and Cheney regime turned their glimmer of hope into an inescapable nationalist reality we still enjoy to this day—and surely for generations to come.

## GETTING AN ART-ON AT THE
# BRAND LIBRARY

Brand Library & Art Center
1601 West Mountain Street
Glendale
818.548.2051
www.brandlibrary.org

*Your copy of L.A. Bizarro is overdue.*

You should get stoned and come here.

Ha ha. But no, seriously, you should get stoned and come here. Glendale might not be the first exit off L.A.'s congested freeway of culture—but if you're an art book geek for whom the thought of losing an entire day foraging through the shelves of a cozy old library makes you all tingly down there, you should drop this book right now, roll a fatty, grab an extra pair of underwear, and run straight for the Brand.

Not that we'd go on record suggesting you use illegal recreational drugs to better enhance the experience of an *L.A. Bizarro* destination—we're only suggesting the recreational drugs prescribed by doctors in the state of California to help manage migraines, chronic back pain, and the free-for-all art book orgy of the Brand Library.

The Brand is at once manageably small yet impossible to experience in its entirety using only one lifetime. The modest facility may be absent the high tech hoo-ha of a fancy contemporary branch, but it also has neither the coldness of the common public library nor the austerity of a university. The Brand feels more like a really great used bookstore, and if they served food, we'd move in. They've got art books packed into every room, squeezed onto every shelf, down every aisle and at every turn, and we don't just mean ancient art or the Renaissance masters—or even a collection limited to sculpture and painting. You'll find graphic design, architecture, photography, and fashion. Art theory, art biographies, and art history. The

classical, the contemporary, and the postmodern. Oversized coffee table books so large you'll need help turning their pages. Magazine racks lined with the latest issues of *Artforum*, *Artweek*, *Aperture*, and *i-D*, plus a host of arcane design magazines you've never heard of. The library's small, comfortable reading areas beg for your time. Outside, the Brand's tranquil lawns, Japanese garden, and surrounding grounds could swallow an afternoon on their own. Did we mention their music room, featuring one of the largest CD collections in the world? The old records? The record players?

They've also got a section of books devoted entirely to Los Angles history, public art, architecture, and popular culture. *L.A. Bizarro* was conspicuously absent from those titles, however, but then why would a library with a Los Angeles section want to shelve a book about Los Angeles that spent twenty-one weeks on the *Los Angeles Times* bestseller list? From *People* magazine to CNN, it got more ballyhooey than most books, and it was in fact rated "a classic" in one of America's major metropolitan newspapers—wouldn't that warrant a spot on the shelf of a Los Angeles section? We're not bitter about it or anything, we were just wondering.

Maybe it was checked out. Or better yet, maybe it was stolen.

The Old Town Music Hall
140 Richmond Street
El Segundo
310.322.2592
www.otmh.org

## ANACHRONISTIC ENTERTAINMENT AT THE

# OLD TOWN MUSIC HALL

There aren't too many places left where a person can see a movie the old-fashioned way. At The Old Town Music Hall you won't lose your way in a labyrinthine cineplex or be forced to take an early withdrawal on your IRA to purchase a small Pepsi. Tucked away on a tiny side street in El Segundo (you know, that less-traveled side of LAX, the one Fred Sanford joked about), this Lilliputian theater served as a silent movie house upon its opening in the 1920s. Today, after nearly a century of innovation, it still serves

as a silent movie house. In fact, their film calendar rarely carries a title that postdates the bombing of Pearl Harbor. Though the Shirley Temple vehicle *Dimples* may not be at the top of your list of must-sees, you'll be treated to an experience pleasingly absent of rowdy teens, soda-slicked floors, and people who eat with their mouths open.

The façade of The Old Town Music Hall isn't much to look at, but the interior of the diminutive 188-seat auditorium is a place where the Asiatic and the rococo collide. Barely large enough to accommodate the two munificent chandeliers pulling at its relatively low ceiling, the cozy space is appointed with an elaborate Chinese gong flanked with fright masks. At stage right, gems of the gumball machine variety encrust a gleaming gold Buddha atop an exotic bell piano. Semi-reclinable seats in rows no wider than four across face a low stage dressed with cherub-topped candelabras emitting electric pink flames, and—making use of every square inch—crammed down front of the proscenium are two concert pianos including a 1917 Steinway once belonging to Nelson Eddy, whose ivories were reportedly tickled by George Gershwin (the Steinway, not Eddy).

The Old Town Music Hall features another attraction even more unique to movie theaters than Chinese gongs and cherubic lighting schemes: Bolted in place at center stage is their 1925 "Mighty Wurlitzer" (at The Old Town Music Hall, the word "mighty" always precedes the name "Wurlitzer"). And mighty it is, because this is hardly your garden-variety El Segundo silent movie theater pipe organ.

As the accompanist takes his seat and commences the pumping of his mighty organ, shaking the floor with a thunder that only a Wurlitzer can generate, the velvet curtain is slowly drawn. What lies behind is not the movie screen soon to be projected with an image of Fatty Arbuckle as one might anticipate, but the vibrating, honking, rattling animation of floor-to-ceiling organ innards: every pipe, air vent, drum, bell, and horn going at once like a mammoth one-man band. "So what?" we can hear you say—jaded, ungrateful, overstimulated product of the digital age that you are, "Organ guts, who cares?" Well, this is El Segundo where the party never stops, and like Ken Kesey's old school bus, these organ guts go "Furthur," each piece painted in different fluorescent colors and illuminated with black lights! The sight of shaking hot-orange tambourines and day-glo blue snare drums is something you just don't see every day, at least not south of the 10, unless, of course, you do a lot of acid.

Rather than screening back-to-back commercials and trailers for the next big blockbuster, Old Town fires up the Mighty Wurlitzer

*El Segundo's Hallucinogenic Hootenanny*

for a musical prologue prior to each feature presentation, leading the audience through a quick series of sing-alongs to time-tested old standards like "After the Ball," and "My Wild Irish Rose" while lyrics are projected from antiquated slides. If you've never sung along to a psychedelic pipe organ knocking out a tune like "Mairzy Doats" then please tell us what exactly you're planning to do with your pathetic excuse for a life?

You may be the youngest one there by fifty years but if you'd rather brave the scene at Universal CityWalk, don't say we didn't warn you.

## GETTING ALL SHOOK UP ABOUT
# THAI ELVIS

When we first heard about Palms Thai restaurant, we were enthralled. We imagined an intimate venue embellished with faux palm trees, bathed in blue lighting, its small stage backed with a red velvet curtain and illuminated by a single spot light. As the familiar strains of *Also Sprach Zarathustra* swell in the background, the lights dim, and the crowd falls silent in reverent anticipation. This, in our mind's eye, would be the perfect proscenium for the art of Kavee "Kevin" Thongpricha, otherwise known as Thai Elvis.

Yeah, well, dreams die hard.

Palms Thai is a cavernous, cacophonous place with large "family-style" tables butted up against each other in rows that seem to stretch to the horizon. Reservations are accepted before 7:00 PM—after that it's first come, first serve, and you're on your own. We were prudent enough to make a reservation, and though we arrived early, the place was packed with an eclectic blend of Asians (always a good sign), hipsters (not always a good sign), and a mixed bag of hip-hoppers, average Joes, and yuppies in love (who really cares?). We requested a table close to the stage, where we could get the best view in the house for Thai Elvis. Our wish was granted—we were seated front and center. Hot damn! Bring on the King!

We were so worked up about seeing Elvis that we almost forgot that Palms Thai is also known for its fare, which is impressively vast and varied. Aside from healthy portions of the usual suspects—we started out pedestrian with some chicken and beef satay, then sampled a variety of curries and vegetable dishes before ordering some of our favorite exotic delicacies, like wild

Palms Thai Restaurant
5900 Hollywood Boulevard,
Unit B
Los Angeles
323.462.5073

*Airvis has reft the beerding.*

boar with curry sauce, frog with chili and holy basil, raw Thai sausage, and crispy maw salad (maw is the dried stomach lining of a large fish). With all that unusual food on the table, it was our pad Thai—that perennial favorite—that seemed particularly robust that evening, boasting an aroma not unlike a freshly opened can of Mighty Dog. It was the only clunker in an otherwise flavorful array of dishes.

The stage at Palms Thai is elevated to ensure that all diners, even those a quarter mile away in the back of the room, get a decent view of the entertainment. Behind a hideously gigantic metal sculpture of Elvis Presley that stands in front of stage right, we could glimpse Kevin getting ready for his first show of the evening. A coat draped over his shoulders, scarf around his neck, Kevin was intently focused—one might even say *meditating*—on the Asian movie playing on the small laptop computer in front of him. As 7:30 drew nigh, Kevin closed the laptop, stripped down to his Elvis regalia, and shook his arms in true Elvis fashion. Showtime, at last.

And yet there was no overture, no change in lighting, not even a cursory intro to announce the arrival of the one, the only, Thai Elvis. Instead, he just strolled onstage, fiddled with a few knobs on the mixer, and without ceremony, launched into "Suspicious Minds." Or was it "Wear My Ring Around Your Neck"? It was hard to tell because of the ceaseless din echoing off the high ceilings. Nary a patron seemed to notice that the

show had started. Had we stepped into an alternate universe? How could so many people be so painfully blasé about the fact that the greatest Thai Elvis impersonator *in the world* was standing right in front of them? Was their pad Thai better than ours? Or were they just typical Angelenos?

Make no mistake about it, Mr. Thongpricha is a consummate performer who delivers an impressive facsimile of Elvis. It's not just Presley's vocal stylings that Kevin has captured, but his mannerisms in general, right down to the way the King curved his fingers on his outstretched hand. For Thongpricha, this is obviously a labor of love, one done out of respect for Presley. So how come the guy can't get a little of the same from the chattering chowhounds packed into Palms Thai?

The first few songs received a polite smattering of applause, as if to say, "Yeah, that's great, pal, but can you come back later? I'm stuffing my piehole right now." Even that tepid enthusiasm soon waned as diners became increasingly more engrossed with what was on their plate rather than what was happening onstage. The applause eventually stopped

# IS THE POPE JEWISH?

We're not sure what—if anything—goes on inside this tiny building in an alley behind the gutted remains of Splash the Relaxation Center. It looks abandoned and no one answered the door, but we really dig the exterior paint job. If the Hillside Stranglers had gone to art school, this is the kind of place where they would have brought their victims.

**Studio KRK / 8044 ½ Third Avenue /
Behind what used to be Splash The Relaxation Spa**

altogether. The room grew even louder. And louder. Looking around, we see that we're the only ones in the entire restaurant who've made even the slightest effort to give Kevin our undivided attention; he seems to appreciate that, throwing a few classic Elvis poses directly our way. If we had been wearing lace panties, they would have been onstage in a heartbeat.

If anything, Thongpricha is a pro. He seemed unfazed by the relentless chatter, the clanging plates, the loud announcement that "TABLE IS READY FOR JOE, PARTY OF FOUR! TABLE IS READY FOR JOE!" Sweet Jesus, if Presley had to deal with that kind of crap, it would have been enough to drive him to drugs.

After a half hour of full-on performances (including a moving rendition of "I Can't Help Falling in Love with You") Thai Elvis was ready to call it quits. Sadly, the act that followed him, an attractive young woman in a silver sequined dress, received even less respect from the audience. The mood had gone from awkward to downright uncomfortable in a matter of minutes. The cackling of the thirtysomething gals at the table next to us, combined with the lingering odor of the pad Thai, didn't make it any better. We decided the show was over for us as well, which came as a relief to the waitstaff who, although quite friendly, are obviously under orders to turn the tables as quickly as possible. At least Elvis isn't the only one getting the bum's rush at this place.

Kevin slipped the coat back over his shoulders, and wrapped the scarf around his neck. With performances every hour, on the half hour, the man has to save his voice. After all, it's not easy trying to sing over a crowd of loud, hungry philistines, even if you are the ersatz King of Rock 'n' Roll.

# AETHERIUS SOCIETY

The Aetherius Society
6202 Afton Place
Los Angeles
213-467-HEAL
www.aetherius.com

Consider the following:

*"He parted the sea!"*

*"He turned water into wine!"*

*"He shot up to heaven like a rocket!"*

*"He wrote science fiction!"*

So what's so strange about the notion that mankind is hopelessly violent, and that we've completely destroyed the human race on this planet not once, but twice? It went down the first time at a place known as Lemuria, which is not, as some believe, the official land of the lemurs. Never heard of it? Does Atlantis ring a bell, then? Yes, the elusive sunken city was also the playing field for the second suicidal Super Bowl that wiped out mankind many eons ago.

As if these two cataclysms weren't enough, it seems we've also lived on another planet somewhere between Mars and Jupiter—and we trashed that, too. Totally.

If there's one thing we humans are good at, it's destroying everything we touch. With any luck, we'll be four-for-four with this global warming thing, and who knows—we may just punctuate our exit from earth with a few nuclear holocausts for good measure. *Go humans!*

If none of this sounds familiar to you, then perhaps you are not acquainted with the teachings of The Aetherius Society.

Like the Church of Scientology and the Unarius Academy of Science, The Aetherius Society is a mélange of earthly theologies augmented with a healthy dose of what some may classify as sci-fi weirdness, but which is really no more incredible than the notion

# GO FOR THE BRONZE

If North Hollywood were to become a modern day Pompeii by a natural disaster akin to Vesuvius, smothering the intersection of Lankershim and Magnolia under hundreds of feet of ash, what might the archeologists make of the excavated ruins in years to come? What might those ruins say about who we were, what we valued, and who shaped our philosophies? Certainly anyone cast in a plaster relief or represented by a bronze bust set upon a concrete pillar would point the scholars of the future in some important directions. So what sorts of cues might they glean from the likenesses of Phil Donahue, Bob Mackie, and Huckleberry Hound?

**Television Personality Bronzes / Academy of Television Arts & Sciences / 5220 Lankershim Boulevard / North Hollywood**

of a virgin giving birth to Christ. Like Unarius, Aetherius is referred to as a New Religious UFO Movement (NRUM). Unlike Scientology, Aetherius will not try to crush you like a bug if you look at its teachings sideways.

Like most religions, Aetherius a is little too complex to lay out in a single entry of a glib guidebook, but the CliffsNotes are as follows: Mixing yoga, UFOs, and a patchwork quilt of eastern and western religions, The Aetherius Society has developed a small but zealous worldwide following since its inception in 1954 by Sir George King. A big hit in England, Australia, New Zealand, Canada, and other countries where they talk funny English, the society's American and Australasian headquarters are located right here in Los Angeles. Sir George King was the "Primary Terrestrial Mental Channel for the Cosmic Masters." In other words, he channeled aliens who had (and apparently still have) a perverse desire to help us out of our violent rut; they just don't want to get too close in the process. With our track record for genocide and global destruction, who can blame them? Fortunately, these "Transmissions from the Cosmic Masters" have been recorded, transcribed, and published by The Aetherius Society for the benefit of all those in search of the Truth. "Blessed is the great being that is the galaxy" is an Aetherius adage that even atheistic cynics like us can get behind.

*Is that a spiritual energy radiator in your pocket or are you just happy to see me?*

As best as we can tell, The Aetherius Society does not appear to be a plot to separate the gullible from their life savings, which is admirable in a world of Ponzi schemes posing as religions. "Service is the most potent religion," says The Aetherius Society, and those who follow this doctrine by performing selfless acts for the benefit of their fellow man will advance up the ladder of enlightenment far more quickly than, say, chronic masturbators, Republicans, and others hopeless atavists—at least that's how we see it.

Indeed, much of the Aetherius mission is to balance mankind's incredibly nasty karma, which is a Herculean task no matter how you slice it. As far as animals go, man is the only one intelligent enough to create something as miraculous as cheese in an aerosol can, yet stupid enough to kill each other over whose Guy in the Sky is better. If we are indeed made in God's image, He certainly has a perverse sense of humor.

That's where The Aetherius Society can lend a helping hand. Take their "Operation Prayer Power," for example. Using "dynamic prayer, eastern mantra, and mystic mudras," members of the society gather together in order to summon up "Spiritual Energy" which is then stored in a radionic battery. This energy is then released through something called a "Spiritual Energy Radiator," and is used when the Earth is in deep shit and in need of Spiritual Energy, like after a Republican administration or the opening of a new P.F. Chang's.

## OUT *'n'* ABOUT
# BEVERLY HILLS: THE CITY THAT TRIES WAY TOO HARD

Sister City Sign / Coldwater Canyon at Monte Cielo Drive / Beverly Hills

The charging sessions for Operation Prayer Power are open to anyone willing to take the time and energy to be taught how to turn mere mantras into a powerful, global healing force. Be an Energizer Bunny for peace—stop by The Aetherius Society to help fill their radionic battery today.

And tell them Tom Cruise sent you!

## PROVING THERE'S NO BUSINESS BUT SHOW BUSINESS AT THE

# CRYSTAL CATHEDRAL

We don't know much about Jesus but we know what we like, and the folks at the Crystal Cathedral sure put on one hell of a show. One might not think laser beams, disco fog, and pyrotechnic displays more befitting the glory days of Siegfried and Roy have their place in church, but here, Christian worship means one thing: *special effects*! The days of sitting on painfully hard wood pews listening to your priest drone on in Latin—or worse, English—are over. Slide your heathen ass into one of the Crystal Cathedral's cushy seats worthy of an AMC movie theater and hold on tight.

In addition to the glass and steel architectural oddity that is the Crystal Cathedral, the church is infamous for their splashy Christian spectaculars staged here twice yearly, each one worthy of a Las Vegas showroom. The Glory of Easter is their fast-paced passion play with a cast of hundreds piling onto the cathedral stage, dragging with them oxen, tigers, peacocks, and enough barnyard animals to fill a dozen petting zoos. Even Jesus milks his entrance vamping down a long catwalk through the center of the theater . . . er, church . . . on a real burro.

Rubbernecking chicken hawks take delight in the Roman soldiers, traditionally played by the St. Paul High School football team, charging down the carpeted aisles on horseback baring their muscled, barely-legal thighs in short skirts and strappy sandals. Showstopping ensues with the heavenly angels, strung up by fine wire to an intricate block-and-tackle apparatus,

Crystal Cathedral
12141 Lewis Street
Garden Grove
714.971.4000
www.crystalcathedral.org

IN-CAR
WORSHIP
ONLY
*please*

*Too much is never enough.*

flying hundreds of feet from the far corners of the balconies and swooshing down just inches above your scalp, straining operatically and circling above the expensive seats down front. If you happen to be positioned in just the right spot, you can look straight up into their filmy gowns and cop a peek of some *real* heaven—which, perhaps, is why those tickets cost a little more.

The magic makers of the Crystal Cathedral are far too savvy to blow their wad all at once; special effects and exotic animals are carefully paced throughout the productions to prevent any downtime, and the finales never fail to thrill. During the crucifixion scene, all three crosses rise from the floor through clouds of dry ice as an enormous section of the cathedral's glass wall opens like an electric garage door, bringing a gust of the cold night wind into your face while green laser beams shoot from behind the Star of the show and out into the evening sky. For anyone who ever saw KISS in concert the first time around, the resurrection sequence will take you right back to an Ace Frehley guitar solo of 1979.

While hardly shy of special effects, "The Glory of Christmas" may lack the fireworks of the Easter extravaganza, but it does boast a camel and special guest stars. We got to see a solo dance performance by Heather Whitestone, the deaf Miss America. Jealous?

Even if it's not Easter or Christmas, there's still plenty to see and spend your money on at the Crystal Cathedral. In fact, free tour guides are available to show you around. Don't miss the parking lot featuring a "drive-in worship" section, in which followers may sit in the comfort of their own SUVs while listening to the Sunday service on giant loudspeakers positioned throughout the lot. One can only fantasize about carhops on roller skates gliding from one driver's side window to the next carrying giant collection plates. What else might you expect from a congregation that held its first service at the Orange Drive-In Movie Theater in 1955? True, all true.

Want to know what the landfills of tomorrow will look like? Take a peek inside the gift shop. Crystal Cathedral postcards, key chains, pins, poster books, DVDs, thimbles, bells, mugs, even Crystal Cathedral cocktail napkins—it's all here, and yours with the simple exchange of U.S. currency. And if you haven't the time to attend Dr. Schuller's Sunday services or read the books he's penned, the gift shop radically simplifies the path to enlightenment: You can purchase a glittery halo here and bypass the mumbo jumbo. Also featured among the wares in the gift shop is Schuller's telling Possibility Thinker's Creed:

*"When faced with a mountain I WILL NOT QUIT! I will keep on striving until I climb over, find a pass through, tunnel underneath— or simply stay and turn the mountain into a gold mine, with God's help!"*

—*Robert Schuller*

Etched onto a glass paperweight the creed sells for twenty dollars, plus tax.

Say what you want about Robert Schuller, but the man knows of what he speaks. A gold mine, indeed.

## GETTING A FIVE-DOLLAR HISTORY LESSON— AND A GOLDEN TAN—AT THE AMERICAN

# MILITARY MUSEUM

Contrary to what one might guess, the American Military Museum is not some bright, shiny, government-funded facility loaded with exhibits that whitewash war with self-congratulatory propaganda. But if your idea of fun is a day spent roasting under the unyielding El Monte sun in a dusty dirt lot perusing the corroded fighting machines of wars past, then brother, have we got a museum for you!

The American Military Museum pushes no political agenda, and has much less to do with celebrating war than it does honoring the veterans who've fought them. Their collection is the largest of its kind in the U.S., with nearly two-thirds of its three-hundred-plus pieces on display. Most remarkably, this is a mom-and-pop business (or pop-and-son as the case may be), the private collection of Don Michelson, an ex-officer for the Quartermaster Corps during World War II. Following the war, Michelson began collecting military whatnot by chance, starting first with uniforms and sundry memorabilia, later moving onto tanks, amphibious vehicles, and bomb loaders—haggling with the government to acquire some his best scores. He established the museum in 1963, originally in the city of Bell, and relocated here in '78.

Informally stationed in a semi-landscaped lot behind a cyclone fence along Rosemead Boulevard, the exhibit arrangements are at once much cruder and far better organized than the sandwich-board sign and the Porta Potty in the parking lot might indicate. The approach is straightforward, and refreshingly low tech. The attention and care with which

American Military Museum
1918 North Rosemead Blvd.
South El Monte
626.442.1776
http://tankland.com

*Tanks for the memories.*

this collection of fighting machines has been assembled and presented is impressive—if not charming—and half the fun is trying to guess what function a particularly confounding piece of equipment originally served. Look it up in the binder provided at the check-in tent, and although some of the book's entries are in need of an update (" . . . We are going to sand and repaint this exhibit in spring 2004 . . . ") most offer letter-specific details about an item's date of manufacture, origin, capabilities, and service history.

Pieces like the *Gebirgskanone 15*, an early First World War mountain gun used by the German Army, number among other museum rarities like the 1952 Soviet-manufactured anti-aircraft gun sold to Iraq in the 1960s and later captured by American troops during Desert Storm—which is pretty damn exotic for South El Monte. Stunners like a repaired 1965 helicopter gun ship (the famed "Huey") that crashed in Vietnam, a World War II searchlight, and lifeboats used in World War II, the Korean Conflict, and Vietnam sit grouped behind a low rope, along with less dramatic but equally compelling pieces like the towable water unit that brought hot showers to GIs on the field. Tanks and

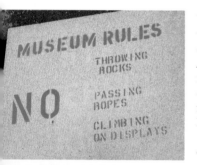

armored personnel carriers are occasionally upstaged by some of the pieces farmed out to studios over time, like the torpedoes used in the movies *Twelve O'Clock High* and *Tora! Tora! Tora!*, the ambulance from *M\*A\*S\*H*, and the Soviet radar simulator featured in the Demi Moore film *G.I. Jane*—which might be exciting for anyone who actually saw *G.I. Jane*. All this for less than a third of what you'd pay to access the Hollywood Wax Museum.

It's a sobering experience to walk among the AMM collection, to get up close and personal (no climbing

on the equipment, please) to tools of war rarely seen by civilians, and to consider the servicemen who occupied these cockpits, steered these tanks, and took aim with these barrels—and to what end. The American Military Museum is more than a collection of outdated equipment sitting in a quiet dirt lot on the border of South El Monte; there are fewer places to better contemplate what war is and what war has been, who's fought them, and how. The sheer mightiness of these machines is no less awe-inspiring to witness as well—although retirement seems to suit them.

# GORDON R. HOWARD

## MUSEUM COMPLEX

Florence has the Accademia, New York has the Met, and Paris, the Louvre. In Burbank, we have the Burbank Historical Society's Gordon R. Howard Museum Complex. While its treasures may not rival the *Mona Lisa* or the *Last Supper,* we'd bet that the Louvre couldn't produce a sport coat worn by Johnny Carson on the *Tonight Show,* or an early animation sketch of Yosemite Sam. *Touché, Paris!*

At the Burbank Historical Society's Gordon R. Howard Museum Complex—or the Howard for short—you'll learn all sorts of fascinating things about the history of the city that made Ed McMahon a household name. In the better part of only one afternoon you'll become a font of knowledge for all things Burbank, which might prove advantageous if you've ever had trouble holding your own in dinner party conversation. Just imagine all the new friends you'll win by casually incorporating what you've discovered at the Howard over cocktails.

" . . . and speaking of *Burbank,*" you'll say, seamlessly making your segue, "isn't it remarkable how it came to be the San Fernando Valley's *first independent city in 1911*?" "Tell us more!" your peers will exclaim, and from that moment on, you'll have them eating from the palm of your hand. Suggestively drag your finger around the rim of your martini glass, and go in for the kill, " . . . of course, it goes without saying that it was the *Great Partition Deal of 1886* that made way for the Providencia Land, Water, and Development Company to eventually acquire the area that would make way for *the city we now call Burbank. . . .* " You'll get laid for sure.

You just don't go strolling into the Howard, however; you have to be buzzed in, just like a speakeasy or upscale apartment. Don't be offended if your buzzing is ignored and you're left standing outside the locked

Gordon R. Howard
Museum Complex
115 Lomita Street
Burbank
818.841.6333
www.burbankhistsoc.com

*Heeeeeeeeeere's yawning!*

# X MARKS THE SPOT

In this house that they called home: a stucco Spanish-style bungalow on the edge of West Hollywood, which once played digs to the seminal L.A. band X.

**Former X Home / 1118 Genesee Avenue / West Hollywood**

door for ten or fifteen minutes to bake in Burbank's unforgiving heat; nobody wants to appear too eager, even at the Howard. Once you're given access, you'll thrill to the Howard's many engrossing exhibits.

Do you think the NBC logo always looked the way it does today? Did you say *yes*? Ha! You uninformed rube! You obviously need to spend some time in front of their NBC logo exhibit, where, through the magic of one-dimensional images mounted to foam board, you'll be whisked through the exciting life of the network icon as it morphs from its early days on radio into the logo we now know and love. If you're still awake after that, check out the turn-of-the-century dentist's office diorama, the History of the Burbank Police Department display, the rousing Burbank Timeline Mural, and the wall of early Lockheed photographs.

After you've squeezed that last drop of excitement out of the Lockheed installation, be sure not to miss the costumed mannequin of James Jeffries, Burbank's own heavyweight champion of the early 1900s. If his original boxing gloves and inspiring story don't get your heart racing, we know what will (we were going to keep this a secret and just let you be surprised, but hell, why not give away the store?). Are you sitting down? The Howard has *the first official seal of the city of Burbank*! The seal reads "City of Burbank, Established 1911" and bears an image of—no, not the face of Ed McMahon, but you're really close—a watermelon.

Did you know that Walt Disney originally planned to break ground for his Evil, er, *Magic* Kingdom in Burbank before he decided to swallow Anaheim whole? It's true! And if you don't believe us, try and stay alert in front of the original plans exhibited right here in the Howard's thrilling Disney display. If you haven't had enough, ask a volunteer to walk you over to the historic Mentzer home on the south end of the complex. The quaint 1887 house is furnished and completely appointed to the period, demonstrating that turn-of-the-century life in Burbank wasn't any less dull than it is today.

There's lots more to see: a diorama of a Burbank ranch house with antique farming equipment, a fire engine, some old dolls, and a gallery of paintings depicting early Burbank.

Hello? Are you still there?

The Gordon R. Howard Museum is owned and operated by the Burbank Historical Society, and the late Gordon R. Howard, a Burbank businessman, was the Historical Society's major benefactor. It was through his generous gift that the museum became a reality. The Burbank Historical Society is a nonprofit organization with a commitment to collecting, preserving, and displaying the history of the Burbank community. The complex is run entirely by its board members and dedicated volunteers. Clearly, the Howard is their labor of love.

And it seems to us that if a love for the city of Burbank isn't blind, then it's probably suffering from glaucoma.

## THREE HUNDRED AND SIXTY DEGREES OF SEPARATION AT THE

# VELASLAVASAY PANORAMA

Before the discoveries of celluloid and the cathode ray tube turned us into a culture of couch-bound Morlocks, people had to get off their fat asses and use something called an "imagination" in order to be entertained. Though the advent of movable type allowed for the mass production of reading materials, and travelling minstrels could be counted on for a bawdy song or two, most other forms of entertainment were to be had in structures that were not so portable. Museums, theaters, and concert halls tended to be large, heavy, and immovable. Only the extremely rich—as in royally rich—could afford the luxury of enjoying the works of, say, Rembrandt, Mozart, and Shakespeare in the comfort of their living rooms.

This doesn't mean that the unwashed masses of centuries past were any less sophisticated than today's average moviegoer, nor were the impresarios of yore less likely than their modern-day

The Velaslavasay Panorama
1122 West 24th Street
Los Angeles
213.746.2166
www.panoramaonview.org

# HIGH SCHOOL MUSICAL

Who'd suspect this quiet and markedly un-rock 'n' roll corner of El Segundo set the scene for cinematic delinquent Riff Randall and her sundry cohorts, as they romped with the Ramones and blitzkrieg-bopped the fictitious Vince Lombardi High to smithereens in the 1979 Roger Corman classic *Rock 'n' Roll High School*? This, of course, was back in the day when detonating explosives in a classroom was considered outrageous.

Gabba Gabba Hey!

**Rock 'n' Roll High School Location / 640 Main Street / El Segundo**

brethren to appeal to the lowest common denominator in order to hype their latest attractions. Then, as now, it was all about gimmick and spectacle, and the spectacle that really knocked them out at the end of the eighteenth century was the panoramic painting. Its gimmick was a manipulation of perspective dubbed *La Nature à Coup d'Œil*, or "Nature at a Glance," by its inventor, Scottish painter Robert Barker, who also coined the term "panorama." By surrounding the viewer and filling his line of sight, the panorama (or "cyclorama" as it would come to be called in the States) presented the illusion of being in the thick of the action. Though it seems incredibly dull by contemporary standards, it was the IMAX of its day.

Yet it is this very dullness—for lack of a better word—that makes The Velaslavasay Panorama near USC so utterly captivating. A noble attempt to revive this nearly extinct art form and its arcane milieu, the Velaslavasay's 360-degree installation is almost cocky in its choice of subject matter, daring us to stay awake by presenting the most soporific tableau imaginable: "Effulgence of the North" is not a tribute to the life and times of Peter North, but a gloriously gloomy exploration of the boundless monochromatic wasteland of the Arctic. Whereas most classic panoramas depicted lush land- or cityscapes or full-on battle scenes, this one assumes the formidable challenge of turning the frostbitten tundra of the north pole into a captivating destination. Yet it is an appropriate subject for a medium that dates back to a time when people were fascinated and even obsessed with Arctic exploration.

## OUT *'n'* ABOUT
# TAG, YOU'RE IT!

Defacing buildings and walls is old-school. This is Los
Angeles, after all, where we enjoy green leaves and flowering
plants year-round—so why should the growing number of
L.A. gangs limit themselves to concrete and cinderblock
when a nicely trimmed hedge is just begging for it?

**Tagged Hedge / West Los Angeles / (maybe your yard is next)**

Located in what is quaintly dubbed "L.A.'s historic West
Adams district" (many are more familiar with its other name,
"L.A.'s historic robbery, rape, and murder district"), the
Velaslavasay Panorama resides in the Union Theater, a 1921 art
deco playhouse that, ironically, was home to the Tile Layers
Union Local 18 for more than thirty years. Painstakingly refurbished with antique fixtures and dark-stained paneling, the Union gives off the same pseudo-Victorian
vibe found at the Museum of Jurassic Technology, and
that's no coincidence: The MJT has served as an inspiration to the Velaslavasay's creator, Sara Velas, and its
director, David Wilson, is one of the panorama's strongest supporters. Indeed, if the MJT had enough room
to accommodate it, the panorama would seem right at
home there.

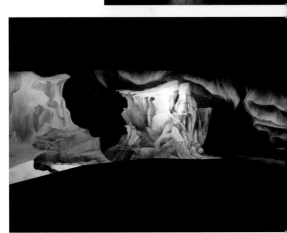

Down a darkened hallway, a circular wooden
staircase leads to another world and another era.
Ascending into the panorama
room—formerly the offices of the
aforementioned tile layers—is an
almost mystical experience. The
circular space is illuminated only by
the light that seems to emanate from
the trompe l'œil painting itself, its
depth further enhanced by the prop
icebergs that appear to float before
it in a moat of black water. The effect
is immediately impressive, and its
stillness elicits an almost churchlike
reverence. In the quiet moments that
follow, as one's eyes become accustomed to the unusual light, the hidden wonders of the cyclorama reveal

themselves. The faint creaks and pops that one first mistakes as the sound of others moving about the room are actually part of a soundtrack by German composer Moritz Fher to emulate the ambience of the Arctic. Then, almost imperceptibly, one notices the light in the room shifting with the elephantine determination of an iceberg, tracing the shadows of an indeterminate passage of time as it recreates the magic of the aurora borealis. We can't be sure if they cranked up the AC in the panorama room or if the visuals had simply induced a sense of chilliness, but the only sensory stimulation that seemed to be missing from the experience was the smell of the north pole, which, as far as we know, is a lot like our grocer's freezer.

Being in the presence of this particular panorama provokes the desire to languish and watch the fading light. To absorb the subtlety of the full thirty-five-minute synchronized cycle of sound and vision is an almost meditative process not recommended for those who need an explosion or a laugh track every seven seconds to hold their attention. Fortunately, a circular bench allows patient observers the opportunity to witness the entire show without burning too many calories. As we discovered, the north pole is a great place to get away from our harried lives, a spot where we can clear our minds and even take a nap.

The Velaslavasay is not just about the panorama, however. Lectures, performances, and other artistic endeavors are often staged in the theater area at the back of the building, and past that, through the rear doors, is The Velaslavasay Garden and Grounds, which promise "lush tropical plantings, a wide variety of succulents, and a copper-roofed exhibit of sinister carnivorous flora." We have to admit we were a bit underwhelmed by our own experience in the gardens, but it did seem to be a work in progress, and perhaps our *Addams Family* expectations of Venus flytraps the size of a man's head were slightly unrealistic. We enjoyed the fake dead raven laying on its side in the dirty water of a birdbath, however.

Attention to detail is The Velaslavasay's calling card, and its plethora of promotional materials utilize the same kind of flowery prose and design elements of the period to which it harkens. Like the Museum of Jurassic Technology, it is The Velaslavasay as a whole that is the work of art: The painting, the gardens, the theater, the building, the events, and the promo materials are but disparate elements that come together like brushstrokes to create the finished piece.

We're not sure if the surrounding neighborhood is controlled by the 18th Street gang or the Harpys, but clearly the Arctic is Ms. Velas's turf, an island of peaceful perfection in an otherwise turbulent sea. We're hoping it'll be a cold day in hell—or a warm day at the pole—before an iceberg is ever tagged with "Flaco," "Spider," or "Little Deuce."

## COMING TO TERMS WITH ONTOLOGICAL SOLIPSISM AND THE NATURE OF PARKING LOTS AT THE

# MUSEUM OF JURASSIC TECHNOLOGY AND THE CENTER FOR LAND USE INTERPRETATION

Whenever we get all hot and bothered about next-door neighbors The Museum of Jurassic Technology and Center for Land Use Interpretation, the uninitiated invariably wipe our spittle from their cheeks and ask why we're working ourselves into a lather about two places that sound so incredibly boring. And that's when we usually clam up, not because the museum and center are boring (far from it, *mes frères*), but because mere words—even from allegedly distinguished connoisseurs of all that is weird and wonderful about our city—cannot do MJT and CLUI justice. And while we wish we could just end it right there and simply encourage you, dear reader, to get your ass over to Venice Boulevard, we realize you expect more from us than that. (Then again, so did our parents, and look where that got us.)

"The Museum of Jurassic Technology in Los Angeles, California is an educational institution dedicated to the

The Museum of Jurassic
Technology
9341 Venice Boulevard
Culver City
310.836.6131
www.mjt.org

Center for Land Use
Interpretation
9331 Venice Boulevard
Culver City
310.839.5722
www.clui.org

# REVENGE OF THE LAWN JOCKEYS

Hancock Park is a wealthy, quiet, and sophisticated area of Los Angeles known for its tree-lined streets, stately mansions, and, at one time, racial intolerance. When Nat King Cole announced he was moving into the neighborhood in August of 1948, the very white, very WASPy Hancock Park Property Owners Association held an emergency meeting to figure out a way to keep one of the nation's top recording artists out of the neighborhood. Their solution was to offer Cole $25,000 more than the $75,000 he had paid for the house, with the understanding that he would spend the money on a new home somewhere outside the boundaries of their lily-white enclave. What were these fine, upstanding citizens so concerned about? "How would YOU like it if you had to come out of your home and see a Negro walking down the street wearing a big wide hat, zoot suit, a long chain, and yellow shoes?" they reportedly asked Cole's manager. Cole moved in anyway, and was welcomed with a sign that read "Nigger Heaven," and later, the same epithet burned into his lawn in large block letters. He remained in Hancock Park until his death from lung cancer in 1965.

Cut to the present day. As if to pay off Hancock Park's karmic debt, Norwood Young, a handsome and flamboyant black R & B singer, lives on the same street where the neighbors once feared the meanderings of the yellow-shoed Negro. Polite, soft-spoken, and amiable, Norwood has used the front of his elegant home—which he's dubbed "Youngwood Court"—to create an homage to Michelangelo's David, and to give a giant finger to anyone who would prevent him from doing otherwise. As Young explained it to us, after cordially inviting us into his well-appointed digs, the first David was erected after the trees in the front yard were cut down, and some protective cover from the street was needed. The other five billion Davids went up, one by one, not only because Young is crazy about that statue, but as answers to each of the complaints he received about them. "Hmm, you say you don't like those two Davids out front? Well, how about . . . two more?!" Complaints escalated from hate mail to eggs to a bullet hole in his front door. Young, like Cole, refuses to back down, which is why we love the guy.

According to the feisty entertainer, not all of his neighbors despise the landscaping at Youngwood Court. But most of them do, and to them we can only say this: thank your lucky stars you live next to Norwood Young. After all, compared to Sheik Mohammed Al-Fassi, who once painted pubic hair on the nude statues that surrounded his bright green mansion on Sunset Boulevard, Norwood Young seems like Frank Gehry. And if you don't want to live next door to Norwood, we'd be happy to switch homes with you. Life's too short to let a homeowners' association pee in your Malt-O-Meal.

**Parade of Davids / Third Street and South Muirfield Road / Hancock Park**

advancement of knowledge and the public appreciation of the Lower Jurassic." Okay, that's their official party line, but dinosaur buffs (and their offspring) will be disappointed—and perhaps even *disturbed*—by what they find at MJT, since it has absolutely nothing to do with fossils or extinct lizards. Indeed, the Lower Jurassic wasn't much to speak of when it comes to technology, especially when one considers the fact that anything remotely resembling a human wouldn't make an appearance on the world stage for another one hundred and fifty million years, but what do trailer parks, crumbling dice, paintings of Russian space dogs, and a bat that can fly through walls have to do with it, either?

To get caught up in that question, as you marvel at stereo-graphic X-rays of flowers and miniature sculptures that fit within the eye of a needle, is something you cannot avoid, but you'll be

better off if you can. The museum's vexing name prompts some visitors to dismiss its unfathomable presentations as merely elaborate hoaxes, but to do this is a mistake. Though a deadpan motif of erudite folly pervades the institution, and some of the exhibits are indeed nothing more than exquisitely wrought bullshit, to get caught up in trying to parse these fictions from the equally unbelievable "realities" on display at MJT is to miss the point of the place entirely—and explains why some disgruntled visitors fail to "get it" at all. The MJT is at once a museum and a send-up of museums, a bizarre

mixture of seemingly disparate elements that appear to have no bearing on one another until the viewer steps back far enough to see that the displays are nothing more than cogs in a greater, far more fantastic machine; the MJT is not merely a repository for academic exhibits—fraudulent and otherwise—it is itself the exhibit.

We've probably already said too much; a joke is not funny when it has to be explained. We can only advise that you enter The Museum of Jurassic Technology with both a sense of humor and a sense of wonder, and don't worry if you are being made a fool of—you are. And, like the flavors of the Tula Tea Room upstairs, that's something to be savored rather than resented.

Next door to The Museum of Jurassic Technology is the equally impossible-sounding Center for Land Use Interpretation, the first agency in the establishment of the American Land Museum, a network of landscape exhibition sites being developed across the United States. The nonprofit center describes itself as a "research organization involved in exploring, examining, and understanding land and landscape issues," and though that sounds about as fun as watching paint dry, we find CLUI to be every bit as engaging as the MJT, if not more so. The Center in Los Angeles is one of four in the United States, the other three being the Desert Research Station in the Mojave desert; the exhibit halls at Wendover, Utah near the Bonneville Salt Flats; and along the Hudson river in Troy, New York.

Neither as playful nor as visually engaging as The Museum of Jurassic Technology, CLUI sacrifices inscrutability for utilitarianism. Exhibits at CLUI tend to be grey monoliths inscribed with succinct preludes to the documentaries that play on the monitors embedded within. Slap on a set of headphones and you will find yourself engrossed in topics with titles as diverse as *Pavement Paradise: American Parking Space*; *Emergency State: First Responder and Law Enforcement Training Architecture*; and *Post Consumed: The Landscape of Waste in Los Angeles*. The exhibit regarding Terminal Island gave us a newfound appreciation for the enormous cranes, containers, and tankers that work gracefully together in a kind of mega-ballet at the center of the largest port of the Americas. The man-made island is a city unto itself, an enormous mechanical organism with a complex "life" process involving importation, exportation, excretion, deportation, and expulsion. Sounds like us after we ate some bad crab at the 94th Aero Squadron.

We're suckers for a great bookstore, and though the offerings at CLUI are limited, they are extremely well chosen. Whether your interests lie in the subterranean underworld of tour caves, heady academic works regarding urban planning and/or

architecture, obscure celebrity death sites, or a guidebook to the top secret nuclear test sites of Nevada, you
will find them all here.

In keeping with CLUI's mission to create a dynamic
contemporary portrait of the nation, the exhibits
change regularly at the L.A. annex, sometimes going
out on the road to other CLUI facilities or partner
organizations. The Center also offers a number of
unique tours that reflect their exhibitions. Past
tours have included *Margins in Our Midst: A Journey
into Irwindale*; *Terminal Island*; and *Diversions and
Dislocations*, a two-day bus tour of the Owens Valley.

*Lay of the Land*, CLUI's newsletter, keeps members
updated on future exhibits and
tours, as well as what's happening
at the center's other facilities across
the country. For a $25 annual dona-
tion, it's well worth it.

CLUI is the perfect place to
get lost for an afternoon . . . and
when you regain your bearings
you will have also acquired a new
outlook on the nature of parking
lots, nuclear test sites, tributar-
ies, trash dumps, loading docks,
skyscrapers, abandoned factories,
suburban tracts, and everything
else we build around us yet invariably take for granted. Combine
this environmental reorienta-

tion with the arcane academia of The Museum of Jurassic
Technology, and you have the formula for what may just be a
perfect day spent indoors. As you question the veracity of, say,
the Stink Ant of the Cameroon, or marvel at the simple efficiency
of a Duncan parking meter (first manufactured in 1937 by the
same company that brought us the Duncan Yo-Yo), you will
find renewed love for an overcrowded, polluted, maddeningly
superficial city that, given the right circumstances, can become
the greatest place on earth, if only for a few hours at a time.

# AFTERLIFE, THEN WHAT?

LA BÊTE
BOROWCZYK

# DEAD MAN'S CURVES

Dead man's curves in Los Angeles are as easy to come by as transsexual prostitutes—and they're almost as fun, especially if you've been drinking. For your driving and dying pleasure, we took two of Sunset Boulevard's most notorious curves at top speed and lived to tell the tales.

## DEAD MAN'S CURVE #1

Few people know that on January 24, 1961, a horrible car wreck almost claimed the lives of Bugs Bunny, Porky Pig, Daffy Duck, Elmer Fudd, Foghorn Leghorn, Yosemite Sam, and a wealth of other cartoon characters. It was 9:30 in the evening when Mel Blanc, the affable king of cartoon voices, lost control of his sports car on Sunset Boulevard just north of UCLA's Drake Stadium and collided head-on with another vehicle. With massive head injuries, a broken pelvis, and two broken legs, Blanc spent weeks in a coma, then even longer in a full-body cast.

The near-fatal accident occurred about halfway into production of the first season of *The Flintstones*, in which Blanc voiced the characters of Barney Rubble and Dino. Rather than replace him, the producers decided to bring the show to Blanc, and recorded him first from his hospital bed, then built a temporary recording studio in his bedroom to finish the season (with Blanc in that body cast the whole time). His fellow *Flintstones* actors would cram into the tiny room to record each show with him. As for Dead Man's Curve, within days of Blanc's accident the city approved changes to reduce the curve's excessive banking, which had already been blamed for twenty-six accidents and three fatalities. Today that patch of Sunset bears little resemblance to the street where Speedy Gonzales almost bit the dust.

## DEAD MAN'S CURVE #2

It was Blanc's accident that inspired the 1963 hit song "Dead Man's Curve" by Jan & Dean, which would in turn presage yet another tragedy that would soon befall singer/songwriter Jan Berry. The overplayed oldie was penned by Berry and Roger Christian and went to number eight on the *Billboard* chart in 1964. The tune tells the story of a race between a Jaguar (Christian's car) and a Corvette (Berry's ride) that begins on the Sunset Strip, winds through Beverly Hills, then slams into a wall at . . . you guessed it, Dead Man's Curve. This one happens to be on Sunset just west of Whittier Drive.

In one of those impossible twists of fate usually reserved for hokier *Twilight Zone* episodes, the story goes that twenty-five-year-old Jan Berry crashed his Corvette Stingray on April 12, 1966, on the very same dead man's curve that had made him a rich man. First thought to be dead at the scene, he was rushed to UCLA Medical Center, where, like Blanc, he spent several weeks in a coma. The accident left Berry with severe brain damage, partial paralysis on his right side, and impaired speech. Jan and Dean were through.

If it seems unbelievable that the co-writer of "Dead Man's Curve" almost died in the very same spot described in his apocryphal song, that's because it never happened. Jan Berry indeed suffered massive injuries when he smashed up his Corvette in Beverly Hills, but the accident occurred when he slammed into a parked gardener's truck on a side street south of Sunset Boulevard, near dead man's curve, but certainly not on it. That doesn't make the accident any less terrible, but it does make it less interesting, which is perhaps why the myth was consistently perpetuated in print. We understand. It's certainly more fun to think that God has a sense of humor and was just getting back at Berry—who died of a seizure in 2004—for writing that cloying ditty in the first place, but anyone who has read Nietzsche knows that God is dead.

*Get your mind out of the gutter.*

## OUT 'n' ABOUT
# KILLS GERMS DEAD

Darby Crash, overrated singer of the overrated punk band the Germs, killed himself in this house with an overdose of underrated heroin on December 7, 1980. Why this is of any importance whatsoever is anyone's guess. How's that for nihilism?

**Darby Crash Pad / 137 North Fuller Avenue / Los Angeles**

# WHATEVER DID?

She sang, she danced, she killed. Baby Jane Hudson had a life that others only dream of, and much of it happened here: the Blanche and Jane Hudson home as seen in the 1962 classic.

**Whatever Happened to Baby Jane? House / 172 South McCadden Place / Hancock Park**

## THERE ARE SOUVENIRS TO DIE FOR AT

# SKELETONS IN THE CLOSET

Skeletons in the Closet
1104 North Mission Road
Los Angeles
323.343.0760
http://lacstores.co.la.ca.us

*Shop 'til you drop... dead.*

If you've been searching for that special gift that says, "I wish you were dead," look no further than Skeletons in the Closet. What began in 1993 as an ingeniously morbid fundraising idea—selling personalized toe-tag key chains to the public to fund a drunk driving awareness campaign—soon blossomed into a full line of apparel, trinkets, and other items available at the L.A. Coroner's very own gift shop. For some reason, it's not surprising that the Coroner's Department has the best sense of humor in the L.A municipal system.

When we tell someone about Skeletons in the Closet—which we do, quite often—the usual response is one of incredulity. And why is that? The L.A. Fire and Sheriff's Departments have their own gift shops, and even the LAPD peddles souvenirs, though they have yet to accept any of our T-shirt suggestions, including "I GOT PULLED OVER BY THE LAPD AND ALL I GOT WAS THIS LOUSY T-SHIRT SPATTERED WITH MY OWN BLOOD" and "MELANIN AND DRIVING DON'T MIX."

In our humble opinion, Skeletons in the Closet got off to a shaky start with "Sherlock Bones," a hokey marketing ploy created in an attempt to personalize the business side of death by presenting a skeleton clad in a houndstooth cape and deerstalker cap. Aside from being incredibly lame, the department's original mascot may also be an infringement on the pet-finding service of the same name, but for whatever reason, they've minimized his visibility to a single T-shirt and mug. That's good news, because the department has since focused its graphic design on far more compelling elements like the chalk outline of a dead body, the Coroner's seal, and the blocky, officious "CORONER" as seen on the backs of jackets at many a fatal crime scene. Any article of clothing bearing that logo is a surefire icebreaker at parties, with the added advantage of repelling anyone you wouldn't want to talk to in the first place.

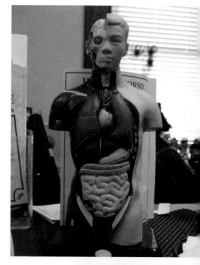

Despite an obvious affinity for puns—groaners like "Boo-verly Hills" and "Pacific Ghost Highway" are used liberally on its Web site—Skeletons in the Closet is surprisingly hip in the merchandise department. The department's clever exploitation of the chalk-outline motif is omnipresent, slapped on everything from knit caps to welcome mats. Personal favorites include the oversized beach towel, which allows one to actually "pose" as the body in question, and the flexible cutting mat that bears the slogan "We have our work cut out for us" (it also makes a great placemat). Besides the expected array of shirts, hats, and other togs, Skeletons in the Closet also sells pens, note pads, Post-its, playing cards, glasses, coasters, luggage, mouse pads, aprons, thermoses, pillow cases, blankets, boxer shorts, and just about anything else you can put a logo on. Looking for a garment carrier with "Body Bag" inscribed on it? It's here. A coffin-shaped hard case that's perfectly suited for purse or lunch-pail duty? Check. "Stay Cool" car shade? You betcha. Thanks to Skeletons in the Closet, never again will shopping for the sulky goths in your life be a challenge that requires you to set foot in Hot Topic, and since most of the items are available in children's sizes, you'll be able to keep your little Wednesdays and Pugsleys happy too.

When it first opened, Skeletons in the Closet was located deep within the main building of the Coroner's Department. Besides being a pain in the ass to get to, it also made for awkward encounters with bereaved citizens who were there on official business. One can only imagine the surreal experience of coming to identify a loved one and having to deal with tourists sizing up T-shirts and asking each other if they should get the barbecue apron or the tote bag. Thankfully, the store has now taken up residence across the parking lot in the old coroner's office, a beautiful brick building that's full of history but bereft of weeping family members. Don't be surprised if you see a ghost or two, however. An employee told us that more than one has been sighted in the building, which still handles the John Doe cases.

Funds raised from Skeletons in the Closet go to the Youthful Drunk Driver Visitation Program, an alternative sentencing option/probation requirement that receives no tax dollar support. First designed for mischievous tykes who have been nabbed operating a vehicle under the influence, the program has expanded to include older drunkards and certain first-time drug, assault, and weapons-related offenders. The lucky criminals get to see a slide show about drunk driving, meet a pathetic soul whose life has been totally boned by a drunk driver, and watch a real live autopsy (no pun intended). According to a department representative, the results of the program have exceeded their expectations, with many of the participants gaining a new sense of responsibility and losing their lunch.

Support a good cause. Drop into Skeletons in the Closet the next time you have a few hours to kill.

## REALLY FEELING LIKE A CIGARETTE AT THE
# SMOKING DEATH BILLBOARD

Smoking Death Billboard
Santa Monica Boulevard at
Veteran Avenue
West Los Angeles

Jesus Jumping Christ, enough about the evils of smoking already! In addition to being a quiet pastime, cigarette smoking creates jobs, generates tax revenue, and helps regulate population growth. That's more than you can say for jogging. Plus—and perhaps most importantly—smoking is cool.

But a reformed smoker and confirmed spoilsport saw the perceived error of his ways, and got the big idea to erect a giant

billboard in order to push the year's tally of smoking-related deaths in the face of everyone traveling eastbound on Santa Monica Boulevard. Allegedly, a small crowd gathers to watch the sign roll back to zero at midnight on December 31, but what kind of a loser would do that?

We'd prefer to see a tally billboard for movie trailers that begin with "There comes a time . . . " or the number of women who regret appearing in a *Girls Gone Wild* video. You know, something *important*.

## OUT *'n'* ABOUT

# FANS: CAN'T LIVE WITH 'EM, CAN'T LIVE WITHOUT 'EM

Actress Rebecca Schaeffer was doing quite well with appearances in movies like Woody Allen's *Radio Days*, Paul Mazursky's *Down and Out in Beverly Hills* and her costarring sitcom role in *My Sister Sam*. Well enough to attract the attention of a disturbed nineteen-year-old weirdo from Arizona named John Bardo.

Bardo had seen Rebecca on the tube and fell in love with her, scrawling out lengthy love letters. The missives weren't violent, or sexual, or even illiterate. They showed no sign of the insanity that gripped their author. He told her he was "a sensitive guy." Rebecca made the mistake of replying—once. She didn't sit down and spill her guts or anything like that— John only received an 8 × 10 glossy with a few stock words of encouragement and an autograph. But that was incentive enough for him to make his hajj to Rebecca. And waste her.

Just before Bardo left his quiet Tucson neighborhood, he wrote a letter to his sister in Knoxville, Tennessee. His intentions were fairly clear: "I have an obsession with the unattainable and I have to eliminate (something) that I cannot attain."

On Monday evening, July 17, 1989, Bardo took a Greyhound bus from Tucson to Los Angeles. He had previously paid a Tucson detective agency to provide him with Schaeffer's address. They did, and at 10:15 on the morning of July 18, Bardo rang the front bell of Schaeffer's building. She had been up for a little bit, having laid her clothes out for a later meeting with Frances Ford Coppola. She came down to the front door, dressed only in her bathrobe.

Neighbors heard a gunshot, two screams, then silence. Bardo had fired one shot into Schaeffer's chest, not quite killing her instantly. Bardo quickly fled the scene, but later turned himself in, and told the police where he'd stashed the items he'd been carrying at the time of the murder. Among them was a copy of *The Catcher in the Rye*, the same book that Mark David Chapman was packing when he gunned down John Lennon.

**Rebecca Schaeffer Murder / 120 North Sweetzer Avenue / West Hollywood**

# MY BLOODY VALENTINE

Ironic that Sal Mineo was rehearsing a play called *P.S. Your Cat Is Dead* when he was murdered in the basement garage of his rented apartment. Ironic, too, that he was knifed in the heart just two days shy of Valentine's Day, 1976. Mineo, best known for his supporting role in *Rebel Without a Cause*, was getting out of his car when he was assaulted by at least two unidentified men. Neighbors heard him shout, "My God! My God! Help me!" followed by a final scream, and silence. Mineo was thirty-seven, and died with the script of his upcoming play clenched in his fist. His murder remained unsolved for nearly two years—but it wasn't his understudy who did the knife work, or a spurned lover as some had speculated, just a tragically botched robbery.

**Sal Mineo Murder / 8563 Holloway Drive / West Hollywood**

## FEELING PLUCKY ABOUT

# SUPERIOR POULTRY

Superior Poultry
750 North Broadway
Los Angeles
213.628.7645

A lot of vegetarians take great pleasure in telling carnivores that if they could only see where their meat comes from, they wouldn't eat it anymore. The same thing can probably be said about babies and cunnilingus, but we see their point. Slaughterhouses are loud, smelly, depressing death factories that have distanced the end user from the final product. If people actually had to kill what they eat, most of them would think twice about that chateaubriand.

On the other hand, we've seen the inner workings of a slaughterhouse or two and we have to say that we still love a good steak. And when we're in the mood for really fresh chicken we don't wait at the back of Ralph's for the Foster Farms truck to show up: We go to Superior Poultry. Located on bustling Broadway in the heart of L.A.'s Chinatown, Superior Poultry is definitely not a place to bring delicate, sheltered children who are fond of baby chicks. Then again, maybe it's time for them to see where their fucking McNuggets come from: "Circle of life, my ass, Timmy—this here is the end of the line!"

The front of the simple store is stacked with metal cages that are teeming with cute, fluffy, chirping chickies, or as we like to refer to them, the kung pao of tomorrow. Step up to the counter and you'll see exactly what kind of fate awaits these adorable little critters, and it's definitely not a trip to Disneyland. The industrious, uniformed chicken murderers at Superior Poultry go about their business with detached efficiency, which, when you think about it, is a good thing. They'd get absolutely nothing done if they spent the whole day weeping over every hen they sent to Chicken Heaven. And for all we know, they may go home at night, lock their doors, and beat their chests with guilt—but our guess is that they probably just eat some delicious stir-fry and watch *Chinese Idol*.

*Meat is murder. We'll take ours to go.*

At Superior, they don't stop at senseless chicken murder: they also pluck, wash, clean, and package your pick of the litter, then hand it to you while it's still warm. No time for dallying in vats of "fecal soup" as institutional fowl tend to do—these pullets are on a mission, and that mission is to get into your digestive system as quickly as possible.

One trip to any Chinatown market—with its comical hanging ducks, slack-jawed suckling pigs, and plastic tubs full of odd, odorous sea creatures (some of them still writhing)—will teach you that when it comes to meat, the Chinese have no pretensions about where it comes from or how it gets to their dinner plates. They have no quarrel with the whole carnivore-death connection: It's just another facet of life, one that involves death, and if you don't like it then get the fuck out and go eat a tofu burger on the Westside. We find that kind of practicality refreshing, and feel that if all grocery stores operated with the same transparency, maybe we wouldn't be so flippant about death. In cultures where death and dying are daily realities rather than fashion state-ments, you don't find a lot of goth kids running around. Why play dress-up when you live it? And let's face it, we Americans view our slaughterhouses the same way we view our wars: as neces-sary evils whose secrets we'd rather not be privy to.

As the story goes, German Chancellor Otto von Bismarck said, "There are two things you don't want to see being made—sausage and legislation." We can think of a lot of things we'd rather not see being made, starting with anything involving Tyra Banks, but it seems to us that if more Americans had to at least *point* at the living creatures they want dead and on the dinner table, maybe our asses wouldn't be the fattest on the planet.

There was a time in this country when you would have raised your favorite pig almost as a member of the family and then summarily dispatched it to provide Easter dinner. Now you can get in touch with that quaint early American spirit—in a chickenshit kind of way, and courtesy of the Chinese—at Superior Poultry.

## GRAVE ROBBING AT

# NECROMANCE

Necromance
7220 Melrose Avenue
Los Angeles
213.934.8684
Necromance East
7208 Melrose Avenue
Los Angeles
323.931.2997
www.necromance.com

For a shopper in search of the outré, there is almost no request that the retailers of Los Angeles can't meet. Should you covet a dog brain, a set of vintage dentures (with the original box), the skull of a twenty-eight-week-old infant or a handful of warthog tusks, you'd have to run all over town to tick off that shopping list if you lived in Peoria. In L.A., the only place one needs to head is Necromance, the city's most unique boutique, and a veritable Toys "R" Us for folks who like to play with dead things.

You may find a shop or two around town inspired by Necromance and dealing in similar stock, but none of them have been doing it longer, better, with more variety, or with the

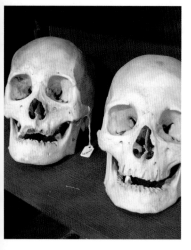

same degree of style. Evoking the Victorian era with its rich color palette and vintage floral print rugs, the Necromance environment effectively seduces with the drama of an old natural history museum and the romance of a witch doctor supply shop. Artfully morbid and laced with deferential irony, exquisitely composed displays are presented within antique wooden cabinets, under bell jars, or inside leaded-glass cases. World-class oddities decorate the walls, while exotic crustaceans, delicate corals, and taxidermied chipmunks line the shelves. Vintage and contemporary jewelry—some fashioned from gold-dipped sea horses or animal teeth—further demonstrate the store's unique ability to celebrate the dark glamour of the dead. It's as much a museum as it is a retail shop, and for those who go gaga over natural curiosities, Necromance ensures adventure.

# SHE CHECKED IN, BUT DIDN'T CHECK OUT

It was October of 1970, and Janis was in town to record what would be her last album, *Pearl*. The raggedy, twenty-seven-year-old Texan was trying her damnedest to clean up her act, but she was still fucked up on booze and speed and downers and heroin. On October 4, she gave herself a massive injection of heroin and collapsed, cracking her skull open as she hit the floor. Suicide was never ruled out, due to the fact that any junkie worth her salt knows her maximum dosage—and Joplin had apparently seen death on the horizon, having put aside a $2,500 fund for her funeral party. The invitation read, "Drinks are on Pearl." Appropriately, the Grateful Dead provided the music at her wake.

**Janis Joplin Overdose / The Landmark Hotel /
7047 Franklin Avenue (former site) / Hollywood**

Necromance is one of the very few places in town where one can legally purchase affordable human remains—a bundle of bones won't cost you an arm and a leg (and Necromance acquires them legally too, FYI). A frog embryo or an Indonesian bat shrink-wrapped onto cardboard are not only inexpensive, but make great low-maintenance pets. You can take home a complete human skeleton for about the same price that you'd pay for Shar Pei puppy—*and* you can grab a sack of edible crickets to munch on for the drive home.

Good news for shoppers predisposed to the macabre: Necromance has an annex just a bone's throw from the original. This second locale nods more towards archaic medical instruments, funerary collectibles, anatomical charts, books, and vintage rarities such as their stupefying cache of personal effects once belonging to Eva Braun. As if the sale of such artifacts would cause any doubt—amidst the wares of a Melrose institution that Hitler himself would have undoubtedly condemned as degenerate—owner Nancy Smith is quick to assure us, "I just appreciate the historical aspect of these items; we aren't Nazi sympathizers or anything. . . . "

We wouldn't have thought so.

*Where the living shop for the dead.*

## OUT *'n'* ABOUT
# DRACULA DIED HERE

It wasn't a stake through the heart that killed Bela Lugosi at age seventy-three, only a garden-variety heart attack. But his years of opium addiction—originally stemming from doctor-prescribed painkillers to manage Dracula's sciatica—probably didn't help.

His battle with the needle punctuated a career fraught with peaks and valleys, beginning with Hungarian silent films, on to major success on Broadway, and then to leading roles in Hollywood features. However, he is perhaps best known as king of the Bs, for credits like *Bela Lugosi Meets a Brooklyn Gorilla*, and the Ed Wood classics *Glen or Glenda* and *The Bride of the Monster*.

After a fourth marriage and a stint in rehab, Lugosi made his final film, *The Black Sheep*, in 1955. He was set to begin work on yet another Ed Wood feature, *The Final Curtain*, when he expired on the sofa in his Hollywood apartment.

**Bela Lugosi Heart Attack / 5620 Harold Way / Hollywood**

## CLOWNING AROUND AT THE CALIFORNIA INSTITUTE OF THE
# ABNORMALARTS

California Institute of Abnormalarts
11334 Burbank Boulevard
North Hollywood
818.506.6353
www.ciabnormalarts.com

If P. T. Barnum and Pee-wee Herman dropped a lot of acid, built a love shack, and moved in together, their place would look a lot like the California Institute of Abnormalarts, a nightclub in Burbank located, appropriately enough, just down the street from Circus Liquor. Once a strictly hush-hush illicit underground operation, CIA finally went legit, got its liquor and food license, and proudly displays its "A" rating from the health inspector right by the X-ray of the two-headed baby. But more on that in a moment. . . .

Proprietors Carl Crew and John Ferguson are former morticians who met couple of decades ago in Marin Country, where they discovered they both had a penchant for collecting the morbid, the outré, and the outrageous—especially if it had anything to do with a circus or sideshow. After spending just a few minutes with them, we realized these two give their previous profession a good name, and that made us feel guilty for ever saying that Nixon had the personality of an embalmer. If Nixon had been anything like these guys, he would have made a much more interesting president, delivering State of the Union addresses in demonic clown makeup or using the mummified arm of Claude de Lorraine to shake hands with Mao Tse-Tung. There would have been no need to break into the Watergate; the Democratic National Committee would have gladly shown Nixon all their papers in exchange for just a peek at Señorita Pulpo, the Octopus Girl. Sadly, however, this was not to be.

Crew, an oversized, bespectacled towhead and the showman of the pair, is a natural-born huckster who would have made a great snake oil salesman back in Deadwood. He's also an actor and writer best known for *The Secret Life: Jeffrey Dahmer* for which he served as both author and star. And, not coincidentally, an evil side of Crew has been said to come out when dealing with some of the boneheaded bands that play at CIA, and we can't blame him. In fact, we're amazed he lets people in there at all, considering the amazing array of oddities he and John have collected over the years (we'd call them priceless, though some would undoubtedly scoff at that estimate). After all, this isn't some Hollywood dump where it doesn't matter where you toss your guitar case or what you fall on when you pass out in a drunken stupor. Hollywood dumps don't have the Alligator Boy or the skull of world's smallest Freemason in a glass case to worry about. Frankly, other than featuring freak shows and bad B-movies, we don't think the stage should be used for anything else. CIA *is* the entertainment, and unless your band has the Incredible Frog Boy for lead singer, you're probably going to get upstaged by the club itself. Still, CIA manages to book some fairly bizarre musical acts (and a few mediocre ones, too, naturally), so when we showed up to get a private tour of the place, we weren't surprised to find Carl out front telling some scruffy goth band to get their shit out of the driveway and to be careful where they set up. Then, the perfect gentleman, he beckoned us to follow him through the door with the grinning clown on it.

*Home of the original poisonous dead clown.*

Inside, it's a funhouse of blacklights and Day-Glo colors, pirates and clowns, stuffed animals and pickled remains, shrunken heads and human skulls, cases of dark exotic curios that are indescribable until Carl describes them. "That's a *real* Fiji mermaid," he said, pointing to a dried-up thing with a tail. "Those things are really rare." Uh huh. Then he nodded towards an X-ray of what looks like a two-headed baby. "Believe it or not, I found that in the dumpster of the 7-Eleven just down the

# DOCTOR CYCLOPS SWUNG HERE

Albert Dekker was a real strange cat. He was also a former California State Assemblyman and a busy character actor who, among nearly a hundred film credits, was best known for his role as the evil Dr. Cyclops in the B-movie of the same name. But it was his 1968 death that got the town talking: a sketchy scene that continues to rank high in the annals of Hollywood self-destruction.

The sixty-two-year-old actor was found locked in his bathroom, hanging by his neck from a rope tied to the shower curtain rod. Simple enough. But the rope was also tightly knotted to one of his arms and to both of his legs. He also wore handcuffs, ladies' silk lingerie, had his final words scrawled across his body in lipstick—*and* sported two hypodermic needles jabbed into his flesh. His death was originally listed as a suicide, but a few days later the coroner said his death was an "accident," and indicated that there was no information to lead them to believe Dekker wanted to kill himself. What was he doing in there, then, in that outrageous getup? Perhaps Dekker indulged in the treacherous masturbatory practice of autoerotic asphyxiation, maybe the suicide of his son just a decade prior was what inspired his path, or maybe he *did* just want to go out in style. Only Dr. Cyclops knows for sure.

**Dr. Cyclops Suicide / 1731 North Normandie Avenue / Hollywood**

street," he said. There isn't a hospital or doctor's office nearby, so how or why an X-ray of an amazing rarity like a two-headed baby would end up in the garbage bin of a convenience store just down the street is anyone's guess, but it seemed amazingly fortuitous to us. "Yes, it is pretty incredible, isn't it?" Carl said with a grin.

Outside on the patio, things just got weirder. It was already too dark outside to get a good look at the Dead Fairy of Cornwall, but we've seen plenty of dead fairies before. We moved on to the severed arm of French nobleman Claude de Lorraine, which looked like, well, a dried-up, severed arm. Carl told us it was the real deal, so we took his word for it—because what we really wanted to see was the dead clown.

# WHY DO BIRDS SUDDENLY APPEAR EVERYTIME YOU ARE NEAR?

Just like me, they long to be close to the two apartment buildings owned by Karen and Richard Carpenter in the 1970s and named after two of their biggest hits.

**Close to You Apartments / 8356 Fifth Street / Downey**
**Only Just Begun Apartments / 8345 Fifth Street / Downey**

Like many of the other attractions at CIA, Achile Chatouilleu is definitely dead. Unlike most of them, however, he's real. An American circus performer who was born in 1866 and died of "chronic nephritis" (read: he drank himself to death), the story goes that Chatouilleu asked to be displayed forever in death as he so often appeared in life: in his clown costume and makeup. Whether or not that's true is up for debate, since Crew says he leased the body from a Gypsy circus family who'd apparently forgotten about their petrified Pierrot; what was supposed to be a six-month gig for the dead clown has turned into years. Hoping that Chatouilleu's family has forgotten about him, Crew has built a kind of cage to protect the glass coffin from the elements, and to protect his patrons from the clown. "He's embalmed with mercury and arsenic," said Crew, again with the trademark grin. "If that glass cracked, it would take a hazmat team to clean this place up. One good whiff and you'd be dead." We took a good look through the bars at the moonlit face of the figure in the glass box, and either it really is a dead guy in clown makeup or a really good fake. "Oh, he's real all right," said Crew, who says he once put on a gas mask and checked Chatouilleu out for himself. "Just a little skin slippage between the thumb and forefinger, but otherwise he's in pretty good shape," chirped Crew, while we made note of the term "skin slippage" for future dinnertime banter. The prison shed setup makes it look like the dead clown isn't going anywhere, but Crew pointed to another corner of the patio and

# THE BOZO FROM HELL

Crimebo the Clown is like the adopted love-child of James Ellroy and Emmett Kelly. Though you can catch his morbid shenanigans on Esotouric's Pasadena Confidential Crime Tour (wherein passengers are enlisted to join the "Crimebo Players" to play the roles of L. Ron Hubbard and Jack Parsons, among others) Crimebo will also come to your next party and read to you from the *Big Book of Terrible Crimes*. Want to find out who was brutally murdered on your birthday? Crimebo knows. Though some may believe that Crimebo's shtick is strictly for grown-ups, we would book this clown for a kids' party in a heartbeat. Nothing will put mollycoddled children in line quicker than seeing photos of Bukowski's nose and learning the grim fate of the Black Dahlia from a wiseguy in greasepaint.

**Crimebo the Crime Clown / 323.573.3445**

said he'd be moving Chatouilleu there soon because he had bigger plans for the space the corpse is currently occupying. "We're going to serve barbecue here," Crew told us. "And we're going to call it Long Pig Barbecue." (Long Pig, for those of you who don't watch Rachael Ray, is cannibal-speak for "human.") Yummy.

Next to the dead clown, we looked up and noticed a hideously amateurish painting of woman who seemed vaguely familiar. "I don't even want to talk about that," Carl said. But of course, he did. "The painting is possessed. People have gone running out of here screaming after looking at. A few Halloweens ago, someone stole it. Two weeks later it was back with a note on it that said "Fuck this." How interesting. Did its eyes move? Did it talk? Did it suddenly morph into something hideous like Laura Ingraham? We wanted to know. "I can't tell you," he said, ominously. When pressed for further info, Crew clammed up completely, so we asked him if we could at least take his picture in front of the painting. He thought about it for a moment and then shook his head. "No. No way," he said politely, *as if he were actually spooked*. Then he turned and walked off under an archway that read "Institute of Nude Wrestling" across the top. We got excited for a moment, thinking we had found the sign from the long lost nudie joint on Santa Monica Boulevard. But just as we remembered the place was called "Academy of Nude Wrestling," Crew snorted and laughed mockingly. "Fuck no, that's not the real sign. I made that!" (For the real "Academy of Nude Wrestling," check out p. 339 in the Lost Strangeles chapter.)

We stuck around for another half-hour of kibitzing with North Hollywood's preeminent charlatan as he attempted to probe the limits of our gullibility by insisting that the cat staring at us from the rooftop was, in fact, a phantom. "Oh yeah," he said, "There must have been a vet around here or something because this place is crawling with phantom cats." When we pointed out that the "phantom" cat on the roof looked very much like a real cat, he laughed once again at our naivete. "You have no idea how real these phantoms can make themselves look." Okie doke. We made some small talk about Marc Bolan and bad movies in an attempt to distract him long enough for one of us to steal the haunted painting, but he kept his eye on it the whole time. We'd have to come back for it. On the way out, we noted what appeared to be a dead "merman" (not Ethel, but a man-fish mutant) on the wall, right next to the head of Sasquatch. "Those are probably fakes," Crew said with unusual candor, then qualified his statement by adding, "Though you can never be sure."

Right after the Ikea cafeteria, we would have to say that California Institute of Abnormalarts is the second-most romantic place in town. If you really want to make the most of an evening there, check out their schedule and go on a night when they're having a real live freak show, or even better, a performance by Shaye Saint John, a performance artist who claims to hold the world's record for having the most problems. "Man, all I can tell you is that she had this horrible disease that destroyed her spine, and then she got hit by a train and lost her limbs and her face got all burned up, but she keeps going, and makes these incredible short films out in her abandoned home in the desert." Right, Carl, and she probably breeds phantom cats out there, too. If you've never been entertained by what appears to be a coked-up, wheelchair-bound drag queen wearing a hideous mask, wig, and loose-fitting mumu, who flails "her" fake arms and legs (which look surprisingly like those of an old, beat-up mannequin), and babbles incoherently in a voice that sounds like one of the Chipmunks on Adrenochrome, then you must check out this exquisitely "handicapped" fucktard who will amuse you in ways

you never imagined possible. We predict she'll be opening for Bobby Slayton at Hooters Casino in Vegas by the end of the year. She's *that* good.

Then again, so is Mr. Crew.

## WONDERING IF MAYBE SUICIDE IS THE ANSWER AT THE

# COLORADO STREET BRIDGE

Colorado Street Bridge
Colorado Street at
Arroyo Boulevard
Pasadena

*Nowhere to go but up.*

A decorative byway for some, a stairway to heaven for others—they don't call it "Suicide Bridge" for nothing. For many, taking the Colorado Street Bridge over the Arroyo Seco had nothing to do with reaching the other side of the gulch. It's been a point of departure for over one hundred-plus despondent Angelenos for whom life in L.A. was not all sunshine and frozen yogurt. The 1913 marvel saw an upgrade and restoration in the early nineties including the addition of a tall barrier, though the nickname Suicide *Prevention* Bridge has not taken hold, as it still hosts the occasional swan dive.

## ENJOYING A COLD ONE AND A MOVIE AT

# CINESPIA

Cinespia
Hollywood Forever Cemetery
6000 Santa Monica
Boulevard
Los Angeles
www.cinespia.org

Okay, we admit it: Sometimes we grow a little weary of the whole "death is neat!" routine that's so popular in this town. That said, we've obviously been guilty of it ourselves, and since it would be bad form to switch horses in midstream, here's our obligatory nod to Cinespia. The nonprofit organization provides an outdoor moviegoing experience during the summer months by projecting Hollywood classics on the marble wall of a mausoleum at Hollywood Forever Cemetery. The terminally hip already know it as a great place for a cheap date, and out-of-town visitors who don't already believe that everyone in L.A. is too cool for their own good will now have solid evidence.

If you're turned on by the idea of spreading out a picnic blanket near Virginia Rappe's grave and noshing on cheese and crackers while watching a movie that may or may not star people buried within spitting distance of you, then you will love Cinespia. Although dogs are not permitted, drinking is, so why not get tanked up on Miller Lite and then take a leak on the headstone of Adolphe Menjou? Though a light brigade of security guards are employed to keep people corralled in the screening area, it's mostly a symbolic show of force. Anyone with even the slightest amount of gumption and a couple of Olde English 800s in them can easily sneak off into the pitch-black boneyard for a little boning of their own. Most of the folks at Cinespia are friendly, if not a little too friendly, and while we happen to enjoy the sweet scent of Sour Diesel weed burning from a nearby pipe, we'd appreciate it if you wouldn't stand directly in front of the screen while you tell your friends all about your day at Amoeba Records or Red Balls or wherever the hell it is you work and/or shop. We don't care about your life. We came to hear Peter Sellers say "Birdie Num Nums," and we'd be obliged if you didn't ruin it for us.

Still, we can't seem to shake the nagging feeling that there's something inherently *wrong* about this movie-and-a-mausoleum motif. Maybe it's the sense that the whole thing tries just a little

## OUT 'n' ABOUT
# HUSH LITTLE BABY, DON'T SAY A WORD...

Long before she'd increased her odds of an early demise with a penchant for champagne, sleeping pills, and Kennedys, life for the infant Marilyn was already off to a rocky start: born to a mentally ill mom, bounced into the first of many foster homes at twelve days old, and—at this site in Hawthorne— nearly suffocated with a pillow by her unstable grandmother only a month after her first birthday.

**Norma Jean Infanticide Attempt Site / 4244 West 134th Street / Hawthorne**

too hard for our tastes, or that we're less than enthusiastic about the concept of turning a graveyard into an ArcLight Cinema. If it's going to be that way, though, we'd prefer to take the whole postmodern deconstructionist over-intellectualized art-imitates-life-in-an-environment-of-death cinephile bullshit to its logical conclusion and only screen hardcore porno movies at Cinespia. Sophomoric references about stiffs aside, how better to reinforce the inherent banality of the circle of life than to project the gushing spasms of *la petite mort* onto the wall of a building filled with dead people who, in all probability, also once fucked like porn stars? (Sorry, Bob Crane is buried in Westwood.)

Now *that*, in our opinion, would be entertainment.

Until that day comes, however, we'll have to be satisfied with the cheap double entendre of titles like Billy Wilder's *Ace in the Hole*. Yeah, we get it.

## CHICKENING OUT AT LOS ANGELES
# PET MEMORIAL PARK

Los Angeles
Pet Memorial Park
5068 North Old Scandia Lane
Calabasas
818.591.7037
www.lapetcemetery.com

If Hollywood Forever is the cemetery to the stars, then Los Angeles Pet Memorial Park is the cemetery to the stars' pets. From Gloria "I'm ready for my close-up, Mr. DeMille" Swanson to Aaron *"Love Boat"* Spelling, this is where the beautiful people come to deposit their beautiful animals. Hopalong Cassidy's horse is buried here, along with Petey, the ring-eyed, four-legged mascot of the Little Rascals. Yep, we're talking megastars—but the real star of this underground show in Calabasas is a chicken you've probably never heard of.

"Blinky" was a typical Foster Farms chicken, not unlike the countless other dead, plucked hens cooling in meat sections across Southern California. What made "Blinky" different from her peers was that she didn't turn up as a main course on someone's dinner table, but instead was the main event of a memorial service and burial at the L.A. Pet Memorial Park in 1978. Conceptual artist and highbrow prankster Jeffrey Vallance bought the chicken at the Ralph's in Canoga Park, took it to the cemetery where it was placed in a powder blue coffin with pink satin lining—along with a paper towel since Blinky was beginning to thaw and leak. The casket was carried out to the grave by pallbearers (how many men do you need to carry a single dead chicken, anyway?), and Blinky was lowered into the ground. Vallance then retreated to the nearby Howard Johnson's for the chicken special.

Ten years later, Vallance had Blinky exhumed and an autopsy was performed. That paper towel became a sacred relic, "The Shroud of Blinky," and was sold to a collector for $1,000. Vallance published a book chronicling the saga and everyone had a good laugh. Except for the folks at L.A. Pet Memorial Park.

When we first visited the park in 1996, we couldn't help but a notice a fire hydrant just outside the fence that surrounds the park. It seemed like a cruel joke to play on all those ghost dogs who, in the afterlife, could do nothing but gaze longingly at the object of their desire from the astral plane. We laughed at this notion, not knowing the mood would soon turn sour.

Moments later we were standing in the humble air-conditioned trailer that functioned as the cemetery's office, showroom, and God-knows-what-else. Everything was going great until we mentioned to Sandy, the park's rep, that wanted like to see Blinky's grave. She visibly stiffened at the mention of Vallance's name. The friendly lady who was just showing us cat caskets and quoting burial fees was now obviously perturbed as she angrily flipped through the grave files in search of Blinky's final resting place. She eyed us suspiciously, and then started in with the questions about Vallance (Doesn't he run some kind of a group? Does he still live around here? What's his deal? How do you know him?). We didn't know the man, we explained, we were just there to pay respects to his chicken. Referring to her map of the cemetery, Sandy begrudgingly led us to a tiny plot less than a hundred yards from her office where, sure enough, a granite marker read:

BLINKY
THE FRIENDLY HEN
JEFFREY VALLANCE
1976–1978

Then Sandy popped the big question, the one that had obviously been bothering her all along: Were we part of a group that visited the cemetery a few years ago? We assured her that this was our first visit, and she proceeded to spin a grim tale about a group of "weird, rude people" who showed up one Sunday after the *L.A. Weekly* had run a mention of Vallance, Blinky, and the park. "They said and did some really nasty things," she said, "Awful things that disturbed the patrons who were here visiting their pets." When pressed for details, Sandy begged off, saying she wasn't there at the time and had only heard the complaints after the fact.

*All dogs go to heaven. Some stop here first.*

# WHEN SILENCE WAS GOLDEN

We thought the worst thing about sound movies was the advent of Foley art, but decades before the age of over-wrought audio embellishment, sound films were wreaking another sort of havoc. With the new technology came a theretofore unseen variety of Hollywood suicide: that of the silent film actor who couldn't successfully cross over.

Like so many silent screen stars, **Marie Prevost** found herself short on jobs and down on her luck when the talkies came around, as her honking Bronx accent didn't complement her classic beauty and did nothing to encourage speaking roles. Even though she died way back in 1937, her story is still interesting today—just because it's so damn disgusting.

Despondent, Prevost hit the bottle—drinking herself into a state of poverty and, ultimately, death. It was days before the body was found, and when cops finally burst into her small apartment, they were treated to a grim scene: The shapely legs that once made the transplanted New Yorker a successful Mack Sennett bathing beauty had been half-eaten by her devoted little dachshund, still mewling at the foot of her bed. Whether he was trying to wake her up or the hunger just got the best of the poor fellow will never be determined. English pop star Nick Lowe eulogized Marie in his 1978 song that bore her name: "She was a winner/who became the doggie's dinner...."

The dashing **Karl Dane** didn't get a song written in his honor, but he did have one of Hollywood's biggest studios—MGM—pay for his burial, which, unfortunately, was due to the tragic fact that when he killed himself in 1934, no one else bothered to claim his body.

After having made MGM proud as a successful silent film comedian, the powers that be decided Dane was better seen than heard, making him an out-of-work actor and a very available carpenter. He didn't spend too many years away from the studio, however. Soon enough, he was back at MGM—outside the front gates working a hot dog stand.

At age forty-eight and with his future looking none too bright, he took a self-inflicted bullet while alone at his apartment, but not before laying his collection of old press clippings on the floor before him.

**Lou Tellegen** had to make do without a gun, but he managed to get the job done quite effectively anyway using only a pair of scissors. While locked into a bathroom at the home of movie producer Joseph Schenck and actress Norma Talmadge, Tellegen stabbed himself seven times in the chest, an abbreviated film career being his source of despair. Neither his former or current wife bothered to show for the funeral. In fact, the funeral for Lou Tellegen—one of the world's first international matinee idols of the silent era—drew less than forty attendees. That's some pretty lousy BO.

Marie Prevost Dachshund Debacle / 6320 Afton Place / Hollywood
Karl Dane's Last Clipping / 626 South Burnside Avenue / Los Angeles
Lou Tellegen Scissor Suicide / 1844 North Vine Street / Hollywood

She also made it clear that she didn't know whether Vallance himself was part of the offending entourage, but one thing was clear: Sandy was still pissed about whatever went down that Sunday, and as far as she was concerned we must have had something to do with it since we knew about Blinky. We asked if we could take a photo of the casket room. "Absolutely not," was Sandy's terse reply as she lit up a long, skinny cigarette. We were done.

Fortunately, prior to heading down the wrong road with our Blinky inquiry, we had managed to cop a folder of materials from the park. This slick package was loaded with helpful pamphlets like "The Proper Goodbye," "Are You Coping?," and "Death of Your Four-Legged Friend"—which obviously excludes owners of birds, fish, chimps, kangaroos, and snakes. At the time, one of us had a cat named "Dr. Gene Scott, God's Angry Cat," and we found out that the cost of burying the good doctor would be somewhere in the neighborhood of $500, which did not include a headstone. This figure seemed a bit high since the cat "casket" looked more like a couple of plastic litter boxes turned upside down on each other and lined with satin, but this is a non-profit organization, so the price had to be reasonable, right? Plus, the fee included the backbreaking task of digging the grave, lowering the litter box coffin (and cat) into it, filling it again with dirt, and installing a permanent vase for flowers—or catnip, as the case may be. (Update: Pet owners please note that swanky wooden caskets are now available, but if you plan to go this route, you'll need to keep a lot of ice on hand. Delivery takes about ten to fifteen days.)

Who can put a price tag on the peace of mind that comes from spending a last special moment with your beloved companion as it rests peacefully in a glorified litter box in the "Slumber Viewing Room," then sticking it in the ground and planting an expensive granite headstone on a grave you'll visit even less than those of your own grandparents? Well, we can. We need to eat, for Christ's sake. Fortunately, as fate would have it, Dr. Gene Scott would be snatched by a coyote a few years later, leaving only a wisp of fur at the scene of the crime. His was a tragic, but affordable death.

Although the park is open to the public (like any cemetery), if you plan to visit, please don't come in a large group and make obscene comments to the grieving patrons while you desecrate the grounds. Instead, why not enjoy a meditative opportunity amidst the scenic beauty of this peaceful, well-maintained park, and let yourself be touched by the love and dedication of non-cheapskates who shelled out good money to give their late house pets a decent burial—and perhaps just a touch of immortality?

But whatever you do, don't ask about "Blinky." That damn chicken is nothing but a troublemaker.

## GIVING THE DEVIL HIS DUE AT
## THE CHURCH AT ROCKY PEAK AND

# SPAHN RANCH

The Church at Rocky Peak
22601 Santa Susana Pass
Road
Chatsworth

Spahn Ranch
Right across the street

First off, there is no Spahn Ranch. Not anymore. The legendary Manson Family enclave was consumed in a 1970 wildfire, bulldozed, regraded, sold, then subdivided into at least three separate parcels. Most of it was eventually fenced off as private property. Sometime just after the dawn of the twenty-first century, a concrete bridge was built over the creek where the stinky, naked hippies once bumped uglies. A gate and intercom suggest that the road leads to some kind of residence which is not visible from the street, and difficult to distinguish on Google Earth. Suffice it to say, if anyone lives there, don't disturb them—they already have enough bad vibes to deal with.

Spahn Ranch enjoyed a colorful history, and we're not just talking crimson red. Over the years, its owners included original screen cowboy William S. Hart, would-be Western movie mogul George Spahn, and, according to locals, Ronald Reagan's son, Michael. Never as popular as a legit movie location as nearby Iverson Movie Ranch or Corriganville, the 511-acre property eked out a meager existence providing horses to film productions, and by renting itself out as backdrop for softcore skin flicks where hirsute harlots and mutton-chopped woodsmen feigned fornication for the cameras.

We did our share of skulking about the property in days gone by, but quite frankly, we're too old to heave ourselves over chain-link fences, or any fences for that matter—we almost killed ourselves getting to Sunken City—and our criminal records are already long enough, thank you very much. While we would never encourage anyone to commit a misdemeanor in search of ancient graffiti etched into the canyon rock by cult members more than forty years ago, should you feel compelled to cut a trail through the wilderness that was once the domain of Charlie's devils, pose under giant rock just like the Manson Family Singers, and carve your own initials on the large boulder where "CM" and his band of merry murders did the same, don't call us to come bail your ass out of jail. We don't even know you.

If you insist on paying a visit to the area and want a bird's-eye view of what used to be Spahn Ranch, drop by the Church at Rocky Peak just across the street, built on the site where Manson allegedly staged mock-crucifixions (and if you take the 118 West from Topanga Canyon, you'll see the church's own giant crucifix, planted atop a stony version of Golgotha, replete with what appear to be fake boulders—it's awesome!). As if to somehow balance what must be a millennium of bad karma, the Church at Rocky Peak serves as the yin to Spahn's yang. Though the church is also located on private property, its staff and parishioners don't seem very perturbed by death-obsessed looky-loos. When we stopped by one sunny afternoon to check out the view from the elevated parking lot, we ran into a friendly staffer who seemed inured to the constant queries about their satanic ex-neighbor. He gladly pointed out where the ranch once stood, and went so far as to share the heartwarming tale of two teenaged lovebirds

*"I'm the devil; I'm here to do the devil's business."*

—TEX WATSON TO THE OCCUPANTS OF 10050 CIELO DRIVE

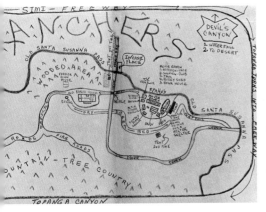

who parked down the street for some heavy petting and ended up murdered. It was almost like a Chick tract come to life!

After you've trespassed on private property in order to pay homage to a cadre of spoiled suburban brats who festered in the desert heat and ate enough drugs to believe that the puerile Peter Pan who led them was actually Jesus Christ, you're going to need the Church at Rocky Peak more than they need you. Rest assured that a quick prayer won't bring back Sharon Tate, her unborn baby, Jay Sebring, Abigail Folger, Voytek Frykowski, Steve Parent, Rosemary and Leno LaBianca, Gary Hinman, or anyone else the Manson Family murdered, but it may just dust off a smidgen of the evil pixie dust you will have undoubtedly collected during your sojourn.

To get to what used to be Spahn Ranch from Los Angeles, take the Ronald Reagan Freeway (118) to Topanga Canyon and head south. Make a right at the light for Santa Susana Pass and keep going until you see the sign for the Church at Rocky Peak on your right. On your left you'll see the bridge to nowhere, and further down the road, a sign for Santa Susana Pass State Historic Park. Spahn Ranch was located approximately between the two.

Tell them Vincent Bugliosi sent you!

## TAKING OUR MEDICINE AT
# PSYCHIATRY: AN INDUSTRY OF DEATH

Psychiatry:
An Industry of Death
6616 Sunset Boulevard
Los Angeles
800.869.2247
www.cchr.org

Since its inception, Scientology has put forth many outwardly benign front organizations with the aim of pulling people into the church: Foundation for Religious Tolerance, Concerned Businessmen's Association of America, and Association for Better Living and Education are but a few of the delightfully Orwellian organizations created by COS. But by virtue of its name alone, Psychiatry: An Industry of Death is not one of the group's more subtle ventures.

Housed in yet another deceptively earnest COS organization, Citizen's Commission on Human Rights (CCHR), Psychiatry: An Industry of Death takes a valid premise—psychiatry is an imperfect science with its own history of failures and abuse—and then, through the miracle of overkill, exaggeration, and omission, proceeds to throw the baby out with the Thorazine by laying almost every conceivable ill in this world at the feet of psychiatry. Apparently the ugly truth just isn't ugly enough for these good folks.

We've never been to CIA headquarters in Langley, Virginia, but we'd like to imagine that its lobby is a more grandiose version of the CCHR reception area: a sterile, officious room festooned with giant CCHR crests on the wall and inlaid in the floor. When you enter the CCHR lobby, you're greeted by a number of fresh-faced volunteers who look and sound exactly like real human beings. These true believers are courteous and ready to answer your questions—right after you "sign in" and provide your name, occupation, and any other information they can wheedle out of you.

"We notice you're a writer, Mr. . . . . *Smegmazoid*. What do you write about?"

"Oh, scam artists, whackjobs, cults . . . you know."

"Hey, that's great. Step right this way!"

After taking a picture of the entrance to the museum—a grim, institutional door above which is emblazoned "Abandon Every Hope Ye Who Enter Here"—we were politely told not to take pictures. We thought that was somewhat odd for a free museum that's open to the public and eager to spread the word about the evils of psychiatry, but one can never quite fathom the logic of the COS. We soon forgot all about it when we were given a set of headphones and a small receiver through which we could listen to the audio portions of the museum's interactive displays. Yes, we're easily amused.

*To the Lobotomobile, Icepickman!*

The museum proved to be a thrill-a-minute adventure from the moment we set foot in the full-scale padded room that also serves as a video theater. As the lights dimmed, we took a seat on one of the metal benches and were soon immersed in a delightfully sensationalistic video that begins with the ominous phrase, "Everywhere you look, there it is." No, silly, not Tom Cruise—they're talking about the "pseudo-science" of psychiatry. For us, the *Current Affair* production style of the ten-minute video, which abounds with slam-bam sound effects, annoying visual gimmicks, and suspiciously staged interviews with talking heads, also brought the word "pseudo-journalism" to mind.

# POTTY MOUTH

Unlike Belushi, who required a woman named Cathy Smith to do his needlework for him, Lenny Bruce could handle a syringe all by himself. And he did it quite often, it would seem, judging by the marks found on his arms when medics who discovered him dead and naked on the bathroom floor of his home in the hills above the Chateau Marmont in August of 1966. Bruce was forty years old.

**Lenny Bruce Overdose / 8825 Hollywood Boulevard / Los Angeles**

Bonus points for the blood-spattered graphics at the finale, however.

Then we moved into the museum itself: a dark, moody, gorgeous labyrinth replete with images of medieval torture, Victorian cruelty, and modern atrocities. Dubious medical devices with wonderful names like "The Bath of Surprise" are recreated in working miniatures, while devices like the penile plethysmorgraph—it cures pedophilia by applying shocks to the wiener!—made us happy we go for grown-ups.

Skillfully mixing fact (pharmaceutical companies get away with murder) and fallacy (B. F. Skinner raised his daughter in a box) to create its own delightfully preposterous reality, the CCHR blames psychiatry for, among other things, the Nazi Holocaust, Islamo-fascist terrorism and 9/11, ethnic cleansing, school shootings, Tim McVeigh, and the death of just about every unbalanced celebrity from Judy Garland to Kurt Cobain (sadly, Albert Dekker is absent from the wall of shame, but for some inexplicable reason, Phil Hartman is included).

The museum portrays psychiatrists as cynical, murderous, sex-addicted quacks who are part of a global conspiracy to . . . well, do something really bad, as far as we can tell. Curiously missing in the main part of the museum is any mention of Scientology itself, Hubbard's alleged appetite for pills, or COS's longstanding grudge against psychiatry ever since some shrinks pooh-poohed the organization as a dangerous cult and called El Ron, in layman's terms, Fruity Pebbles. We suppose that would have made us mad, too.

Other highpoints in the museum: the 3-D illusion of a TV monitor bursting through the wall, red bricks exposed like an open wound; lots of disturbing footage of real lobotomies being performed; a rare glimpse of Walter Freeman's "Lobotomobile," in which the operation's most ardent proponent toured the nation to give demonstrations; an interactive electroshock exhibit with a Tesla-like glass head; and enough authentic pill bottles to make Elvis sit up in his grave and beg. On the other hand, we were disappointed by the exhibit called "Whores of the Court," which was devoid of any explicit photographs of judges being fellated.

At the end our self-guided tour, we left the glum confines of the museum and entered a bright, futuristic room. Under a sign that reads "You're Safe as Long as We're Here," a large video monitor touted the successes of CCHR, and also mentioned the group's connection with Scientology. A list of board members and contributors on the wall also contained the names of the usual COS celebrity suspects. No sooner had we complimented the church on this uncharacteristic display of transparency than we were accosted by a staff member who asked us a lot of personal questions and wanted us to fill out an extensive survey. Some things never change.

To its credit, Psychiatry: An Industry of Death is an extremely well-designed and entertaining exhibit that hard-pedals its scandalous message with enough multimedia exhibits, interactive demonstrations, and Fox TV–esque hype to capture the imaginations of the most ADD-challenged among us. A lot of bucks and brainwork went into this museum, and, after parsing fact from fiction, there's definitely a message here about evil that cannot be ignored. Whether or not it has anything to do with psychiatry is for you to decide.

## DINING OUT IS A LIFE-OR-DEATH PROPOSITION AT

# THE PRINCE

Imagine sitting in a crimson red Naugahyde booth, tucked into the corner of a dark, oak-paneled English pub, surrounded by still life oil paintings, redcoat lamps, and miniature knights in armor looking over your shoulder. As you contemplate scotch or *soju*, you start to feel a bit peckish. Perusing the menu, you can't decide what you're in the mood for. Chicken? Sea snails? Silkworms? Live octopus tentacles?

Oh, the decisions one must make at The Prince.

Located in perhaps our favorite part of Los Angeles, historic Mid-Wilshire/Koreatown, The Prince is nestled on the ground floor of Windsor Apartments, a former hotel in the grand tradition of the Gaylord, the Bryson, the Talmadge, and other fine old

The Prince
Windsor Apartments
3198 West Seventh Street
Los Angeles
213.389.2007

haunts built in the 1920s. Just as so many of these architectural riches have been lost to the wrecking ball or an overzealous makeover, so too have the dark, womb-like restaurant/lounges that once serviced the stars in their shadowy recesses. There was a time you could have stood in front of the Windsor and hit the Coconut Grove with a rock. No more.

Koreatown's sprawling growth has been both a bane and a salvation for these endangered edifices. The sad, tawdry migration of the Brown Derby to its unrecognizable state atop a mini-mall is a prime example of the former; the preservation of The Prince by its Korean owners is testament to the latter. (Ironically, the interior of The Prince subbed for the Brown Derby when Nicholson and Dunaway got together there in *Chinatown*.)

Despite the ill-informed opinions of naïve, inebriated Yelpers, make no mistake about it: The Prince is *not* a dive bar by any stretch of the imagination. In fact, anyone fortunate enough to have ever sipped a martini in the Oak Room at New York's Plaza Hotel will experience a sense of familiarity here. The dim and moody lighting, in conjunction with the preponderance of red in every aspect of the decor, magically combine to produce a sense of security and secretive adventure.

**If the booze doesn't kill you, the food will.**

That's where the sautéed silkworms and live octopus tentacles enter the picture. Yes, there are other places in Koreatown that serve such peculiar and potentially dangerous dishes, but eating something so incredibly otherworldly amidst the stately, anglicized charm of The Prince is a downright surreal experience.

Fans of insects will find a plateful of pleasure in the sautéed silkworm larvae, which possess neither the tactile quality nor the flavor of silk—whatever that may be—but at least they're dead (and probably from a can, judging from their mushy consistency). The same can't be said of the live octopus tentacles, which you should order even if you can't find the courage to eat them. We can recall no experience that compares to sitting at an elegant dining table covered in a deep red table cloth and witnessing a plate full of furious, writhing, dismembered cephalopod appendages, the suckers still flaring and contracting in vain, as they literally crawl off the plate in a last-ditch attempt to kill everyone at the table. Should you decide to indulge your taste buds, we advise you to be firm with the roiling bastards and chew your food like you've never chewed it before. When one grabs hold of your tongue, mouth, or teeth—and it will—be prepared

# HARMFUL IF SWALLOWED

Florence Lawrence wasn't the first movie star to kill herself, but she was the first movie star to kill herself with insect poison. She was also the first movie star.

During the infancy of the motion picture industry Flo-Lo blazed trails, and over her career appeared in nearly three hundred (mostly silent) movies. She was the first film performer to sign a studio contract, the first to receive a screen credit by name, and the first woman to co-head her own film company. Oddly, she's also given credit for an automotive innovation: she invented a primitive form of the first brake light and turn signal.

Injuries and recovery time from a 1915 studio fire—as well as four months of temporary paralysis the following year—were professional setbacks from which Lawrence was unable to rebound, and by age twenty-nine her film career was all but over. The stock market crash, a bone marrow disease, and three husbands later, Lawrence—understandably—lost her lust for life. She exterminated herself with ant paste at her West Hollywood apartment in 1938.

Now, more than a century after her first screen appearance, the name Florence Lawrence doesn't register much outside a small community of silent movie geeks and serious film historians, but it's just as well: Most Angelenos don't know how to operate a goddamn turn signal either.

Suicide of the "First Movie Star" / 532 Westbourne Drive / West Hollywood

for a fight when you pry it off with your fingers. If you do not manage to get the entire tentacle in your mouth, you will have to use the same technique to wrestle it from your lips and face. Whatever you do, chew *completely* and make sure the damn thing is dead before you swallow it. Should it still have enough fighting spirit to take hold of your esophagus, the Heimlich maneuver will not help you. If such a situation arises, please be aware that you very well may choke to death.

Have a nice day.

AFTERLIFE, THEN WHAT? / 281

# FARMER JOHN

## SLAUGHTERHOUSE

Farmer John Murals
3049 East Vernon Avenue
Vernon
323.583.4621

Hot dog and Dodger fans alike are well familiar with the folks at Farmer John (aka Clougherty Packing, LLC), who have been cranking out the world-famous proprietary "Dodger Dogs" since 1964. That was the year tragedy struck L.A.'s television airwaves when the locally produced hit show "Polka Parade" went national and dropped all local advertisers. Sadly, the weekly polka program was Farmer John's biggest advertising vehicle, and though we're not quite sure how to interpret that, good news soon arrived at the slaughterhouse doorstep, swaddled in Dodger blue. The Dodgers were looking for sponsors for their new TV and radio telecasts, and as fate would have it, the legendary union was born. Since then, anyone tuning into a game has heard announcers singing the praises of the "superior Eastern-bred, corn-fed pork that is Farmer John's Meats."

Located in the exquisitely dismal industrial area of Vernon, Farmer John is one of the last slaughterhouses in a region that once teemed with factories that turned mammals into meat. By the 1970s, most of the competition had closed down or moved to the rural Midwest to mitigate shipping costs for both the animals and the grain they ate. But not Farmer John: They narrowed their lucrative beef, lamb, and pork processing empire to accommodate hogs alone, and in doing so, eventually built a $325 million-dollar-a-year pork business that proudly stands as the biggest

west of Oklahoma—and L.A.'s best-selling brand. Despite the double whammy of the 1994 baseball strike as well as a fire that wiped out the weenie production line that same year, Clougherty Packing bounced back and was purchased a decade later by Hormel for a whopping $186 million. The new owners have promised not to fuck with the company's signature murals.

Spoiler alert: Farmer John is about as real as Santa Claus or the Easter Bunny.

It took a few decades, but eventually Francis and Bernard (Barney)

## OUT '*n*' ABOUT

# THIS ISN'T ALICE'S WONDERLAND

It might look like an unremarkable split-level box to you, but for its neighbors, 8763 Wonderland Drive will forever remain an ugly thorn in the side of an otherwise tranquil Laurel Canyon community.

This was the scene of the bloody "Four-on-the-Floor" murders, the victims of which were the coke-tootin', house-robbin', drug-dealin' pals of the late porn star John Holmes, who had led them to the house of a rich club owner/coke dealer named Adel Nasrallah (aka Eddie Nash) to rip him off. They did, and Nash—who also foolishly counted Holmes among his friends—figured out who had screwed whom. He forced Holmes at gunpoint to take him and a club-toting crony to the Wonderland house, where they proceeded to usher the slumbering occupants into an even deeper sleep with bludgeonings so brutal that their faces were left unrecognizable. Holmes's palm print was found on a wall over one of the victims, indicating that the killers probably dragged the well-hung, whimpering drug addict up to face his old friends for one final look.

**Wonderland Drive Murders / 8763 Wonderland Drive / Los Angeles**

Clougherty, the brothers who started the company in 1931, got tired of people getting their name wrong (it's pronounced clow-er-tee). They also knew that "Farmer Francis" and "Farmer Bernard" lacked a certain common-man appeal. Thus, in 1953, the fictitious agrarian in overalls and straw cowboy hat known as Farmer John was born. Four years later, in 1957, the Farmer's creative legacy would reach its pinnacle as work commenced on what is quite possibly L.A.'s greatest work of art: the gloriously underrated Farmer John murals.

If the odor that emanates from the Farmer John plant is any indication of what goes on inside, it can't be a pretty scene. All the more reason to decorate the walls surrounding the enormous complex with bustling, bucolic scenarios that depict a less lethal side of farm living. Originally begun by Hollywood scenic painter Leslie Allen "Les" Grimes, the murals span entire city blocks

*Death to pigs!*

# JESUS SAVES;
# MOSES INVESTS

Originally a fixture atop the now-demolished Church of the Open Door, the red neon Jesus Saves signs (a twin was erected on the same rooftop some years after the original's 1935 debut) were once unmistakable beacons of hope amidst an otherwise dreary downtown skyline. Perched over the cityscape, the signs, with their enormous capital letters, were anything but subtle in their conveyance of salvation. It seemed only fitting when they fell into the holy hands of the gruff, cigar-chomping, horse-loving, money-grubbing televangelist Dr. Gene Scott, who moved the beauties atop his Los Angeles University Cathedral (formerly the United Artists theater) where the iconoclast's widow, an alleged ex-porn star, still carries on his distinctly acerbic tradition of fundraising—er, preaching. The historic signs are still there, though somewhat hidden by the city's shifting architectural façade. Once the sun goes down and they begin to glow, their stark beauty is almost enough to make us see the light.

**Jesus Saves Signs / 933 South Broadway / Los Angeles**

and reach enormous heights. For eleven years, Grimes worked tirelessly on the peaceful, pastoral vistas of playful pigs blissfully unaware of their impending doom. Along with the happy hogs, Grimes painted laughing children, stacked hillbilly chicks, and

a veritable menagerie of animals, barnyard and otherwise. His incessantly upbeat attention to detail is impressive, but apparently Grimes couldn't resist an occasional stab at gallows humor: besides a pig peering out from behind prison bars, he also painted a line of hogs trotting happily to a smokehouse where, rather than being served dinner, they become it.

In 1968, while painting clouds and sky on one of the building's higher walls, Grimes fell to his death

## OUT 'n' ABOUT
# (NOT QUITE) FASTER THAN A SPEEDING BULLET...

Just up the bend from the site of the former Sharon Tate house is the pad where, at age forty-five, George "Superman" Reeves—the chunky hero of the early TV series—was found in his bedroom, naked, with a gunshot wound to the head. The gun was found at his feet, so the coroner's office ruled his death a suicide. Reeves's mother, however, smelled something foul and ordered her son's body to be put on ice until they could positively rule out murder. Eventually Reeves was cremated and his mother passed away.

Maybe mom knew best after all. Reeves had been tangled up in a ten-year affair with Toni Mannix, the wife of MGM studio exec Eddie Mannix. George was also a kept man; Toni not only regularly supplemented Reeves's income, but also helped to set him up in his Benedict Canyon home. In 1958, George told Toni the affair was over, and that he had proposed to a young New York socialite named Lenore Lemmon. Toni was destroyed . . . and vengeful . . . and crazy. She threatened to expose Superman's alleged bisexuality, harassed the new couple with phone calls at all hours of the day and night, and was even suspected of having the brake fluid drained from Reeves's Jaguar to ensure a deadly car wreck. Reportedly Reeves's death was at the hands of his spurned benefactor, who hired a hit man to use Reeves's own Luger, an earlier gift from Toni. Although evidence for both arguments was inconclusive, his death was officially classified as suicide.

**The Superman Murder Mystery / 1579 Benedict Canyon / Beverly Hills**

from a fifty-foot scaffolding. His work, considered by some art historians to be the apogee of West Cost vernacular painting, was carried on by an Austrian immigrant named Arno Jordan, who, as a teenager, fled war-torn Europe to fulfill his dream of painting slaughterhouses in the New World. A skilled artist with a modicum of architectural training, it was Jordan who maintained Grimes's whimsical style and added some of his own distinctive flourishes during the thirty years he worked on the murals. The "official" story is that Jordan retired for "health reasons" in 1998, but an anonymous source at the company told us that Jordan

The Federal Humane Slaughter Act of 1958 requires that animals be electrically stunned prior to slaughter so that they will feel no pain. Neat!

simply failed to show up for work one day and never returned. The source also speculated that any number of reasons might explain Jordan's disappearance—including his alleged fondness for drink or an inexplicable longing to return to his homeland—but vehemently denied our persistent attempts to suggest that Jordan had fallen into the hot dog machine and been turned into a thousand wieners. "That's ridiculous," said the source, "Mr. Jordan would only have made a few hundred franks, at most."

After Jordan's "retirement," the gauntlet was taken up by Philip Slagter, his nephew A. J. Slagter, and graffiti artist Eddi Milan, aka Ed1. Extensive restoration and preservation was the first order of business; common house paint had been used for most of the original murals, which were peeling and fading because of the salts leached by the concrete and brick masonry. In addition to the massive amount of scraping, repainting, and sealing of the older work that covers the outer walls of Farmer John, A. J. and Eddi painted the sweeping skies (complete with flying pigs) that completely encompass some of the main buildings, creating a breathtaking 3-D effect that can be especially appreciated from the Bandini Street vantage point.

The Famer John murals are the company's way of putting a positive spin on the ten-acre death factory and its plentiful, dee-licious output. And you know what? It works. No matter how updated and modernized a slaughterhouse may become, the process of turning live pigs into crates of wieners, breakfast sausages, and holiday hams cannot be a pleasant affair. It never ceases to amaze us how easily a gigantic, jolly mural of life on the farm can distract one from the ugly business that goes on just behind it. Rarely do art and industry collide in such an effective manner.

One can only imagine if other less-than-palatable institutions would similarly benefit from a Farmer John-style makeover. What if the outer walls of the county jail depicted men gleefully reading books, lifting weights, and otherwise going about the process of rehabilitation, rather than dealing drugs, carving shivs from soap bars, and getting gang-raped in the shower by hulking brutes with swastikas tattooed on their bellies? Perhaps the odor of our local sewage treatment plant would be diminished, if only in our minds, by a festive depiction of gleaming toilet bowls and festoons of fresh white toilet paper rather than an endless,

# NOT SIMPLY DIVINE

Cult film legend and disco icon Divine (née Harris Glenn Milstead) was about to make his long-awaited crossover from cross-dressing into the mainstream with a gig on a hit sitcom playing a male character. He was to begin his first day of rehearsals for *Married ... With Children* the morning of his death at the Regency Suites. The 375-pound actor died peacefully in his sleep from an enlarged heart. It took six men to carry Divine's body from the hotel.

**Divine Departure / 7940 Hollywood Boulevard / Hollywood**

turd-studded river of urine and excrement. Would the haunting nightmare of nuclear holocaust be somehow mitigated if the San Onofre and Diablo Canyon nuclear power plants were covered with bright daisies instead of ulcerated keloids, swollen tumors, and oozing, pus-filled ... well, you get the picture.

If you don't have the time to take the family out to the *real* countryside (is there any left around here, anyway?), why not make some liverwurst sandwiches, grab the kids, and head on down to the Farmer John slaughterhouse for the next best thing? Like the stench, it's an experience you won't soon forget!

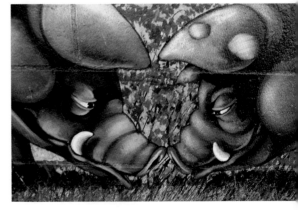

WHEEL INN

GO AWAY

CHAPTER
№ 7

# GETTING OUR KNUT AT THE
# INTEGRATRON

The Integratron
2477 Belfield Boulevard
Landers
760.364.3126
www.integratron.com

From Los Angeles:
Take the 10 Freeway East
towards Palm Springs.
From the 10, take Route 62
towards Yucca Valley. From
Yucca Valley, take Highway
247 (Old Woman Springs
Road). Drive 10.5 miles to
Landers. Turn right on Reche
Road, and travel 2.2 miles to
Belfield Road. Turn left on
Belfield, travel one mile to the
Integratron.

For the record, we hate the desert. Fucking hate it. It's too hot, too sunny, too dry, and the people who live there either tend to be really strange or to suffer from chronic asthma. We've never understood why someone would choose to camp in Joshua Tree or spend a weekend in Palm Springs for fun, but whatever; people are weird and as much as we'd like to, we can't fix them unless they want to be fixed. Even then, we charge an exorbitant fee.

Objectionable as the desert may be, we'd probably visit with greater frequency if there were more people like George Van Tassel living there. Van Tassel is precisely the sort of fellow we'd expect to find living in the desert of Southern California, except that he's dead. When he was alive, however, he made his home in Landers—just south of the restricted area of the Marine Corps' Combat Center in the Bullion Mountains of the Mojave—and he put every other desert eccentric to shame.

From the sands of Landers rises Van Tassel's Integratron: a never-realized electrostatic cellular rejuvenation generator designed to add decades to a human life. The device wasn't about longevity for longevity's sake, however, but rather an attempt to minimize the amount of reincarnations needed to reach moral and spiritual maturity by extending each successive lifetime. In other words, longer lifetimes = fewer reincarnations = shortcut to spiritual perfection. Simple.

In case you're immediately dismissing Van Tassel as some New Age crackpot, we should probably make note of his impressive resumé: He was the widely read author of the books *I Rode a Flying Saucer* (1952), *Into This World and Out Again* (1956), and *The Council of Seven Lights* (1958). He also once worked for Lockheed and Howard Hughes, and they certainly wouldn't have hired anyone weird. He also received the concept, design, and engineering instructions for The Integratron on good authority: Solgonda, the leader of four aliens "with perfect teeth," traveled to the Morongo Basin all the way from Venus just to give it to him. Soon afterward—enabled with funding from generous donors— Van Tassel contracted a Montebello roofing company to build the Integratron's shell, which was constructed entirely of wood and without the use of metal nails so as not to interfere with the rejuvenating properties of its electrostatic field. Although the building looked really cool, George never actually hammered out the rejuvenation part. With his structure completed in 1959, Van Tassel continued to tinker with the works until his death nineteen years later, just prior to which he had declared The Integratron "ninety percent complete." So many cells to rejuvenate, so little time.

Nonetheless, Van Tassel was a prolific man who enjoyed an exciting life out there in Landers, publishing his own quarterly newsletter, *Proceedings*, establishing the College of Universal Wisdom, and hosting the Giant Rock Spacecraft Convention. Eager to hear the lectures of famous UFO contactees—and anxious to witness Van Tassel channeling space brothers like Knut—attendees flocked to the annual event by the thousands. After more than twenty years, however, his conventions lost speed—but not before going out in a blaze of glory. Like the storyline of a really excellent drive-in movie, some rowdy bikers crashed the UFO event in 1970 and set a car on fire. Even we'd have trekked out to the desert for that one.

After Van Tassel's death in 1978, The Integratron's future looked uncertain. A San Diego developer leased the property with plans for conversion into a disco (another twist on life rejuvenation, certainly), and the dome was rumored to be a meth lab for a time (temporary rejuvenation, to be sure, followed by certain death), but it wasn't until 1987 that Van Tassel's inspired erection fell into the hands of a new owner, one who was down with the space brothers. For the first time, the Integratron was open for public tours, albeit infrequently.

In 2000, the landmark was sold once again, itself receiving the very sort of life rejuvenation The Integratron originally promised others. Three groovy sisters from New York found The Integratron's happy medium, hitting somewhere between trance channeling and pyromaniacal bikers. They've equipped the grounds with an outdoor living room, a telescope for nighttime stargazing, a fire pit, and a shaded courtyard. Restrooms marked "Mars" and "Venus" now stand in the shadow of the infamous dome, which has been significantly spiffed up with a fresh coat of paint. A Von Tassel exhibit occupies some of its ground floor, featuring photos, models, news articles, and The Integratron timeline. The top floor features a nondenominational altar, and plays host to the best damn time to be had in Landers: weekend "sound baths"—The Integratron's "sonic healing sessions"—conducted right under the dome itself.

Don't get excited: in these baths you remain clothed, although you are required to remove your shoes. The Karl sisters bill their scheduled sound baths as "Kindergarten Nap Time of the Third Kind," wherein bathers grab a blanket or quilted mat, stretch out on the floor at the foot of a set of singing quartz crystal bowls, and immerse themselves in a cascade of soothing sounds as elicited by one of the sisters. Before your bath, you're given

*Is that a natural cone of receptivity in your pocket or are you just happy to see me?*

# YESTERDAY'S INN OF TOMORROW

White vinyl donkeys and silver foil elephants wearing space helmets hung from the ceiling in the lobby, and rooms were appointed with "daring new interior colors" and "a newer than tomorrow space-age decor." This was Stovall's Inn of Tomorrow: a Best Western motel that offered a Monsanto-cum-"Small World" alternative to Anaheim's overabundance of cut-rate lodging for Disneyland-bound families. They boasted "Moon level luxury . . . Down to earth rates."

Unfortunately, "tomorrow" didn't end up looking anything like Stovall's ebullient prediction, and although the motel is still in business, today the decor is relatively earth-bound.

**Stovall's Best Western / Formerly Stovall's Inn of Tomorrow / 1110 West Katella Avenue / Anaheim**

a brief history on The Integratron and the life of Van Tassel, and provided with a dubious explanation of the building site; The Integratron didn't just land here by chance, certainly. Van Tassel claimed The Integratron's location is one of exceptional geomagnetic activity, a site he determined by coordinates that have something to do with the great pyramid at Giza and a Landers curiosity called Giant Rock, which is often referred to as "The World's Largest Single Boulder." Giant Rock (which sits just up the road) was also a Native American hot spot and the short-lived home of Van Tassel's eccentric friend Frank Critzer, a prospector and suspected—but unlikely and unsubstantiated—Nazi spy who lived in a hole burrowed beneath the stone. Critzer died in a dynamite explosion after he barricaded himself inside his subterranean hideaway and police attempted to smoke the human gopher out with a tear gas grenade. Unfortunately, the grenade ignited the cache of explosives Critzer kept under his kitchen table. Oops.

Regardless of its inconvenient location and checkered past, one thing is certain: The Integratron's acoustics are impeccable, and once those bowls start singing—each one tuned to resonate with each of the seven chakras, so we're told—you may as well be on Solgonda's spacecraft. Sound waves resonate through you, around you, above you, and beneath you. Tones morph into other tones, traveling through one ear and seemingly passing out the other; their source points shifting with the aid of The Integratron's amplifying architecture, bouncing, echoing, and reverberating into each other, pulling you into another dimension, massaging the brain, tranquilizing your thoughts, and suspending you in an altered state from which you return only with the greatest reluctance. Maybe it had something to do with finally being able to lie down after the two-and-a-half-hour drive,

but we had to scrape ourselves up off that floor when our bath was over.

After staggering down the stairs, we sat for a while on the ground floor, pawing over The Integratron reference library. Some of Van Tassel's writings and press coverage are archived here, along with reference books on UFO phenomenon and inventors like Nikola Tesla, by whom Van Tassel was greatly influenced.

Hate the desert as much as we do? The Integratron is worth the trip. Check their Web site for the next sound bath weekend, and make your reservation. You're unlikely to find many spots more steeped in weirdness, wrought with intrigue, and riddled with lore.

## OUT 'n' ABOUT
# IT NEVER RAINS IN (SOUTHERN) CALIFORNIA

Where the weather is always warm, the skies are always blue, and the sun shines every single goddamn day.

Flooded Sign / Seen almost every time it rains / Greater Los Angeles County

# A PROPHECY IN MUD AND BROKEN CONCRETE AT

# SUNKEN CITY

Sunken City
Point Fermin Park
San Pedro

We all have those days when we're down on L.A. "Fuck this bullshit place!" we cry, pounding our fists against the steering wheel while stuck in another two-hour freeway standstill, gazing at the fade-to-brown horizon line, idling gallons away beneath yet another billboard telling us—for one reason or another—that we're just not good enough. *I wish this whole goddamn city would just BREAK OFF AND SINK INTO THE PACIFIC!"*

It's in those moments that we must catch our breath, dab our tears, and find solace by reminding ourselves that a lot of Los Angeles already has sunk into the Pacific—and there's more on the way. What a relief!

Before L.A. County had the benefit of the red flags provided by Malibu—the periodic lessons learned when prime oceanfront real estate travels southwest and rides the wild surf subsequent to a heavy rainfall—there was a seaside neighborhood in San Pedro unwittingly about to hang ten at the close of the 1920s. South Paseo Del Mar, indeed. Never was a street more aptly named.

Even now, over seventy years later, South Paseo Del Mar leads the way, more or less, to what's left of the neighborhood that was literally swallowed by the land mass at the edge of Point Fermin. What remains of the street passes underneath an iron fence, finally breaking over the edge of a sharp drop. But the fragmented asphalt of Paseo Del Mar only hints at the story, which all occurred over a period of about five years, with much of the block sinking at a rate of nearly a foot a day. All but two of the homes were moved to more solid ground, and the rest of the neighborhood finally went south. The fabled Sunken City is all but hidden from public view these days, teasing us from behind a barrier of eight-foot fencing, but that certainly needn't stop you. It's dangerous to access and completely illegal, but if you allow nitpicky details like that scare you away from an adventure why the hell did you buy this book anyway?

If low-end attractions that require trespassing make your heart race as they do ours, Sunken City will take your breath away—it's like reaching Oz (and almost as difficult to access). Head down to Point Fermin Park and over to the concrete lookout pavilion at the edge of the grass facing the water. Hop the low barrier wall—making sure no one sees you—and follow the well-worn trail to your left. Scale the edge of the iron fence hugging the side of the cliff and continue beyond the broken edge of Paseo Del Mar. There the majestic remnants of the neighborhood streets and sidewalks lie broken and buckled, once host to San Pedro residents who felt they made a good real estate investment, and now host to Jäger-chugging graffiti artists for whom Sunken City is a fertile canvas.

After a heavy rainfall this area gets muddy. And slippery. You may discover firsthand that there are some very good reasons why this neighborhood caved in on itself. So if you should lose your footing, fall to the shoreline and break your neck on the rocks below, don't come crying to us. It's not like we didn't warn you.

For those less intrepid, Sunken City may be viewed from a turnout where Pacific Avenue meets with Paseo Del Mar, just a block away. But you have to stand behind a fence and it's not nearly as much fun.

*Women and children first.*

OUT 'n' ABOUT

# FLEE MY BABY

The southeast corner where Melrose joins Santa Monica at Doheny in West Hollywood and the corner of Spalding at Wilshire in Beverly Hills are important sites in the annals of rock 'n' roll history. It was these spots that played host to the great escapes of sixties hit mistress Ronnie Spector from her eccentric then-husband Phil. After a quick but brilliant career as lead singer of the Ronettes, by age twenty-four the Spanish Harlem beauty had been all but forced into an early retirement, as Phil virtually held her prisoner behind barbed wire and cyclone fencing in a rented mansion on the edge of Beverly Hills. On the rare occasion she ventured off the property—sometimes barefoot, as Phil commandeered her shoes to prevent a long-term departure—she'd head down the hill to Carl's Market (now Petco) and find solace connecting with the outside world by way of the magazine rack. When she finally did break out for good, barefoot, on June 12, 1972, she headed straight to her lawyer's office to commence divorce proceedings, and settled into the Beverly Crest Hotel (now the Mosaic). Ronnie later commented, "Being married to Phil Spector was a picnic compared to getting divorced from him."

Carl's Market / 508 North Doheny (former address) / West Hollywood
Beverly Crest Hotel / 125 South Spalding Drive (former address) / Beverly Hills

# DEANZA SPRINGS RESORT

DeAnza Springs Resort
1951 Carrizo Gorge Road
Jacumba
877.2GO.NUDE
www.deanzasprings.com

Seems that nearly everyone has a life to-do list. Whether kept on paper or in the back of your head, we've all got those entries we anticipate ticking off, one by one, over our lifetime: "See Paris," "Get Scuba Diving Certification," "Open a Roth IRA," "Vacation at a Clothing-Optional RV Park," and the like. But whether you live a long healthy life or not, the reality is that either way your days are numbered, so maybe it's time to start editing said list down.

Since the U.S. dollar is like Monopoly money against the euro, don't worry about Paris for now. The Eiffel Tower isn't going anywhere, and maybe it's actually worth waiting to see how they're going to tart that thing up after everyone gets tired of those twinkly lights. And unless you're looking into a career as a marine biologist, how much use do you really think you're going to get out of that scuba certification anyway? With respect to retirement investments, a Roth IRA certainly isn't a bad idea, though we make it our policy not to offer retirement advice unless you pay us.

However, when it comes to clothing-optional recreation, we're here to tell you that it's time to start making some plans.

On the edge of the Jacumba Mountains, just a stone's throw north of Baja, and barely sixty miles east of San Diego as the nude crow flies, sits California's largest clothing-optional resort. Nestled into five hundred acres of high desert, DeAnza Springs is a surprising world unto itself—and a remarkably well-appointed playland of nude recreation. Horseshoe pits and shuffleboard beckon if you're in an old-school nudist sort of mood—just like in those naturist films of the 1960s—and there's an outdoor fitness area, two tennis courts, and volleyball (grass, sand, or water) if you prefer your clothing-optional recreation with a little less irony. Nude pool sharks can work their cues at the billiard tables, and there's a dance every Saturday night. Though most of the DeAnza property is clothing-optional, there are nudity-required zones: the two pools (one indoor, heated, and open twenty-four hours a day), the hot tub, and the encompassing deck, skirted with lounge chairs just like the ones at the best hotels in Las Vegas.

The amenities are staggering. DeAnza serves as a year-round vacation spot—affiliated with the American Association of Nude

Recreation—featuring 311 RV sites, a handful of "park models," Wi-Fi–ready rental units and motel rooms, and virtually unlimited desert campsites for those who prefer to rough it in the raw. Laundry facilities are available should you need them, as are public restrooms and showers for those pitching tents or hanging out on a day pass. You can bring your pets along for your clothing-optional adventure too, and even keep them in the enclosed pet park if you don't feel like being a slave to the leash. Forget to bring sunscreen? Don't let your no-longer-so-private parts get fried by the desert rays—take a nude stroll over to the gift shop housed in their 7500-square-foot clubhouse where you can pick up fun-in-the-sun staples, along with DeAnza beach towels and beer cozies. And even if you've left your laptop at home, you can still blog your "wish you were here's" from their computer room and library.

The Oasis Lounge and "Come As You Are Bar" are located across from the Cactus Flower Café, DeAnza's very own restaurant (Department of Health Rating: A). The café keeps a limited but varied menu for dinner, five or so options, clean and simply prepared. The generous plate of king crab legs served one Sunday evening was fresh, not overcooked, and served with drawn butter and lemon alongside steamed vegetables and rice. This was practically spa cuisine, and the added advantage of being able to take your meal nude (with a small "sitting towel" placed over the seat cushion, as is the protocol in clothing-optional environments, FYI) was certainly not reflected in the price of our entrée. Breakfast had fresh blueberry pancakes, eggs, and sausage at the table—pun not necessarily intended—which was a pleasant departure from the greasy-spoon variety and just the right kind of fuel for an active day of nudeness.

DeAnza's promo brochure promises a friendly, accommodating, and accepting environment, and from the moment of check-in DeAnza walks the walk. With a brief but detailed on-the-spot orientation, guests are ushered into the fold with a grounds map, a rundown of the resort amenities, a quick walk-through of the clubhouse, and an off-the-cuff dinner recommendation. The personal attention given to guests ensures that all visitors—whether accustomed to a clothing-optional getaway or not—feel included and encouraged to share in DeAnza's bounty. Ultimately, your RV park experience is what you care to make of it: busy weekends play host to upwards of three hundred guests, and there's a small but close-knit community of full-timers keeping the grounds active through the week. Want to chat up other naturists at the hot tub and take advantage of the unique poolside milieu? As long as you're not a masher, you'll find a polite and well-socialized bunch. Want to lay low after water aerobics class and indulge in a little desert solitude? No one's going to force you into a game of nude bocce ball if you're not up for it and the retiree

*Bare bums and RVs: it's a beautiful thing.*

# WHAT IS THE SOUND OF ONE HAND UNZIPPING?

After spending a few hours exploring downtown Los Angeles, it might become unequivocally clear why the place smells like pee: There are no public restrooms. Anywhere. Not even at Starbucks. Why else do people go to Starbucks?

You won't find a public restroom on Onizuka Street either, but you will find peace of mind and fresher air if you slip into Weller Court. Three flights up and through two sets of glass doors sits a tranquil half-acre oasis of impeccably manicured botanicals and glassy brooks, yours for the strolling. Park yourself on a bench near the waterfall, and in about thirty seconds—breathing easier—you'll forget about downtown altogether. Soon, the peaceful sound of running water will remind you that you need to take a whizz like nobody's business, and you will suddenly see the forest for the banzai trees . . . so to speak. Be discreet.

**Japanese Rooftop Garden / 123 Onizuka Street / Los Angeles**

strumming a uke under the shade of the patio certainly isn't one to pass judgment, so go ahead and get lost; you won't be breaking any hearts and you'll find plenty of room to roam.

Walking the impeccably kept property, dotted with both palm and deciduous trees as well as the occasional rock garden, can be a surreal experience for those new to the clothing-optional RV park scene. The novelty of crossing paths with naturists taking their morning power walk around the grounds or feeling the breeze of a passing golf cart zipping by with an unclothed driver at the wheel are some of the subtle reminders of your amply advantaged alt-adventure. And if you need a getaway from your getaway, DeAnza offers that too, either by mountain bike or on foot with eight desert trails (graded easy to challenging) wandering off their grounds and into the vast hills of the Anza-Borrego State Park (though not within DeAnza property lines, still completely hikable sans hiking shorts). There are archeological sites to explore, remains of old railroad camps, even a great photo op at the fictional Heartbreak Hotel, a set built for the television show *Manhattan, AZ.*

If you don't want to commit to an overnight stay, day passes are cheap—and discounted for couples—but if you're going to bother with the trek to Jacumba the deal is sweetened by the unbeatable rates for their immaculately kept rooms and rentals. Rising with the sun and stepping out for a nude stroll along the sandy path to the heated pool followed with a nude breakfast and a desert hike is an experience you just won't get at a Best Western.

Check out the DeAnza calendar of weekend and holiday events. Among poker, bingo, and trivia nights, the list also includes the Glow in the Dark Dance, Kamikaze Karaoke, the Gender Bender Dance, and even a special event for Cher's birthday (the Gypsies, Tramps, and Thieves White Elephant Flea Market). Will you book your stay for Martin Luther King's Bloody Mary Monday, or the Party Like a Rock Star Variety Show?

Choices, choices. And you thought taking your clothes off was all there was to it.

## GETTING HIGH ON ADVENTURE
# HELICOPTER TOURS

We've said it before and we'll say it again: Pacoima is for lovers. So where better to wow Ms. or Mr. Right Now than at the Whiteman Airport? For thrill seekers who've exhausted their options for an exciting first date, take to the skies on a private helicopter tour and you're sure to get lucky. Not in the copter of course, but maybe in the airport parking lot after. Like we said, there's something about Pacoima.

A forty-five minute helicopter trip over busy freeways, through skyscrapers, and above some of L.A.'s ugliest swimming pools may not be for everyone. Nothing spoils a first date like crapping yourself, and there's really no sexy way to puke into an airsickness bag—so before making any commitments, do a little research. Prior to every first date comes the "screening" conversation—the dating job interview—in which you'll undoubtedly

Adventure Helicopter Tours
Whiteman Airport
10500 Airpark Way, Unit M3
Pacoima
888.WE.FLY.LA
adventurehelicoptertours.com

discuss personal interests, hobbies, favorite cuisine, and such. Use this opportunity to slip in a few extra questions related to helicopter flight, but be subtle, because if it's a good fit you won't want to ruin the surprise. For instance, does your date like dogs, enjoy live theater, or suffer from vertigo? Do they love the beach, dig jazz, or freak out when confined to small spaces? Do they eat sushi, adore Paris, or experience recurring aircraft catastrophe dreams? If they pass the preliminaries, consider taking the plunge. Dangerous? Feh. If you've driven to Pacoima and survived you've already beaten a stiffer set of odds, not to mention the fact that Adventure Helicopter touts a flawless safety record, which is more than you can say for dinner at El Coyote.

Conveniently calm any preflight jitters over drinks at Rocky's, the aviation-themed burger and booze joint just at the edge of the runway. Then head over to Adventure Helicopter's pistachio and mellow yellow lobby, relax on the big leather sofa, and soak up the splendor of their safety video (it isn't necessary to pay too much attention beyond the seatbelt fastening part; after that point, you're in God's hands). After payment processing and the quick signing of some release forms, you're shuttled off to the runway by golf cart, feeling as important as Tiger Woods or the Pope.

Think L.A. looks crappy at ground level? It's just as crappy from the air. Crappier really, depending on where you fly, but there are a lot of advantages to touring L.A. while snugly nestled inside AHT's cozy Robinson R44. For one, downtown Los Angeles doesn't smell like urine from five hundred feet in the air. In addition, you certainly won't get a bird's-eye view of the trampoline in the backyard of the Playboy Mansion from the window of a Gray Line tour bus—or the chance to take a photo of the Hollywood sign, looking down, not up. And you definitely won't make it from the Santa Monica surf to the back lot of Warner Bros. in fifteen minutes by rental car. Upgrade to their bitchin' Notar MD520, the rare "Ferrari of helicopters," an aircraft virtually exclusive to law enforcement ("with the speed of a cheetah, the agility of a hummingbird and the presence of an eagle"), and treat yourself to a new perspective on the soul-sucking 405. Rather than a 5-mph crawl while staring into the back end of the same vehicle for an hour and forty-five minutes, you can instead whisk overhead like Superman at 100 mph, lean out the Notar's open side, and hock a big loogie onto the odious belt of pavement below—an experience, in itself, worth the extra fee. Good news if your date shares such hatred of the 405, as this is the sign of a healthy mind.

With a helicopter tour, uneasy first-date chatter is avoided thanks to bulky headsets, which effectively muffle the noise from the propeller whirling above, and prevent any real conversation from taking place. Better yet, if you're not feeling any chemistry or your date turns out to be a big fat drip, simply ignore him or her and look out the window. It's a win-win!

AHT offers nine superlative tours, from a piggish hour-long joyride of helicopter madness to a feisty fifteen-minute quickie. You can explore Hollywood landmarks, spy on celebrity homes, or try a heli-surfing adventure down the coastline, hovering close to the water. They also offer an evening tour—where the badly bungled civic engineering and brown air of the L.A. Basin is lost with the night and reduced to a dramatic and mesmerizing expanse of twinkly lights. Pretty.

The AHT staff treats their clients like royalty, the pilots are cool, and everyone gets a free T-shirt. It's not cheap, certainly— starting at about a hundred bucks per passenger—but can you really put a price on adventure? You'd easily spend more on dinner, drinks, and Cirque du Soleil tickets—*and* you'd have to sit through all those fucking jugglers and clowns. Do we need to say it again? *Pacoima is for lovers.*

Don't bother with competitors; book your adventure now (and don't forget to tip your pilot generously—after you make it back down to the landing pad, of course).

*"When you're beside me, we can fly . . . oh, we can fly."*
—THE COWSILLS

## SPREADING GOD'S LOVE IN LATEX PAINT AT

# SALVATION MOUNTAIN

Why do Christians seem to have the market cornered on monomaniacal folk art? You'll never see a Jew building an effigy of Moses in their front yard out of hubcaps and broken bottles. Show us the Muslim with passages from the Koran hand-lettered over every inch of their thirty-five-year-old station wagon. A celebration of L. Ron in flattened soda cans and salvaged plywood? Even a Scientologist draws the line somewhere.

Yes, there most definitely seems to be something inherent within the Christian faith that drives the non-trained artist to express their love of God with found objects and sundry recyclables.

Salvation Mountain
No phone
Beal Road
Niland

Deemed folk art by many and a toxic hazard by some, one of the more awe-inspiring examples of faith-based outsider art lies on the edge of Highway 111 in arid Niland, a scant five miles east of the Sonny Bono Salton Sea Wildlife Refuge (we couldn't

make this up). Salvation Mountain, standing about three stories tall and constructed mostly from mud, hay, and a blend of oil and latex paint, is the work of Leonard Knight, a sprightly septuagenarian who began the indefinite work-in-progress, he explains, "because I love God and I love people," some twenty-five years ago. Over a massive, sculpturally graded hill with a treatment calling to mind marzipan and Easter candy, Knight honors nature with simply rendered waterfalls and flowers crafted from window putty, inter-mittently inscribed with prayers, affirmations, and passages from his favorite book.

A native Vermonter, Leonard discovered God in the late sixties and headed west—possibly because latex paint doesn't take to the hills of Vermont quite the same way it does in Niland—where he's made his home, in the back of a 1951 Chevy dump truck, since the early eighties. Although Knight is technically squat-ting on government land, ironically enough he seems to be keeping

under the radar. He got a little heat in the early nine-ties when Salvation Mountain was allegedly tested by a hazmat team, who tagged his rainbow-glazed mound of God-loving goodwill a toxic wasteland. The county threatened to bulldoze but the mountain was saved by an outcry of public support. Sometime later, Knight took soil samples himself and sent them to a San Diego lab that, according to Leonard, determined the soil was "positively safe." Efforts are currently being made by way of a letter-writing campaign to have the site secured by congressional support.

Salvation Mountain is also now home to an annex: a fantastical, cavernous grotto composed of hay bales, tires, car doors, and salvaged tree branches, reminding us of God's love at every turn. In spite of

# LEAP OF FAITH

Peg Entwistle was a successful Broadway actress who came to Hollywood in the early 1930s to break into the movies. She also has the distinction of being the only known individual to leap to her death from the iconic Hollywood sign. Despondent after being dropped from her RKO contract, she could have just as well gone back to New York; she certainly had plenty of good theater years left in her, seeing she was only twenty-four. But Peg, being the true drama queen that she was, jumped from the top of the second "D" (the sign used to spell out H-O-L-L-Y-W-O-O-D-L-A-N-D) to her early, but admirably stylish, death.

**Hollywood Sign / Beachwood Canyon / (Don't even bother, it's completely off-limits these days) / Hollywood**

his inventive choices, creative vision, and large-scale execution, Knight has never considered himself an artist, crediting God with "everything really good" on Salvation Mountain, and holding himself responsible for "everything that's falling apart."

Leonard is pretty much always around, working in the morning and leading tours until sundown. And although access to the Mountain is free, it's always polite to offer a donation—because, toxic or not, we'd kind of like it to stay right where it is.

*Go tell it on the mountain.*

## RISKING MORE THAN SUNBURN AT THE

# NUDE BEACH

Free your mind, and your clothes will follow: There's nothing quite so liberating as the nude beach experience. It's so much more than the simple act of taking to the sand with nothing but a little SPF between you and the warmth of the sun on your skin. It's the comfort of knowing how many people look even worse naked than you do—and that in itself is worth the extra drive.

With the revision of zoning laws for both Los Angeles and Santa Barbara counties in recent years, however, such fun in the

# LOVE MEANS NEVER HAVING TO SAY YOU'RE SARI

Don't get us wrong, it's not that we think the Hindu faith is "bizarre"—Catholics have had the market cornered on religious weirdness for quite some time—it's just that the dusty canyons of Calabasas are the last place we'd expect to find a little bit o' Calcutta?

**Hindu Temple / 1600 Las Virgenes Canyon Road / Calabasas**

sun is now considered a sex crime in the free and easy state of California. Aggressive policing and vigilant ticketing effectively squelched almost all the long-standing nudie haunts once dotting the So Cal coastline, to the extreme that Beach Patrol took to the surf on Jet Ski, by boat, and to the air with helicopter, tenaciously sniffing out the naked as though they were Al-Qaeda operatives or undocumented Mexicans.

*Where your body is a crime punishable by law.*

The Japanese have enjoyed mixed bathing for centuries. Germany's *Frei Korper Kultur* allows for nude sunbathing in public parks. Australia? Brazil? Don't get us started. A woman bares so much as a little areola in Malibu and she's risking life as a sex offender. While our brethren to the East—*Russkies* no less— splash freely in the waters of an officially sanctioned nude beach along the sunny shores of the Moscow River, we watch American liberties slowly whittled to little more than the right to bear semi-automatic weapons and shop at Wal-Mart. Excuse us, but didn't we used to be the leaders of the free world?

The good nudes is that not all of Southern California's clothing-optional beaches have been obliterated by clothes-minded county law. An exceptional, precious few remain—drawing hundreds on the hottest summer weekends—where hedonists still enjoy an all-over burn without an accompanying court date. It's not that these beaches are legal, but local authorities—in practice—tend to look the other way. Maybe it has something to do with all those dimpled white asses.

In any case, a nude beach neophyte needs more than a legal briefing before hitting the tar-soaked sands of

# UNDER A SPELL

If only more of Beverly Hills looked like this. This 1921 design by Henry Oliver was originally built on the lot of the now defunct Willat Movie Studios in Culver City. It was moved to its current location in the 1930s, where it now functions as a private home. Boo!

**The Witch House / 516 Walden Drive / Beverly Hills**

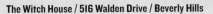

Southern California; there's clothing-optional protocol to consider. When on a nude beach, do as the nudists do (well, most of them, anyway; as things go, one should never take one's cues from the potbellied man in dark sunglasses and a baseball cap lurking behind a rock with a single-use camera). Yes, looking at naked people beats the hell out of boogie boarding, but it's not polite to gawk, so at least do your staring surreptitiously or wear aviators with reflective lenses like the perverts do so no one will be able to tell. Also, stay mindful of the fact that private inlets and cliffside coves are favored by those of easy virtue—employ your peripheral vision skills when exploring the shoreline in your best effort to appear as though you were just passing by and didn't even happen to notice the fervid finger-banging going down on that bright orange beach towel. And should you get carried away and find yourself on one side or another of such banging, you'd best be damn discreet. Sure, sex on the beach beats the hell out of boogie boarding, but you certainly wouldn't want a little seaside sumpin'-sumpin' to land you in the slammer just because some kid went hunting for sand dollars in the wrong place at the wrong time—not to mention Beach Patrol, who make a career of being in the wrong place at the wrong time.

## GAVIOTA BEACH: AS NATURE INTENDED

A scenic, secluded spot with clear, swim-friendly waters—*and* it's easy to locate. Being at one with the natural world doesn't get too much better than this, unless of course you happen to be arrested or inadvertently brush against the poison oak skirting the access trail, but such are the rigors of nude beachgoing. A favored spot for lower-key naturists, Gaviota stays sparsely populated and there never seems to be more than a few dozen people here at any one time. A lengthy strand allows for a long walk through gently crashing surf, and it's not unusual to spot a school of dolphins jumping along the shoreline or giant starfish holding tightly to its rocky points.

**TO GAVIOTA FROM LOS ANGELES:** Take the 101 Freeway north past Santa Barbara. About thirty miles west of Santa Barbara take the Mariposa Riena exit. Make a U-turn back onto the freeway going south and drive a half-mile to a dirt parking area just to the side of the road on your right; look for railroad crossing lights as a landmark. There is a cluster of blue garbage cans left of the wide and well-worn trail down to the beach. The trail provides an easy and beautiful walk to the water, and close proximity to poison oak, so wait until you reach the sand before you drop trou.

## MORE MESA: MORE, MORE, MORE

Grade A. This is just how nude beaches look in nudist magazines. Actually spotted: cute naked people playing acoustic guitar. At More Mesa, beach recreation that would normally annoy—like Hacky Sack, Frisbee, and volleyball—is really entertaining when you can watch naked people doing it. The vibe is easy and though you'll spot an occasional swimsuit, those wearing them are out-numbered by about twenty to one.

**TO MORE MESA FROM LOS ANGELES:** It's a bit of a schlep, but well worth it. Take the 101 Freeway north just beyond Santa Barbara. Exit on Turnpike Road and turn left. Take Turnpike to Hollister Avenue and turn left. Take Hollister to Puente Drive and turn right. Take Puente to Vieja Drive and turn right. Start looking for Mockingbird Lane. Park on Vieja, as close to the intersection of Mockingbird as you can get (parking is prohibited on Mockingbird Lane). After you park, walk all the way down Mockingbird; it will end at a dirt trail. Take that trail (it's an easy walk, but not a short one) to a steep and seemingly endless stairway down to the beach. Once you hit the sand, you're still not there; the only reason More Mesa remains unfettered is because nude use is respectfully contained to the north end of the beach. Keep on walkin'.

## SAN ONOFRE: OUR MEN IN UNIFORM, OUT OF UNIFORM

What do Annette Funicello, naked Marines, and nuclear power have in common? San Onofre State Beach, that's what. Celebrated by Annette's eminently forgettable surf song "The Battle of San Onofre," a unique location has this spot sandwiched between a nuclear power plant to the far north and Camp Pendelton to the near south. Though the beach draws a mixed crowd, it's favored by the U.S. Marine Corps' freer spirits, and their ardent admir-ers. We didn't ask, they didn't tell. Frequent fly-bys from military helicopters make for a less peaceful afternoon, but beggars can't be choosers. Get there early, or you'll never find a place to park.

**TO SAN ONOFRE FROM LOS ANGELES:** Take the 5 Freeway south toward San Clemente. Take the Basilone Road exit. Signs for the beach will appear on your right. Enter the San Onofre State Beach parking lot, and follow all the way to its end. At the very end of the lot, you'll see a sign for Trail Six. Take the trail to the shore, and head left, to the southern end of the beach. You'll know when you're there.

# NOT REALLY CARING ABOUT HOW IT ALL HAPPENED AT THE

# MUSEUM OF CREATION

## AND EARTH HISTORY

Did you know that the Ice Age occurred after Noah's Ark landed on Mount Ararat, or that Neanderthal man was a descendent of Adam and Noah? If you experience difficulty wrapping your mind around such fantasies—facts, rather—then you might want to motor down to Santee and get yourself a heapin' helpin' of Creationist hoo-hah. Just a short drive from San Diego State University there's a museum that will illustrate how God (you know, *God*, the guy in the Bible) created the Earth and our universe in six twenty-four-hour days—just like on one of those design makeover shows or *Project Runway*. More importantly, it will fill the gaps your flimsy myth called evolution has failed to explain.

"*Fascinating, tell us more!*" you say? We assure you, the Museum of Creation will be happy to oblige. In fact, within their seemingly endless four-thousand-square-foot labyrinth you'll saunter through God's much-ballyhooed workweek day by day, while being pummeled with evidence and arguments explaining just exactly how God did it. Although the Getty this is not, they have made the very most of the sterile, industrial park-like facility, with video exhibits, fossils, live animals, interactive displays—even a plastic Rosetta Stone and the tawdry Ishtar Gate of Babylon.

It's the Institute for Creation Research at work here, and this location also doubles as their education and outreach center. The ICR is hardly subtle about their mission, which—plainly stated in one of their many free pamphlets—is to "tear down the strongholds of evolutionary thinking . . . (and) . . . win back the church, sciences, and society to a creation world view." They don't mess around; theirs is not a presentation of the Sunday School variety. The ICR doesn't expect anyone to swallow creationism without a fair scientific debate. They've done their homework for sure, and they've done it with the help of a team of seventy-four associates: astronomists, geologists, biologists, zoologists, biochemists,

Museum of Creation and Earth History
10946 Woodside Avenue North
Santee
619.596.1104
www.icr.org

From Los Angeles:
Take the 101 Freeway South to Interstate 5. From Interstate 5 take Interstate 805 South, and merge onto CA-52 East. Take the Mission Gorge Road exit, and turn left on Mission Gorge Road. Mission Gorge becomes Woodside Avenue. Turn left onto Woodside Avenue North.

geophysicists, geohydrologists, and a whole slew of other Ph.D.s, M.D.s, D.Sc.s, and Th.D.s, all of them ready with arguments, evidence, and answers.

"What about the Grand Canyon?" you might say, "Surely God didn't do that in a single day." Evidently God did the Grand Canyon before his lunch break, and you can watch their video exhibit and pick up the pamphlet "Mount St. Helens and Catastrophism," which will also explain why the so-called "petrified forests" of Yellowstone were probably created simultaneously. Queries concerning fish fossils found hundreds of miles from water or Noah's improbable six-hundred-year life span are small potatoes for the folks at ICR. And don't get all Day-Age Theory on their asses by daring to suggest that God actually used evolution as a tool in his design process. They can answer to that as well. In detail.

Using alternative dating methods—for instance, the rate of addition of helium to the atmosphere from radioactive decay—creationists date the earth somewhere between ten thousand and twenty thousand years old. Perhaps such a notion may strike you as absurd, not to mention the creationist argument that we're all descendents of Adam and Eve (ICR's molecular biologist has analyzed blood type origins to support this theory), but see if you have the wherewithal to laugh after you've dredged through their exhaustive parsing of genetic variation, the laws of thermodynamics, radiometric dating methods, plasma cosmology, and—leaving no strata unturned—the systematic gaps in the fossil record. Ready for the bookshop?

Scale models bring many of these points to life, like the Tower of Babel and Noah's Ark. The great flood is taken quite seriously—and quite literally—by creationists, and is central to many of their arguments. For the heretic, it's also perhaps the hardest theory to swallow. Their deconstructed scale model of the ark (placed beside a toy Hot Wheels car to gauge its size) is offered along with a detailed accounting of the types and numbers of species aboard the ark (estimated to be between twenty thousand and fifty thousand). How did Noah feed them all? Why didn't predators attack their prey? They've got the answers. Think Noah is purely Christian folly? Using an etymology study, the ICR demonstrates that the concept of Noah and the great flood are, in fact, recalled in the ancient traditions of *all* nations.

By exposing the gaps and lack of evidence in evolutionist theory, the creationists make their case. "The entire absence of proof is the strongest possible proof that evolution is a myth," they argue, with their "proof" ultimately lying in the Bible—their all-encompassing history textbook—but not without refreshingly strong, oftentimes valid, and more often than not far-fetched, scientific arguments (even one for Noah's advanced age). While debunking Darwin's work as simply a "revival of ancient paganism" (even robbing him of the credit for developing evolutionist theory in the first place), the museum will draw a straight line from his theory—the same "poisonous philosophy" that infected Hitler and Margaret Sanger, the founder of Planned Parenthood—to abortion. With each exhibit, free pamphlets featuring related articles reprinted from the creationist science magazine *Impact* elaborate on every theme ICR presents: "Hitler's Evolution Versus Christian Science," "The Heritage of the Recapitulation Theory," and "Evolution and the American Abortion Mentality" are but a few of the page-turners destined for the top of your toilet tank.

The museum's final corridor, in which portraits of ruthless eighteenth- and nineteenth-century evolutionists like John D. Rockefeller and Andrew Carnegie are lumped with Darwin, Marx, and Nietzsche, hang juxtaposed with eighteenth- and nineteenth-century creationists like Michael Faraday, Charles Babbage, and Samuel Morse. ICR's rogues' gallery is also more than ready to demonstrate with its twisted evolutionary tree how evolutionist theory is, in fact, the root cancer for many of society's woes. Evolution's fruits include the "Harmful Philosophies" of Nazism, humanism, atheism, racism, and many other ugly-isms. The "Evil Practices" of pornography, slavery, bestiality, homosexuality, genocide, abortion, and child abuse hang from those branches as well, sadly turgid with ripeness and ready for the picking.

It's not that we're so terribly opposed to another take on the origins of our universe, and for the record, some of our best friends believe in God. We love the fact that we live in a country that allows freedom of speech, even in San Diego County. Everyone's entitled to their own beliefs, certainly, but what causes us the greatest pause with respect to creationist theory and leaves us feeling, well, sort of icky, is that it's never referenced as "theory." The museum favors the terms "model," or, when appearances are down, "the truth." They argue that the creation model is just as scientific as the evolution model, and is at least as nonreligious (although, ironically, it's entirely biblically-based), but at the same time argue evolution is unscientific because no one has ever observed it in action. "Religions," they say, like atheism, humanism, communism, and Nazism, are all evolution-based, a theory compatible with Taoism and Buddhism, demonstrating that evolution is no less religious than creationism, and therefore, can and should be taught in schools as science—and without reference to the Bible.

Although we find such divisiveness exhausting, not to mention colossally depressing, the Museum of Creation is hardly a bore. To their credit, they present their model as best as anyone can. There was no proselytizing—except for the exhibits—and no one ever asked for money, although donations are accepted. There is no admission fee, and the staff at the front desk were not only

*And on the fifth day, God created the chicken. And she was fully functioning. And God saw that it was good. And delicious.*

quite pleasant, they gave us about twelve pounds of free pamphlets, books, and CDs upon our departure.

The most interesting side effect of our visit to the Creation Museum was how little we cared about the origins of the universe anymore. However, getting an explanation as to why Christians believe that strong environmental policy is akin to pantheism made it worth the drive. Defend the earth as God's creation, but go ahead and destroy it. Really, God *wants* you to. The things you learn in San Diego County.

## SOAKING IN A SQUATTER'S PARADISE AT

# WARM SPRINGS CAMP

Warm Springs Camp
Death Valley

Directions from Shoshone: Take Highway 178 west approximately twenty-eight miles, and turn left onto West Side Road. Take West Side Road approximately four miles and turn left onto Warm Spring Canyon Road. Follow Warm Spring Canyon Road for approximately thirteen miles, and after passing through a low canyon, you'll spot some large cottonwood trees. Veer left at the cottonwoods, and follow the road to the compound.

Has your honey been hinting about a romantic getaway spent luxuriating in the desert—a long, lazy weekend of hot tubs, massage tables, and blistering sun? If a Palm Springs spa just isn't in your budget right now, why not surprise your sweetie with a desert getaway they'll never forget—try as they might—to wonderful Warm Springs Camp.

If you aren't one to turn your nose up at an abandoned cinderblock mining compound with no indoor plumbing located nearly fifty miles from the nearest gas station on a remote and bumpy dirt road leading into some of the most barren land in Death Valley, you'll have yourself a ramshackle vacation playland of sun and sand that won't bite the wallet.

Warm Springs Camp is an off-the-beaten-planet adventure for intrepid campers who know good sunscreen and pack their own toilet paper. It's also an ideal hideout for anyone who might be running from the law with a hogtied hostage in the trunk of their car (note: no cell phone reception out here). The site lies west of the Black Mountains accessible only by the kind of dirt roads represented as faintly dotted lines on a good map, just beyond a region peppered with names like Funeral Peak, Deadman Pass, and Coffin Park, deep within the groin of Death Valley. This secluded "oasis" is the result of a natural spring, hence the name, and was once home to the Panamint Shoshone who actually farmed this wasteland until it was destroyed by a flash flood in

# MY, THAT'S A BIG ONE

Michelangelo took a subtle potshot at the Roman Catholic Church in the famous Creation scenario on the ceiling of the Sistine Chapel (note God's outstretched hand and man's lazy, I-can-barely-hold-the-remote-control pose). There's no telling whether the sculptor who created the statue of Santa Monica intentionally made the thing look like a gigantic dildo or if he just had other things on his mind, but it doesn't take a fertile imagination to make the phallic connection. Could it be that the church's penchant for pederasty was an inspiration even back in 1934 when the statue was—wait for it—erected?

**Santa Monica Statue / Ocean Avenue and Sunset Boulevard / Santa Monica**

1897. In the 1930s, a lady miner, Louise Grantham, established the camp adjacent to the spring, which is still free flowing, as a home base to her eleven booming talc mines.

Travel begins with a three-and-a-half-hour drive from L.A. to Shoshone, in Death Valley National Park. From there, deeper into the desert you go, taking the well-maintained Highway 178 onto the more neglected West Road, then onto a dusty single lane better suited for vehicles with good clearance. The dirt road stretches for miles, seeming to lead positively nowhere. And miles feel longer here because the road requires them to be slower and there's nothing on the horizon to satisfy anticipation but rocks, in every direction, as far as the eye can see. After a clump of reassuring cottonwood trees indicate that you have in fact taken the correct path, you'll park, wait for the dust to clear, and find yourself upon the scene of an eerily vacant, mustard-colored encampment nestled into the "oasis" of Warm Springs. The word "oasis" is used only at its most literal here, being that this is merely a spot in the desert that produces water—you will find no tropical fruit trees, lush grasses, or sparkling waterfalls. Reaching Warm Springs camp is a lot like finding a single shoe and a pair of jeans alongside a jogging path in a city park, moist with morning dew. There's a story to tell, and no doubt this canyon has seen life, but those who can tell it and those who lived it vacated long ago.

*Like* **Green Acres** *without the green.*

The adjacent mines still gape with the promise of talc; several of the largest are immediately nearby and completely accessible for exploration, should you wish to engage in a game of chicken with a sandy hole in the ground supported with wooden posts that have long since succumbed to dry rot. The camp facilities themselves may look less like those of Desert Hot Springs Resort and more like an SLA safe house, but it's technically a national park so it's yours for the squatting—at you're your own risk—year-round. The main structure formerly housed the camp kitchen, now a ghost of its former self, beyond which lies a row of "cabins" fronted by a screened porch, one featuring a handsome stone fireplace. Perfectly inhabitable, while crudely rustic, the accommodations come modestly equipped with an honor system of dry goods, packaged instant food, and firewood conscientiously left by previous campers, many of whom journaled their stay at Warm Springs in a spiral-bound notebook left in an otherwise empty basket. You've also got use of the swimming pool out front, which even boasts a diving board. The pool doesn't have any water in it, but if you're looking for a place to shoot your music video, finish that student film, or indulge in some freaky outdoor sex, Warm Springs Camp will not leave you short on possibilities.

The focal point of Warm Springs of course is the spring itself, the primary reason to make such a trek unless you're a complete road-tripping masochist. An easily ascended trailhead begins just behind the outhouse, and as you follow the trail into the fissure of the hillside you'll begin to hear water. After maneuvering your way though a dense but perfectly manageable tunnel of brush you'll find the spring trickling from a tiny grotto and filling a sandy pool settled into the crook of the stones. The pool itself is only a little deeper than a standard bathtub, and it's barely wide enough to accommodate maybe three people who aren't interested in being physically intimate with one another. More importantly, there's a reason it's called Warm Springs and not Hot: it's only warm. It doesn't get hot—but that's not exactly a disadvantage for a campground that reaches 115-plus degrees in the summer months, and for a chilly winter morning, Warm Springs is okay. Not great, but okay. And since this isn't costing you anything, okay will have to do.

The downside to Warm Springs Camp—assuming there's an upside—is that your accommodations come with no policy to prevent overbooking. The chance that you might arrive for your weekend getaway only to discover a gaggle of naked, beer-soaked desert rats who had the very same idea does exist. But really, isn't that what travel's all about: seeing new faces, meeting new people, and sharing the same bathwater?

# DUME COVE BEACH

So Cal is so laid-back.

Save the occasional deadly earthquake, devastating wildfire, or real estate–munching mudslide, life in Southern California is one long, lazy, sun-drenched afternoon, where the weather is always perfect, the skies always clear, and even the homeless have nice tans.

Dume Cove Beach
Dume Drive at Cliffside Drive
Malibu

One of the greatest advantages to life on the left coast is the luxury of being able to roll out of bed on a balmy January morning, pull on a pair of board shorts, toss on the flip-flops, and head down to one of our clean and beautiful beaches, arguably the finest in the world. There, with the warm sand under our tan feet, we—the laid-back inhabitants of So Cal—simply soak in the sun, share in the love, and celebrate the overall good vibe of what it means to be here, the single most beautiful, casual, laid-back and sunny place on this planet.

That's why we want you to enjoy Dume Cove Beach. Often. And bring all your friends.

Dume Cove is the epitome of laid-back So Cal—or just call it "Cali," all the natives do—and best of all, it's a well-kept secret beach, frequented almost exclusively by nearby residents. Although it's public land, there are no signs announcing it from PCH—in fact, it's not even shown on some maps—and it's accessible only through the Malibu neighborhood that would like very much for you to go away. But anyone—and we do mean absolutely anyone—can enjoy this beautiful, private slice of laid-back Malibu, anytime. It's even free to park.

Drive north on PCH up to Malibu and make a left on Heathercliff Road. Watch for the quick left onto Dume Drive and take it all the way to its end, at Cliffside. From there, just kick back and enjoy the laid-backness of free-and-easy Malibu. If you arrive early enough, you might be one of the fortunate few to score a parking space; Malibu rolls out the red carpet to nonresidents with a spacious lot that can almost

## Paddle fags unite!

accommodate nine cars—as long as you only stay two hours and have absolutely no plan whatsoever to enjoy a sunset. But don't let that spoil your new favorite beach; you can park all day and into the night along Dume Drive (or the next block or two over on Fernhill or Grasswood), just be sure to take heed of the many signs dotting the neighborhood's tow-away sector. You can't park within about a quarter-mile of the trailhead to the beach, but no worries, the short walk in the sunshine will prove a nice warm-up for an afternoon of paddleboarding. From there, it's an easy jaunt to the end of Cliffside Drive, past the security cameras, motion-sensitive spots, and fortress-like fencing around some of Southern California's most refined residential architecture. And pay no mind to the suspicious glare from the occasional car slowly driving from behind an electric gate: It's not that they aren't laid-back, they're just not accustomed to seeing anyone on foot who isn't saddled with a leaf blower or trimming a hedge.

Cliffside Drive tapers to an entry leading to a stairway down to the south side of the beach. When you spot the sign hand-scrawled with the message "no paddle fags in surf zone," you're there. A stucco arch leads the way, with a hand-painted reminder that surfers do, in fact, have exclusive proprietary rights to select areas of Pacific. It's a little-known fact, but with the territorial gain of California during the presidency of James Polk, it was expressly understood that surfer's "zones" would be remain protected in perpetuity because—by virtue of the fact that they can stand upright on a piece of fiberglass-coated polystyrene along the crest of an ocean wave—surfers are a superior race of human beings with an inalienable right to keep regions of the world's largest ocean zoned exclusively for their use, and not for paddle fags. Sorry for the history lesson, but surfers are really important.

The gate is frequently chained shut—and topped with razor wire just in case anyone thinks they get to enjoy the beach without losing some blood—but there's an alternate point of entry through the Point Dume Natural Preserve. Here, at the edge of the aforementioned parking lot, you'll find a clearly marked trail through the lush botanicals native to the Malibu cliffs, eventually meeting a stepped descent to the easily accessed north side of Dume Cove.

If you've been waiting for the perfect place to break out the inappropriate swimwear you purchased in a delusional but inspired sexy moment (read: string bikinis, Brazilian tangas, and neon banana hammocks) or just need a spot to expose some infected body piercings to a little fresh air, Dume Cove awaits. Don't bother to depilate, that extra twenty pounds can wait, and by all means bring your paddleboards, Water Weenies, and anything else that bears no resemblance to a surfboard but does an effective job keeping beach lovers afloat.

Because here in Cali, laid-back is what it's all about.

# A YABBA DABBA DOO TIME AT THE
# CABAZON DINOSAURS

It's not always easy writing a book like *L.A. Bizarro*. For every gem that makes it into these pages, there are probably five more that were bulldozed. Our favorite haunts of yesterday too often become the condo developments and mini-malls of tomorrow. Red hot leads routinely turn ice cold, and just because a place has been an undisturbed So Cal institution for forty-plus years doesn't mean some jackball won't buy it and turn it into a sports bar, with absolutely no regard for how we might fill our pages.

On the other hand, sometimes it feels like we've been goosed by the hand of God, and thrown a bone so turgid with strangeness that even we couldn't have made it up. Take the Dinosaurs of Cabazon, for example: a 1970s roadside attraction lionized by a registered sex offender and now enjoying a second life as a venue promoting creationist theory.

Thirty years before Steven Spielberg made the term "Jurassic" part of our pop vernacular, a septuagenarian Knott's Berry Farm portrait painter named Claude Bell was slaving away on a seemingly senseless Jurassic project of his own. He broke ground in 1964 and when construction was completed a decade later Claude had realized a life-long dream, having built himself a four-story bron-tosaurus complete with little windows, a fire escape, and air conditioning, that he christened "Dinny" (pronounced *Die-nee*). Bell, who developed his flair for exhibition as a child at the turn of the century by sculpting sand for spare change on the beach in Atlantic City, quickly commenced production on a second structure: a sixty-five-foot Tyrannosaurus rex with a lookout station in its mouth and a slide mounted upon its tail. Unfortunately, shortly before fine-tuning the details Claude left us for the big Jurassic roadside attraction in the sky. So many dino-saurs, so little time.

Enter Paul Reubens. From the obscurity of Cabazon onto the small screen of the multiplex, iconic status was effectively secured when Pee-wee Herman shared

The Cabazon Dinosaurs
50800 Seminole Drive
Cabazon
951.922.8700
www.cabazondinosaurs.com

Wheel Inn
50900 Seminole Drive
Cabazon
951.849.7012

# WELCOME TO THE NEIGHBORHOOD

Don't you hate it when a heavy smoker moves onto your block? The residents of Hancock Park sure did. In fact, when Nat King Cole—the prolific jazz singer, songwriter, pianist, political activist, and three-pack-a-day puffer—took up digs on Muirfield in 1948, the community demonstrated their disapproval of the hitmaker's nasty habit by burning a cross on the front lawn of his classic Tudor—or so the legend goes (it was actually a racial epithet, burned into the turf). He refused to quit, however, believing his penchant for Kools contributed to the resonance of his famous voice. Fortunately for the neighbors, Cole died of lung cancer in 1965.

**Nat King Cole's House / 401 South Muirfield Road / Hancock Park**

a scene with the Bell Dinos in *Pee-wee's Big Adventure*. Then, some years later, pervert status was effectively secured by Reubens, with a 2001 raid in which 30,000 images and more than 650 hours of film were seized from his personal erotic library, some of which allegedly included "minors engaged in sexual conduct." Perhaps in an effort to distance themselves from the scandal, neither Dinny nor Mr. Rex made any comments to the press.

Although Reubens has always maintained that magazines like *101 Boys*, *Young And Ready*, and *Teen Nudes* were part of his "vintage art collection," the Reubens debacle whipped up a frothy legacy for the colossi of Cabazon, particularly given the next

## WHEEL INN
"Home of the Dinosaurs"          Cabazon, California

stage of their once quiet life. In 2005, the property was purchased by Gary Kanter, an Orange County developer (red flag) who saw fit to transform the imposing roadside tourist trap into an imposing creationist "place of worship" with the help of Pastor Robert Darwin Chiles (yes, a creationist pastor named Darwin—as we mentioned earlier, goosed by the hand of God), featuring a store, museum, and "science" center, with future plans for a water park.

If creationist theory leaves you with a taste for honey-dipped fried chicken as it does us, mosey on over to the Wheel Inn. Dwarfed by the shadow of Bell's inspired masterworks, this cowboy-cum-atomic coffee shop has been host to hungry travelers en route to Palm Springs since 1958. As heavy on charisma as it is on cholesterol, the Wheel Inn sports a phone on every table and a clientele who possess all the idiosyncratic qualities that typically distinguish the sort of people you tend to find living in a desert. An adjoining mini-mart just off the main dining room sells everything from Indian-head-nickel belt buckles and cuckoo clocks to single rolls of toilet paper and the Native American–inspired feather-and-leather craft catastrophes known as "dreamcatchers."

*Gimme that ol' time religion, it's good enough for a stegosaurus.*

The angle for Kanter's new venture is, of course, to bring truth to the absurd notion that dinosaurs somehow roamed the earth "millions" of years before man. Poppycock. If that were the case, how did those dinosaurs manage to board Noah's Ark, smartypants? Too big for the ark, say you? Well that just shows you don't read the Bible, because according to the Christian organization Answers in Genesis, Noah was obviously poaching *teenaged* dinos, doofus, which apparently fit snugly into the ark's overhead compartments. You don't honestly believe that after single-handedly constructing a floating zoo the size of a football stadium that Noah had the strength left to leash a full grown brontosaurus, do you? The man was six hundred years old, for Christ's sake! Use your head.

## CELEBRATING THE MAN BEHIND THE SQUEEZEBOX AT THE

# LAWRENCE WELK MUSEUM

There probably aren't a lot of musicians who would name Lawrence Welk as their idol. With respect to music he was hardly a trailblazer. He didn't experiment or take risks, and he always played to the safest common denominator. It might seem that Welk's output was downright bland, and that the reputations of his longtime sponsors, Geritol and Sominex, preceded him. After a visit to the informal museum occupying the lobby of the

Lawrence Welk Museum
Welk Resorts Theater
8860 Lawrence Welk Drive
Escondido
888.802.7469
www.ewelk.com

Welk Resorts Theater at Welk Resorts in Escondido, however, you'll discover an inspiring American success story of almost mythic proportions, one certain to encourage some serious reevaluating. You may even come to understand why Lawrence Welk, in fact, rocks.

The exhibit shows us that Lawrence Welk was a man of many surprises. For instance, who'd have thought—with his thick accent of ambiguous European provenance—that he did not in fact emigrate from Poland, Romania, or Hungary as one might guess, but that he was actually a native of North Dakota! It was no speech impediment: He came by the accent honestly. As

the product of immigrant parents who lived and farmed in a German-speaking community, Welk didn't actually learn to speak English until he was a young adult. Making the very most of a fourth-grade education and a hard-line work ethic—as well as a burning desire to get the fuck out of North Dakota—he became the second wealthiest entertainer in Hollywood for a time (following Bob Hope), and it all started with a mail-order accordion and a big dream.

After dazzling us with the mammoth sparkling

THIS CRYSTAL CHAMPAGNE GLASS WAS CREATED FOR MR WELK'S TWENTY-FIFTH ANNIVERSARY T.V. SHOW.

champagne glass created for *The Lawrence Welk Show*'s twenty-fifth television anniversary, the museum takes us from his farming days in North Dakota (with a replica of his farmhouse bedroom), to his days of early broadcasting (with a radio station diorama), and on to his touring years of hot jazz and big band. Engagement posters and historic photographs illustrate the text inscribed on the wall, and you can see his television and recording careers represented with original gold records, awards, and even his baton. Alas, there is no mention of the rumored colostomy bag.

You think a band like Aerosmith has enjoyed a long touring career? Ha! Welk could've taught them how it's done. Maybe the reason he didn't take risks with his television show is because he worked so goddamn hard to get there that he didn't want to blow a good gig once he had it. Don't let the Geritol and the Sominex fool you; he was a traveling musician, after all. His orchestra toured for *twenty-seven* solid years, playing ballrooms (and in some cases empty storefronts) right on through the Great Depression. His band would change form—and name—over its career on the road, performing as Welk's Orchestra, Lawrence Welk's Novelty Orchestra, Lawrence Welk and the Hotsy Totsy Boys, Lawrence Welk and the Honolulu Fruit Gum Orchestra, and Lawrence Welk and his Champagne Music Makers. After long-term hotel gigs in Pittsburg and Chicago, the Champagne Music of Lawrence Welk (so named because of the light and bubbly quality to their sound) finally landed at the Aragon Ballroom in Los Angeles in 1951. An astonishing thirty-year television career soon commenced, starting on a local station, then moving to network, and finally into syndication—*until 1982!*

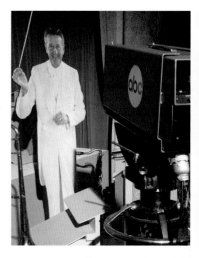

*When champagne and Sominex made beautiful music together.*

For our money (and it should be noted that access to the museum is free) the drive to Escondido is worth—if nothing else—the museum's superlative photo op: a life-sized cardboard stand up of the Man himself, baton and all, set upon a recreated bandstand of the television show, upstage of a vintage ABC camera. Step in, and for a moment, you can join the ranks of a Myron Floren, Jo Ann Castle, Arthur Duncan, or a Lennon Sister. An adjacent gift shop offers a disheartening selection of Welkabilia: no bobbleheads, snow globes, or giant pencils, but they do have a fantastic collection of DVDs and videos.

With little deviation from waltzes, polkas, and big-band standards, *The Lawrence Welk Show* stayed true to its namesake's entertainment philosophy. He didn't believe in taking chances with new material, instead holding steadfastly to the proven standards and keeping his arrangements simple, sweet, and no longer than three minutes in case people didn't like a particular tune. He wanted *The Lawrence Welk Show* to provide his audience with "joy, happiness, and relaxation," with television that was "always in good taste."

Leaving the Welk Resort parking lot and heading back onto Champagne Boulevard, as we drive past its rolling green lawns and the tall palms swaying gently in the breeze, we ask ourselves: What's so wrong with Welk's style of entertainment anyway? After all, we like happiness and relaxation, and why does life need to get any more raucous than a cold glass of champagne and an accordion solo? Sometimes an easier, gentler sort of music—one that almost aids the digestion—suits us just fine. Inspired by the Welk success story, we pause to reassess. Looking at life through LW's simple lens, we wonder: is it that we're getting older, or did Lawrence Welk—the baton-wielding master of the mediocre— have it right all along?

# TIJUANA PHARMACIES

**Tijuana Pharmacies**
**Tijuana, Mexico**

Naive, slutty, under-21 coeds from San Diego party colleges have made Tijuana THE destination for aspiring date rapists. But they're not the only attraction. Sedatives, narcotics, and other drugs lure Angelenos and other Southern Californians to the multitude of *farmacias* just over the border in Tijuana. Working moms, retired seniors, and citizens of every social stratum have chosen to skirt our government's price-fixing collusion with Big Pharma by crossing the border to get affordable pharmaceuticals, from antibiotics to antidepressants.

If TJ's income were derived solely from *yanquis* who come there for the drugs they need, it would still be a formidable cash cow. Factor in all the visitors who make the hajj for the drugs they *don't need* and you're really talking about some big bucks. According to the Substance Abuse and Mental Health Services Administration (SAMHSA), prescription drug abuse is more popular as ever, which means that Tijuana probably ranks high on any recreational drug user's top ten list.

For decades, Tijuana farmacias have been illegally peddling pills and injectables without prescriptions, a practice that came under fire in the nineties when Rohypnol, the so-called "date

rape drug," better known as roofies, became a darling of the news media. While there's no doubt that the drug, which is not legally available in the U.S., was slipped into many a woman's drink with criminal intent, the nationwide publicity only served to inspire legions of frat boys to seek it out, and, ironically, provided a convenient new excuse for college girls with nary a drop of the drug in their bloodstreams but who regretted the previous night's debauchery just the same. "Surely someone must have spiked one of Taffy's twenty Long Island Ice Teas before she took on the water polo team, the homeless guy who lives in the bushes behind the Jolly Jug, and a goat."

The ensuing hysteria over Rohypnol prompted a Claude Raines–esque response from Mexican authorities, who were shocked, *shocked* to discover illegal activities in Tijuana, and promised a swift crackdown. As you might have guessed, nothing really changed in our favorite border town, although potent painkillers like Oxycontin and Vicodin now make roofies seem as quaint as Quaaludes.

If Tijuana was a medical flea market ten years ago, it's now become a veritable Wal-Mart for Americans who are either too poor or too twisted to get serviced stateside. Besides cheap medicine, the town offers everything from affordable orthodontics to cut-rate cosmetic surgery. If the thought of a border-town boob job gives you the shivers, imagine this: apotemnophiliacs (literally, those who love amputation) have been known to come to Tijuana to voluntarily have their limbs sawed off. And you thought Britney was nuts for shaving her head.

Getting your hands on prescription drugs in Tijuana is fairly easy, though you sometimes have to jump through a few hoops to do it. Some farmacias still let you write your own prescriptions— especially once they get to know you—but most play dumb and force you to see a "doctor" just down the street before they will dole out the good stuff (now we know where California's medical marijuana scheme came from). It's all part of the game that begins the moment you cross the border. To put the odds of winning in your favor, we suggest you go directly to the same person you can rely on to take you straight to the action in any town around the world: a taxi driver.

Rather than drive over the world's busiest port of entry, park your car on the U.S. side and stroll into Mexico; it'll save you a lot of time when you're coming back the other way. Past two large metal turnstiles and an onslaught of hustlers and peddlers (ignore them all), you'll find the taxi zone, where a wealth of cabbies will help you get exactly what you came for. They don't do it for their health or yours, or even for the fat tip you should give them once they've come through. They do it because the farmacias give them kickbacks for bringing in business. Competition for *turistas*' drug dollars is fierce in Tijuana, and cabbies are an essential part of the process. Pay close attention and you'll notice someone at the farmacia writing down not only the taxi driver's name and cab number, but also how much money you spend. At the end of the year, when the farmacias tally up just how much revenue the cabbies have delivered, the drivers are rewarded for their loyalty in the form of an appliance or color TV. Kind of warms your heart, doesn't it?

Once you make it to a pharmacy, keep in mind that the friendly person behind the counter is not a doctor, and quite often, not even a pharmacist. If a store doesn't have a particular drug in stock, don't be surprised if they try to sell you something else and tell you it's essentially the same thing. Sometimes they're right, sometimes they're way off. Any druggie worth his smelling salts knows the difference between Zanaflex and Xanax, but if a clerk thinks he can pull a fast one on you, he'll try. Many of the better farmacias keep an ancient, dog-eared copy of the Physician's Desk Reference under the counter, so ask for it and look up whatever it is they're trying to pawn off. If it doesn't remotely fit the bill, don't buy it.

Whether you're looking for ampicillin or Ambien, the up side to buying drugs manufactured in Mexico is that they are incredibly cheap. The down side to buying drugs manufactured in Mexico is that they're manufactured in Mexico. An authentic-looking package does not guarantee the authenticity of what's inside, and as with almost anything you buy in Tijuana, there's a good chance it's fake. If you get ripped off, live with it—the possibility of getting a refund at a Mexican farmacia is about the same as eating from a street vendor without contracting diarrhea.

It's easy to be lulled into the notion that Tijuana is a lawless town where you can get away with having your leg sawed off, but trust us when we tell you it's not. This is the land of the shake-down, and if you think you got burned because you purchased counterfeit drugs, just wait until you get arrested for it. As in the States, Mexican law forbids the sale of controlled substances (Valium, Vicodin, pseudoephedrine, etc.) without a valid pre-scription. Unlike in the States, many pharmacies sell controlled substances over the counter without a valid prescription. When this happens, it's not just the pharmacist who's broken the law—you have, too. The sentence for possession of a controlled substance runs from ten months to fifteen years, and there are some medications that are considered controlled substances in Mexico that are not controlled in the United States. In other words, buying drugs illegally in Mexico is a complicated mess that is inherently risky. Do your homework before you go. Should you be arrested, be prepared to do time in jail, or bring plenty of cash to bribe your way out of it. Mexico is a progressive country, but they still do not accept credit cards for graft.

If you avoid the *federales*, congratulations. Now you have U.S. Customs to contend with. Although scrutiny of those crossing the border has increased since 9/11, customs will allow you to bring back a "reasonable amount" of medications for personal use. Be advised that though you may think thirty Percocet a day is a "reasonable amount," the feds will undoubtedly frown upon the 1200 tablets in your fanny pack. Rule of thumb: if the medi-cation is a controlled substance, a reasonable amount as far as customs is concerned means up to fifty combined total doses. You will also be expected to declare any controlled substances you are bringing back from Mexico, and be able to provide a valid prescription from a U.S. doctor. The prescriptions must be in your name, as well as in their original containers. Some farmacias think they're doing you a favor by placing the drugs in vitamin bottles or other innocuous containers to help you get through customs. Unless your intent is to smuggle in a more than reasonable amount, this ploy is not only unnecessary but illegal, and will likely earn you a cavity search from disgruntled customs officials. If you get caught, the least that can happen is they take your drugs away; the worst that can happen is that you go to jail.

In order to avoid either, we suggest you follow the letter of the law. Should you choose to ignore our advice, here are four helpful hints that may or may not help you get across the border with your stash:

1. *Look like a tourist rather than the drug addict that you are.*
We recommend picking up a shirt while you're in Tijuana—preferably one that sports a slogan like "Party 'Til You Puke at Señor Bullfrog's Cantina!" This way you will appear to be just another stupid kid whose parents were duped into sending him/her to a San Diego party college.

2. *Bring back plenty of junk.*
Buy enough turista crap to discourage customs agents from wanting to deal with you. Bottles of mescal and Kahlúa, statuettes of Jesus and Elvis, hot sauce, papier mâché flowers, Day of the Dead tableaux, serapes, blankets, sombreros—bring back enough of this garbage and they will peg you for just another American asshole rather than a drug smuggler and leave you alone.

3. *Use decoys.*
This is the inverse philosophy of #1. Bring back a few Cuban cigars or an extra bottle of Kahlúa and make sure to declare them. Officials will think you're too dumb to be packing four hundred Placidyls in your pooper.

4. *Don't be greedy.*
If you are dumb enough to pack four hundred Placidyls in your pooper, you deserve to be caught. Remember the fifty dose/reasonable amount rule. If you try to smuggle in an "unreasonable" amount of drugs, customs may think you're a dealer. You do not want customs thinking you are a dealer because they will send you to prison where you'll get a lot more than four hundred Placidyls up your pooper. Bribery tends not to work on this side of the border, but on the bright side, at least you won't be getting your pooper packed in a Mexican prison.

With all the rigmarole and risks involved in smuggling controlled substances from Mexico, you have to ask yourself, "Is it really worth driving all the way to Mexico to buy drugs and possibly end up in prison where I will have things forced up my pooper? Or should I just stay home and drink Nyquil?" If you

*Is that a bottle of Rohypnol in your pocket or are you just planning to date-rape me?*

answered yes to either of these questions, you may want to check out the many fine Malibu rehab treatment centers which we discuss in our "Dipsomania" chapter.

# BOTTLE VILLAGE

Bottle Village
4595 Cochran Street
Simi Valley
805.584.0572
http://home.roadrunner.com/
~echomatic/bv/index.html

## *Village of the damned bottles.*

You may think Simi Valley's only claim to fame is a jury that can plummet Los Angeles into a week-long orgy of rioting, looting, and arson, but maybe you've never heard of Grandma Prisbrey's Bottle Village. Or maybe you did and you just forgot about it.

As you cruise down the wide, clean, suburban thoroughfare that is one of Simi Valley's main drags, you realize that Cochran Street is a long way from the intersection of Florence and Normandie. Yet you can easily miss Bottle Village even if you don't blink. Wedged between a faux–Cape Cod apartment complex and a private home, the registered landmark sits on a long, thin lot and can easily be mistaken as condemned property when casually viewed from the comfort of a passing car. But pull over and peer through the locked gate, and you'll start to notice some distinct oddities: a wishing well fashioned out of cobalt blue bottles; a concrete walkway studded with license plates and toy guns; a thirty-one-foot Royal Spartanette trailer; even a garden made of decapitated doll heads impaled on long sticks. That's right—babies' heads on stakes. Mistah Kurtz got nothin' on Grandma Prisbrey.

Simi Valley was still called Santa Susana when Tressa Prisbrey began assembling her "Bottle Village" on a third-acre lot in 1956, just downwind from the stench and feathers of a local turkey farm. At a time when most sixty-year-olds were preoccupied with the imminent invasion of the Red Menace and Elvis Presley's pornographic hips, Prisbrey was breaking ground on an empire of junk that would be her artistic legacy. Some say Bottle Village

began as a retaining wall to divert the heavy rains; others contend it started as a way to stanch the relentless odor from the turkey farm. In a 1982 documentary, *Grandma's Bottle Village: The Art of Tressa Prisbrey*, the aging artist said she needed a place to house and display over seventeen thousand of her most prized possessions—namely, her pencil collection. Regardless of the inspiration, Prisbrey needed a cheaper alternative to concrete blocks, and turned to the local dump where she

would load her Studebaker with a plentitude of colorful discards. Aside from the bottles that she collected in every conceivable shape and size, Prisbrey had an excellent eye for other building materials that probably went unnoticed by the average contractor, but which sometimes attracted the attention of the local gendarmes. As Prisbrey herself explained in the aforementioned documentary:

*They sold the dump for an airport, and they closed up. So I took my Studebaker—I have a Studebaker pickup—and I went down there the last day, see what I could find. And boy, did I ever have a load! I was comin' down the pike there and I saw a red light and heard a horn. I knew what that meant. But I didn't stop; I come home. That's resisting an officer, you know!*

*I says, "Now what have I done?"*
*He says, "You got a license to carry that stuff?"*
*I says, "No, I haven't."*
*He says, "Your back window's broke."*
*I says, "I know it."*
*He says, "You haven't got no tail light."*
*I says, "I know it."*
*He says, "You haven't got no muffler, either."*
*I says, "I know it."*
*Then he went and opened the door where I get in at.*
*He says, "You haven't got no horn, neither."*
*I says, "I know it."*
*He says, "You haven't got no emergency brake, either."*
*I says, "I know it. And I haven't got no license, either. Do you know that?"*

One can only imagine what would happen if an inebriated black man in, say, Lake View Terrace, spoke to an officer like that.

We like to think of Bottle Village as sort of a poor woman's version of the rambling Winchester House in San Jose, only Prisbrey wasn't afraid of no ghosts: She just couldn't stop building. Among her finer achievements were the Leaning Tower of Bottles; the

sweat lodge–inspired Round House; Cleopatra's Bedroom; and the Meditation Room where Prisbrey would often play the piano and sing bawdy songs from the Roaring Twenties to visitors who had shelled out twenty-five cents for a personal tour of the grounds.

By 1981, when naïve art and folk art were coming into their own among the cognoscenti, Bottle Village was declared a California State Historical Landmark. Seven years later, at the age of 92, Prisbrey passed away in a nursing home just outside of San Francisco, having allegedly told a reporter the day before her death that she was "going home to my Bottle Village." By that time, the property housed over twenty-three individual buildings and life-size sculptures, with too many smaller, quirky details to even count.

Though the '94 earthquake did considerable damage to Bottle Village, it's impressive to see the number of buildings constructed from junk by the hands of an elderly woman that remained intact, while so many nearby tract homes took it in the shorts. Even so, the earthquake took a cruel toll, tumbling a good number of the walls and edifices on the property. When the state appropriated money to fix the landmark, art-hating earthquake victims howled bloody murder. The plan to reconstruct Bottle Village was scuttled by weak-willed politicos seeking reelection, and it has lingered in disrepair ever since. Well, not complete disrepair: Joanne Johnson and the nonprofit, all-volunteer group, the Preserve Bottle Village Committee, have done their best to keep the weeds at bay, as well as to pick up and organize the many bottles scattered about the property. They also hold the keys to the kingdom. Tours of Bottle Village are by appointment only, and a donation of money and/or manpower is much appreciated. Bottle Village doesn't get the attention of, say, Watts Towers, but it's well worth your generosity and time to check out one woman's rebellious enthusiasm for the outré, the discarded, and the magical. Through Grandma's myopic eyes, anything was possible.

# FISHING FOR DOLLARS AT
# TROUT DALE
## AND DINING ON A WHIM AT
# THE OLD PLACE

Fishing is a study in paradox. Next to baseball, it is the dullest sport in the world. Unlike baseball, it has moments of excitement. As kids, it seemed to us that grown-ups used fishing as a convenient excuse to get away from the spouse rather than a bona fide activity, but as we ease into middle age we're beginning to understand the appeal of doing nothing more than staring at the water all day and drinking beer. And perhaps getting away from the spouse.

Whether you're trying to escape your family or spend more time with them, Trout Dale might be the answer. Located just off Kanan Road in the Agoura Hills, Trout Dale is a lazy angler's dream come true. For $7 they'll give you a bamboo pole, some bait, and let you fish to your heart's content. While bearing a slight resemblance to the great outdoors, each cement "pond" at Trout Dale looks more like an oversized puddle with a fountain in the middle, and the abundance of space heaters is more of a distraction than a convenience.

Unlike real angling, which requires infinite patience and a modicum of skill, fishing at Trout Dale is apparently designed for those with ADD. The well-stocked ponds ensure an experience akin to shooting fish in a barrel—without the need for a gun. But be prepared to commit to whatever you hook; catch and release is strictly *verboten* at Trout Dale, which means you'll have to pay an additional fee for every fish you catch (around $7 to $8 for a thirteen- to fourteen-inch fish), and $1 to clean each one. Unless you enjoy cutting open live fish and scraping out their guts, we think that's a bargain.

If you're not rushing home to eat your trout, you may want to stop

Trout Dale Inc.
2468 Troutdale Road
Agoura
818.889.9993
Allyoucanfish.com

The Old Place
29983 Mulholland Highway
Agoura Hills
818.706.9001

## *Trout 'n' about*

by the Old Place just down the street, which is perhaps L.A.'s sketchiest restaurant. The Old Place is operated by an elderly, idiosyncratic couple who open the glorified shack whenever the spirit moves them, offer a menu of no more than two main items (if you're lucky), and cook your meal whenever and however it pleases them, giving "rustic" a new meaning. Just for fun, ask them if you can use the pay phone on the wall, then stand back and enjoy the fireworks.

The Old Place closes when people stop coming or when they run out of food. Fortunately, you'll always have your trout to fall back on.

## STOCKING UP ON KANGAROO MEAT AND SWASTIKAS AT

# CHARLIE BROWN FARMS

Charlie Brown Farms
8317 Pearblossom Highway
Littlerock
661.944.2606
www.charliebrownfarms.com

### *Welcome to Hell-Mart.*

You know the feeling. It's happened to all of us—and can strike at any time. You could be sitting at a stoplight, weeping at a funeral, presenting the annual fiscal report, taking holy communion, getting a prostate exam, walking the dog, shooting heroin, giving birth to octuplets, peering through your neighbor's blinds, being sworn in as the president of the United States, or polishing off a bag of Funyuns when you are overcome by an indiscriminate longing that is sudden and utterly irresistible.

We are speaking, of course, about the undeniable urge to purchase a Hong Kong Phooey action figure set.

Or an alligator steak.

Or, perhaps, a life-size caveman and his lovely, hairy girlfriend.

Or a Betty Boop doll in camouflage gear or a deep-fried Snickers bar or a pencil sketch of Tupac drawn by a hillbilly or a bottle of Brain Wash Soda or a framed photo of Pope John Paul II or a bust of Queen Nefertiti that looks like Anjelica Huston or a Chick-O-Stick or a real ostrich egg or a cast-iron Aunt Jemima notepad or a corncob pipe or a shirt that says "I'm with Stupid" or a smoking donkey or Stalin-era commie propaganda postcards or an "I Love Lucy" decal or a full-scale fiberglass moose or an 8 × 10 of Eva Longoria or a homosexual garden gnome or an Elvis Presley *Viva Las Vegas* folding chair or a jar of pickled okra so big you could fit a human baby in it or a porcelain bulldog wearing a star-and-stripes top hat with the slogan "These Colors Don't Run" embossed on the base.

You know, *that* feeling.

Located in the northernmost nether region of Los Angeles County, a desert wasteland better known for its concentration of meth labs, tract homes, and white supremacists, Charlie Brown Farms is Southern California's sprawling retort to the redneck souvenir shacks commonly found littering the tourist routes of the Deep South. While it may look and sound like a happy place, Charlie Brown Farms has, beneath its manic exterior, all the charm of a Third Reich Stuckey's (Google it if you've never driven east of Arizona), perched seductively beside a forlorn stretch of asphalt known as Pearblossom Highway, or, more commonly, the Highway of Death. Every year, scores of motorists are killed and hundreds more are injured along this godforsaken two-lane deathtrap once known as a shortcut to Vegas and now more notorious as a feeder for desperate wannabes driven to move to the far-flung badlands of Palmdale and Lancaster so they can proudly proclaim "I am a homeowner." Sad crosses adorned with ribbons and faded teddy bears are common roadside spectacles in this desolate wilderness, and one can only wonder how many of these poor souls unwittingly enjoyed what was to be their last meal—most likely a brisket sandwich and a date shake—at Charlie Brown Farms before they earned a starring role in that ultimate reality show, a Driver's Ed movie.

There was a time, before eBay made buying junk a point-and-click activity, when Charlie Brown Farms was a veritable godsend. Where else could one find so much cultural detritus under one roof? (Okay, make that about seven roofs, because Charlie Brown Farms goes on and on and on with one addition after another. In fact, there are three rooms devoted to frightening dolls alone.) Now, however, we get a different vibe as we stroll through the place. What was once giddy elation has been transformed into a kind of a depressing creepiness. It's not the ghosts of everyone who died out on Highway 138, nor the freezer case packed with exotic animal meat, nor the room full of Christmas ornaments and Jesus paraphernalia, nor or the loads of Southwestern crapola like Lone Stars and Kokopellis that lend

the place its subtly sinister vibe, but the odd feeling that we may open a door and stumble into a Klan meeting at any moment.

Make no mistake about it, we saw employees of all skin colors manning the aisles of Charlie Brown's, so it's not like this is some secret Aryan outpost (though we couldn't help but notice the preponderance of white nerdy management types scuttling around in embroidered Charlie Brown Farms sport shirts). And maybe we're just being too sensitive about the shelves of African-American figurines that are seemingly aimed at black customers, yet are stocked cheek-by-jowl with the aforementioned big-lipped-mammy notepad, which is decidedly *not* geared towards the discerning African-American consumer. Is this just Charlie Brown's well-intentioned but misguided way of saying, "Hey, we're not really racist out here in the sticks," which, in turn, leads us to our next question: Just how many blacks make it a point to stop at a souvenir stand in the Hate Crime Capital of Southern California? We have no clue, but our guess is they're not the ones who collect these things. "Honey, you have just *got* to see these adorable Negro figurines" is probably not a common phrase in the African-American parlance.

We imagine that Jews are equally ill at ease at Charlie Brown Farms, and not because of the heavy Christian vibe, either. Despite a rich history of wandering in the desert, the last thing a Jew wants to see when he stops in the middle of nowhere with his family for a nosh on the way to Vegas is a glass case proudly displaying replica lapel pins of every possible variation of swastika dreamt up by the Nazis. Hitler Youth? *Check*. Storm trooper? *Check*. SS? *Double check*. For $30.99 you can own the complete set in a handsome commemorative plastic case, *plus* a beautifully detailed swastika arm patch. *Oy vey*, now *that's* a bargain!

Again, maybe we're just being your typical bleeding heart liberals, but there's something disturbing—and you may have noticed that we're not easily disturbed—about the insensitivity of these displays. If this were Melrose, and the store were called Schvarzes and Jewboys, and run by some hip-hop Hasidim, then sure, it would be distasteful, but at least we'd get the joke. Here, there is no joke. These hideous trinkets are sincerely presented as curios without even the slightest hint of irony, and that's what makes them so fucking frightening. It's like finding out that Lillian Vernon and Harriet Carter are lynch-happy white-power freaks with Aryan Brotherhood tramp stamps.

None of this, of course, is to imply that anyone should avoid patronizing Charlie Brown Farms. Good Americans of all colors work here—it was a young black woman who unlocked the display case and showed us the Hitler Youth pin—and the barbecue is pretty damn good, as is their selection of fresh candy and obscure sodas (almost as many as Galco's). Sure, it's at least an hour drive from the city, but that's how long it takes to get from the Hollywood Bowl to Sunset Boulevard on a busy night. Best of all, it will seem like you're in another world entirely—like the lunar surface! In fact, we encourage everyone, especially African-Americans and Jews, to take the high road and drop in on Charlie Brown Farms, if only to say "Howdy" and get a taste of Americana that is sadly dying off. In fact, what would be the harm

in turning your trip into a cultural exchange of sorts, painting on some Jolson-esque blackface or donning a striped Dachau prisoner outfit with a crude Star of David sewn to chest and then energetically questioning the staff about their unique gifts? Proclaiming "Do you have a mammy with nappier hair or even bigger lips?" or "I won't give you more than a dollar fifty for the Luftwaffe dagger—and that's my final offer!" at full volume will surely elicit peals of uproarious laughter and make Reginald Denny proud of all of us, in his own special way.

And don't forget to order a deep-fried Snickers bar before heading out on the Highway of Death. You'll need it for the long trip into the afterlife.

The Ambassador, Los Angeles, California.

# LOST STRANGELES

# NO, VIRGINIA, THERE ISN'T A
# SANTA'S VILLAGE

Santa's Village
Skyforest

## *Bah humbug!*

Want to slide your fingers down Santa's frosty pole? See the world from atop a giant mushroom? Take a ride on the back of an anabolic bumblebee after stuffing your gut with pumpkin-spice pastries dripping with gooey icing?

Well, sorry, you can't, because Santa's Village closed in the nineties.

Imagine if you were to create an environment by cross-pollinating choice cuts from the early Pia Zadora vehicle *Santa Claus Conquers the Martians* with select chapters from Terence McKenna's *Archaic Revival*, and asked Lewis Carroll to fill the gaps. Maybe then could you begin to grasp the enigmatic glory that us regulars called "The Village."

What was really odd about Santa's Village wasn't that it was an entire amusement park erected in honor of a pagan holiday nestled in a forest clearing high in the San Bernardino Mountains. The weirdness was its candy-coated jumble of Santa Claus idolatry and Christmas tree worship, four-foot-tall polka-dotted mushrooms, miniature horses that bit, a pumpkin-headed man, a lollipop lady, and—just in case the scene got too heavy for you—a nondenominational chapel. It was the mind-expanding juxtapositions like happy snowmen and flying dragons, or live peacocks and giant candy canes that pushed Santa's Village way beyond the "Rudolph the Red-Nosed Reindeer" mindset. And, ironically, they were open every day but Christmas.

Perfectly manicured pathways trimmed with three-hundred-foot pine trees and psychedelic mushrooms crisscrossed through the grounds, leading visitors past freak-out focal points and surrealist masterworks like the Crooked Tree House, a jack-in-the-box that stood two stories high, or a twenty-foot-tall box of popcorn. Santa himself would casually stroll the grounds with a leashed reindeer or two, while the sounds of the Beach Boys' "Merry Christmas, Baby" blared from speakers perched high in the treetops throughout the park. Children ran from the petting zoo—hands good and filthy with goat saliva—over to the Candy Kitchen for some homemade sweets, while adults grooved to the Santa's Village kaleidoscopic color palette of lemon yellow, acid green, sky blue, hot pink, and orange Popsicle. Young and old, Jew or Gentile, everyone was tuned in and turned on in The Village. Maybe it was the calming effect of the forest. Maybe it was the magic of Christmas. Maybe it was the sugar.

Disneyland this was not. The park was small enough that you didn't need to sacrifice Cinderella's Pumpkin Coach Ride in order to visit Mrs. Claus's Spice Kitchen, and you never had to wait in long lines for anything except Santa's House. The Christmas elves at the control panels had no qualms about allowing you extra time on a favorite ride, lines permitting, to the extreme that you'd be *begging* to get off the spinning Christmas tree or the body-bruising bobsled. The Alice in Wonderland installation offered a reprieve from the madness, with voice-over narration telling Alice's story while you zigzagged through corridors past staggering dioramas of her life and times.

This is this age of instant gratification. We can kiss off a clingy partner with a five-word text message and find a rebound on Craigslist five minutes later. We can avoid time at the gym with a visit to a plastic surgeon. We can terminate a pregnancy legally, or at the very least, avoid cooking for the children we bothered to have with the aid of a microwave oven—or better yet, a drive-thru. Why then, Santa, why have we been robbed of Christmas in June?

Why, you bastard?

Miniature Horse Do Not Feed He Will Bite

## DEAD AND VARIED:

# DR. BLYTH'S WEIRD MUSEUM

The side streets of Hollywood Boulevard have played host to freak shows for decades, but only one was housed indoors and charged admission.

Ever see a twenty-three-pound tumor swimming in formaldehyde? If you were looking to add punch to a lackluster afternoon or simply wanted to sicken some out-of-town guests, Dr. Blyth's did the job for a mere three bucks. The museum consisted of only one small, dark room, discreetly tucked beyond a doorway draped with a curtain of wooden beads behind the front counter

Dr. Blyth's Weird Museum
1641 Cahuenga Boulevard
Hollywood

of Panpipes Magickal Marketplace, a small shop still dealing in sorcery and witchcraft accouterments to this day. Text typed onto yellowing index cards thumbtacked to the wall or resting inside dusty glass cases offered the abbreviated backstory and questionable provenance of exhibits like the three-hundred-year-old head of Hamander the Warlock, who was burned at the stake; the especially curious corpse of the alleged Vlad Dracula (1431–1476), fangs and all; and the head of Henri Landru, the Bluebeard of France, guillotined in 1922. There was a Cyclops baby, a dwarf fetus, and even Siamese twin infants—not to mention a host of cancerous human organs. Dr. Blyth's delivered.

And of course there was Elinane. You know, Elinane—*the devil child*.

It's unclear whether or not Dr. Blyth actually ever earned a Ph.D., but he did earn the title "Eighth Wonder of the World" by Ripley's Believe It or Not, and he was a genuine yogi celebrated for his ability to eat light bulbs, sew buttons on his arm, and stop the beat of his own heart. He had an obvious affinity for the outré, and the museum showcased some of the more noteworthy pieces of his collection.

Sadly, Dr. Blyth's Weird Museum was shuttered in '96—something about a license to exhibit human remains or some such bureaucratic nonsense. Even so, there's still plenty on the side streets of Hollywood Boulevard to sicken out-of-town guests, and one probably needn't walk too far down Cahuenga before spotting a human deformity or a twenty-three-pound tumor—but damn, we sure miss Elinane.

*Honk if you love human remains!*

## TESTING OUR COLOR BLINDNESS AT

# SAMBO'S

Sambo's Coffee Shop
(defunct)
Vermont Avenue at
Sixth Street
Los Angeles

The Last Sambo's on Earth
(still going strong)
216 West Cabrillo Boulevard
Santa Barbara
805.965.3269

Anyone who remembers Andy Kaufmann's brilliant exercise in video verité, *My Breakfast with Blassie*, will recall Sambo's Restaurant on Vermont Avenue as the setting of the titular meeting between the soon-to-be-dead comedian and the aging wrestler. By the time that video was released in 1983, all but one of the chain's 1200 coffee shops had shut their doors forever. The popular franchise that began in Santa Barbara in 1957 had spread across the country by the 1960s, but as the civil rights movement gathered steam, Sambo's became more known for its racially charged name than its ten-cent coffee and dollar pancakes. By the late seventies, the chain was under attack: Some

communities passed resolutions for-
bidding the use of the name, while
others simply refused to grant or
renew the chain's permits to operate.

As kids, we had a feeling that
something was not quite kosher
about Sambo's, but we loved it anyway. As adults, we were well aware
that it had become a cultural anachronism and its days were numbered.
That's why we ate at the Vermont
Sambo's as often as possible.

There was nothing particularly
special about Sambo's, other than
the fact that the chain's mascot
and decor was based on a popular
children's book, *Little Black Sambo*.
Ironically, the name wasn't chosen due to any great love for the
turn-of-the-century tale, but rather because its founders, Sam
Battistone and Newell Bonette, were commonly referred to as
Sam and Bo. It doesn't take a rocket scientist to make the leap
to Sambo's, but then again, if two partners named Bob Jigg and
Abu Mohammed opened a diner, one would hope they'd have
the common sense not to combine their names to create an ugly
racial epithet. Still, one can only assume that calling a restaurant
"Sambo's" in the 1950s was as acceptable as calling a tobacco
product "Nigger Hair" in the 1920s.

Though the restaurant's original mascot appeared to be a
young boy of African descent, the owners displayed enough
common sense to soon change his racial heritage to one that was
clearly East Indian (in line with Helen Banneman's original 1899
story), and that's the character most remembered by Sambo's
patrons. On the menu and in panels on the restaurant's walls, the
main character was depicted with light-brown to pale skin, wearing a turban and pointy shoes, and carrying a sun umbrella—all
of which he gave away to outwit a hungry tiger. For the record,
there are no tigers in Africa nor the American South. Even so,
explaining to a predisposed lefty that this particular Sambo was
Indian and not African was about as easy as explaining the difference between a Nazi swastika and the Buddhist symbol for good
fortune to Irv Rubin. Rotsa ruck.

As America juggernauted into the heady, hypersensitive era
of political correctness, Sambo's became increasingly construed
by far-left nitwits as little more than Denny's in Uncle Tom's
clothing. Despite the clearly Indian protagonist on its walls, the
name alone carried enough pejorative baggage to raise eyebrows
as well as temperatures among those engaged in an already
heated national debate. Though some Sambo's franchises tried to

*He's little,
he's black,
and he's
not going
to take it
anymore.*

forestall the inevitable by taking new names like "The Jolly Tiger" or "No Place Like Sam's," the damage was already done. By 1982, the Sambo's saga had come full circle; the first shop in Santa Barbara was also the last. It's still open to this day, and even sells a T-shirt with the original "black" Sambo on it, though he still looks Indian to us.

Vermont Avenue doesn't seem the same to us without Sambo's, but if you don't mind the drive, get your ass up to Santa Barbara to experience it for yourself. If you're like us, you'll probably wonder what all the fuss was about in the first place.

## CRYING CROCODILE TEARS FOR THE

# CALIFORNIA ALLIGATOR FARM

**The California Alligator Farm**
**Adjacent to Lincoln Park**
**Los Angeles**

There once was a time when Florida had nothing on Los Angeles. The City of Angels also boasted acres of orange groves, a booming community of Jewish retirees, and eventually, a bevy of overly tanned coke addicts and circuit party homosexuals. It may come as a surprise, however, that L.A. was also once home to a thriving alligator park.

*Gitalong, little gator.*

Joy Riding. California Alligator Farm. Los Angeles, California.

At the time, the California Alligator Farm was the biggest in the world, claiming "The Most Stupendous Aggregation of Alligators Ever Exhibited!" Here spectators could watch reluctant reptiles coerced into performing "tricks," witness gator hypnosis, and even saddle one up for a ride around the park. At feeding time, the bloody reality of the food chain became a spectator sport, as anxious crowds watched an attendee take a full-grown live chicken by its legs and swing it over the open jaws of a hungry adult alligator before dropping the unlucky bird to its quick and apparently tasty demise. Afterwards, you could further demonstrate reptile appreciation in the gift shop, throwing karma to the wind over an enticing selection of handbags, wallets, shoes, and luggage.

Unfortunately, our alligator farm went the way of our orange groves, and it's probably just as well. The spoilsports at P.E.T.A. would probably picket to have the place shut down anyway.

# THE EFFECT OF NUDE-WRESTLING TRAINING AND UNAVOIDABLE INTERVENTIONS ON SELECTED PHYSIOLOGICAL PARAMETERS INCLUDING INCIDENTS OF UNINTENDED TEABAGGING AND WHAT IT'S LIKE TO GET SMACKED IN THE FACE WITH A PAIR OF ENORMOUS SWEATY KNOCKERS

Yes, Virginia, there really was an Academy of Nude Wrestling, but it's unclear as to exactly what happened there. We imagine it was a place where men paid to get naked and "wrestle" with nude women, but why pay for that when you can get it for free at just about any frat party? Then again, perhaps the place was not just a front for titty-grabbing, but offered wrestling of a more philosophical nature, wherein a man paid to sit across from a nude woman and argue whether consciousness is a formal system involving the direction, choice, and synthesis of nonconscious processes, or if consciousness exists outside the realm of scientific scrutiny, confabulated and deluded in its pretended access to cognitive processes, and is therefore ultimately nonfunctional. Then again, it was probably just a front for titty-grabbing. The Academy of Nude Wrestling only lasted about a year, circa 1973, but what a year it must have been. While its brief tenure may seem tragic, one must keep in mind that had it endured it would have eventually been put out of business by Craigslist.

**Academy of Nude Wrestling /**
**7736 Santa Monica Boulevard (former location) / West Hollywood**

# NAKED CITY

**Naked City**
**Hemet**

It's not often that one gets the opportunity to wax nostalgic about a nudist swingers' retreat owned and operated by a paraplegic hippie ensconced in the sun-scorched hills of Hemet, but that's just one of the many advantages of being us.

With its twenty-two acres of dry, rocky desert hilltops dotted with abandoned trailers and crumbling carports, Mammary Mountain was the stuff of which depraved and marginally misogynistic fantasies were made. There just aren't many places left in Greater L.A. where you can get lap dances in a room with red carpet on the walls, watch strangers having sex alongside an over-chlorinated swimming pool, or view porn videos from a tanning bed—not that we did any of those things.

A prurient playground for the skanky, out-of-shape, and markedly unrefined, Naked City's creative roster of special events included the "Jack-off and Jill-off Chili Cook-off," the "Select and Connect Wesson Oil Sunday Splash," the "Pretty Pussy and Damndest Dick Contest," and "June Is Bustin' Out All Over Day,"

*Love, American style.*

where visitors who tip the scales at 210-plus pounds were admitted free.

Such was the wonder that was Naked City, which claimed a population of 36-24-36, and advertised as accepting Visa, MasterCard, and Masturbate.

Those were some good times.

# SPLASH THE RELAXATION SPA

**Splash The Relaxation Spa**
**8054 West Third Street**
**Los Angeles**

Until it closed sometime in 2006—no one really noticed—Splash The Relaxation Spa was the kind of place that made you feel like you needed a delousing just for driving by it.

For more than twenty years, Splash was a refuge for connoisseurs of sleaze, a haven where every dark, cramped, mildewed room boasted a Jacuzzi and mattress, each rife with the genetic material of a thousand lurid encounters. Its intoxicating aroma of chlorine and Lysol was the siren song for a generation of cheating spouses, streetwalkers, cokeheads, college kids, and other assorted perverts who were not repulsed by the idea of bathing in a roiling broth of used bathwater and bodily fluids. Here is where the not-so-beautiful people used to come, and often come again before leaving. Unlike motels and hotels, most of which do not sell their rooms by the hour, Splash allowed harried individuals to escape the rat race for sixty minutes at a time to pursue their inner peace in a hot tub ringed with human grime, its foamy surface reminiscent of boiled chicken scum. Whether one's pursuit of pleasure entailed smoking rock and cornholing a ninety-pound hermaphrodite named Quantasia, or simply date-raping a Tri-Delt whacked on the Rohypnol you slipped in her Zima, it didn't matter at Splash as long as you paid your bill.

Splash was a symbol of those heady Reagan years where anything seemed possible with an eight-ball of coke and a bag of dildos, a shining beacon of freedom that made us long for communism and a hot shower. But as the years went by, this damp den of decadence became little more than a sad anachronism and a parody of its own folly. Though it was inevitable that this eighties relic would go the way of muscle pants, Flock of Seagulls, and *Miami Vice*, if history is any indication, they will all be back again. In fact, that's probably them at the door right now.

*Please don't drink the water.*

## FIGHTING OFF THE ZOMBIES AT
# TRADER VIC'S

We consider Victor "Trader Vic" Bergeron to be the granddaddy of the theme restaurant, which kind of puts him in the same class as Albert Einstein. Both men were brilliant thinkers; both men gave us concepts that may very well expedite the end of the world. Einstein got the ball rolling on nuclear weapons. Bergeron begat Trader Vic's, and thus ignited a chain reaction that would eventually result in the cultural meltdown that is Bubba Gump Shrimp Co., and other mega-themed eateries that herald the coming apocalypse. It can also be argued that Bergeron was the first celebrity chef, which means we also have him to blame for Wolfgang Puck, Emeril Lagasse, Rachael Ray, and a host of

Trader Vic's
9876 Wilshire Boulevard
Beverly Hills (former location)

other kitchen clichés we'd like to see kneecapped.

Bergeron began his empire in Oakland in 1932 with a pub called Hinky Dinks, which he wisely renamed Trader Vic's in 1936. By the time the popular Polynesian playground made it to Los Angeles (as part of the newly opened Beverly Hilton), the year was 1955, and the Mai Tai, also a Bergeron concoction, was just eleven years old, the same age we were when we started drinking them. Such was the auspicious start of a tiki trend that would spread throughout the Southland, spawning knockoffs large (Seven Seas) and small (Tiki-Ti) and everything in between, along with a spate of potent fruity drinks that came with toys as condiments. Cheap paper umbrellas were the norm, but Bergeron adorned his upscale drinks with colorful plastic Menehunes dolls, which resembled a cross between a Trobriander and Burl Ives.

*I think I just pee-peed in my pu-pu platter.*

When it came to Polynesian-style inebriation, Trader Vic's was always our number-one choice—especially when we were underage. From eighteen until we finally hit twenty-one, not once were we ever carded there. Though the Mai Tais were delicious, the Zombies were even better, and the Scorpion Bowls—imbibed through straws that would have made Daniel Plainview proud—were the Rophies of their day. The food, though delicious, was an afterthought for serious drinkers like us. We kept it simple and made it easy on ourselves by ordering the Flaming Pu-Pu Platter, sometimes several at a time. (We invite you to insert your own childish joke here about "flaming" and "pu-pu." We're already worn out.)

After more than fifty years, the Los Angeles Trader Vic's poured its last Mai Tai in April 2007 to make way for the new Waldorf-Astoria adjacent to the Hilton. The San Francisco location closed a mere eight months later. The good news is that similar closings—like the Trader Vic's in Dallas—were followed by re-openings in which the original décor and menus were painstakingly recreated. Though a few original Trader Vic's restaurants are still going strong at other locations around the globe, we were at first cynical that the remakes would be anywhere near as magical. But the Dallas rebirth has proven that anything is possible with a lot of money and a little respect for the past, and we're hoping the new and improved Trader Vic's in downtown Los Angeles will follow in its footsteps. Then again, after a few Scorpion Bowls, who gives a rat's ass?

## OUT *'n'* ABOUT
# GET LEIED AND PAY WHAT YOU WISH

Accented with rock grottos, palm fronds, and neon flowers, the façade featured a waterfall cascading three stories above the sidewalk. Inside, Clifton's Pacific Seas kept its promise: Owner E. J. Clinton and his architects proved that you don't need to sacrifice glamour just because you're dishing up cafeteria meals served from steam tables or warmed under heat lamps with a "pay what you wish" policy. The exotic glitz of the Pacific Seas rivaled any Hollywood nightclub, all the while catering to senior citizens, families on a budget, and down-and-out winos. Opened in 1931, and scuttled four short decades later.

**Clifton's Pacific Seas Cafeteria / 618 South Olive / Los Angeles**

## SNIFFING OUR FINGERS AT
# MARINELAND

Of all the betrayals in world history, the closing of Marineland ranks up there with the assassination of Julius Caesar and NBC's cancellation of *Manimal*. The world's first "oceanarium" opened in 1954, a year before Disneyland, and has been called California's first major theme park, though we would probably hand that distinction to Corriganville, the western movie ranch that began admitting guests in 1949.

Even so, Marineland was a special place. Built on the tip of the Palos Verdes peninsula at Portuguese Bend, it was the largest oceanarium in the world at the time, and offered a more mellow, educational experience than the Wild West hooey peddled by Corriganville, or the manic, Technicolor hubbub of Disneyland. Locals and tourists alike were entertained by Orky and Corky, the first celebrity killer whales, Bubbles the pilot whale, and a host of dolphins, seals, and other sea creatures. Baja Reef offered

Marineland of the Pacific
6610 Palos Verdes Drive
South
Rancho Palos Verdes

## Psst. Wanna buy a used whale?

visitors the unique opportunity to slap on a snorkel and swim through a life-sized aquarium, and who could resist sniffing their fingers after heaving dead fish at the barking seals and sea lions? Marineland also housed research and teaching facilities, and was a favored location for movies and TV shows looking to goose their ratings, though as far as we can tell, Fonzie did not jump the shark here. *Benji Takes a Dive at Marineland*, *Sea Hunt*, *The Beverly Hillbillies*, and *The Lucy Show* were but a few of the entertainment vehicles to employ Marineland's milieu as a backdrop. Sadly, *Manimal*, which only lasted eight episodes, never had the opportunity to shoot here, but we're sure that Dr. Jonathan Chase turning himself into an abalone would have made for riveting television.

The architecture at Marineland was as noteworthy as its animals. Designed by William Pereira, the mastermind also responsible for CBS Television City, most of USC, and San Francisco's Transamerica pyramid, Marineland was a modern marvel of circular structures. The array of giant glass-lined exhibition tanks were fed with fresh seawater by a complex of hidden pumps and pipes, and the Marineland

GREETINGS FROM *Marineland* OF THE PACIFIC

Restaurant and Porpoise Room Cocktail Lounge offered some of the most beautiful ocean vistas on the Pacific coast.

In 1986, the park was purchased by Harcourt, Brace, Jovanovich (HBJ), the parent company of the SeaWorld parks that had flourished in Marineland's wake (the first SeaWorld opened in San Diego a full decade after Marineland's debut). Despite promises to keep the park open, HBJ abruptly closed operations six weeks after the purchase, and moved Orky and Corky to SeaWorld in San Diego. Orky died a year later; Corky lives on to this day, and performs under the stage name "Shamu." You may have heard of her.

Marineland was summarily abandoned, though the restaurant remained open as the Catalina Room until 2004. Other than the occasional movie shoot, the park grounds suffered a slow deterioration for the next twenty years, until they were finally bulldozed to make way for a massive resort and enclave for the über-rich. Hey, screw the whales. We need more oceanfront condos.

SERVING JUSTICE AT

# LAW DOGS

All rise!

The line at Pink's could vanish, Tail o' the Pup could tap dance down La Cienega, and Oki Dog could wrap its special in the Shroud of Turin itself—but none of these miracles would match the marvel that was Law Dogs. Forget about Los Angeles; for twenty-five years, on every Wednesday after 7 PM, Law Dogs cooked up something you couldn't find at any other hot dog stand *in the world*: free legal advice.

**Law Dogs**
**14114 Sherman Way**
**Van Nuys**

Law Dogs' owner and operator, attorney Kim Pearman, knew how to win a court case, but had no idea how to run a hot dog stand, so he did what any intelligent entrepreneur would do: He went through the competition's trash. Digging through the garbage bin at Cupid's, Pearman lined up his vendors and perfected the art of putting together a good dog before opening Law Dogs in December 1980 (he was going to call it Stupid's Hot Dogs, but his wife talked him out of it).

Pearman was as surprised as anyone when his experiment in fast food and free counsel soon blossomed into five more joints, and caught the attention

of Hollywood and points beyond. Disney knew there was a story there and optioned the film and TV rights. While the Mouse wrestled with whether to cast Dean Jones or Kurt Russell in the lead, Pearman showed up on every conceivable TV and radio show, and Law Dogs became something of a cult phenomenon.

Sometimes he would get over fifty people in line on Wednesday evenings, with questions ranging from immigration to murder. Pearman never solicited cases for his business and guaranteed each Law Dogger the same confidentiality his paying clients received. This was not a gimmick: Pearman lost sleep worrying about his customers and their problems, and though he wasn't sure how the state bar might view his generosity, he never had a single malpractice case arise from his Law Dogs' counseling. As Dickens might have said, "It was the best of times, it was the wurst of times."

Some of the folks who dropped in for advice were unable to parse the difference between "Free Legal Advice" (as offered on the sign out front) and "Free Legal Representation." Some expected him to draw up their divorce papers or mount their embezzlement defense *gratis*. Pearman is generous, but not crazy. What he offered free of charge was his legal expertise to many individuals who could not afford an attorney, or who were baffled by the daunting, often frustrating process of navigating our legal system. This wasn't about offering someone a helpful hint and telling him to get lost: Pearman guided many folks through entire legal proceedings—like preparing an appeal— which, all told, could easily take months and sometimes more than year. Considering how much lawyerly advice tends to cost by the hour—even over the phone—Pearman's generosity added up to a pretty penny. A lot of pretty pennies, in fact.

In time, Disney's interest cooled, and competition from places like 7-Eleven left all but one of the Law Dogs to carry on the good fight; and carry on it did, to the tune of about $2000 of debt every month. Graduates of Wharton Business School will be quick to ask: What kind of businessman keeps his operation going when it loses over $24K a year? Well, how do you spell philanthropist? Pearman wanted to give something back to the community, and his successful law practice allowed him to absorb the loss—for a while. If you didn't know better, you might think that Pearman was trying to give lawyers a good name.

Undoubtedly, some will argue that Law Dogs couldn't stand up to Pink's in the flavor department, but that's hooey. Law Dogs got its franks from upscale distributor Young's Market. And if you had to wait in a long line at Law Dogs, you were waiting for free legal advice, and that's the best condiment of all. Sure, sautéed onions are delicious, but they're not going to give you pointers on preparing your last will and testament, are they? In a town filled with ambulance-chasers who peddle their services on TV

*Give me a Super Judge Dog with extra chili and a divorce on the side, please.*

with all the subtle panache of carnival barker, Pearman's noble venture was truly an oddity, and an exception to the clichéd rule. Unfortunately, even philanthropic lawyers have their limits, and Pearman decided to throw the book at Law Dogs in 2005. Our objections were overruled; now it's a taco stand.

In closing, let us propose this hypothetical scenario: It's 1994. You've just murdered your ex-wife and her handsome young friend in a fit of rage, and worked up an appetite in the process. Would it make more sense to go straight to Law Dogs— or to hide in the back of a Bronco and lead police and news crews on a low-speed chase halfway to San Diego? We all know the answer, and though it's clear that at least one man was not smart enough to take advantage of Pearman's largesse, plenty of other customers will fondly remember the humble Van Nuys hut where, in addition to Jury Dogs, Plaintiff Dogs, and Super Judge Dogs, justice was also served.

Court is now adjourned.

## SHARING THE ROAD AT

# LION COUNTRY SAFARI

It seemed like a great idea. It was sort of like a zoo, except at Lion Country Safari it was the humans who were caged—within their cars—passing slowly through Irvine's ersatz Serengeti with the AC cranked, doors locked, and their windows rolled tight.

Lion Country Safari
Adjacent to the Verizon
Wireless Amphitheater
Irvine

The park may have thrilled many a vacationing family, but let's not forget that this is Orange County after all, the very same pocket of Southern California responsible for Richard Nixon, the Trinity Broadcasting Network, the Mighty Ducks, and *The OC*. Evidently Lion Country Safari was destined to cause harm one way or another.

Most of Lion Country's suburban adventurers made it though the 140-acre property and past its exit gates unharmed, but there were others less fortunate. Rhinos routinely dented auto bodies and scraped paintjobs, monkeys pounced on hoods and ripped sundry rubber detailing from car doors, and giraffe tongues lashed though the open windows of those who didn't

# Where the wild things were.

follow park rules. In some cases, it wasn't even necessary to enter the park to experience the mischief firsthand. A freeway traveler was killed because of an escaped elephant with wanderlust that apparently went looking for greener pastures on the 405.

Wayward animals posed many problems over the park's fourteen years. Bubbles the hippo met her untimely death after meandering from familiar territory and getting trapped in a pond. Days of failed retrieval efforts ended with a dart gun that proved a little too tranquilizing, as Bubbles collapsed and suffocated, killing both her and her unborn baby—in pro-life Orange County, no less. A second death-by-elephant occurred when a park handler tried to scuttle another AWOL attempt. The elephant never made a successful escape, but he undoubtedly got the last laugh.

As fun as that all seems, Lion Country Safari was no Disney movie. This was *the wild* (sort of) where animals lived their lives unedited: humping, shitting, and spraying the sides of vehicles with urine, requiring startled parents to provide quick explanations for what Junior had witnessed from the back seat. Lion County promised adventure, and it delivered.

"No Trespassing" read the sign on the park's admissions gate, "Violators Will Be Eaten!" Apparently ticketholders could be eaten too, as demonstrated by a three-year-old who nearly became an unruly tiger's lunch during one of Lion Country's stunt shows. Though only seriously mauled, the incident didn't do much to improve the park's compromised reputation. Like a pack of hungry hyenas, mounting insurance claims and fiscal losses eventually devoured what little hope was left. Lion Country Safari finally called it quits in 1984, reportedly leaving many of the park's four-legged denizens for dead. Rescue efforts by Martine Collette's Wildlife Waystation allowed a chimp or two to live out the rest of their lives a healthy distance from Orange

County, just a couple hours north in Little Tujunga Canyon. Others were pawned off to various animal-centered attractions.

What's left of the park is now slated for development: 3,700 houses and condos will soon occupy the land formerly home to the displaced African wildlife once subject to errant handlers and the daily procession of exhaust pipes.

We'd like to think Bubbles would have wanted it that way.

## EXPOSING TOPANGA'S NAKED TRUTH AT
# ELYSIUM FIELDS

Elysium Fields
814 Robinson Road
Topanga Canyon

Topanga Canyon's reputation as L.A.'s free-and-easy hippie holdout is total bullshit. "The Canyon," as the locals say, has never been short on tight-assed elitists, and there is perhaps no better proof than the twenty-five-year-long zoning battle against Elysium Fields, Topanga's infamous family-friendly nudist resort.

Elysium was the dream of Ed Lange, a fashion photographer and former art director for Paramount Studios. Lange was an early advocate of nudism's new wave, moving away from the regimented ideological European model of total health, and toward a sort of G-rated hedonism of body acceptance and personal freedom. Elysium Fields was exactly the sort of place that typified Topanga's perceived public image. With over seven hundred members and nine private acres, Elysium was the apogee of the California cliché, offering a Native American sweat lodge, nude yoga, Balinese dance, tarot readings, and tribal massage. The hot tub was a popular meeting place, and vanilla recreation like tennis or lap swimming served those for whom "movement class" wasn't a draw. In its later years, Elysium's Ankh Room hosted "Second Saturday Night Live" with musical acts like Buck Naked and the Compact Cowboys. Curious first-timers could peacefully commingle with longtime regulars, families shared the lawns with singles, and in spite of what their neighbors thought, Elysium

# THE SHAT IN THE HAT

L.A. is a town where stars come crashing down as quickly as they are sent into orbit. If fame is fleeting, then respect is virtually nonexistent in La-La Land, and there is no better iconic metaphor for this phenomenon than the original Brown Derby, the one shaped liked a hat (there were other Brown Derby restaurants scattered around the city, but this was the only one modeled after an article of clothing). Once a world-famous symbol of Hollywood's golden era—more famous than any movie star during its heyday—it is now the architectural equivalent of a babbling bag lady, almost unrecognizable in its perch atop a Koreatown mini-mall. The original Brown Derby on Wilshire may have become the Barbara Payton of Tinseltown restaurants, but at least it never had to blow guys behind a dumpster for booze money.

Carcass of the Original Brown Derby / 3377 Wilshire Boulevard / Los Angeles

## Meet me in the Ankh Room.

was no more debauched than the early-bird breakfast service at Denny's.

Lange founded Elysium in 1967 to a vitriolic reception from Topanga's neighboring community, who were no more accommodating of hippie ideals than Lange's members were of tan lines. Soon, helicopters were circling Elysium's park-like setting, with an ensuing raid resulting in twenty-four indecent exposure arrests. The following year, a Malibu judge struck down the area's anti-nudity ordinance, and Elysium's future looked bright. Topanga residents, however, were unrelenting. Aided by legal counsel they took aim elsewhere, filing complaints about everything from traffic congestion to fire truck clearance. In one particularly heinous sabotage attempt, an Elysium neighbor even went so far as stationing beehives on his adjoining property line, effectively creating a serious nuisance for the park's vulnerable targets. This was the "Summer of Love," mind you, in Topanga Canyon, L.A.'s alleged hippie haven.

After a year of concerted efforts by Topanga's moral gatekeepers—and much to their delight—the Los Angeles County Board of Supervisors reversed zoning in 1970, precluding clothing-optional anything from taking place on the Elysium property. Although most would guess that Elysium Fields had enjoyed a quiet and peaceful existence privately nestled into the oak trees of free-and-easy Topanga, the truth of the matter is that for most of its life—from 1970 to 1993—the park was engaged in an ongoing zoning war. Finally, after twenty-five years of community resistance and over one million dollars spent in legal fees, Elysium was granted a conditional use permit. Ed Lange died two years later.

The property was left to Lange's daughters, who decided to sell. Attempts by the Elysium board of directors to purchase the property and keep the resort operating were unsuccessful, with Elysium's last bare ass seen sometime around the summer of 2000.

Now, with its truest vestige of hippie-ness long gone and a canyon more populated with soap opera stars, real estate agents, and music industry millionaires than with nudists, "hippie" and "bohemian" are nothing more than Topanga's brand: a promise as empty as it was when Ed Lange and his sun-kissed cohorts were fanning away the bumble bees and smarting from the sting of their acrimonious neighbors—all the while trying to steal a little peace in their ill-fated, clothing-optional Shangri-La.

## DOUBLE PENETRATION AND A LARGE PEPSI: THE SUNSET

# PUSSYCAT THEATER

Porn on the big screen was an experience riddled with nuance—like electric typewriters and Walkmans, analog subtleties lost with the digital age. A Pussycat matinee meant there was no such thing as skipping forward through the dialogue sequences or jumping back to slo-mo the money shot. The Pussycat required an audience to savor each moment as it happened, and when it was over, it was over. Pulling up the soles of your shoes from a tenacious theater floor knowing the adhesive in question wasn't that of a soft drink spilled from two rows behind only compounded the theatergoing adventure with a disconcerting sleaziness that no surreptitious download on company time can match. There was nothing virtual about the embarrassment of being seen passing beneath a marquee bearing a double bill like *Wad Busters* and *Nagasaki Nymphos,* and simply settling

The Sunset Pussycat Theater
1508 North Western Avenue
Hollywood

*That darn cat.*

into your red velveteen seat—its cushion a veritable library of DNA—was an exercise in trust for which a "back" button could offer no safety net. Spectacle? You haven't really seen a cream pie until you've seen one two stories tall. Today, kids need only click a mouse to witness any perversion known to man, but in those pre-Internet salad days, eager teenagers clever enough to gain entry to the Pussycat could ascertain the mysteries of womanhood through a 35mm anatomy lesson on the scale of Mount Rushmore. And it was possibly the only time in motion picture history that previews for coming attractions not only had double meaning, but were actually entertaining.

Sadly, the last of L.A.'s Pussycat Theaters purrs no more. Having nearly gone feral in the age of the home video market, she finally saw the last of her nine lives and was quietly laid to rest in the shadow of DVDs and high-speed downloads. But what goes around often comes around, and since there are already two movie theaters in L.A. regularly running silent films—and one earnest attempt to bring back the drive-in—perhaps one day we can look forward to a time when nostalgia trumps public shame, allowing popcorn and cum shots to join hands once again.

## GET OUT OF OUR WAY, WE'RE GOING TO THE

# ATOMIC CAFE

**The Atomic Cafe**
**422 East First Street**
**Little Tokyo**

It seems to us that "The Atomic Cafe" would have been about as appropriate for Little Tokyo as "The Zyklon B Diner" would be for the Fairfax District. But . . . whatever.

"The Atomic," as it was fondly known, opened in 1946 on the corner of First and Alameda, but didn't really become an L.A. hotspot until the local punk scene adopted it in the late seventies as one of its official downtown hangouts (the Holy Trinity being rounded out by Al's Bar and Gorky's). Characterized by its delightfully shitty menu (fried baloney chop suey, Go-Go chicken, and the titillatingly named wiener bang), great jukebox (Dead Kennedys, Germs, Sid's "My Way," etc.), and ever-present hostess (Atomic Nancy, daughter of the original owners, and a total freakin' hottie), The Atomic was almost too good to be true. Throw in a cantankerous junkie short-order cook who would shuffle around the place in a housecoat and slippers, a cigarette dangling from his lips, and it really *was* too good to be true— especially when he closed the kitchen at one in the morning so you could give him a ride to get a fix. The transformation was a

*Try the mushroom cloud omelette.*

testament to the efficacy of opiates. What an hour before had been a listless grouch was now the happiest short-order cook on earth. And on his face was plastered a grin so frightening, it made the Joker look like Kathie Lee.

When The Atomic was packed with punks, i.e, on weekends, it tended to be intolerably obnoxious, even if you were into the scene. We found it much more interesting on weekdays, usually after midnight (the place was open from 4 PM to 4 AM), when Hollywood punks, downtown artists, Little Tokyo yakuza, and the occasional Skid Row bum could easily be your potential booth neighbors. In the wee hours, the cook often played waiter as well, and he appeared to hate both jobs with equal passion. If he didn't ignore you altogether, he would often pretend to take your order, then bring you whatever he felt like cooking. You learned not to argue, lest he take your plate away completely. If he wasn't nodding off in one of the booths, he was in the kitchen, banging pots and pans to create the illusion that he was hard at work. If the ash fell off his cigarette and into your wiener bang, he considered it a condiment.

You can't get service like that anymore.

The Atomic Cafe closed on Thanksgiving Day, 1989, the final nail in the coffin for a decade that began with such promise, and that anyone in their right mind was happy to finally see come to an end.

## WAXING TANGENTIAL FOR THE
# COPPERTONE BILLBOARD

For travelers en route to the vacation destinations of the Greater Orange County area, no car trip through Buena Park was complete without passing the gigantic, double-sided Coppertone billboard on the 5 Freeway.

In the days of the early seventies the billboard was animated, the frisky terrier rocking up and down while tugging at the bikini bottoms of an overly tanned child. *"Beautiful Tan . . . Beautiful Skin . . . COPPERTONE."* With its palette of bright blues, muted yellows, and golden browns, the Coppertone billboard was the definitive symbol of summer fun: suntan lotion, clear skies, and

**Coppertone Billboard**
**Santa Ana Freeway at the**
**Beach Boulevard Exit**
**Buena Park**

sandy Southern California beaches. Like the tip of Disneyland's Matterhorn, the billboard offered a vicarious twenty-second escape from reality, at 55 mph, without leaving your driver's seat.

The mid-eighties saw the billboard in a serious state of disrepair. The little dog wasn't animated anymore, and looked more rabid than playful. The little girl was beginning to sunburn. The ensuing years were less kind. The Coppertone billboard became the perfect argument for vigilante justice when it was defaced with gang graffiti, and although attempts had been made to maintain the sign by retouching the vandalism, soon after it was graffitied again, then retouched, and graffitied, ad absurdum, until eventually the battle was lost and the maintenance abandoned. The original paint began to flake, and the pigtailed girl with the formidable tan line (urban legend says it was child model Jodi Foster; it wasn't) was in desperate need of a higher SPF, clearly unable to withstand summer after summer of relentless Orange County heat. By 1993 she looked like she had been dragged from a burning building. It was like watching the torch fall from the hand of Lady Liberty.

Soon afterward, without any fanfare and—understandably—without any fight, the billboard was taken down. For some of us, driving that portion of the 5 Freeway is now like passing an old house where a childhood friend once lived. It never gets any easier watching treasured parts of Southern California disappear.

*"Tan, Don't Burn, Use COPPERTONE"*

## SHOOTING UP AT THE

# AMBASSADOR HOTEL

The Ambassador Hotel and Cocoanut Grove
3400 Wilshire Boulevard
Los Angeles

You have to hand it to the Los Angeles Unified School District: They really know how to fuck something up royally. As if the Belmont Learning Center disaster wasn't a big enough turd in their cap—almost a quarter-billion dollars down the toilet to build a school on a toxic waste dump and then about another quarter-billion to tear some of it down and rebuild it again—the nation's second-largest school district fought tooth and nail to seize the historic Ambassador Hotel and Cocoanut Grove nightclub through the right of eminent domain, just so they could tear

The Ambassador, Los Angeles, California.

it down and dance on its grave. Why they were so hell-bent to demolish this vintage crown jewel is anyone's guess, but the LAUSD's obsession to build on that spot and that spot alone, when others were available nearby, bordered on what amounted to a collective case of OCD. After rounds of negotiations with the L.A. Conservancy, school district officials promised to maintain the integrity of the hotel and club by incorporating both into the new school's architecture. Preservation of the hotel was soon deemed too costly, but the Cocoanut Grove would be turned into the school auditorium. Yes, and the check was in the mail, too. No one was terribly surprised when LAUSD officials changed their minds once again and decided at the last minute to go with blueprints that would erase every last vestige of the Ambassador from the face of Los Angeles.

A 22 ACRE RESORT IN THE CENTER OF LOS ANGELES

*The Los Angeles*

# AMBASSADOR

LOS ANGELES, CALIFORNIA

Beautiful modern guest rooms, suites and cottages in a setting of twenty-two acres of luxury and convenience.

Home of the world-famous
**COCOANUT GROVE**
*Rooms from .. $8 single, $11 double*

New York Reservation office:
MUrray Hill 8-0110
Chicago: ANdover 3-6222

And we thought Donald Trump was a dick for wanting to raze the place back in 1990 so he could build the world's tallest building there. If L.A. had only known what the future held, they would have been better off letting The Donald have his way. Then at least people could point to the skyscraper blotting out the sun and say "See that monstrosity? That's where the Ambassador was." Knowing what a class act Trump is, he would have probably kept a piece of the old hotel open as a gift shop or spa, which is more than we can say for the LAUSD. Not that the area doesn't desperately need a new school, but did one of the city's most distinguished landmarks have to die for its sins? The answer, of course, is no, but it's too late now to do anything about it.

Built in 1921, the Ambassador Hotel and the Cocoanut Grove were impressive even by the opulent standards of the day, occupying almost twenty-four acres of prime real estate on Wilshire Boulevard. It's hard to name a performer, business mogul, or head of state from the first half of the twentieth century who didn't stay or play there. Presidents Hoover, Roosevelt, Truman, Eisenhower, Kennedy, Johnson, and Nixon were all guests of the Ambassador, as were world leaders ranging from Winston Churchill to Nikita Khrushchev. The Ambassador was no stranger to royalty, including queens: Merv Griffin got his start here at the Grove, where Liberace also played a number of successful runs. Frank Sinatra, Gene Kelly, Judy Garland, Bing Crosby, Diana Ross, Barbra Streisand, Sammy Davis Jr., Louis Armstrong, Nat King Cole, Sarah Vaughan, and Julie Andrews were just a few of the stars who illuminated the Grove's stage. Six Academy Awards ceremonies took place there, including the twelfth, in 1940, when

*Gone with the Wind* swept the Oscars. Howard Hughes lived there for a time, as did Albert Einstein, Jean Harlow, John Barrymore, Gloria Swanson, and Ronald Reagan when he was running for governor in 1966. Tragically, all of this history would be over-shadowed by Bobby Kennedy's assassination in the pantry of the Ambassador's kitchen, a few minutes after midnight on June 5, 1968. RFK had just won the California Democratic primary when he was gunned down by Sirhan Sirhan, a pissed-off Palestinian immigrant with a name like a Def Jam recording artist. There have been many conspiracy theories over the years as to Sirhan's motives, including conjecture that he may have been hypnotized, *Manchurian Candidate*-style, but until now no one has suggested that his "handler" was Pat Collins, the Hip Hypnotist from the Sunset Strip.

## Someone's in the kitchen with Sirhan.

As the last best hope for the Democratic party in the 1960s, it can be argued that Kennedy's death opened the door for the Republican ascendency that, despite brief respites with Carter and Clinton, would eventually lead this country to economic and moral ruin. The Ambassador followed the nation on a similar path, as the assassination would indelibly taint the hotel and mark the beginning of its long decline. As business dropped, so did efforts at upkeep, but even so, the hotel managed to impress well into the eighties. In its faded glory, there was still something special about the Ambassador's Mediterranean Revival–style architecture and regal appointments. You had the feeling you were stepping back in time when you strolled across its hand-crafted tile floors and red-carpeted lobby replete with fountains and columns. The opulent marbled corridors and vast, high-ceilinged ball-rooms were breathtaking, and the expansive lawns and two-story bungalows that surrounded the vintage pool and cabana area created an oasis in the middle of the city. On the lower floor, the hotel boasted its own branch of the U.S. Post Office and a sunny, modern coffee shop, one of the first in America to be designed by

a black architect, Paul Williams, who is not to be confused with the albino dwarf singer/songwriter/seventies sensation of the same name. In short, the Ambassador was a classy old broad who had survived good times and bad, and was truly the last of her kind. So it only made sense to tear her down to build an overcrowded school that would require its own on-campus police station for what would be described as "a mini-city of juveniles."

Before and after its closure, the Ambassador was a popular location for movie productions—too many to mention, in fact, but our three faves are: *The Graduate*, in which Dustin Hoffman had to deal with Buck Henry at the front desk of "The Taft Hotel" before he could *shtup* Mrs. Robinson; *Defending Your Life*, in which Albert Brooks was depressed because Meryl Streep got a better hotel than he did in the afterlife; and *Fear and Loathing in Las Vegas*, in which the Ambassador not only doubled for the Beverly Hills Hotel, but was also used as the car rental

agency terrorized by Johnny Depp as Hunter Thompson.

If life were like a Hollywood movie, there would have been a last minute reprieve for the Ambassador and a happy ending for all of us. But life rarely turns out like a Hollywood movie, and the Ambassador is now just another beautiful memory in a town that is decidedly uglier without it.

## TAKE THE LAST TRAIN TO CORRIGANVILLE AND WE'LL MEET YOU AT THE

# SANTA SUSANA RAILROAD

## HISTORICAL SOCIETY

---

Back in the fifties, dressing up like a cowboy was, for many young white men, a rite of passage not unlike the present-day trend wherein white boys dress up like inner-city hoods and wear their fucking stupid-looking pants around their knees. The big difference, of course, is not that Eminem is the Fess Parker of the twenty-first century, but that should a kid in a coonskin cap ever have wandered into a real cowboy camp, it seems highly unlikely that the cowboys would have popped a cap in his ass on the spot.

Hey, times change.

Corriganville Park
7001 Smith Road, east of
Kuehner Drive
Simi Valley

Santa Susana Railroad
Historical Society
Santa Susana Depot
6503 Katherine Road
Simi Valley

Before Disneyland or even SeaWorld, the first theme park in California was Corriganville, named after its founder, Ray "Crash" Corrigan, a D-list Western actor who also was the guy in the gorilla suit in any Three Stooges film that required simian comic relief. In 1937, he started Corriganville in the then wasteland of Simi Valley as a working Western movie ranch, and later had the brilliant idea of opening it to the public on weekends. It was a smashing success, and for a time was one of Southern California's most popular tourist destinations. With the arrival of the space age, however, interest in playing cowboy waned, and eventually the ranch closed and parts of it were sold off to housing developers, to create a new sort of wasteland. A good portion of Corriganville is still standing—or at least the foundations are—at Corriganville Park in Simi. It's an interesting hike, especially when you reach the concrete bowl that used to be Jungle Jim Lake. The underwater camera rooms are still there, and if you listen closely, you can almost hear the sound of the cameras rolling as Tarzan wrestles a rubber alligator just below the surface of the lake.

Over at the Santa Susana Depot, there's a scale model of Corriganville and lots of brochures and other souvenir crap that they used to sell there. While you're checking out the rest of the restored vintage depot, be sure to drop in on the Santa Susana Railroad Historical Society and thrill to the sight of an HO scale model train setup that loosely represents Southern Pacific's coastline route in the mid-1950s. The guys who are into this

## OUT *'n'* ABOUT
# GOATS AND THE GHOSTS OF BURLESQUE

Up until 2006, a ten-room converted goat shed finished with cottage cheese ceilings and powder blue sculpted wall-to-wall carpet was the place where anyone willing to make the drive out to Helendale could take a crash course in burlesque's golden age. Visitors could peruse the pasties, boas, and breakaway beaded gowns that once hugged the ample curves of the trade's bigger names, one of whom was burlesque queen Dixie Evans, who also served as museum president, curator, superintendent, and personal tour guide. Walls covered with original 8 × 10s that once graced the lobbies of burlesque houses and the box office windows of classier strip joints across the country underscored Exotic World's costume collection, prop cache, and the shrines to diseased bra-busters like "Bazoom Girl" Jennie Lee (the museum's founder) and Sheri Champagne—which included urns holding their ashes.

After fifteen years, the institution was unable to withstand the relentless hassling from county officials, weather damage, and the death of Jennie Lee's widower—who held the deed to the property. The museum was forced to close. But like an old stripper who lives for the warm glow of the footlights, Exotic World refuses to hang up its G-string. Rebranded as the Burlesque Hall of Fame, the institution aims to reestablish itself with a new facility in Las Vegas. And sure, maybe Vegas is a more appropriate locale for a stripper museum than a San Bernardino County goat ranch, but no matter how nice the new place might be, we'll sure miss the way Dixie's rhinestones and brightly dyed marabou offset the desert dust, providing a much needed jewel in Helendale's crusty navel.

Exotic World / 29053 Wild Road (former address) / Helendale

stuff are some of the nicest geeks on the planet, but they make computer nerds look like Hugh Hefner. We don't know the official lingo, but there's even a head honcho guy in a control room who overlooks the entire operation. He's kind of like the Gene Kranz of the Santa Susana Railroad Historical Society, a detail-oriented guy who makes sure there are no small-scale catastrophes by saying things like "Hey, Tim, I already told you twice to slow down when you're coming out of that tunnel, and if you take that turn any faster you're going to be in a world of trouble." We forgot his name, but he had a mustache. We think.

If only more hip-hoppers, gangbangers, and stupid white boys would get into model trains, perhaps we could return to a kinder, gentler, more Corriganville-y kind of time, when the worst things we had to worry about were commies and Sputnik and the Creature from the Black Lagoon.

## REMEMBERING THE SMELL OF BURNING HAIR AT
# THE FIREFLY

Not to be confused with the still-very-much-alive bar of the same name in Studio City, The Firefly of our salad days was located on Vine Street just south of Hollywood Boulevard. It was a long, narrow affair with mirrored walls, Naugahyde overtones, and the usual dive-bar accouterments; yet there was also something special about The Firefly not apparent at first glance. If you took a moment to look up at the mottled acoustic drop ceiling, you'd notice an odd, smoky streak that ran the length of the bar. Like a great river, this dark stripe took years to form, but was forged by fire, not water. You see, The Firefly lived up to its name.

The Firefly bartenders (some say they owned the place as well) were twin brothers who looked like members of the Young Republicans, shared a taste for matching velour tuxedos, and hated each others' guts. Towards closing time, they would peel up the rubber mats that lined the bar and stack them neatly behind them. One of the brothers would dispense a *very* generous amount of lighter fluid into the shallow trough that ran from one end of the bar to the other, and then, without a great deal of fanfare, his twin would produce a lighter and ignite it. *Fwoosh!* A wall of flame would leap up and race down the bar with an intensity that would literally take your breath away—along with your eyebrows, lashes, bangs, and other facial hair if you weren't careful. The entire spectacle would happen so quickly that if you were really drunk or not paying close attention (or both), you might only feel the flame's warm kiss on your cheek, followed by the distinct smell of burning hair, quite possibly your own. The mats would then be replaced, only to be removed again minutes later for another performance. What began as a spirited gesture to announce last call soon became an unscheduled ritual that was repeated as needed—and as the natives grew restless as last call drew nigh, it was needed a lot.

As one might expect, the fire marshal was not thrilled with this practice, and paid frequent visit to issue citations. Worse, The Firefly was allegedly selling more than just liquor from behind the counter, a convenience that did not go unnoticed by the local authorities. Whether The Firefly played with fire one time too many, or the owners decided to quit while they were ahead, we'll never know. It closed without fanfare one night in the late eighties and never reopened.

Over time, we've come to miss The Firefly like a lover who taught us to live dangerously, only to vanish without even saying goodbye. It was a slice of heaven, and as such, we thought it would be immortal; but like all of man's creations, The Firefly has gone to a place where moth and rust (and flame) doth corrupt.

*Cocktails for pyros at the greatest bar on Earth.*

## JUST SIT RIGHT DOWN AND AND YOU'LL EAT A TAIL AT

# ALAN HALE'S LOBSTER BARREL

These days, you really can't say you've made it until you own your own restaurant. And isn't that ironic? In a town where today's superstars are inevitably tomorrow's has-beens, the only thing more fleeting than fame is a thriving bistro. Many attempt it, few succeed, but none can compare to the white-hot supernova that once blazed across the constellation of celebrity-owned eateries. Yes, we're talking about Alan Hale's Lobster Barrel.

For fifteen years, from the seventies to the early eighties, the Skipper from *Gilligan's Island* greeted diners at his eponymous

Alan Hale's Lobster Barrel
826 North La Cienega
Boulevard
Los Angeles

*"Try the Land Crab, Little Buddy!"*

# HE STUFFED HIS HORSE

Are the Sons of the Pioneers absent from your iPod playlist? Have you always thought "Dale" was a man's name? Would you reckon "Happy Trails" has something to do with a teenager's underpants?

Although Roy Rogers and Dale Evans might not mean much to anyone under age sixty, a trip to their eponymous museum in Victorville had plenty to offer visitors with little knowledge or appreciation for the First Couple of B-Westerns.

Having never seen Trigger in action on the silver screen didn't preclude the perverse thrill of viewing the celebrity equine stuffed and forever rearing on hind legs behind plate glass. Among the museum's incongruous taxidermy collection—which included among its hundred-plus specimens a hyena, a penguin, and a polar bear—the horse Roy pimped in nearly two hundred films stood freshly preserved alongside Dale's gelding, Buttermilk, and their German shepherd costar, Bullet. Merely an array of glittery cowboy outfits, fancy saddles, and some early career photos this was not. Morbidity abounded with displays including those devoted to three of their ill-fated children—only one of whom lived to see high school—that included report cards, clothing, and childhood toys. The amateurish memorials gave museum visitors a bit more than they had anticipated upon entering the pecky cedar Western-style lobby, and an assortment of telling knickknacks like photos of Roy and Dale shaking hands with the Reagans, a three-dimensional portrait of Billy Graham, and a bicentennial edition of the Bible, had others looking nervously for the nearest exit.

Roy was known for his impromptu weekly visits, when he could be seen holding court in the lobby chatting with old fans, posing for pictures, and signing the 1950s publicity shots of him and Trigger for sale in the adjacent gift shop—but by the mid-nineties, those visits were dwindling, and then became especially rare after his death in '98. Roy's passing marked the end of an era for both the golden age of Hollywood cowboys and the Roy Rogers and Dale Evans

Museum. Three years later Dale sidesaddled after him, and in 2003, the museum packed up and moved to Branson, Missouri. Renamed the Roy Rogers – Dale Evans Happy Trails Theater & Attraction, its new location sits opposite the roller coaster of Celebration City Amusement Park, and is undoubtedly enjoying more tourist traffic than the museum did in its days on Roy Rogers Drive in Victorville. That might be all well and good for Branson, but now our drive from Los Angeles to Las Vegas offers few of the salient roadside pit stops we once so relished. The World's Largest Thermometer or a Fresh Date Shake just doesn't compare to old-time cowboy taxidermy or a private peek into the untimely death of a twelve-year-old, so you might as well take advantage of those cheap airfares and bypass the I-15 Freeway altogether. So much for the thrill of the road.

Roy Rogers and Dale Evans Museum /
15650 Seneca Street (former address) / Victorville

seafood joint on La Cienega's infamous "Restaurant Row," which, during its heyday, was the apogee of unintentionally kitsch L.A. dining. Almost every night, Hale would don his signature captain's hat and roam the eatery like a shaved circus bear, spreading his avuncular charm like herpes. It was not unusual for the Skipper to give away hats just like the one he was wearing, or to autograph the color postcard of himself that sat on each table, even if you didn't want him to. He was just that kind of a guy.

If the Skipper wasn't your bag, you could always walk down the street to Casa Cugat, a Mexican restaurant owned by Cuban bandleader and Desi Arnaz prototype Xavier Cugat. If you were lucky, Cugat's wife, Charo, would be playing hostess. There wasn't a red-blooded hetero boy alive in the seventies who hadn't dreamt of Charo's bee-stung lips engulfing his chorizo—which may explain why our parents never took us there. They obviously knew the potential was high for an embarrassing boner incident at Casa Cugat, a factor they knew would never enter into the equation with Mr. Alan Hale, Jr. at the helm.

So we will never forget our encounter with Hale back in 1979, when he sat at our table, asked us

if we were enjoying our meal, and—we shit you not—called us "Little Buddy." Perhaps he always sported an unusually red nose and boisterous disposition, but on that particular night his affability bordered on mania, which caused our parents to speculate as to what he may have been drinking. We should have been thrilled to be hanging out with this icon from all those after-school reruns we had so rapturously endured, but we couldn't keep our thoughts from straying first to Charo, then to Ginger and Mary Ann naked, and finally—horribly—to the singular image of Mrs. Howell fellating a Great Dane.

Other than professional attention whores like Paris Hilton and Tyra Banks, we can think of few contemporary celebrities who would so lovingly pander to their fans with this kind of play-along hospitality. Though plenty of stars fancy themselves as restaurateurs, it is highly unlikely that Robert De Niro will ever greet you at the door of Ago by shouting "Suck on this!" and shooting you in the stomach. Even so, that doesn't stop us from envisioning the Skipper's mantle assumed with gusto by another actor who, like Hale, is famous for playing a cantankerous but lovable TV character. Hugh Laurie comes immediately to mind, limping around his own restaurant—called something like "SteakHouse MD"—popping Vicodin like Tic Tacs, grumbling about the stupidity of his customers, and spitting in the salad dressing.

We can dream.

## GLOWING WITH PRIDE ABOUT THE

# SANTA SUSANA

## FIELD LABORATORY

Boeing (née Rocketdyne) Santa Susana Field Laboratory/ United States Department of Energy Energy Technology Engineering Center Top of Woolsey Canyon Off of Valley Circle Boulevard, Chatsworth

Quick—where did the worst nuclear disaster in U.S. history take place?

If you answered Three Mile Island, you're absolutely wrong.

If, however, you said it happened at the now-defunct Santa Susana Field Laboratory (SSFL) in the northwest corner of the San Fernando Valley, give yourself a brownie point—and get out your Geiger counter.

The almost three-thousand-acre facility was built in the mid-forties to research nuclear reactors and rocket engines; the remote location was chosen because the work being done there was so dangerous. Unfortunately, someone forgot to plan for the expansion of that little city just two dozen miles to the

## OUT *'n'* ABOUT
# FAGOTS WELCOME

Once upon a time (not that long ago, actually), Barney's Beanery, the perennial saloon and chili house on Santa Monica Boulevard in the heart of West Hollywood, issued a heady decree heard 'round the world . . . or at least 'round the block: "FAGOTS — STAY OUT." The quaint spelling of the epithet on the carved sign that hung over the bar told a story in and of itself, the only thing missing being the sound of *Deliverance* banjos twanging in the distance. With this inflammatory warning also emblazoned on matches and other store paraphernalia, Barney's flaunted its homophobia in the center of a neighborhood in which the so-called "fagot" population was growing exponentially. When the Beanery was taken to court by the locals to have the slanderous slogan removed from the premises, the owner finally relented and took it down of his own accord, grumbling that it was all a joke and that gays have always been welcome at Barney's—which sounds like a load of bulshit to us.

Of course, the irony in all this brouhaha is that the restaurant never really needed to ban "fagots" or even "lezbeens" from the premises, since no self-respecting homosexual— other than a culinary masochist—would bother to patronize this overrated L.A. cliché. It's strictly for breeders. Proof: the place has hardly been overrun by "fagots" since the matchbooks were reprinted, though the occasional homosexual has been known to drop in for a burger and beer.

**Barney's Beanery / 8447 Santa Monica Boulevard / West Hollywood / 323.654.2287 / www.barneysbeanery.com**

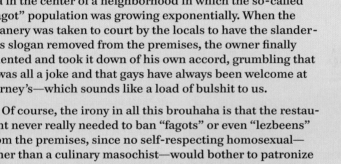

south called Los Angeles. Though the site technically resides in the Simi Hills in the southernmost corner of Ventura County, it overlooks the densely populated Valley suburbs of West Hills, Chatsworth, and Canoga Park to the south, and the city of Simi Valley to the north, all of which have been poisoned by SSFL's toxic waste and nuclear mishaps.

The facility is noteworthy for many reasons. Wernher Von Braun's early V-2 rockets were tested here, as were the rocket engines that took the Apollo program to the moon. Laser testing for Reagan's "Star Wars" missile defense was carried out on the grounds, along with a myriad of black ops that we will never

*Get a load of San Fernando's very own Chernobyl!*

know about. What we do know is that the nation's first commercial nuclear facility (the Sodium Reactor Experiment, or SRE) came online here in 1957, and for a short time, the small, uncontained reactor provided power to more than 1100 homes in nearby Moorpark. Then, on July 13, 1959, the reactor suffered a partial meltdown—the first nuclear meltdown in history—releasing what one study estimates to be well over four hundred times the radiation released by the 1979 Three Mile Island meltdown in Pennsylvania. Another independent advisory panel estimates that the meltdown led to somewhere around 260 cases of cancer within a sixty-square-mile radius of the reactor (and all this time you thought Grandpa had just smoked one White Owl too many).

You'd think that the worst nuclear meltdown in our nation's history (and the third worst in the world)

would be hard to top, but SSFL soldiered on. Over the years, approximately *ten* nuclear reactors were built on the Rocketdyne-operated site (parent company Rockwell International also had secret nuclear reactors at its facilities on Canoga Avenue and DeSoto Avenue) and at least half of those reactors failed and/or leaked radioactive contaminants into the atmosphere. The site also contained plutonium and uranium carbide fuel fabrication facilities, the nation's largest "Hot Lab" for decladding and examining irradiated nuclear fuel that was shipped to SSFL from Department of Energy facilities across the nation, and, most disturbingly, an open burn pit used to incinerate radioactively and chemically contaminated whatnot.

The Hot Lab lived up to its name, suffering a number of fires involving radioactive materials, often resulting in massive contamination. The sodium burn pit was an *open air* pit for cleaning sodium-contaminated products, but it also turned out to be a cheap and easy way to dispose of highly toxic materials as well. The radioactively and chemically contaminated smoke would waft gently across the valley to the south or over the hill into Simi, depending which way the wind was blowing. The neighboring children's camp at Brandeis-Bardin Institute in Simi still gets the worst of it, as runoff from the 1959 meltdown still flows directly into their property whenever it rains. Another practice involved barrels of highly toxic waste that were filled to capacity, then shot with a rifle so they would explode and disperse their contents into the air.

Sure, burning toxic waste is cheap, easy, and fun, but it can also be deadly. Twenty-two of the twenty-seven men who worked on one sodium pit crew in particular died of various cancers. In 1994, two SSFL scientists were killed when the illegal crap they were incinerating blew up. Their deaths led to a grand jury investigation and an FBI raid on SSFL, which is how most of this info came to see the light of day. But it's only the tip of the iceberg.

There's no telling just how much poison has leached into the soil and groundwater of the cities that surround SSFL, but the state has estimated that almost two million gallons of toxic trichloroethylene were dumped on the grounds and that half a million gallons also of trichloroethylene have saturated the bedrock, soil, and ultimately the water table beneath the lab.

The U.S. Environmental Protection Agency reviewed the site in 2003 and gave it two big thumbs up, saying that there was no risk of exposure to contaminants in the area, and though three other studies failed to find any evidence of increased cancer rates in the area, Boeing still agreed to pay $30 million to settle a lawsuit alleging that pollutants from the site caused nearby residents to get cancer. Hmm. Perplexing.

The DOE has been anxious to turn the prime-view property over to residential developers who are just, uh, *dying* to build there. We can only imagine some of the creative names that marketing gurus will devise for the gated communities that will inevitably populate the radioactive hilltop: Keloid Crossroads . . . Glowing Oaks . . . Plutonium Estates . . . Uranium Acres . . . Tumor Hills . . . Metastasize Manors.

And just think of the creative marketing campaigns they could use to bring the suckers in:

*Your nuclear family deserves a nuclear neighborhood!*

*Ask about our fallout move-in special!*

*Where the glow of sunset is surpassed only by the glow of your front yard.*

*Active lifestyles need radioactive living!*

Of course, the ultimate irony here is that SSFL was built to develop weapons to stop the Soviet Union from bombarding us with radiation, and yet it was the facility itself that poisoned and killed the nearby residents in the worst possible way, never once warning them that they were in danger, that their water and air were deadly, and that their children may very well turn into flesh-eating mutants.

With a government like that, who needed the commies?

# ABOUT
# THE
# AUTHORS

**Anthony Lovett** is an avowed hermit and the proud recipient of the St. Augustine Award for Outstanding Procrastination Skills. Out-of-body experiences aside, he has lived in Los Angeles since 1979.

**Matt Maranian** gave Los Angeles the best years of his life, and then ran as far as he could possibly go without a visa. However, he still finds himself in a 405 Freeway standstill more often than he should.

Want more Bizarro? Discover the latest L.A. weirdness and share your own depraved experiences at www.labizarro.com.